The Politics of Regional Identity

Focusing on the politics of representation and constructions of identity, this book analyses the impact of European regionalism on the Mediterranean.

The Mediterranean – as a region, as an area of EU policy and as a locus on the fringe of a rapidly integrating Europe – has, so far, been a theoretically under-researched area. Containing empirical research on Greece, Malta and Morocco, this theory-led investigation into the political effects of the Mediterranean's symbolic geography complements work done on the constitution of entities such as nations, Europe and the West. *The Politics of Regional Identity* draws on the fields of critical international relations and critical geopolitics to examine both the theoretical and empirical manifestations of these changing geopolitical images and discourses.

The Politics of Regional Identity is essential reading for all students, policy-makers and researchers of politics and international relations seeking a deeper understanding of European Mediterranean policies.

Michelle Pace is Roberts Fellow on EU Enlargement at the European Research Institute, University of Birmingham. She also works on an EU Fifth Framework project called the 'European Union and Border Conflicts: The Impact of Integration and Association' co-ordinated at the Department of Political Science and International Studies of the same university. She is Research Associate at the Europe in the World Centre, University of Liverpool, and member of the editorial board of the journal *Mediterranean Politics*.

The New International Relations
Edited by Barry Buzan, *London School of Economics* and
Richard Little, *University of Bristol*

The field of international relations has changed dramatically in recent years.
This new series will cover the major issues that have emerged and reflect the
latest academic thinking in this particular dynamic area.

HW
Kispess R
06/01/003

The Politics of Regional Identity
Meddling with the Mediterranean

Michelle Pace

Routledge
Taylor & Francis Group

LONDON AND NEW YORK

First published 2006
by Routledge
2 Park Square, Milton Park, Abingdon, Oxon OX14 4RN

Simultaneously published in the USA and Canada
by Routledge
270 Madison Ave, New York, NY 10016

Transferred to Digital Printing 2006

Routledge is an imprint of the Taylor & Francis Group

© 2006 Michelle Pace

Typeset in Sabon by
HWA Text and Data Management, Tunbridge Wells
Printed and bound in Great Britain by
Antony Rowe Ltd, Chippenham, Wiltshire

British Library Cataloguing in Publication Data
A catalogue record for this book is available from the British Library

Library of Congress Cataloging in Publication Data
Pace, Michelle, 1970–
The politics of regional identity : meddling with the Mediterranean /
Michelle Pace.
p. cm. – (The new international relations)
Includes bibliographical references and index.
1. Regionalism. 2. Regionalism–Mediterranean Region.
3. Regionalism–European Union countries. 4. Mediterranean
Region–Foreign relations–European Union countries. 5. European
Union countries–Foreign relations–Mediterranean Region.
6. Geopolitics–Mediterranean Region. 7. Geopolitics–European
Union countries.
I. Title. II. Title.
JF197.P33 2005
327´.09182´2–dc22   2004011916

ISBN 0–415–33396–2 √
ISBN 978–0–415–33396–2

Communitarian International Relations
The epistemic foundations of international relations
Emanuel Adler

Human Rights and World Trade
Hunger in international society
Ana Gonzalez-Pelaez

For my mother, who would have liked to have seen this day so much, and for dad and Egil. I also dedicate this book to my students who share with me my passion for the Med!

Contents

Illustrations

Series editor's preface

This book adds to the growing, but still small, literature that approaches the study of foreign policy through the method of discourse analysis. Using Mediterranean regional politics as its case, it shows how this method can be refined to analyse the nexus of language, culture and power in foreign policy making, and how this in turn can generate insights into, and prescriptions for, the multilateral political processes that go on within and between states. Iver Neumann has been closely in touch with this work, and I turn over to him the task of introducing it in more detail.

Barry Buzan

Preface

In the 1980s, the music industry underwent a technological-driven change. The old vinyl-based medium of the long-playing record gave way to the new metal-based medium of the compact disc. Where the programming of the music was concerned, the change was one from analogue storage, where music was physically engraved by means of a groove that varied incrementally in depth, to digital storage, where music was coded according to the zero-one binary formula. According to some aficionados, the music suffered in the process.

It is perhaps time that those of us who have studied identity politics in terms of self and other face the music as well. The self–other nexus is a digital code, by means of which complex social realities are reduced from the polyphonous to the binary, from the analogue to the digital. Since we are social scientists and not music programmers, there is no *ipso facto* problem with this. It is part of our business to draw out general patterns, and this invariably means flattening details. You cannot produce knowledge about the social without making a distinction between what is more and what is less important, and you cannot produce a model without simplifying reality. If we drew up a map of the social that was full-scale, no-one would have any use for it. The point of studying identity politics in terms of the self–other nexus was to demonstrate that it is impossible to have inclusion without exclusion. Integration of some spells expulsion of others. To those of us who tried to make this point in late 1980s and early 1990s Europe, the political point was to counteract the easy assumption made by a number of politicians and academics alike that with the Cold War gone, Europe would once again be whole and problems with delineation and relations with neighbours would evaporate together with communism. This was an erroneous view, and there was no need to look further than to the fate of Morocco's bid for EC membership in 1987, which Michelle Pace discusses below. Rabat sent a letter to Brussels asking for membership and was told that, since Morocco was not a European country, it could not join. The challenge was simply refused in the shape that it was given by the challenger. In this case, the relationship between the EC and Morocco was reduced by the EC itself as being a digital one between zero and one, between 'non-Europe' and 'Europe'.

The fact that digital thinking exists amongst the people that we study is, however, no excuse for engaging in such thinking ourselves. There is a difference between the models of the world that exist amongst our informants (folk models) and the models that we draw upon in our analytical work (scientific models). The downside, or better limitation, of treating Europe's relationship to its environment in terms of the self–other nexus was that, in availing ourselves of such a problematique, we were scoring an ontological point about identity formation in general, rather than engaging in the substance of politics. Now that those who wanted to hear have taken on board that point, it is time to turn to other ways of posing the problem.

Dr Pace's book tries to do exactly that where the Mediterranean is concerned. One way of reading her work is in terms of how she brings insights from the field of symbolic geography into international relations and, one may hope, Mediterranean studies as well. The key idea in symbolic geography is that any thing – a land-mass, whatever – has an inside that is material (a territory) and an outside that is represented (a map). When we talk about geography within international relations, what is at stake is geography as a represented entity. Now, symbolic geography makes it an object of study to look at the preconditions and effects of operating with one set of geographical delineations rather than another. Let me illustrate by means of two key studies. Larry Wolff's *Imagining Eastern Europe* demonstrates how, historically, Europe was represented as having two key parts: North and South. At some point (Wolff says at the end of the eighteenth century, others say at the beginning of the nineteenth century), this division gave way to a division between East and West. That the effects of such a shift carry enormous political relevance should be immediately clear. To any Swede alive during the Cold War, for example, it would make a difference if she had been trapped in a symbolic geography that bracketed her with the Communist other. Now, that's a counterfactual, so let us simply leave it at that and turn to the other key study, which is Maria Torodova's *Imagining the Balkans*. Her argument is that the chaos in parts of the Balkans in the 1990s brought back a symbolic geography where the entire Balkans (her native Bulgaria included) was represented as the armpit of Europe.

What is at stake, then, is classification. In order to exist as a social fact, the Mediterranean has to be defined in terms of territory, functions, institutions and sundry diacritical markers. A number of different agencies will bring their own representation(s) of the Med to this semantic fight. To the extent that somebody's Mediterranean emerges as dominant, power is at work. In turn, those who have succeeded in ramming through their own representations may harvest effects from the social fact that 'their' representation of the Mediterranean dominates a certain discourse.

Dr Pace's wide-ranging work details a number of relevant aspects of this process. She labels her approach 'discursive constructivism', but she could equally well have categorised her work as symbolic geography. Either way, the approach has deep roots in the social sciences. The idea that what we study are things (like the Med) that have an inside that exists materially, and an outside that is represented, that the representation is a social fact that is the true and exclusive domain of social scientists, and that these facts should be studied in terms of classification all go back to one of the founders of the social sciences, namely Émile Durkheim. Michelle Pace's work is, therefore, not only a nice contribution to the new field of symbolic geography. It is also a contribution to the movement within the discipline of international relations back to the broad tradition of social science understood as a unitary undertaking that transcends narrow empirical specialisation.

Iver B. Neumann
7 July 2004

Acknowledgements

This book would not have been possible without the financial support and critical encouragement of many people. The Centre for European Studies Research at the University of Portsmouth funded my PhD research including field trips and conferences that formed the basis of this monograph.

I finalised the writing up of the monograph as research fellow on the research project 'The European Union and Border Conflicts: The Impact of Integration and Association' (EUBorderConf), funded by a grant from the European Union's Fifth Framework Programme (SERD-2002-00144), with additional funds from the British Academy, and co-ordinated at the Department of Political Science and International Studies (POLSIS), the University of Birmingham, UK. I am particularly grateful to Colin Hay, Thomas Diez, Ingrid van Biezen, Jeremy Jennings, Karim Knio, Alessandra Buonfino, Cornelia Navari and Maureen Waugh from POLSIS for their encouragement and support. I also thank members of the security studies research group at POLSIS, where I presented parts of this book, for their feedback and suggestions. Thanks especially to Stuart Croft, Chris Browning, Donna Lee, Julie Gilson, Terry Terriff and Paul Williams.

This manuscript has been in the making for some time and I have benefited enormously from many discussions of my key ideas over the years. While it would be difficult to thank each and every one individually, I would like to extend my special thanks to the following people:

First and foremost, Iver Neumann who has not only been a great mentor but also a very special and supportive friend. Thanks for ploughing with me through all these times and for your continuous support and encouragement; I would like to extend another special thanks to Michael Shapiro for your useful comments, suggestions and support; many thanks to the anonymous reviewer of my book proposal for his/her constructive comments as well as the series editors Barry Buzan and Richard Little for allowing me such a great opportunity, and Heidi Bagtazo, Grace McInnes, Harriet Brinton and Digby Halsby at Routledge.

The participants at the BISA Poststructural Politics Group workshop on 'Other Europes' held on the 16 May 2003 at SPIRE, Keele University, School of Politics, International Relations and Environment particularly Costas

Constantinou for inviting me to present my thoughts on Europe and the Mediterranean and Christopher Brewin, Rob Walker and Jef Huysmans for an extremely thoughtful discussion; Richard Gillespie, Tobias Schumacher, Gordana Berjan, Xavier Guillaume for reading parts of the book and Sergei Prozorov for reading all the manuscript and for their very useful feedback and comments; all interviewees in Brussels, Greece, Malta and Morocco for their invaluable time and dedication.

A grateful thanks to Egil who ploughed with me through some tough periods and even commented on drafts of my work, for the way in which he supported me, encouraged me and gave me confidence in my work. Thanks also to my families in Malta, Greece, Morocco and Norway.

All the other people I met along the way for making my research so meaningful and such an enjoyable and interesting experience.

Abbreviations

AAs	association agreements
ACP	African Caribbean and Pacific countries
AMU/UMA	Arab Maghreb Union
ASEAN	Association of Southeast Asian Nations
CAP	Common Agricultural Policy
CEECs	Central and Eastern European countries
CESDP	Common European Security Defence Policy
CFSP	Common Foreign and Security Policy
CIS	Commonwealth of Independent States
CNI	Campaign for National Independence (Malta)
COM	Commission document
CSCE	Conference on Security and Co-operation in Europe
CSCM	Conference on Security and Co-operation in the Mediterranean
DG	Directorate-General
DG1B	Directorate-General for External Relations
EC	European Community
EEC	European Economic Community
EFTA	European Free Trade Association
ELIAMEP	Hellenic Foundation for European and Foreign Policy
EMFTZ	Euro–Mediterranean Free Trade Zone
EMP	Euro–Mediterranean Partnership
EMU	European Monetary Union
ENP	European Neighbourhood Policy
EP	European Parliament
EU	European Union
Eurofor	European land or ground rapid reaction forces
Euromarfor	European maritime or naval rapid reaction forces
EuroMeSCo	Euro-Mediterranean Network of Foreign Policy Institutes
EUROSTAT	European Union statistical information
FDI	foreign direct investment
FEMISE	Euro-Mediterranean Forum for Economic Institutes
FIS	Front Islamique du Salut

FP	foreign policy
FPA	foreign policy analysis
FT	*Financial Times*
FTA	Free Trade Area
FTAA	Free Trade Area of the Americas
GAFTA	Greater Arab Free Trade Area
GDP	gross domestic product
GERM	Groupe d'études et de recherches sur la Méditerranée
GMP	Global Mediterranean Policy
GNP	gross national product
HD	human development
HDI	human development index
HDR	Human Development Report
IMF	International Monetary Fund
INSEA	National Institute of Statistics (Rabat, Morocco)
IR	international relations
Med	Mediterranean
MEDA	Mesures d'accompagnement financiers et techniques à la réforme des structures économiques et socials dans le cadre du partenariat Euro-Méditerranéen (Financial and technical measures to accompany the reform of economic and social structures in the framework of the EMP)
Med-Campus	a programme to support cooperation between Mediterranean and community universities
Med-Invest	a programme to support Mediterranean small and medium-sized enterprises (SMEs) in association with community SMEs and professional bodies
MEDSTAT	regional programme for Mediterranean partners statistical information co-operation with EU member states
Med Urbs	a programme to support co-operation between Mediterranean and community local authorities
MENA	Middle East and North Africa
MEP	Member of the European Parliament
MEPP	Middle East Peace Process
MERCOSUR	Mercado Común del Sur
MFA	Ministry of Foreign Affairs
MLP	Malta Labour Party
MNCs	Mediterranean non-member countries
MP	Mouvement Populaire
MPs	Members of Parliament
MPC-12	Mediterranean partner countries (of EMP until 30 April 2004)
MS	(European Union) member states
NAFTA	North American Free Trade Area
NATO	North Atlantic Treaty Organisation

ND	Nea Demokratia
NGOs	non-governmental organisations
NMCs	non-(EU)member countries
NMP	New Mediterranean Policy
NNP	New Neighbourhood Policy
N+S	North and South
OSCE	Organisation for Security and Co-operation in Europe
PASOK	Panellino Socialistiko Kinima
PHARE	Poland and Hungary aid for economic restructuring
PLO	Palestine Liberation Organization
PN	Partit Nazzjonalista
PSOE	Partido Socialista Obrero Espãnol
RMP	Renewed (or Redirected) Mediterranean policy
RSC	regional security complex
SADR/RASD	Saharawi Arab Democratic Republic/République Arabe Sahraouie Démocratique
UK	United Kingdom
UN	United Nations
UNDP	United Nations Development Programme
UNHDR	United Nations Human Development Report
UNFP	Union Nationale des Forces Populaires
US	United States
USA	United States of America
US$	United States dollars
USFP	Union Socialiste des Forces Populaires
WEU	Western European Union
WTO	World Trade Organisation

1   Introduction

The geographical term 'region' usually refers to a homogenous area of the earth's surface with characteristics that make it distinct from the areas that surround it. Moreover, a geographical area is generally specified as a 'region' when there is a certain pattern of regular relations and interactions among the countries in that area. The distinction between areas may be based on natural or man-made characteristics or a combination of both. Scale distinctions are made between large-scale regions of continental proportions (*macro regions*) down to very small structures (*micro regions*). Moreover, regions with common region-wide characteristics (*uniform regions*) are distinguished from those in which the characteristics are most strongly discernible at or near the centre of the region and least strongly at the boundaries (*focal regions*). In the case of the Mediterranean, the classification of this '(macro) region' is a rather contentious one.[1] In fact, there are two different representations of the Mediterranean commonly found in the literature: the Mediterranean as a 'region' (with sub-regions) or the Mediterranean as an interface between coherent regions. In the case of the former, the Mediterranean is said to embody many 'sub-regions' (geographically speaking).[2] These can broadly be said to be southern Europe, which includes southern European Union (EU) member states (which now includes Malta and Cyprus since the EU's 1 May 2004 enlargement) and at least parts of Turkey; North Africa which consists of Algeria, Libya, Mauritania,[3] Morocco, and Tunisia; and the Levant which comprises Egypt,[4] Israel, the Palestinian Territories, Jordan, Lebanon and Syria.[5] These classifications are debatable: some would further differentiate between southern Europe (now six EU states) and south-eastern Europe. Moreover, many would call southern Europe and North Africa regions (or something other than sub-regions). One may argue that these can be both regions and sub-regions, namely that, for example, North Africa can be classified as a region but also as a sub-region of the Middle East.

Despite these controversies, there is a growing inclination to consider the Mediterranean in a holistic fashion in all Western institutions, as a geopolitical unit that ties the nations around its rim with common 'concerns' and shared 'interests'. Various academic studies, especially those within the field of international relations (IR), also treat the Mediterranean as a 'region' due to the interdependent nature of the political, economic and social issues affecting the area as a whole.[6] Before presenting the manner in which this book addresses its undertaking, there is a question which needs to be dealt with: One may ask, but why the Mediterranean? The Mediterranean is an area that involves the leading states and international organisations in the world. Also, it is often conceived of as a meeting point of the 'North' and 'South' and of different cultures in the area: as an interface between three continents, North Africa, Europe and Asia: as a 'region' with diversity and as a complex case which presents challenges – perhaps more than other areas. It is also a reasonably contemporary theme to codify the conditions and effects of discourses on regionality. Moreover, there seems to be a gap in the available material with a critical approach to the study of the Mediterranean area.

As its title suggests, this book seeks to problematise conventional conceptions of regionality and to specifically re-think the Mediterranean 'region' in an open, relational, political context. It also aims to suggest a re-imagining of this 'region' politically, geographically, socially and culturally. In an era of globalisation, boundaries are constantly shifting and changing. The major objective of this book is to *conceptualise* the social construction of this area (as a holistic 'region') and the underlying assumptions of such imaginings, and in so doing to reveal how regions, in particular the Mediterranean region, are produced and reproduced over space and time. Despite the several references to the Mediterranean as a taken-for-granted concept, there does not seem to be one common, shared understanding of this area. So, what is the Mediterranean? On the one hand, any attempt to map the (social) relations of the Mediterranean and their overlapping points runs the risk of misinterpretation. On the other hand, there is an obvious need (especially for an academic investigation like this one) to ensure that the Mediterranean is recognisable as an object of study and that all those interested in this area are in fact talking about the same 'thing'. The boundary lines that govern the physical and political relationships of the Mediterranean region may provide such a common understanding. However, to draw such precise boundaries is bound to lead to misunderstanding and misinterpretation. Once such lines are drawn, they give the impression that all relations pertaining to this 'region' fall neatly within these boundaries. The result in effect is to fix the Mediterranean's changing geography and to leave the 'region' without meaning. Therefore, whether one takes the view of the Mediterranean as a region or as a meeting place between regions, one runs into this problem, so neither is satisfactory. But one can ask does this mean that we stop talking about 'regions'? This chapter has started by criticising the notion of the Mediterranean as a region sufficiently to put the term 'region' in inverted commas. The next question that follows from such a stance is then whether there is any justification for continuing to refer to the 'region' (even in inverted commas) or whether one should advocate a policy of referring to the Mediterranean as 'the Mediterranean area', thereby adopting a more neutral term (and which implies a focus on the society/people of a particular space).

The latter option is the one chosen for this book since it holds that, inasmuch as the sustained political relevance of regions depends on people considering them to be relevant to their activities, the study of regions must in some way include the study of meaning and identity, particularly processes of identification, categorisation and self-understanding.[7]

It is important to clarify here what is meant by identity – as this concept will often be used in this book – particularly the relation of identity to culture. Is identity a substitute for political culture? As the above section explored a problematisation of region, so too the concept of identity needs to be explicated. Identity is understood here as the process of associating oneself closely with other individuals or reference groups to the extent that one comes to adopt their goals and values and to share considerably in their experiences. However, the notion of identity also includes those processes of *disassociation* from other individuals or reference groups, thereby incorporating a rejection of certain groups' goals, values and experiences. In other words, identity is a process of the 'continuous making of the self' through othering. It is therefore a flexible, fluid concept rather than a static, fixed notion. Hence, it follows that national identities as well as collective identities have their internal and external others who may be threatening while others may be inspiring.[8] It may well be argued then that identity is neither an independent nor the dependent variable but rather an *element*, an important one indeed, that influences foreign policy (for example, the European Union's foreign policy) in interaction with other factors. These factors include: ideology, member states' domestic politics and party-political differences and national policy-making style(s).[9]

This rethinking of the Mediterranean has been encouraged by the fact that this area is a complex space in the making and involves overlapping and intersecting relationships. It also involves some concept of evolution, of dynamics. Since this author finds it problematic to talk about the Mediterranean region, the latter will be treated as an area to which theories of regionalism have been (controversially) applied.

Regionalism is often said to result from increasing interdependence between states. For instance, after the Arab–Israeli war of 1973, the Euro–Arab Dialogue was created as a means of regularising, controlling and manipulating the emerging system of Euro–Arab interdependence.[10] The then European Community (EC) member states attempted to influence the economic policies of oil-rich Arab states through economic aid to resource-poor Arab countries (what one author calls 'the evolving substance of associative diplomacy').[11] The Euro–Arab Dialogue was rather unsuccessful because European policy remained politically motivated. Europeans advised Arab states to avoid capital-intensive industries and to concentrate on labour-intensive industries geared for Arab markets rather than for export. Thus, the Europeans anticipated the potential danger of competition resulting from a possible future Arab industrial surplus and thereby sought to protect European markets.[12] During the early 1970s, the EC also looked at the Mediterranean and perceived this area's potential as an interface between the two regions of Europe and Africa. In seeking to establish relations with its southern neighbours, the EC launched its (so-called) Global Mediterranean Policy (GMP). Following the end of the 'Cold War' and the collapse of the bi-polar international system, regionalism once again appeared as a natural phenomenon in the new international order. The EC saw the transition to a new European order as a positive opportunity to develop its external role. (The Maastricht Treaty of December 1991 adopted a Common Foreign and Security Policy (CFSP).) Euro–Mediterranean relations were enhanced through the New Mediterranean Policy (NMP, also known as the Renewed or Redirected Mediterranean Policy or RMP) that was introduced in December 1990. EC–Mediterranean initiatives, however, failed to adopt the necessary long-term policies required to tackle the increasing disparities between the two sides of the Mediterranean.[13] In an effort to revive the potential of the Mediterranean (to become a region), the EU launched the Euro–Mediterranean Partnership (EMP) in November 1995. To date, this policy is believed to be the most successful of all EU Mediterranean initiatives since it addresses political, economic and cultural relations between European and Mediterranean partners. But have EU member states reflected on the actual 'substance' of the Mediterranean? Or is the Mediterranean just an 'other' in Europe's self-identification process? Few works have considered the EMP in such identity terms. This book therefore hopes to contribute to studies of the EMP by looking into the process of negotiation in the EU's identity formation and how EU identity (that is, the EU's identification processes) is forged as the effect of a securitisation process *vis-à-vis* the Mediterranean area.[14] Before going any further, it is worth introducing the theoretical framework that has informed the approach adopted here.

Theoretical framework

The questions of 'place', boundaries, borders and space have raised issues of theoretical approaches to the study of 'regions' and even of the nature of theory itself; of the conceptualisation of regions and their practical definitions and of the criteria that make regions, or what should be studied 'within' them.[15] These questions have recently found themselves on the agenda of IR.[16] The following brief outline relates to conventional theories that mostly focus on regional arrangements based on security co-operation issues. These will lead us on to the more critical theoretical approaches to the study of regions (which have influenced this work and) that look into the processes of region making through the practice of foreign policy and identity politics.[17]

   In the edited book of Lake and Morgan, Pervin claims that '(T)he transformations generated by the end of the Cold War and the demise of the Soviet Union as a superpower create an opportunity to re-evaluate the interrelation between regional subsystems and the global system, and to distinguish the autonomous dynamics of the region from the impact of external influences'.[18] The historical development of the past 15 years, together with advances in IR theory, have led to a renewed interest in explaining the origins and the management of conflict at the regional level. The authors' theoretical framework is based on the basic unit of analysis being the regional security complex (RSC, a term introduced by Barry Buzan, see below) that is defined as 'a set of states continually affected by one or more [positive or negative] security externalities that emanate from a distinct geographic area'.[19] Membership in an RSC includes great powers whose actions generate externalities in the region or who are affected by the externalities produced there.[20] Morgan proposes a 'ladder' of regional order ideal types where successive rungs on the ladder represent greater levels of interstate co-operation with the final stage being integration. The very fluidity of one of the empirical cases cited in this book – that of Pervin on the Arab–Israeli conflict – reflects the complexity of the concept of regional order. As Lake points out, 'negative security externalities will always be greater, and positive security externalities smaller, than the states of a regional security system desire'.[21]

In his 1991 book, Buzan claims that 'In security terms, "region" means that a distinct and significant subsystem of security relations exists among a set of states whose fate is that they have been locked into geographical proximity with each other'.[22] He also introduced the notion of a security complex theory. For Buzan '(A) security complex is … a group of states whose primary security concerns link together sufficiently closely that their national securities cannot realistically be considered apart from one another'.[23] Building on the work of Deutsch *et al.*,[24] for Buzan, a security community is one of the extreme relational possibilities along the spectrum of a given complex that defines security interdependence. In a security community 'disputes among all the members are resolved to such an extent that none fears … either political assault or military attack by any of the others'.[25] Moreover, for Buzan, a mature anarchy is a position on his continuum of regional security configurations, related to the idea of a 'security community'. For Buzan the movement on a spectrum of weak to strong states directs attention to the domestic level, and the corresponding movement from immature to mature anarchy (or in regional terms from security complex to security community) introduces the possibility and need for change at the international level. However, this advance depends on maintaining the realist doctrine on state primacy. The agency of change in the domestic as in the international sphere cannot be attributed to sub-state or supra-state actors. Following Buzan's work there has been further exploration of such a security 'problem' at the former Centre for Peace and Conflict Research in Copenhagen. This so-called 'Copenhagen School' of security studies – which includes Buzan – took a new turn and refined the concept of security. The new focus and emphasis shifted from the primacy Buzan originally gave to the state, to society and identity. It was recognised that societal identity is a core value vulnerable to threats and in need of security. As examples, the authors state that identity has been a source of resistance to integration in the EU and the major cause of upheaval in central and eastern Europe.[26] In this revised work, Wæver *et al.* gave an old idea a new angle in *discourse* on international affairs.[27] Identity was no longer consigned to the neorealist category of soft security concepts. The analysis of collective identity started to be approached from a deconstructionist, sociological angle, focusing on the practices and processes by which people and groups construct their self-image.

However, this work appears to have remained somewhat realist. The term 'society' is not meant to connote a process of negotiation, affirmation and reproduction, or even to embrace the 'system of interrelationships which connects together the individuals who share a common culture', as in Giddens' more traditional sociological formula.[28] The work of Wæver *et al.* implies a less fluid reality. Their work remains at a level of reification that excludes discussion of questions of process. If they were concerned with the process of social construction, they would not regard society as 'a social agent that has an independent reality'[29] and they would have to conduct an analysis at the sub-social level. Some analysts have criticised the notion of 'societal security/insecurity' put forward by Wæver and the Copenhagen School arguing that this is a communitarian concept that is quite at odds with human rights-based concepts such as the Commission on Global Governance's concept of civic security.[30] In the Bosnian war, for example, societal security, in the sense of the security of ethnic identity, could be said to have been strengthened at the expense of individual security or the identity of secular multi-cultural society. Thus, critiques argue that this notion of societal security can have authoritarian dangers.

Wæver *et al.* acknowledge that economic and other threats to particular groups within a society can affect the security of society as a whole.[31] This focus on the multi-dimensionality of threats was taken up in a later work.[32] In this influential work, Buzan, Wæver and de Wilde develop an innovative distinction across five different sectors of security according to the different relationship prevailing within each sector between the threat(s), the referent object (the target of the threat) and its perception of vulnerabilities, and the securitising actors (the actors in charge of defusing the threat). The *military* sector refers to the traditional core of national and regional security concerns, namely relations of forceful coercion. In this case, the referent object is the state, whose sovereignty and territorial integrity are endangered by an external threat and defended by the ruling elites. The *political* sector focuses on relations of authority, governing status and recognition. The social order and the organisational stability of a governance structure are at stake here. The EU, for example, may be challenged by an external ideology in terms of its internal or external legitimacy. The *economic* sector covers relations of trade, production and finance and evaluates how dependence on external supplies constitutes a vulnerability, in case of interruptions of imports or, more generally, of threats to the welfare of the 'people'. The *environment* sector also refers to the welfare and well-being of a country's citizens, albeit with a specific focus on the natural environment. The *societal* sector concerns the collective identity of a political entity and the referent objects are groups that can legitimately demand institutional protection (of the polity) from threats challenging their identity and cohesion. The 'Copenhagen School' suggests that a security threat entails an existential danger, justifying emergency measures. Such an existential threat is recognised and singled out through 'speech acts'. Therefore, the utterance of the term is constitutive of security, as it presents a claim to use special rights to counter the threat.[33] Observers argue that although the debate on expanding the security agenda to non-military sectors and non-state referent objects launched an interesting discussion about the security (studies) agenda, it has not really dealt with the meaning of security.[34] For some analysts, the debate has focused too much on adding adjectives such as 'societal', 'environmental', etc. to security but has largely neglected the 'signifying work' or what security signifies – that is, the noun 'security' itself.[35] Huysmans, for example, approaches security as a 'thick signifier', in which case the enunciation of security creates the (in)security condition.[36] What then, makes an issue a security issue? Bicchi argues that two elements must be present: (a) a discourse defining it as such; and (b) a series of decisions translating the discourse into practice. The discursive element is crucial in order to single out the interpretation it receives from relevant actors that can thus clarify its conceptual context and political relevance. It is thus the *interpretation* that classifies the security issue as such.[37] Therefore, it is interesting to reflect on the usage of the term 'securitise'. There is a sense in which Buzan *et al.* use 'securitise' mainly in a 'negative' sense. For example, one can say that in the recent US-led war in Iraq 'the US securitised Saddam Hussein' where the sense of the word is to convey that a discourse exists defining Saddam Hussein as a threat. This is commonsensical, and perhaps unavoidable, but it does seem that it distorts the 'whole' meaning of the term by putting all the emphasis on the supposed source of threat, and none on the specification of the referent object. In this example, is the US not securitising itself as much as Saddam Hussein? This observation emphasises Wæver's own point about the multi-layered nature of discourse.[38] A broader question relates to the relationship between the sectors. Is the economic sector not sometimes a part (or subset) of the identity/societal sector? Is an overlap of sectors possible? The synthesis of sectors and the process of securitisation therefore are in need of more explication. Are sectors defined by their referent objects or by the means used? What is and what is not a sector? How can one distinguish between political and military sectors? This leads to a further interesting discussion as to why select these five sectors – economic, environmental, military, political and societal – specifically? Where does religion fit in this schema of sectors? For example, in the context of Morocco, the Moroccan king has a dual role: one as the representative of the people (state role) and another as the prophet (a religious role). Hence, what is the nature of 'religion' as such and does this potentially open up another sector? Recently, Bagge Laustsen and Wæver have argued that religion should be seen as a sixth separate sector.[39] The authors explore the logic of securitisation of objects of a religious nature (for example, what 'fundamentalists' fear and how fundamentalists are seen as a security threat). Their work shows why it is often particularly tempting to securitise religion, how it is done, and what doing it does. This focus has shed light on further questions in the debate. Which evidence counts in the process of securitisation? Whose recognition counts? Does recognition of a security issue depend on who or what is targeted? In the earlier example, for the USA, is it American society that counts? How do we mark a successful securitisation, for who and for what? The position of the Copenhagen School in this debate has clearly evolved through time and is unquestionably coming close to encompassing the effects of inter-unit relations. Whom exactly is being marked a securitisation? Is it the international community as the ultimate audience? The debate may benefit from a further discussion on the role of individual leaders as referent objects. Moreover, if we take collective identity as a constructed and reproduced issue then this can embody all five or six dimensions of security. The 'old' Copenhagen School seem to approach the apparent fact of societal identity as a taken-for-granted reality that defines the security problem. However, identity (and the processes of identification that are entailed) is not a fact of society; it is a process of negotiation among people and interest groups. Being Maltese, Greek, Belgian or Moroccan is a consequence of a political process, and it is processes of identification and self-understanding, that is, identity formation, not the label symbolising identity/identities, which constitute the reality that needs explication.[40] Moreover, where identity is relevant, it is just as likely to be the *effect* of a security problem rather than its cause. This may be analysed by deconstructing the process of identity formation/identification at the sub-societal level. Identity is often constructed and articulated as a result of a labelling process that mirrors a conflict of interest at the political level.[41] The 'new' or 'revised' Copenhagen School has moved in this direction:[42] yet, in terms of the School's 'societal security' it is still unclear whether there is a distinction between the 'social', identity and society/societal: society in non-identity-defined terms seems to remain a problem in the School's schema. In some senses, the School's 'societal' sector appears as an 'identity' sector. But the question remains: what if actors look at threats to the functioning of society in other terms – for example, in terms of societal cohesion, group solidarity and trust as threatened by crime, or neo-liberal agendas (as some Mediterranean partners read the EU's project for the Mediterranean)? This is not covered by society, because it is not identical to identity, but in all its diversity, at the core of society lies social cohesion of which 'identity' is just one element. Thus, identity and society may overlap, as do all the other sectors, but they have different focal points. How then is 'society' to be understood? This leaves room for debates on 'society' in non-identity terms.

The perennial struggle between and across different discourses about the definition of the categories and phenomena that make up our 'social' world is not only the agenda of the Copenhagen School but more broadly of the work of critical theorists/constructivists.[43] The seminal work of Steve Smith has been very instructive in this thinking.[44] Smith's starting point is that although social constructivism offers an improved explanatory power in studies of European governance, it has largely been ill-defined in the literature. He therefore argues that there is in effect a range of social constructivisms within IR, ranging from rational choice theorists (rationalism) to middle ground theorists (social constructivism) to postmodern scholars (reflectivism), with divergent meta-theoretical assumptions. This range of constructivisms share a similar starting point in that they reject assumptions of rationalist accounts but diverge in social ontologies, that is, in how to characterise European governance.[45] Smith is not very happy with the label of 'middle ground' for social constructivisms and therefore develops a distinction between 'thick' and 'thin' constructivisms: to the extent that constructivists treat reasons as causes, they can easily relate to (neo-liberal institutionalist) rationalist arguments (thin constructivists). But, to the extent that they cannot, they are then involved in telling a different type of story about the social world, one that differs from the rationalist story on ontological and epistemological grounds (thick constructivists). The approach followed in this book is a reflectivist one where social constructivism is combined with discourse analysis, thus emphasising the power of enabling discourses in foreign policy (policy is part of discourse). As Foucault claims 'discourse in general and scientific discourse in particular, is so complex a reality that we not only can but should approach it at different levels and with different methods'.[46] Discourse analysis can be used as a method to analyse the social world, specifically those statements which point to the varied nature of this world. Foucault's methodological works can therefore be seen as tools for studying the world in the light of statements that constitute our social world. Those who follow a Foucauldian, radical constructivist analysis hence point to the need for pluralist methods in an analysis of discourses. This radical strand of constructivism offers tools that can be applied to regionalism and region-building and which can then highlight the social/political creation of spaces and specifically of regions. Boundaries have a crucial role in the construction of regional consciousness. Therefore, this process of region-construction is linked to the politics of identity since regions can be formed in response to discursive formations of an 'other'. Some 'thick' constructivists work within the field of regional and identity studies.[47] Within the 'soft' or 'thin' constructivist works in IR, some hold that the structures of human association are determined primarily by shared ideas rather than material forces.[48] Hence, along the constructivist continuum, it follows that regions are determined by discourses and practices. Moreover, identities and interests of purposive actors, including states, are constructed by these shared ideas rather than given by nature. Critical theorists in general criticise neo-realists and neo-liberals, who see the structure of the international system as a distribution of material capabilities, with the neo-liberals adding institutions to the material base. They maintain that it is ideas and culture that constitute the meaning and content of material factors. They further state that ideas shape the identities and interests of actors. Wendt, for example, develops a complex theory of structure, agency and process based on three distinctions: macro and micro levels; causal and constitutive effects; and effects on behaviour and on identities and interests. Since Wendt argues that social structures (such as regions) may constitute agents (states), 'the nature of states might be bound up conceptually with the structure of the state system', and that 'the ideas held by individual states are given content and meaning by the ideas which they share with other states'.[49] In contrast to Waltz's *Theory of International Politics*,[50] Wendt demonstrates that many of the states' essential qualities (including identities) are contingent and socially constructed. Whereas neo-realists explain structural change in terms of the distribution of capabilities, Wendt sees it in terms of the evolution of identities through natural and cultural selection. He also discusses how interdependence, common fate, homogenisation and self-restraint may be responsible for collective identity formation/identification processes (that is, including regional identity).[51] Hence, Wendt's strand of constructivism is not arguing that material interests are irrelevant or about trying to privilege ideational over material explanations. Rather, Wendt's point is that material factors become intelligible only in light of ideational factors that attach meanings to them.[52] Wendt's work brings us back to the discussion of regions and how it is to be approached throughout this book. This book has been influenced by the works of critical theorists, particularly the strand of constructivists labelled as radical or reflective. Rather than applying conventional, static theoretical approaches which reify a social configuration of a region as an entity that exists, this book adopts a process-based framework, adapted from the *discursive constructivist* strand of social constructivist approaches, where the project of region-making is analysed as an ongoing process and not as a fixed concept;[53] and, moreover, as a process through which collective identities are negotiated and continuously in the making. This approach is more akin to the work of radical constructivists where the main focus lies on the role of language in the construction of entities such as the Mediterranean. Discussions of the Mediterranean are then not simply descriptions of an existing reality but are instead part of the process of constructing that reality and where discursive practices enable such an entity to be conceptualised, talked about and addressed in policy statements, etc.[54] This approach does not imply discarding conventional theoretical frameworks. Rather, in order to have a more informed view of 'reality', we need to work with theories in parallel, that is, to take a multi-disciplinary approach to the study of regions.

Methodology

This book analyses the construction of the Mediterranean region from the emergence of the EC's bilateral relations with Mediterranean countries during the 1960s up to the present day and illustrates *how* varying discourses of *Mediterraneanness* have been central in framing the possibilities of available action for EU decision makers.

It does this through a dual methodology: first, a textual analysis of EuroMed documents from 1960s to date (EU statements and texts: EuroMed publications prepared and distributed regularly by the Commission services, including EuroMed synopsis, EuroMed special features, EuroMed reports, EuroMed calendars and EuroMed information notes;[55] Commission reports and brochures on the EMP, the latter given more importance since it is the most recent and considered to be the most successful EU Med policy to date). In the case of EU discourses on the Mediterranean, the discursive practices of three selected and specific EU member states, namely France, Italy and Spain (on the Mediterranean), were added on in order to double check which member states influence EU policy on the Mediterranean. This analysis is reduced to these three EU members since it is assumed that they share a similar Mediterranean sensibility that is more pronounced than that of other EU member states.[56] Second, through interviews/fieldwork to complement the documentary approach.[57] A first set of interviews were conducted in Brussels with EU policy-makers involved in policy-making towards the Mediterranean. A second set of interviews were conducted in three case study countries: Greece, Malta and Morocco. The objectives of this dual methodology were to:

- understand the rationale of policy-makers within the EU in their policies towards the Mediterranean;
- chart the policy instruments used by EU policy-makers towards the Mediterranean;
- map out the EU's policy-making process towards the Mediterranean;
- analyse the images and perceptions of the Mediterranean in EU policy-making, and the impact of these images and perceptions on policy;
- contrast images and perceptions of the Mediterranean in case study countries with those in Brussels;
- contrast perceptions of EU policy on the Mediterranean in case study countries with EU actors' perceptions of EU Med policy.

Thus, this methodological framework attempts to understand and assess the EU's influence – through discursive practices and the provision of legitimacy to policy decisions – on the Mediterranean. Moreover, this framework provides a platform for an analysis of the degree to which the EU becomes an important point of reference in the political debates within Mediterranean countries over time.

Interviews

The majority of interviews were carried out between May 1998 and January 2004. Some of these interviews were taped (with interviewees' consent) and transcribed – the transcription was then sent to interviewees for approval. In those interviews that were not taped, detailed notes were taken during the interview, which were then transcribed and sent to the interviewee to approve and amendments made where necessary. In such cases, this resulted in additions and clarifications being made to (rather than subtractions from) the transcribed material, which further improved the value of the material.

Who was interviewed

In terms of material for the implementation of discourse analysis as method, the model adopted here followed that of Ole Wæver[58] and aimed mostly at 'responsible' politicians acting in their official function but also others who contribute to shaping public discourse. These include intellectuals/academics/researchers, policy-makers (government representatives at ministerial level, representatives of political parties at higher levels, professionals otherwise involved in policy-making), diplomats/officials, and journalists/opinion leaders (from opposition parties as well as government), through whom one can gauge the logic of the 'Mediterranean' concept examined more explicitly, and then check whether the same mechanism is more implicitly or explicitly at play with politicians. (The position of the interviewees within their organisational structures was also important.) When observing politicians, it has been fruitful to select 'difficult situations': contexts in which heated debates are underway (for example, on Malta's membership of the European Union) where they need to mobilise rhetorical power and therefore they draw on those semiotic structures that generate most *meaning* for their purpose. These elite groups were the final choice of the sample of interviewees selected for this research since it was assumed that these groups are the most informed on Mediterranean affairs, EU affairs and on the EMP – the topics for the questions of this investigation. These elites were also assumed to have an impact and influence on the foreign policy-making process in the EU or in their respective countries and they were also easier to reach. Interviews were carried out with politicians and policy -makers on both sides of the Euro-Mediterranean space. The interviewees in Brussels included Commission officials and case study representatives based in Brussels. These key players were selected on the assumption that they play important roles in the EU's production of the Mediterranean as a concept and have a crucial influence on the EU's Mediterranean policy. In Brussels, interviews were conducted in either English or French.

The fieldwork also benefited from a number of open interviews in a selected number of countries in the Mediterranean area. These were aimed at codifying the actions that forged an idea, if any, of the Mediterranean, in this area. The cases of Greece, Malta and Morocco were selected since during the time of writing, they were at different stages and in different positions in their relations with Europe and the EU: Greece, an EU member country, Malta going through the process of negotiating accession with the EU and Morocco an associate of the EU.[59] In Malta, Maltese and English were the main languages used during interviews, while in Morocco, French was mainly used with some Arabic at times, and in Greece most interviews were conducted in

English or French. The aim of this selection is to show that those features these cases have in common provide a basis for a systemic comparison and explanation of their differences. The aim is not to neglect any fundamental and fairly obvious differences that exist between these societies by fitting them into a procrustean bed of structural similarities.

The interviewees in Malta, Greece and Morocco were selected amongst influential policy-makers who have been in office during critical turning points in EU–Mediterranean relations, particularly from the early 1990s onwards (when the EMP was formulated and launched). Consequently, these targeted individuals were selected because they represent a spectrum of perspectives and experiences in relation to the EU's policy-making on the Mediterranean. Currently, these policy-makers also play a role as public intellectuals in the case study countries; some of them have columns in their respective countries' national newspapers, most regularly feature in foreign policy debates on television and in various public conferences. Therefore, they were valuable sources not only for assessing the developments that occurred in the past, but also for relating those past events to current developments.

How selection bias was avoided

The temporal span in which these interviews were held slightly complicates the way in which the interviews represent various actors' views of the EU's policy-making process on the Mediterranean. Because of the ever-changing political developments that take place in the Mediterranean, these interviews document viewpoints based on a general notion of 'EU Med policy', but also take as concrete examples of the EU's Med policy at particular times and during particular political events. The complication lies in the fact that these two levels, the general and the concrete, do not always lead to convergent assessments of EU Med policy. For these reasons, slightly different issues were raised in the different interviews that reflect not only differing political opinions, but the temporal context as well. (I had initially directed a similar set of questions to my interviewees, but later allowed the interviews to evolve in an open-ended fashion.) After describing the research question, I first asked interviewees to evaluate the nature and the extent of EU policy-making on the Mediterranean, then directed specific questions relating to developments that occurred since the 1960s, and finally asked interviewees to discuss how and whether their personal views regarding the European Union and the Mediterranean have evolved over the years. In this sense, the interviews are very helpful in tracing a diachronic change of opinions across the EU and Mediterranean countries' political spectrum. At the same time, they also present a highly complex set of data because of the different variables involved. The possibility of holding a second set of interviews with some of the interviewees at a later stage was for this reason left open and some interviewees revisited.

How the interviews were structured

November 1995 marked the crucial political decision made by the EU and its Mediterranean partners to adopt a refreshed, global and comprehensive EU Med policy. This concerted effort aimed at turning the Mediterranean basin into an area of dialogue, exchange and co-operation guaranteeing peace, stability and prosperity and culminated in the Barcelona Declaration. In terms of this research, this has meant that the assessment of the EU's Mediterranean policy focused, in the main, on the Barcelona Declaration which has been treated as a seminal text since it has a broad reception among European as well as Mediterranean actors (policy-makers, academics, practitioners, etc). This means that it plays a prominent role in EU conceptualisations of the Mediterranean and in Mediterranean partner countries' perceptions of the EU's policy on the Med. Niels Akerstrom Andersen calls such texts 'monuments' and encourages discourse analysts to perform monument criticism.[60]

How the discourses were extracted from the interview material

This work has followed the methodological approach taken by Ole Wæver in selecting the concept of Mediterranean 'region' and investigating ways in which the Mediterranean is thought of. The application of discourse analysis as a method thus establishes a model by fitting material from different contexts, actors and years into a structure. By moving through time and looking at differentiated actors, one can see *how* structures shape, get reproduced and modified. The analysis was also undertaken across time with the aim of showing how these structures constrained or suggested arguments and positions. For these reasons, fieldwork was carried out on the ground in Brussels, Greece, Morocco and Malta and extensive reading was made about the history of the latter three countries. This helped to establish a general sense of the countries and their politics, which in practice, as well as for theoretical reasons, helped to gradually recognise recurring patterns and identify puzzling formulations that in turn revealed important general insights after the fieldwork was carried out.[61]

It is often argued that this method is not always received with enthusiasm in political science: the analyst can only investigate a limited number of countries, because one needs to know the language, the history of the country and a rather broad spectrum of its culture and politics. A culture is a closed *meaning* system, defined by its unique traits, exhibiting an organic inner coherence, and therefore only possible to understand from within – preferably through living it.[62] Keeping in mind the critical, theoretical approach adopted in this work, this book does not attempt to offer ultimate causes for explanation. Rather, it seeks to better understand the pattern of regularities in discourses on the Mediterranean, as these find their way into EU foreign policy processes.

Thus, by taking a discourse analysis approach, this methodological framework aimed at developing an assessment of the EU's policy-making process of the Mediterranean. In doing so, it centred on comparing ways in which different concepts of the 'Mediterranean' are presented in public discourse by different actors, in Brussels and in Mediterranean partner countries and at different points in time, especially following specific political developments.

The writing process – how the interview data became text

Analysts have highlighted the challenge of foreign policy analysis of how to deal theoretically with general beliefs to which actors adhere: not only in relation to political ideology but in relation to beliefs about concepts such as Europe, the Mediterranean, national identity, etc.[63] A discourse analysis approach to foreign policy-making takes into account the impact of language and societal foundations of these beliefs. This approach is based on linguistics and the concept of political discourse. The main idea of discourse analysis as method is that this discourse framework can help to analyse differences and similarities in, for example, French, Italian and Spanish policies towards the Mediterranean since the 1960s and how these in turn impact upon EU Mediterranean policies. In this context, this framework also assists in our understanding of Greek, Moroccan and Maltese interviewees' perceptions of the EMP. The different meanings, signified in different discourses, of concepts which are assumed to be critical concepts in the policies of these countries and those of the EU towards the Mediterranean are analysed. The discourse of concepts such as the EMP, Mediterranean, regionalism, 'regional' identity (European identity and Mediterranean identity), national identity, 'Partnership', 'North and South', security, economic development, dialogue and co-operation can account for French, Italian and Spanish policies towards the Mediterranean since in the 1960s and how these feed into EU Med policy. They can likewise account for ambivalent attitudes to the EMP from the case study countries. Discourse analysis as method therefore provides an empirical evaluation of one of the 'reflectivist' approaches.[64]

For this purpose, two questionnaires were prepared in an attempt to capture these general beliefs. The questionnaires attempted to capture beliefs within foreign policy-making processes and take into account the language in which beliefs are expressed by interviewees and their social nature. The conclusion is that, although certain aspects of French, Italian and Spanish policies towards the Mediterranean since the 1960s and of Maltese, Greek and Maltese critical views on the EU's EMP could also be explained through external factors, the discourse/'understanding' aspect is indispensable for a general analysis of the period. Rather than focusing on individual decision makers alone (agency), the questionnaires aimed at focusing and including in the analysis the context in which agents operate, with the related constraints and embedded norm-structures impacting on the process of decision making. Thus, this methodology highlights that what matters in policy-making is *how* policy-makers *imagine* the Mediterranean (milieu) to be, not how it actually *is* and which determines agents' behaviour. Hence, the questionnaires aimed at explicating the language dynamics in which actors operate. The analysis which is presented in this book helps explicate and understand the depth and persistence of particular views and of the possibility of continuity of beliefs (across changes of persons or even of governments). A discourse analysis approach to foreign policy-making focuses on understanding beliefs and on long-term political decisions and more general factors or regular markers across time and space, where social, widespread beliefs prevail.

Why interviews and documentary approach/analysis were chosen

In line with the theoretical framework adopted in this book, the methodology selected in order to inquire into the social construction of the Mediterranean area aimed at investigating the processes of social practices that constitute this notion. In this book, discourse analysis is therefore being used both as a way of interpreting the world and also as a method for doing so. In adopting a language approach to the construction of the Mediterranean in EU foreign policy-making processes, the author has found it useful to frame her research question through discourse analysis as a useful dialogue on *how* best to critically evaluate foreign policy theory as practice, specifically the EMP as practice. Following the work of other IR theorists,[65] the main research materials used in this context have been EU documents, transcripts' materials and academic sources (books and articles). In order to test the reliability of discourse analysis, the researcher encounters the problem of *when to stop* analysing texts. Milliken and Wæver suggest that the analysis is complete 'when upon adding new texts and comparing their object spaces, the researcher finds consistently that the theoretical categories she has generated work for those texts'.[66]

An analysis of the data collected from documents and the fieldwork aimed at revealing whether there was any regularity in markers across discourses on the Mediterranean (across Mediterranean countries and across EU discourses and Mediterranean discourses) or whether there was a specific position in one country or between countries. In so doing, it also attempted to navigate through the multitude of *meanings* which are attributed to the Mediterranean in different social/political contexts and to explore their articulation, competition and disarticulation.

The reasons why this dual methodology was chosen to investigate the EU's foreign policy on the Mediterranean include the following:

- Discourse analysis as a method makes theory about 'signification' (that which is signified) or what often appear as rather abstract and vague concepts, researchable through the actual processes of a sign system.
- This method for 'reading' EU practices on the Mediterranean makes research better organised and easier to carry through.

- This method can also assist in bringing greater insight into *how* a discourse is organised through its control over interpretive processes and into *how* discourses differ in their construction of social reality.
- Discourse analysis can facilitate communication and debate among scholars (and for this reason it may appear to be more appropriate for an academic audience).[67]

It is hoped that the empirical coding of the processes involved in the construction of a 'region' such as the Mediterranean will shed light on the viability and appropriateness or otherwise of a language approach to the study of regions. The overarching finding in this context has been a *securitisation* discourse, in that EU policy-making on the Mediterranean can be detected in terms of regular references to:

- Values: EU documents often reflect references about *common* security, that is, stability and security in the Mediterranean is equated with security and stability in Europe.
- Institutional context: The EU is portrayed as the only institutional context in which all Mediterranean partners can sit together and participate in political dialogue.
- 'Reality': The European security system often incorporates the Mediterranean as Europe's *southern flank*.

Potential contribution to policy-making processes

The methodology adopted here will contribute not only to the development of the academic study of regionalism, but has the potential to contribute to the EU's policy-making process on the Mediterranean.

At the European level

- The analysis of the EU's three areas of involvement in the Mediterranean (the three baskets of the EMP: political, economic and social) will clarify and evaluate the range of policy instruments available to EU policy-makers and will allow for critical reflection on previous EU policies on the Mediterranean, as well as provide guidelines for EU's future policy in the Mediterranean.
- The analysis of the history of the case study countries will allow for the development of EU policy-making in accordance with the specificities of the Mediterranean.

At the Mediterranean level

- The analysis of EU policy on the Mediterranean will clarify and evaluate the range of possibilities for Mediterranean partners' involvement with the EU. This will allow policy-makers in the Mediterranean partner countries to integrate the potential EU role in the Med more consistently and thoroughly in their planning.

• The analysis of EU policy-making towards the Med will clarify the access points for actors in the Med to the EU. This will allow for a better integration of the EU in the decision making of both Med politicians and civil society actors.

The next section will briefly present the structure of this book.

The structure of the book

The structure of this book is a relatively straightforward one. Chapter 2 is devoted to an analytical review of IR theoretical literature as it relates to regions and of various strands of constructivist approaches (in IR) for a better understanding of the study of regionality. Constructivism as a theoretical 'approach' in IR is widely wrought by controversies, bifurcated and difficult to pin down. What unifies all constructivists is a concern with *understanding* how meaning emerges in social interaction.[68] The approach adopted here situates itself within what has been labelled '*discursive constructivism*'[69] which entails a multi-level of analysis approach and seeks to suggest this as the way forward for a better understanding of regions, since this involves both agency and structure in its focus on the aspects involved in the process of region making. What is being proposed here is a flexible tool of analysis for the study of region building based on an understanding of *processes*, which lead to discourses on regionalism and regions. In such a framework, actors are free to operate in structures and in turn these structures can be altered through actors' actions. Hence, actors can modify structures. It is not being denied that structures can place constraints on actors as to how much can be changed. But certain limits can be overcome in order to make a discourse such as that on the Mediterranean area a valid one.

Chapter 3 offers a background chapter before advancing to the discourses of the EU on the Mediterranean (Chapter 4). In order to contextualise and foreground EU practices on the Mediterranean, Chapter 3 takes a snapshot of the levels of economic development (of countries from EU member states, accession countries, Turkey, Israel and Arab partners) that give rise to the hegemony of the EU in the Mediterranean. This 'reality' check offers an analysis of the structural conditions that bring about the development gap between 'North' and 'South'. This chapter also serves as a context chapter on the Euro–Mediterranean Partnership, which is presented in detail, prior to the empirical chapters that follow.

Chapter 4 presents the EU's discourse on the Mediterranean by using a discourse analysis approach. The textual analysis of EU documentation and the fieldwork carried out in Brussels were aimed at codifying the geopolitical claims (of the Mediterranean) that are implicit in the practices of EU foreign policy. This analysis is carried out through a deconstruction of the EU texts and the data collected from interviews with EU Commission officials and others in Brussels. Therefore, by taking a critical standpoint towards EU practices on the Mediterranean, this chapter aims to contribute to the understanding of such action. The aim of this chapter is to critically evaluate EU Mediterranean policy as 'practice' (in line with the theoretical framework discussed in Chapter 2). Policy, like discourse, defines its object (the Mediterranean in this case): it organises it, regulates it, categorises it and constructs it. Hence, the EMP (as the selected EU Mediterranean policy) defines the Mediterranean and constructs it through a continuous process of policy-making.[70] It is hoped that this chapter will highlight the processes of symbolic constructions in the EU's Mediterranean policies (including any regular markers across EU discourses on the Mediterranean), especially in its most recent attempt, the EMP. This chapter also seeks to find out whether the Mediterranean offers a discursive framework for EU political action.

Chapter 5 presents the results from textual analysis of EU documents and interviews which were conducted in Malta, Greece and Morocco, during which the EMP was discussed with a selected number of policy-makers and people who influence them. It aims to present the extent to which there are differences and commonalities in (and including regular markers across) discourses on the Mediterranean between these three case studies. Through an analysis of secondary sources, the chapter outlines the social historical background to each case that will assist the interpretative analysis of EU documents and the interviews' data in outlining whether discursive practices are due to historically or culturally embedded notions of the Mediterranean or whether they contain specific discourses that may connect to other discourses. The case studies' historical background sections thus serve as the doxic backdrop to ongoing debates in Greece, Malta and Morocco on the Mediterranean and on Europe: in effect, the history of each case serves as a way of presenting the past as part of the present discourses (and also, texts as background to interviews).

In order to tie up the research results with the theoretical framework adopted in this book, Chapter 6 compares the discursive statements of the Mediterranean in EU discourses (statements and texts) and discourses of the Mediterranean in Greece, Morocco and Malta. In so doing, it highlights the varied practices underlying political discourse and action on the Mediter-ranean. The political and academic elites' views and textual analysis of background readings from the three Mediterranean case studies are contrasted with EU texts and Commission officials' (and other interviewees') discourses of the Mediterranean. Thus this chapter seeks to question whether the EU constructs the Mediterranean as a static concept (thus giving the Mediterra-nean a fixed meaning) and whether the discourses emanating from within the 'Mediterranean' countries selected make a more complex reference to the term Mediterranean (and, if so, through which processes of action). The study of the action, structure and thought/process in the societies investigated seeks to bring out the *constellation* of ideas on the Mediterranean.[71] Is there an absolute true Mediterranean? Or is it rather that contexts and embedded notions about the Mediterranean make a discourse on the Mediterranean meaningful and viable? The chapter concludes that awareness of such practices is especially important for researchers and political analysts.

Finally, the conclusion returns to the discussion of whether the Mediterranean area is in fact a region in light of the textual/documentation analysis and interview findings. The conclusion also considers the efficacy of codifying the theoretical and empirical approaches used in this study for an analysis of the process of the social construction of other areas in the world and explores some areas of policy relevance in light of the EU's recent European Neighbourhood Policy (ENP) initiative.

Preliminary concluding remarks

There is a need to understand regions as processes of overlapping dimensions, each with its own patterns of change and development and we need to redraw political and cultural maps of the post 'Cold War' period. Regions are the products of processes of identity construction in which the 'self' and the 'other', or multiple others, are constituted. The region structure is just one way of organising the significance of space and theories of regionalism have so far helped us in conceptualising the latter. However, in order to analyse specific forms of region-formations and how these are reproduced by the activities of actors acting in the international system we need to enhance our theoretical frameworks through the addition of identity politics. Regionality becomes socially relevant, meaningful and 'real' when someone/a society points out 'a region', talks about it, attempts to classify it, categorise it, regulate and administer it.

From a theoretical point of view, the study of the Mediterranean requires an eclectic approach to theory: in other words, it cannot be analysed simply in terms of traditional theories of regionalism. In practical terms, the Mediterranean mosaic must be analysed in terms of the processes that lead to its shared meaning – these can then enable analysts to cope with the multi-dimensionality of the Mediterranean. The Mediterranean does not correspond to any existing structure of IR. Rather, it comprises a unique blend of a number of different societies within the international arena. Therefore, it is a question of developing multi-disciplinary theories for a multi-issue Mediterranean. Images of the Mediterranean as a number of concentric circles suggest that the concept of the Mediterranean may *make more sense* if different views are put together. The complex processes involved in the making of the Mediterranean correspond to the heterogeneity of the Mediterranean, its blurred boundaries, its varied historical experiences and its diverse political and economic requirements. This therefore means that any analysis of the Mediterranean (as for any other area) needs to be flexible to reflect these processes and transformations. This book, in recognising the complexity involved in understanding the social construction of the Mediterranean, attempts to provide a framework in which analysis of the Mediterranean continuously in the making can be furthered. It adopts a strand of constructivism known as discursive constructivism that focuses on understanding the processes and mechanisms through which the political fiction of the 'region' can crystallise, at certain moments, as a powerful compelling 'reality'. In so doing it emphasises the need to avoid unintentionally reproducing or reinforcing any such reification of 'regions' that comes about when we uncritically adopt categories of practice as categories of analysis. What is problematic is not that a particular term is used, but *how* it is used. The theoretical attempts to conceptualise region making processes will be elaborated in the next chapter.

2 Regionalism in international relations
Theoretical overview

This chapter aims to discuss how the analysis of foreign policy – as a process that organises the international environment – can be applied to the study of regions. The main argument here is that if foreign policy analysis (FPA) is taken as a framework in which to study world politics, then regionalism can be taken as one level of analysis. Behind this focus lies an understanding of foreign policy as a discursive activity – in line with critical theoretical writings that show how empirical phenomena are constructed discursively.[1] In the case of the EU's Mediterranean policy, this involves processes of defining implicitly what the EU is and what the Mediterranean is. It is argued that foreign policy (as a discursive activity) is a process of othering, constructing the self and the 'other'. In other words, when analysing foreign policy, analysts are not only concerned with the strategies devised to utilise a nation-state's capabilities to achieve the goals its leaders set – but they are also in effect looking at constructions of identity.[2]

The Mediterranean as an area of EU policy, and as a locus on the fringe of a rapidly integrating Europe, offers us a fresh empirical story, thus lending added substance to an emerging research programme.[3] This chapter will be divided as follows: the first section will examine approaches to FPA. This will be followed by a critical analysis of the study of regionalism that groups approaches into conventional and newer approaches. The boundaries between the latter may appear too artificial but this approach is adopted for purely analytical purposes. The main rationale for such boundary-drawing between traditional and other approaches to regionalism is in fact to facilitate the link between more recent IR theoretical works which focus on elements of foreign policy theory based on discourse analysis, what has been referred to as *discursive constructivism*, and studies of regionalism.[4] The application of such works is aimed at developing a process-based approach to the topic of elite discourses in relation to the EMP, which is developed more fully in Chapters 4 and 5. Since this book is about how the EMP is perceived, Chapter 4 will focus on the hegemonic EU discourses. In Chapter 5 the main focus will be on national elites who may have different perceptions of the Mediterranean as a region and of the EMP as an EU policy on the Mediterranean. The importance of discursive constructivist approaches lies in the fact that different discourses may create different conceptions of and [mis]understandings about the EMP. Such an approach is thus important to help us understand problems between partners of the EMP. A separate section will therefore attempt an application of a discursive constructivist approach to the study of regions through a focus on the Mediterranean. As will be shown in Chapter 4, there is a certain regularity in the markers of the Mediterranean across EU discourses. For this reason, this chapter argues that such discursive constructivist works offer an alternative approach to conventional FPA[5] as they uncover the regularity of discourses on the Mediterranean and therefore show *how* European identities are negotiated through the marking of otherness.

The following section presents the theoretical approaches to FPA within the field of IR.[6]

Approaches to foreign policy analysis

IR analyses of European foreign policy have been dominated, in the main, by structuralist theories; in particular, variants of neo-realism and neo-liberalism/institutionalism. In these frameworks, state behaviour is assumed to be highly restricted by the nature and the operation of the international system, making the latter the appropriate level of analysis from which to explain state behaviour.

In the introduction of his book on *Foreign and Security Policy in the EU*, Eliassen defines foreign policy as 'the part of a state's policy that determines its relations with other states and with the international community'.[7] With the emergence of the EC, foreign and security policy areas were initially left to national sovereignty. The Community was empowered to deal with so-called 'external relations' which included economic and commercial relations with 'third' countries. It was difficult to consider the EC as an international, coherent and unified actor while member states arranged bilateral agreements with various 'third' countries. When the Treaty on European Union came into being, it incorporated a CFSP pillar. The end of the Cold War, 9/11 and the war against terrorism have brought about a change in security thinking amongst member states. The Gulf Wars also exposed the weaknesses of the lack of an integrated European approach to foreign and security policy.[8] Contemporary scholarship on European foreign policy focuses on the manner in which authors see the EU, which varies according to each contributor.[9] Some see the EU as a fragmented entity,[10] others as a supranational state[11] and yet others as a nation state with nation state-like foreign policy strategies.[12] Piening focuses on the Union's (international) capacity as being that of a 'world power in its own right' (with power mostly residing in the economic sphere).[13] Bretherton and Vogler offer an analysis of EU foreign policy as being *sui generis* and reject attempts to characterise it along a continuum from international organisation to federal superstate. More recent contributions to this debate reflect upon the significance of collective identity in the development of concepts of EU 'actorness' with some arguing for multiple identities in the EU – supranational, national, regional and local.[14] Various strands of constructivist approaches highlight ways in which notions of the EU's presence and resulting actorness derive from shared internal beliefs about the Union and more specifically from external expectations of the Union by third parties.[15] This can be seen in the Council report on relations between the EU and the Mediterranean countries, in preparation for the conference on 27–28 November in Barcelona which states that:

> An ambitious policy of co-operation to the south forms a counterpart to the policy of openness to the east and gives the EU's external action *its geopolitical coherence*.[16]

In a similar vein, Brian White engages in an earnest debate about what European foreign policy – as an empirical domain of foreign policy – is and about the potential of a revitalised foreign policy framework, which incorporates both positivist and post-positivist approaches.[17] White's main argument is that there is a need to enhance theory and to see what foreign policy-making entails. The EU deems it fit to deal with a multitude of countries as groups and to devise 'Common Strategies' to deal with these countries, to 'govern' them.[18] In the case of European foreign policy this strategy clearly defines 'Europe' through a process of excluding 'the non-European'.[19] White notes that the assumption that systemic imperatives determine the behaviour of the units within the system does not allow room for an understanding of those occasions when the unit – be it a state or some other actor – does not behave in accordance with the dictates of the system.[20] In other words, a focus on structural imperatives leads to a simplified view of the policy process.[21] Hence foreign policy analysts need to look at structure, agency *and* process, a perspective that has been presented in more recent foreign policy work and which has been referred to as *discursive constructivism*.

A recent study, *European Integration and National Identity: The Challenge of the Nordic States*, elaborates a discourse analysis theory of foreign policy.[22] In this work, Wæver addresses challenges identified with rationalist materialist-based theories to European integration and highlights how rationalist materialist explanations of integration have failed to capture the significance of identity-based arguments in explicating the Nordic countries' approaches to European integration. Wæver argues that such identity insights do not just affect how we should understand these particular countries' attitudes to Europe, but also indicate a need to rethink predominant understandings of the EU more generally. Other contributors to this edited volume focus on how, for example, in Denmark and Norway, the 'nation' was constructed in anti-elitist terms so that those encouraging greater integration came to be seen as motivated by narrow self-interest and not by the interests of the nation. Such insights can therefore help explicate these countries' reticent attitudes to further integration.

Another effort at bridging the gap between rationalist and reflectivist approaches in IRT can be found in the work of Henrik Larsen. Forming part of the 'Copenhagen School', Larsen gives discourse analysis a prominent place in the study of IR in general, and foreign policy in particular. He goes a step further and criticises the way that ideas have been treated in IRT for not having taken language seriously enough. For Larsen, discourse refers to 'systems of values and rules in a given linguistic context'.[23] He suggests that discourse accounts for the way that foreign policy – defined as the government's activity concerned with relations to international actors[24] – is conceptualised. He draws upon a metaphor developed by his colleague, Ole Wæver, of discourse in terms of a discursive 'tree' structure in which change is more likely to take place at the branch level rather than at the root, where it would be a revolutionary turn.[25]

Another contribution from this group of critical analysts comes from the work of Browning who develops a narrative theory of identity, action and foreign policy. In contrast to traditional and dominant approaches to foreign policy analysis that take the identity of states as unproblematic and universal, Browning argues that identity needs to be understood as historically specific, inherently unstable and in constant need of reaffirmation and renegotiation. Neglecting processes of identity construction, traditional foreign policy analysis is not simply incomplete, but misses the fact that it is only in the process of narrating a constitutive story of the self that the self is able to attain a sense of its own subjectivity in relation to others at any given time and that action becomes meaningful. His work, which focuses on Finland as a case study, analyses the construction of Finnish national identity from the emergence of Finnish political subjectivity from 1809 through to the present day and illustrates how varying discourses of Finnish identity have been central in framing the possibilities of available action for Finnish decision makers. The analysis draws out contending representations of Finnish identity, points to how and why changes and reorientations in Finnish foreign policy have occurred, and re-establishes foreign policy as a highly political process concerned with power and the right to define reality and national subjectivity.[26]

Such critical works shed light on how discursive processes constructing national identity and subjectivity are central to an understanding of foreign policy. In problematising categories and concepts, usually taken for granted, and showing them to be imbued with power and politics and notions of inclusion and exclusion, these works open space for critical self-reflection.

When applying European foreign policy-making, in particular to the case of the EU and the so-called 'South' (that is, the Mediterranean), one notes that a structuralist EU foreign policy approach is very limited in its explanatory power. As Marjorie Lister notes 'the EU is best understood as a unique type of institution,[27] itself in the making, rather than an embryonic state'.[28] Moreover, the EU's policy in the Mediterranean 'suffers from a gap between its apparent potential to act and its actual performance'.[29] This discrepancy can be understood by examining 'the particular institutional and procedural constraints of the Union's 'dual' system of foreign affairs'.[30] Rather than a unitary actor, the EU acts as a clearing-house for national interests that lead to an internal bias towards economic means and create problems for its Mediterranean partners in terms of predictability and transparency. This misunderstanding between EU–Mediterranean partners often leads to policy being directed by the lowest common denominator principle. Moreover, policy is often influenced by which member state happens to be running the Presidency at that particular time.[31]

It can then be argued that FPA requires an opening to a thorough framework that helps us analyse EU action/discursive practices. Here action is a generic term under which all official practices are incorporated. Action is thus constitutive, that is, a social term. This includes the manner in which EU foreign policy may be informed by different individual foreign policies of the member states. This will be covered in more detail in Chapter 4. What is important in this *discursive constructivist* framework is to find out which action is giving *meaning*[32] to the construction of the Mediterranean in the EU's Mediterranean Policy and which EU practices carry such narrative functions. By participating in Mediterranean affairs, the EU's policies attempt to redefine the area through a developmentalist discourse. Most references to the Mediterranean are related to problems of resources and the lack of development in the 'region'. The EU attempts to be involved in the Mediterranean by exporting its own values and its own model of regionalism. But as was observed by the Egyptian president, Hosni Mubarak, recently, third parties (like the US and the EU) do not allow for indigenous dynamics to evolve in the particular region they are involved in.[33]

Hence, European foreign policy can be informed by discourse analysis.[34] Policy is here understood as discourse as it in effect defines its object/field of knowledge. In other words, discourse is there to organise, regulate, categorise and construct: policy does exactly what discourse does – it constructs our knowledge of the international field and the parameters of our actions in it. In the case of the EMP this policy defines the Mediterranean and Europe. It is therefore worth seeing not only the discourses surrounding the EU's Mediterranean policy but also *how* policy itself institutes and constructs social (international, bilateral and multilateral) relationships and hierarchies and how it constructs its objects/fields of knowledge (be these states, civil societies, the Mediterranean region and the Euro-Mediterranean area).[35] The study of foreign policy must be analysed as 'a continuous process', which means that a broad definition of the foreign policy of the EU must be used when the EU's external policy is examined.[36] Through this critical approach to FPA, EU elite representations of European identity through foreign policy will also be uncovered. The politics of identity in EU foreign policy requires, on the one hand, the production of identity and foreignness and is a boundary-producing political performance, while on the other hand, it is the conventional EU-based practice that can be reinterpreted as one instance in the operation of a generalised foreign policy and which serves to reproduce foreign policy (the constitution of identity).[37]

Tracing the development of FPA through the classification of regions. Regionalism and its discontents

Having presented the different approaches to FPA this chapter now moves on to examine how the classification of the world into regions has informed the development of FPA. Hence, this section presents some of the main theoretical approaches dealing with regionalism in IR. This analysis is aimed at uncovering the underlying assumptions, shortcomings, limitations and expectations of these approaches on regional arrangements in order to arrive at a better understanding of the study of regions.

In the late 1960s, an attempt was made within the field of IR to present regionalism as a framework for a better understanding of world politics. This relatively young approach has generally focused on the plausibility of taking the 'region' as a distinct level of analysis. Theories of regionalism are often based on a number of regular markers and a set of assumptions under which a 'region' makes sense and is thus given a shared meaning. In turn, the concept of 'region' implied by these assumptions infers homogeneity.

The concept of 'region' has traditionally been thought of in geographic terms as a natural, real entity. A general understanding of region is often construed as 'sub-systems of states linked by geographical relationship, mutual interdependence and subjective perception of belonging to a distinctive community'. Moreover, 'it is a firm assertion of regionalist studies that the sharing of common features brings about peculiar forms of political interactions among the countries of an international region'.[38] Economic relations are often said to naturally follow these political links in the process of region-formation (the spill-over effect of functionalism). Regionalism is thus often portrayed as something smooth and functional: a phenomenon that comes naturally to the forefront especially since the so-called 'end of the Cold War' and the collapse of the bipolar system.[39] In mainstream theories, regions are seen as 'objective' entities based on criteria that are 'objectively' detectable.

I shall discuss some of the images of regionalism, grouping these images under what I shall term actor-based theories and structure-based theories of regionalism. It must be emphasised that the boundaries between those approaches labelled as conventional and new approaches is an artificial one and this division is only applied here as it facilitates the presentation of the discursive constructivist perspective which is the strand of constructivism chosen here. The actor and structure classification is informed by social and critical theory, in particular the works of Giddens[40] and Berger and Luckmann,[41] who argue that research in the social sciences cuts across different dimensions of their subject matter, namely structural, institutional and action-related. Structures are said to shape institutions and together with them they shape social action in the sense that they set the parameters of their operation. On the other hand, action establishes and reproduces institutions and, combined with the latter, they inform and construct structures. Seen in this framework, institutions can be understood as processes or sets of practices/

social action repeated in a similar and regular fashion over long periods of time, thus acquiring a sense of stability and durability. Along this frame of thinking, it can be argued that the regularity of markers in and across discourses gives meaning to a field of knowledge.[42] Structures can then be seen as even longer reproduced sets of action, meaning and discourse that provide a frame for the operation of institutions as well as of action. In this process-based framework for regional studies, structures and institutions are thus not seen as only constraining but also as enabling, that is, providing resources for thinking and acting.[43]

The objective of this section is to show how most of the main, existing theories of regionalism fall under either the actor-based or the structure-based framework for the study of regions, or somewhere in-between. This study seeks to suggest that for an improved understanding of regions, regional analysts would do justice to their subject matter by looking through a process-based 'lens', which combines the actor-based and structure-based frameworks into a dynamic and flexible structure. The latter framework seeks to imply that these theoretical dimensions should not be seen as distinct but as being all related to each other in a variety of ways. The underlying premise of this alternative way of understanding regions rests on the basic assertion of this book, namely, that regions are socially constructed and that a critical study of regions must therefore analyse the process in which this construction occurs.[44] Although some of the critical theories referred to do not directly address regionalism, they offer useful tools for a better insight into the study of regions. Sometimes, typologies erect artificial boundaries between perspectives that share common ground and assumptions. However, for heuristic and analytical reasons, I opted for a detailed examination of the theoretical debate. As pointed out above, the classification of theories under the headings of actor-based, structure-based or process-based should therefore be considered as such for purely analytical purposes. A crucial contribution of this classification is that it leads us to new questions on aspects related to discourse analysis. In the following sections, the traditional perspectives on regionalism will be discussed in the light of this understanding.

Traditional approaches

Neo-realism

A neo-realist perspective on regionalism would lead to the following expectations: first, any regionalist arrangements among countries in the so-called semi-periphery or periphery or between these countries and developed countries will be predominantly security-related. Second, it is expected that the existence of a regional hegemonic state will enhance the success of regionalist projects. There are theories of middle-ranking powers or states that fit this specific expectation of a regional arrangement. According to such so-called structural realist approaches, a state's behaviour in conditions of international co-operation can be explained either through its national preference formation or through its interstate strategic interaction. Systemic change is characterised by an alteration of power in the international order; its focus is the rise and decline of the dominant states that govern the particular international system. The implicit realist position assumes that the world is logically coherent. This assumption involves the view that theory and the external world should be of the same structure, that is, one can match one against the other: one is therefore an empiricist. Thus, world politics was seen to have undergone a systemic change when it experienced a shift in power of the formerly dominant state – the Soviet Union. A middle power such as Turkey plays an important political role within the limits of its 'region'; it is by definition a local power whose demands are restricted to its own and immediately adjacent areas. When placed within the hierarchy of states, Turkey is greatly influenced by the actions of the major players, but it also exerts some influence in the 'region' in which it is located. Therefore, its ability to form regional co-operation and structures and the fact that it has the power to have an impact on regional co-operation makes it affect the whole system. Although a middle power has marginal value for the major powers, it still has the capacity to disturb the balance of power and its alliance with or defection from one camp has serious implications for the distribution of power in the international order.[45]

Neo-realists claim a third expectation from regional arrangements: bearing in mind that state interest is the primary interest – in regions without a clear hegemon, entry into regionalist projects is subject to 'relative-gains' accruing to the different partners in the arrangement. In other words, a regional arrangement has to satisfy states' interests for realists and neo-realists to conceptualise of such a 'region'.[46] According to neo-realists then, a regional grouping would be very difficult to maintain since co-operation depends on the calculation of gains by the states involved in the project. Neo-realists would adhere to such views on regionalist arrangements.[47] Like realist approaches to the study of world politics, neorealists claim that power is central to co-operation among nations.[48] However, unlike the post-classical or modified structural realists, the structural realists of the Waltzian type do not acknowledge that regime-based interstate co-operation is in need of understanding. In fact, neo-realists pay little attention to international institutions and their role in regional co-operation arrangements.[49]

At an analytical level, one notes that beyond the empirical proposals put forward by neo-realist scholars, the theory has certain implicit assumptions that commit it to certain political positions.[50] For example, neo-realism is what Cox calls a 'problem-solving' theory – it works to resolve certain problems set out within certain frameworks; it never problematises the assumptions on which those frameworks are established. Thus, with its rationalist metatheoretical orientation, neo-realism works to resolve problems established in the framework of the state-system, without questioning all the assumptions that make up the conditions under which the idea of a state-system makes sense (that is, sovereignty, autonomy, rationality, agency and so on). This would lead us to say that neo-realism is inherently conservative (it is not interested in transformation(s) of the conditions of existence – merely in solving problems understood according to pre-existing implicit assumptions). Thus, when one applies the neo-realist perspective to regional studies, regionalism is then based on a set of assumptions that constitute the conditions under which a 'region' is given meaning. Therefore, according to these assumptions, for a 'region' to exist states in this regional arrangement need to share some complementarity, division of labour and responsibility to achieve a specific desired aim. A region might therefore be seen as a subsystem of the international system that functions precisely on the basis of a division of labour and complementarity. For this strand of neo-realists, a perceived commonality of interests is crucial for the establishment of a regional project (functionalist argument). Accordingly, as regards regionalism, one needs to question the main assumptions under which a 'region' makes sense. Critical theorists have, for a long time, tried to bring out the implicit assumptions on which different ways of understanding world politics have been grounded. Such approaches will be considered in a section below which develops the framework for process-based theories of regionalism.

Neo-liberal institutionalism

Like neo-realists, neo-institutionalists expect regional arrangements to be negotiated in situations where states have clearly defined common interests.[51] Unlike structural realists however, these theorists perceive regionalism as the creation of international institutions and regimes for policy co-ordination. This school of thought in fact emphasises the role of international regimes in helping states to realise common interests. In a world of uncertainty, which makes co-operation between states hard to achieve, regimes are said to reduce this uncertainty thus making it easier for states to embark on collaborative ventures. Thus, neoliberalism also advances a functionalist argument for the study of regionalism.[52] Moreover, this school of thought also tends to stress the influence of domestic social groups. Hence, the state will act as a negotiator at the inter-governmental level but will be limited by national political considerations. This thinking is in line with that of middle-ranking states' theory mentioned in the section above which claims that domestic politics is a major obstacle for such a power.[53] For example, Turkey's economic and political structures have been influenced by changing economic conditions within the EU – its main trading partner – but its domestic politics has limited its process of adaptation.[54] For neo-liberal institutionalists, the main motivations of actors involved in regionalist projects would be the procurement of public goods from interdependence.[55] Although it deliberately appropriates essential elements of the realist approach to world politics, neo-liberal institutionalism is still a rationalist theory that portrays states as rational egoists who care only for their own absolute gains.

The main limitation of the neo-liberal institutional approach to the study of regions is that regionalism is perceived as an ultimate goal, when regionalism can actually be a stepping stone to a higher goal. For example, a regional grouping might have tariff barriers to trade and the regionalist project might be aimed at reducing these barriers or knocking these down altogether for the regional group's integration into the global world economy. One of the main objectives of the World Trade Organization is such elimination of all barriers to trade.[56] Hence, regionalism must be perceived as a process rather than an ultimate goal in itself.

Neo-Marxism

According to neo-Marxist perspectives, the study of regional arrangements could be interpreted in the context of a general understanding of imperialism, involving the subordination of the periphery and the semi-periphery to the interests of the core, presumably industrialised countries: regions are located in the context of a capitalist world system. Neo-Marxists claim that such regionalism would have the intention of dividing the developing countries, by entering into distinct arrangements for different groups.[57] This would result in the exploitation of the 'underdeveloped' countries and the maintenance of the privileged position of the industrialised ones. Moreover, multinational corporations would try to block the establishment of regionalist schemes among all developing countries because of the risk that such schemes would place these countries in too powerful a position *vis-à-vis* international capital.[58] Thus, for neo-Marxists regionalism is expected to enhance the role of the 'market' and to institutionalise unequal exchange and investment relations: the society of states is a second order phenomenon when compared to global capitalism. Like the neo-realist and the neo-liberal institutional approaches, regionalism in the neo-Marxist sense is hence primarily interpreted as power-related.[59] This sometimes involves core countries prompting it, encouraging it or even imposing it. It could also involve a local peripheral but middle-ranking power or even several peripheral countries coming together to create regions in attempts to counter centre or core imperialism (the formation of the EU can be seen in this way *vis-à-vis* US domination in the economic sphere). Moreover, a peripheral core/peripheral type of relationship might be formed by middle-ranking countries enjoying some relative autonomy in order to reinforce their position in the global division of labour (not necessarily in order to counter imperialism; the attempt of Turkey to become a regional power in the Black Sea through its Black Sea Co-operation initiative can be regarded a case in point).

Neo-Marxism assumes that developing countries have a lot in common.[60] Similar to the literature of the functionalist political theory and the political development theories of the 1950s and 1960s, such assumed homogeneity in the 'Third World' leads to a distortion of 'reality' – which means that little or no account has been taken, until recently, of spatial or temporal disparities in states as diverse as Brazil, Argentina, Taiwan or Nigeria. One may also question the neo-Marxists' claim that regionalism divides and rules. Regionalism may be taken as a step towards globalisation or 'Third World' unity as the ultimate goal, rather than as an end in itself. For instance, multinationals are very interested in the development of MERCOSUR and also in its linkage with NAFTA[61] and/or the EU. For neo-Marxists, the value of MERCOSUR is not as an end in itself but a means to another end, namely a linkage between, for example, MERCOSUR and NAFTA in order to secure economic access for the US under the most privileged terms (that is, the widening and deepening of the capitalist system).[62] In the context of the study of regions, neo-Marxism is perhaps best taken as a research programme rather than a paradigm. Regions are in the making and the study of regions is therefore best seen as a process, a gradual encroachment of ideas and knowledge. Therefore, rather than focusing on the nature of regionalism *per se*, the alternative approach to the study of regions presented later in this chapter suggests that analysts focus on the nature and roots of ideas and theories about regionalism.[63]

Other approaches

The literature of the 1960s emphasised how regions could be seen as developing around a centre, a core area where the internal defining characteristics are more similar, and interaction more intense, than in the regional periphery.

World-systems theory

Stemming from the theories of dependency which were developed during the 1960s and 1970s, a world-systems approach to the study of regionalism posits that the role of the semi-peripheral state in regional projects is a subordinate one to the core states, but the former state still plays a political 'buffer' role and also occupies a middle position in the division of labour. The motivations of the actors involved in such regionalist projects would include the creation of new forms of capital accumulation and the adaptation of the international division of labour to new needs. Regionalism is thus expected to be market-led and subordinate to the creation of regional production networks.[64]

In their seminal work, Cantori and Spiegel suggest a division of all regions or what they refer to as 'subordinate systems' into a core and a periphery.[65] They argue that 'the core sector consists of a state or a group of states which form a central focus of the international politics within the region'. According to the authors, a region is then 'the total interaction of relations within that region'.[66] Under a set of assumptions, Cantori and Spiegel describe the factors delineating a region, namely political/foreign relations (that is, whether antagonistic or co-operative relationships exist between states within the 'region'), geography, social, economic, organisational factors and historical background. The authors also include the role of outside powers (that is, the influence of the international system), the relevant *Gestalt* that they refer to as 'the intrusive system' in defining the subordinate system (that is, to the internal dynamics within the region itself).[67]

Although a useful, analytical framework for analysing the extent to which a particular 'region' fits their model, Cantori and Spiegel's work seems to prejudge the nature of regions as world-system theorists also seem to do when their views are applied to regional studies.[68]

At this point, one needs to stress that world-systems theory is very often related to the neo-Marxist perspective. In fact, many would find it very difficult to draw the line between the two.

Neo-Gramscian world order approach

According to this approach, political-economic elites in the semi-peripheral state will attempt to 'lock in' the semi-peripheral economy with that of the core in order to serve their own economic interests. Regionalism is perceived as a disciplinary instrument for the achievement of deregulation and limited government interference in the economy. Actors involved in regionalist projects are assumed to be motivated to achieve the hegemony of the neo-liberal type of economic order. Neo-Gramscian theorists attempt to supersede conventional IR perspectives on the notion of global hegemony and developed this concept further.[69] In this perspective neo-liberalism should aim at globalism and anything falling short of this is seen as protectionist. In fact, these works have been crucial in the challenge they offered to neo-realism that takes the existing order for granted: neo-Gramscians argue that one should not just focus on states but should rather look at the interaction between ideas, states and social forces in the construction of regions.[70] By seeking to identify counter-hegemonic forces such as nationalist movements, socialist groups and cultural movements within the global order, neo-Gramscian perspectives challenge the neo-realist claim that explaining the reproduction of international anarchy is the primary task of international theory. Neo-Gramscians have a lot in common with critical theorists who question *how* the existing order came into existence and whether it might be changing. Neo-Gramscian works can also be said to have rehabilitated neo-Marxist approaches. Some neo-Gramscians, for instance, trace the development of modes of production, states and the world systems, stressing how production shapes other realms such as strategic interaction and how these realms in turn shape production.[71] Moreover, in the neo-Gramscian school of International Political Economy, global hegemony operates through alliances between elites in core and industrialising societies and through the mechanisms of control provided by global economic and political institutions.

However, the term hegemony is used far too loosely in this perspective.[72] In its original Gramscian use, it refers to cultural hegemony and values of the dominant class, that is, the group permeating the subordinate class.

Global hegemony is thereby said to exist when the dominant state and dominant social forces sustain their position through adherence to *universalised principles* that are accepted by a sufficient proportion of subordinate states and social forces.[73] In this manner, the hegemon is made legitimate.[74]

Globalism

In the perspective of globalists, the state is seen as an essentially conservative force and its role perceived as declining when compared to transnational actors.[75] Regionalism is expected to stimulate regional free trade and will be a building block towards globalisation. Regionalist projects are a counterweight to a system that attempts to conserve centralised power.

Global processes pose many challenges to individual and collective groupings. This approach is therefore another useful stepping stone into new thinking on regionality or spatiality which must recognise that the world is not just 'out there' but is 'here' and 'now'.[76] In this context, a territorial remapping in the context of globalisation is inevitable. Boundaries are shifting, forcing analysts to remap what has until recently been familiar terrain. What is needed is a problematisation of conventional conceptions of regionality as a result of boundary changes.[77] This theme will be further developed in the section on critical approaches below.

Regional governance approaches

Regionalism is expected to work as a programme to upgrade the national interest by grouping states with like-minded states and larger political entities. According to theorists following this approach, actors in regionalist arrangements are motivated to direct projects to protect values and maintain state autonomy *vis-à-vis* economic forces.[78] Thus, in this perspective, the state is the prime mover in politics, the central unit of decision making and the object of political allegiance.[79]

This approach is similar to notions of 'pooling' sovereignty where regionalism can often be seen as a tool for resisting further globalisation more effectively.[80] (For example, British interests are believed to be protected in this manner.) In this scenario, the challenge is not just the growth of supranational bodies, but also internally from the market itself, for example, from financial centres. The UK is not part of the European Monetary Union (EMU) and the Bank of England, which acts as the Central Bank of England to control rates of interest, sets its exchange rates. Thus, it is not just a case of seeing the state as the primary actor. The issue here is much more complicated. The notion of pooled sovereignty and supranational bodies (themselves fast evolving in this case) reveals a 'grey' area. Such issues are very challenging for regional analysis since our views of today must be revised very often and abruptly.

Summary of theoretical approaches

In light of the above analysis of some of the main theoretical IR approaches and their application to the study of regions, it is apparent that some classifications and subdivisions are somewhat too elaborate and artificial. For example, world-system theories and neo-Gramscian approaches can be grouped with neo-Marxist theories since they are compatible in their thinking. Indeed, one can describe all these approaches as diverse aspects of neo-Marxism or the group of neo-Marxisms.[81] Various strands of contemporary social and political thought are either reworking the cosmopolitan spirit, which animated so much of Marx's thought, or more frequently continuing the critique of a world organised around the exclusionary principle of sovereignty.[82] Therefore, following the images of regionalism derived and presented above, one can summarise these theories into two main strands: one strand which can be classified as actor-based theories which speak of actors who have choices to make, such as, for example, states, and a second strand which will be termed structure-based theories of regionalism which describe a given structure that sets the parameters for actors' actions. A world capitalist system is such a structure. Neo-realism, neo-liberal institutionalism and regional governance approaches may be classified under actor-based theories since the state is the primary actor in the international arena for these theorists.[83] Neo-Marxism, world-systems theory, neo-Gramscian world-order and globalism approaches can be grouped under structure-based theories since all of these theorists take the world capitalist system as a given (fixed) structure in the international economy. This classification of theories is here being presented for analytical purposes and should be treated as such.[84]

A common shortfall in these theoretical approaches is that they all reify a social configuration of region as an entity that exists.[85] Some approaches speak of states or institutions as actors in the regionalist project. For this set of theories, the game of power and interests is based on the actor as the unit of analysis. Individual actors have the autonomy and choice to create measures of how they think or act and they also form networks – in other words, a very fixed, theoretical structure. For the other approaches, the superstructure is important – there are no autonomous states because states or any other actors are subject to a capitalist world-system. This overarching system reduces the ability of agents to act. The common deficiency with these actor-based or structure-based theories of regionalism is therefore the fact that they both present *static* frameworks for the analysis of regions.[86] What is needed is a shift from these two extremes of how to see the international system, that is, a move beyond these 'actor' and 'structure' discourses into a 'process' discourse where the project of region-making is analysed as an ongoing process and not as a fixed, static concept. In sum, in order to have a wider, more informed view of 'reality', analysts need to work with theories in parallel.[87]

An alternative framework for the study of regions: process-based theories

As mentioned above, the thinking of neo-Marxists and other theorists, earlier classified under the structure-based approaches to the study of regions, has been a pivotal source for the contributions of many critical theorists.[88] For regionalists, regionalism is conceived as a 'state-led or states-led project designed to reorganize a particular regional space along defined economic and political lines'.[89] The word 'defined' here immediately conjures up notions of rigidity in the manner in which the international system has been perceived. For a long time, critical theorists have tried to build on this premise in order to bring out the implicit assumptions on which different ways of understanding world politics have been grounded.

A third group of theories looks into the process of the evolution of the international system. This means that one has a dynamic, analytical framework to assess processes of region-formation. In such a framework, actors are free to operate within a field of action demarcated by structural restrictions but sustained by resources generated by these very same structures. The latter can hence be altered through actors' actions. Actors are therefore said to be able to modify structures. Although structures often put limits on actors' ability to change the existing structure, some constraints may be modified and overcome. In the field of IR, critical theorists have been trying to establish parameters in which processes unfold and it is under such a framework that the process of region-formation should be analysed and assessed. Analysts have to see actors as products of a process; in other words, the subject is a product of the structure. But whilst structures create actors, actors also create structures. Therefore there is a process of interaction between actor and structure. Critical theorists often draw upon studies of the history of ideas on how human beings impose *meanings* to the world. It is important to note that opting for a constructivist approach to study regionalism implies a very different view of the nature of language from that accepted by traditional, rationalist accounts. Rationalist approaches understand language in purely referential terms, with linguistic practices assumed as merely revealing the beliefs and understandings of decision makers.[90] Thus, traditional approaches see language as passive, as merely a conduit and container of our beliefs and ideas that enables us to communicate our thoughts to others.[91] In contrast, critical approaches take language as partly constitutive of the world, that is, phenomena can only become objects of knowledge through interpretative discursive practices.[92] Therefore, language is here understood as powerful in the sense that it is active, it is *doing* something: it conveys meaning and representations that construct social reality and constitute it, thereby making certain courses of action more meaningful than others, as well as regulating what is meaningful at any given time. Although most of these studies do not directly address the study of regions, their work offers important tools for the investigation of this book. The following section presents a synthesis of critical works which offer an axis along which analysts can study alterity (otherness), the regularity of markers across discourses which define fields of knowledge and a framework in which to locate power and notions of power which lie behind attempts at the classification of regions. By understanding discursive practices on regions we can then understand how such practices construct specific subject identities and thereby construct a particular 'reality' in which policy becomes possible as well as through which future policies would be justified in advance.[93]

One can read critical approaches as criticisms of Marxism and as alternatives and radical philosophies. In locating power, I side with the radical constructivist strand and take Foucault's notion of power, in discarding the classical Marxist view that revolution entails the seizure of the state and thereby of power, on the grounds that power itself is not centralised in the state. The social world consists of power struggles that cannot be resolved because power is a necessary and inherent part of any relationship. Fragmentation becomes both politically and theoretically explicit. Following this thinking one can then concentrate on representations of an external world as an 'extra-discursive' order – the institutional structure out of which discourses develop and that embodies discourse.[94] Discourses or discursive practices of regionalism, regions and regionality are thus taken as the main units of analysis. It is important here to broaden out what is considered to be 'discursive'.[95] Discourse could be said to be the production of meaningful ensembles. This includes the manner in which 'objects' become objects in particular meaningful ensembles (one should recognise that 'object' is merely another meaningful category). In the social construction of reality, it is only when a society points out 'something', talks about it, attempts to classify it, categorise it, regulate it and administer it that this something becomes 'real', that is, socially relevant and *meaningful*. Rather than seeing ideas and beliefs as 'belonging' to individuals, a critical account focuses on ideas and beliefs as social phenomena that structure reality: a constructivist argues that it is only in light of ideas, identities and beliefs that action becomes intelligible and meaningful (that is, language understood as constitutive of social reality). When these practices are repeated thereafter in a regular fashion and in a similar manner over long periods of time, they then acquire a sense of durability and stability. It thereby follows that discourse is always a kind of 'event', in the sense that it is always in the making.[96] In this manner, one can analyse the whole context in which things are uttered and understand the varied nature of the social world. Accordingly, the world is a product of our ideas; one is left only with general *meanings*. Social actions can then be analysed as part of a wider process of the social construction of 'reality'. In the case of region building, one can see this in terms of an attempt by international organisations to define and extend their 'power' over wider geographical spaces.[97] It is as if region-formation constitutes a realm of an area's reality that in turn defines the reality of those empowered to carve this area out. The process of region building can also be seen as part of a wider process of political control – a sort of 'political engineering' by means of which a politically, economically or socially desirable area is constituted. Such control implies that there is somebody who does the controlling, and hence regionalism can be seen as one of the multitude of power centres which might, often in contradictory ways, be involved in the constitution of political, economic and social control. These (linguistic) practices have also been investigated and developed in the social sciences.

Drawing from sociology, the theory of structuration offers an appropriate framework for the analysis of the social reproduction of regions; that is, the ways in which regions, or specific forms of region-formation, are reproduced by the activities of actors acting in the international system.[98] This theory also provides a framework within which the analysis of power and ideology can be recast.[99] In this work, notions of power – as rules within a structure – are taken as both enabling and constraining: the subject that acts is enabled and constrained by the structure. Therefore, in studies of regions analysts need to see the whole genealogy of a discourse on regions. Regions can be seen as products of actors' social action or what one may call discourses or policies. Accounts on the dualism of action and structure therefore provide a framework for a systematic study of processes of regionalisation and the social reproduction of regions (and underlying processes of identification).[100]

Drawing upon the strengths of some of the main theoretical orientations in the social sciences, the theory of structuration presents a way of thinking on the relation between actor and structure which 'should be regarded as the complementary terms of a duality, "the duality of structure"'.[101] Hence, 'social structures are both constituted *by* human agency, and yet at the same time are the very *medium* of this constitution'.[102] Thus, 'the structures that render an action possible are ... reproduced'. Hence, in the case of the study of regions, even a discourse that disrupts the social order, breaking conventions or challenging established hierarchies, is mediated by structural features that are reconstituted by the action, albeit in a modified form.[103] Thus, social life is characterised by its 'recursive character' which is continuously produced and reproduced. Agents are said to reproduce the conditions that make social activities possible in and through their activities.[104] Furthermore, much action is 'purposive' in the sense that it is *monitored* by actors who continuously watch their actions, their reactions to their own actions and the circumstances in which they are acting. This *reflexive* monitoring of action gives actors the ability to give reasons for their actions and thereby makes them *knowledgeable* actors. This framework thus offers us the possibility to locate power contexts and processes in which specific actors create fields of knowledge through regular markers across discourses.

Such a 'stratification model of action' shows the limitations of any attempt to analyse action by focusing on the individual agent. Clearly the process of action must be analysed since unintended consequences of action and unacknowledged conditions of action may have an impact on the resulting action of an agent[105] (in so far as the unintended consequence of action is the reproduction of the *structure* which renders further action possible).[106] Structure refers to 'rules and resources which are implemented in interaction, which thereby structure interaction and which are, in that very process, reproduced' or in short 'the systems of generative rules and resources'.[107] Underlying this definition of structure is power in interaction. Such relationships uncover structures of domination. In this manner, *power cannot be separated from the communication of meaning.* Thus, structures are not structures in themselves but they are structured by rules, resources and actions.[108]

To the theory of structuration, one can also add the ways in which the concepts of time and space enter into this framework. According to this theory, time and space are perceived as boundaries to social analysis or as frameworks within which social life takes place. This leads us to analyses of the time–space constitution of social systems in connection with power relations. Echoing the work of historians of ideas, this theory focuses on the development of writing which has increased the capacity of societies to monitor and control the actions of their populations. Interpreted in this framework, the process of the social construction of regions is therefore a game of power and control. Analysts may therefore be mistaken in thinking about societies as somehow continuous with geographical borders; rather, one should aim to talk about systems that are more or less open and can cut across geographical boundaries.[109] An ontology of time–space as constitutive of social practices is basic to the conception of structuration and, likewise, when applied to the study of regions, to the conception of regionalisation.[110]

Drawing upon social theory, analysts can then read IR in terms of self/ other relations and analyse how regions are constructed in identity discourses.[111] Such an approach opens up the debate about the existence of regions, on those who define regions and with what interests, and how such interpretations and the use and re-use of these views (as practices) help to construct a specific notion of regions. At the core of these theoretical ideas lie two interrelated aspects of nation/region building: social spatialisation and spatial socialisation. The social construction of regions can be interpreted as a process of social spatialisation.[112] Aspects of spatial socialisation include 'the attachment of the population to [this] region in various ties which are constructed in the practices of everyday life and social action' – in effect, a double treatment of space and society which uncover the manner in which the idea of a nation or region is connected to territory and particularly to boundaries.[113] Essentially, the imagination of a nation or region is constantly produced and reproduced in social and institutional practices, including school education and media broadcasting, to which people are connected in their daily lives. Boundaries play a crucial role in the construction of national and regional consciousness in that they attach the social distinction between 'us' and 'them' to the spatial ones between 'here' and 'there'. Thus, regions can be constructed in response to the perception of an *'other'*. Any identity, whether of a state or social group or entity, is always 'established in relation to a series of differences that have become socially recognised. These differences are essential to [its] being'.[114] Identity can therefore be established only in relation to what it is not, that is, to difference. Difference in turn is constituted in relation to identity. Thus, identities are always contingent and relational. When analysing regions, one needs to acknowledge this relationality in the formation of identity/ies (that is the processes of identification, categorisation, etc.) due to the fact that otherness is often fundamentally treated as something significant only in relation to ourselves and from our perspective. In other words, the Other is interpreted as an essential opponent when constructing the Self. Following this line of argument, one can argue that regions are socially constructed and constructions of such 'realities' reflect, enact and reify relations of power.[115] Relations between the West and the rest of the world have been analysed through such a perspective and focus on how Western references to any part of the rest of the world end up with images of an area that shadow overlapping and interdependent identities.[116] Definitions of the Rest in this vein often serve functional purposes. Such doctrines pose as attempts to dissolve differences and preserve similarities (if any) rather than encouraging and celebrating differences.[117] Thus, in terms of these critical reflections, any categorisation of a 'region' brings forward specific affinities and overlaps while often disguising diversity. In West–Rest relations, the West is presented as *the* model and the Rest have to embrace Western values and systems without questioning whether these may be appropriate for other areas of the world. Moreover, the creation of regions 'do(es) not merely reproduce the outlying territories: they work them out, or animate them, using narrative technique and historical and exploratory attitudes …'.[118] A good example of such constructions are expressed in travel guides which tend to orientalise the unfamiliar, the Other. In turn, such a construction of the Rest is the result of a securitisation discourse reflecting the need for stability and security.[119] Hence, although the term 'region' is often used in a geographical sense, one has to analyse carefully the implications on the political spectrum because:

> All cultures tend to make representations of foreign cultures the better to master or in some way control them. Yet not all cultures make representations of foreign cultures *and* in fact master or control them. It requires the study of Western knowledge or representations of the non-European world to be a study of both those representations and the political power they express.[120]

Thus, in short, when one is dealing with representations or constructions of a 'region', one is indirectly involved in analysing a (language) power game. Analysts therefore need to trace out markers across hegemonic discourses that construct fields of knowledge to understand how the latter are given meaning, created, produced and re-produced. Locating power centres and referent objects of power has been the concern of theorists of modernity who attempt to deconstruct developmentalist discourses in light of global-isation forces and contemporary global changes.[121] In this perspective one can interpret how modernity developed at the intersection of national and international conditions and processes. The West, for example, started to forge its identity and interests in relation to endogenous developments in Europe and America and through relations of unequal exchange with the Rest, the Other – the often excluded, colonised, conquered and exploited. By focusing on the issue of *space* and *time*, one can understand how the spread of electronic media and the global movement of people, goods, capital and services has rendered communications between different cultures incredibly rapid. Thus, political, economic and cultural reference points for different people across the globe are at one and the same time both more uniform and more diverse. Therefore, any reference to identities, whether national, regional or international, has as much a homogenising implication as well as a heterogeneous content. Thus, globalisation can be said to bring about a tension between allegiances towards a national identity, a regional identity and an international identity: not an unfamiliar notion in Europe today.[122] Hence, modernity can be said to spread various images worldwide through symbolic forms which are reflected in our cultural identities and which place our sense of *self*, or who we are and where we come from, in considerable flux and disarray. Thus, 'in the 'marginal' countries (or regions), identities evolved from once-stable rural or traditional cultures compete with those borrowed from or disseminated by 'the West'.[123] In other words, Western hegemonic discourses on the Rest enter local, whether Mediterranean or Arab or any of Europe's Other discourses.[124] Such readings reveal how historically the colonised defined the colonisers who in turn defined the colonised and how these practices are still played out in the contemporary global world. This suggests that notions of 'self' and 'other' are interdependent notions and not separate concepts. Analysts therefore need to go beyond such dichotomies – especially the one between identity and difference – by seeing them as inherently relational. In order to understand otherness one needs to recognise identity markers which require difference but not necessarily 'otherness' and to highlight the indebtedness of self to difference, because it enables the self to be. This does not mean that plurality is not equally important.[125] In the context of regionalism, regions are themselves products of processes of identity construction (identification, categorisation) in which the self and the other, or multiple others, are constituted. Regions, therefore, become part of our taken-for-granted world and one hardly ever queries their existence. In this manner, regions can appear to be natural phenomena. Regions are not natural entities but rather social constructs. 'Regions' do function as a way of organising the international system for political, economic or cultural reasons, a manner in which politics can be organised. One needs to keep in mind, however, that hegemonic concerns for boundaries and their maintenance wanes with the changing interests of the 'core' countries or the 'outside' powers. What is needed is an 'unmapping' of the familiar order of the world and a reversal of conventional ways of thinking about IR by distancing ourselves from familiar accounts.[126] Our concern should focus on 'how historically developed, socially embedded interpretations of identity and space give rise to the objects scrutinized in both policy discourse and the disciplinary conceits of IR and FPA',[127] in other words, a 'struggle over the language of analysis'.[128] Through this perspective, the region structure can be interpreted as an imaginary idea and as 'one way among others of organizing the significance of space'.[129] What is needed is to locate discursive formations of regions and their contexts in an effort to better understand the social construction of such spaces.

Critical perspectives offer a very useful organising tool of inquiry: a tool for questioning rather than taking concepts for granted, that is, rather than an attempt at partitioning and wrapping up reality in any definitive manner.[130] Process-based perspectives offer an appropriate framework for the analysis of the social reproduction of regions. In such frameworks one can investigate ways of conceptualising the manner in which regions, or specific forms of region-formations, are reproduced by the activities of actors acting in the international system. The emphasis here is the fact that one deals with the world in terms of constructions, not in a way that is somehow 'direct' or unmediated; discursive practices therefore construct our world. Since the constructive nature of social practices is an aspect of social life that is taken for granted, analysts need a method that examines issues of power and knowledge underlying such constructions. Discursive constructivism as a methodology allows us to question our assumptions and the ways in which one makes sense of one's world.[131] Therefore, discursive constructivism, as the perspective adopted in this book, does not seek to replace conventional IR theories – in effect, it supplements the latter.[132]

Before understanding issues such as the meaning of regions, the institutions of international society, sovereignty or the regulation of immigration, analysts need to question what and who actors are, how they relate to one another and what methods are appropriate for the type of research one needs to understand the process of region formation. Discourse analysis is concerned with these fundamental questions and it can therefore *advance* IR theory, it is not a substitute for it. A combined theory/method by way of discursive constructivism can thus provide a framework within which one can analyse power and the processes or sets of practices/social action repeated in a similar and regular fashion over long periods of time, thus giving the concept of region a sense of stability and durability. Before moving on to the application of this proposed theoretical framework, it is crucial to note the close similarity between critical theory and discourse analysis: both schools are critical in that they problematise the social order and they are also both preoccupied with the relationship between knowledge and power. The main objective of critical writings is precisely that of showing how all supposedly empirical phenomena are constituted discursively through relations of power and knowledge.

The implications of this perspective as far as research on region-formation is concerned can be summarised as follows: a 'region' is said to 'exist' when social actors include it in their discourses as such, attempt to classify it, categorise it, regulate and administer it. In other words, when politicians, elites, peoples, international organisations or any other relevant actor consider a region as such and devise policies to administer it, organise it, integrate it, etc., they are in effect constructing it discursively. The 'truth' of social construction is that the empirical reality is the truth established by the social constructions – which may well be heuristic/interpretative. A concept such as that of 'region' is always in the making and therefore requires flexible analysis. 'Regions' are not created out of thin air but with the recourse to a number of structural, cultural or institutional factors that make regionality meaningful, saleable to electorates or other constituencies and workable. Often, structural restrictions related to identity render the construction of a region difficult or lead to failure; on other occasions, social or historical structures provide the material necessary for perceiving, making sense and constructing a 'region'.

This is why a process-based theoretical framework for the study of regions is so apt. Such an approach builds on what Jackson and Nexon refer to as a processual relationalism or a 'p/r approach'; that is, taking social interaction as logically prior to the entities doing the interacting. Such a process-based approach explores the ways in which different 'configurations' of meaning, of 'regions' in this case, constitute specific practices of international politics.[133] By adopting a discursive constructivist approach to the study of regions, a region is taken to be constituted through the meaningful practices of social actors which, when repeated in a similar and regular fashion over long periods of time, acquire a sense of stability and durability. A region is also constructed through structures understood as even longer reproduced sets of action, meaning and discourse/discursive practices that provide a framework for the operation of institutions as well as of action. One of the effects of regionalist projects is to produce and reproduce the very division of the social world into inside and outside giving rise to international organisations, like the EU's meta-political authority.[134] All this means is that early social activity – including the colonial project – has cut the world up in particular ways, forming the 'raw material' on which a regional project may begin to operate. The region project must be seen as involving the persistent drawing and redrawing of boundaries, establishing and re-establishing those demarcations which make it possible to speak of the region. The configurations of regions thus become the focus of analysis, rather than agents or structures. A process-based, discursive constructivist approach reverses the basic assumptions of conventional IR theories and depicts social reality instead in dynamic, continuous and processual terms.[135]

As the title of this book shows, such an understanding of the Mediterranean offers wide implications for Mediterranean studies as well as international relations and European studies. Through a combined methodology of textual study and codification of interviews this book hopes to provide a potentially in-depth analysis for these disciplines. The main argument here is that the EU treats the Mediterranean as an entity that is developing along the same time-line as itself, and is even a former instantiation of itself (ancient Greece, the Roman empire, and so on) where instantiation refers to how processes produce entities (regions). It is one thing to assert that the Mediterranean region gives rise to insecurity and instability and quite another to account in a precise way for the processes at work behind such assertions.

The question then becomes, to what extent a particular collective – such as the three states singled out as case studies in this book – is ready to tear itself away from 'the Mediterranean' and into 'Europe' (keeping in mind the complex debate here on the formation of European identity). The three cases studied fall neatly along this time-line, with Greece having made the 'transition' (the remnant being a debate about what has been lost by way of 'Eastern' spirituality), Malta being about to attempt it (at time of writing), and Morocco not really having comprehended the 'need' to take the plunge. Much could also be made of how national debates are structured according to the same logic, with nay-sayers appearing as backward looking and 'Europeans' as forward looking.

To sum up the discussion drawing upon alternative frameworks for the study of regions, it may be argued that for a thorough analysis of the process of region-formation, the most concrete level of analysis is concerned with 'elements' or discursive practices of regionalisation.[136] In other words, one must attempt to distinguish several structures/levels/actions/processes of regional analysis.

Traditional as well as alternative theories of regionalism are not without their critics. In fact, in the prescribed process-based theoretical framework, there are various strands of constructivism[137] or critical theorists who certainly fit under this framework as has been described above. However, some works in this broad category of critical theorists would also fit under the category headings of actor-based and structure-based theories. This supports the validity of the analysis here, which points to the need to look at theories in parallel when analysing the social construction of regions.

Critical approaches do not always directly address issues of regionalism and region building. However, their contributions have offered useful tools in pointing to the social and political creation of spaces and specifically of regions. Through a critical perspective, the process of region-construction is linked to the politics of identity and discourse analysis: regions are formed through processes of discursive practices that incorporate an 'other'. Discursive practices can be analysed and such practices taken as the units of analysis (a processual level of analysis). Discourses are here understood as processes or sets of practices/social action repeated in a similar and regular fashion over long periods of time, thus acquiring a sense of stability and durability. Therefore, adopting a discursive constructivist approach, this book employs a methodology to investigate the discursive practices that constitute the Mediterranean as a region. I will briefly present critical theory/constructivism and discourse analysis as the research programmes which lead to the adoption of a discursive constructivist approach to the study of the Mediterranean (as a socially constructed region). In the field of IR, the employment of discourse analysis as a research method is not so well developed but is changing more recently.[138]

Discursive constructivism

As mentioned earlier, there is a close affinity between critical theory and discourse analysis: both schools are critical in that they problematise the social order and question how this is produced and how it functions.[139]

Critical theory and constructivism

An attempt to form a critical theory was made by the 'Frankfurt School'. The theorists associated with this school, including Theodor Adorno, were concerned with the way the system dominates: that is, with the ways in which it forces or manipulates people into ensuring its reproduction and continuation. The 'Frankfurt School' also wanted to demonstrate that social variation is possible: the existing order is not fixed and is not the only possible one.[140] Constructivism has its intellectual roots in critical social theory.[141] In fact, constructivists have been labelled 'the new generation of critical theorists' because of their characteristic concern with the social construction of world politics. Constructivists argue that systems of *meaning* define how actors interpret their material environment. They also hold that social identities constitute actors' interests and shape their actions: 'Identities are the basis of interests'.[142] Hence, all institutions have a structural dimension made up of constitutive principles and agents and structures are therefore mutually constituted.[143] As in structuration theory, structures are enveloped in action.

Constructivism has undergone an intense debate within IR. Critiques argue that it is an ill-defined concept.[144] Smith proposes a range of constructivisms ranging from 'thin' constructivism to 'thick' constructivist approaches, having a similar starting point in that they reject assumptions of rationalist accounts but with divergent metatheoretical assumptions. He argues that there is really no point in trying to classify the different constructivisms (from Ruggie's classification of constructivist thought ranging from: (a) neo-classical, (b) postmodernist, and (c) naturalistic, to the classification put forward by Katzenstein, Keohane and Krasner which ranges from: (a) conventional, (b) critical, and (c) postmodern to Adler's classification ranging from: (a) modernist, (b) rule-based, (c) narrative knowing, and (d) postmodernist to a possible fourth classification ranging from: (a) sociological, and (b) Wittgensteinian) but rather hold that there is no one social constructivism, instead there are many.[145] One can agree with Smith in his conclusion that there is no one social constructivism: the literature seems to be more united on what is being rejected than on what is being proposed. Very broadly, though, social constructivist work can be split into two: one rationalist, the other more reflectivist/radical. It is crucial to keep in mind that these approaches adopt fundamentally different epistemological assumptions: the foundationalist, or modernist, 'soft' constructivists can debate easily with rationalists because they share epistemological assumptions. Reflectivist constructivists aim to explicate a different story. The approach adopted in this book situates itself within the reflectivist strand of social constructivism and combines this with discourse analysis.

Discourse analysis

The philosophical roots of discourse analysis lie in particular in the work of the German philosopher Nietzsche. In his work there are themes that have reappeared in discourse analysis: the relationship between knowledge and power and the relativism of knowledge; certain things become social facts with the institutionalisation of language; things do not exist as such, they acquire their meaning by being included in certain contexts with other things.[146] Discourse analysts argue that the world is a product of our ideas and that political and ideological phenomena are constituted in and by discourse. Discourse analysis thus focuses on a specific level of social reality, that of general *meanings*. If language is taken to create its own objects/field of knowledge one then has a *theory of meaning*.[147] This formulation is based on the premise that meaning is never present but always lies elsewhere and is not guaranteed by anything outside itself. The world one sees is therefore created in and by meanings. Any order that exists is seen as coming from a process of differentiation within the chaos: the 'process of signification/identification' is the drawing of these differences. When one makes a statement, one brings a momentary order to the world – one defines something according to its relationship with something else. Thus, the concern of discourse analysis is the structuring of relational distinctions, posited to be a 'center that organizes and makes them coherent'.[148]

What is discourse?

Discourse therefore consists of an important concept – of re-presentations of reality. When practices (of speaking subjects) of the same representations are institutionalised they make up a position in a discourse. Discourses operate as background capacities for persons to differentiate and identify things, giving them taken-for-granted qualities and attributes and relating them to other objects.[149] Discourse analysis is concerned both with the organisation of texts in various practices and with the discursive resources that those practices draw upon.[150] Thus, discourse analysts are concerned with the repertoires of discourse. They set out to show how representations are constituted and become widespread and what range of different representations contributes to a given discourse at any one time. Discourse analysts also examine the knowledge/power nexus. Discourse analysis has been given a prominent place in the study of IR in general, and FP in particular, by the 'Copenhagen School'. Members of this school have striven to bridge the gap between rationalist and reflectivist approaches in IRT. In fact, they try to combine elements from the various approaches on both sides. The School criticises the way that ideas have been treated in IRT for not having taken language seriously enough.[151] In the case of FPA, discourse analysis offers a useful dialogue on how best to 'critically re-evaluate foreign policy theory as practice' and 'divest power politics "practice" of its legitimacy', these being the stated goals of discursive critique.[152] Discourse in this context is understood as 'systems of values and rules in a given linguistic context'[153] and accounts for the way that FP – understood as the government's activity concerned with relations to international actors[154] – is conceptualised. Consequently, discourse operates on various levels, from producing highly abstract but very fundamental concepts to more detailed elaborations on rather specific issues. In turn, this results in a discursive 'tree' structure in which change is more likely to take place at the branch level than at the root, where it would be a revolutionary turn. Hence, the way in which discourses are framed provides the language in which policy options can be conceived: thus, policy is part of discourse.[155]

As a research programme, discourse analysis is more concerned with epistemological characteristics rather than ontological ones. For discourse analysts the world is in constant flux. Rather than focusing on the extant, discourse analysts concentrate on how the world came about to be the way it is, how it is upheld, and how it is challenged by other possibilities – that is, with the 'becoming of' or how and why things appear as they do. Discourse analysis is therefore concerned with how one can have knowledge about the world (epistemology). Any social scientist that attempts discourse analysis therefore aims at studying the world, or rather social reality, in a hermeneutical or interpretive way. The purpose of such research is thus to understand the actions, and the meaning actors ascribe to their actions that are to be found among the practices of those actions.[156]

This radical version of how one sees the social world takes discourse as statements or 'events'. It follows that 'subjects' are created or 'constituted' by 'signifying practices', that is, by the production of statements in discourses. No discourse has a fixed meaning – its meaning always depends upon its relationship to other discourses. Therefore one ends up with a multiplicity of possible interpretations.[157] There are, however, sources of fixity or points at which meaning becomes comparatively stable: these points of fixation have to do with power. One can locate power at the institutional level/structure out of which discourses are 'fixed' by the power relations inherent in them. Knowledge is power – power to define others. There are rules within a discourse about who can make statements and in what context, and these rules include some and exclude others. Those who have knowledge have the power to fix meaning and define others. Thus, the world consists of power relations and because power generates resistance, the world is made up of power struggles. Hence, analysts need methodologies that develop rules for studying the world in light of knowledge/power relations (or statements about discourse and meaning and power).[158] Discourse studies that include the implementation (and not just the formulation) of policy practices can potentially problematise labels used in the documentation and record implementation practices and expose readers to power in IR. A discursive constructivist perspective provides IR scholars with the tools to theorise the production of foreign policy and international practices. The focus on how speaking subjects order, control, and shape spaces has been fruitfully pursued in development anthropology and geography.[159] From a discursive constructivist perspective one can either see a multiplicity of orders as a desired end or one can look at disorder as a reflection of what is actually happening.[160] One is therefore left with a complex network of different language games. Our grasp of the rules of these games is the key to understanding the social construction of reality. On the one hand, society is produced and reproduced through human action. On the other hand, structures and action are mutually constituted or produced and reproduced (and thus change each other) – this leads to the notion of reflexivity, that is the way in which one actually constitutes one's social world.[161]

Why a combined methodology?

Discourse analysis is often criticised for not giving enough attention to the question of agency:[162] constructivism may answer this. Constructivists hold that the forms of fixation that establish identities and social orders are always precarious. The concept of subject-position provides an important construct that can link the notions of discourse, practice, agency and structure.[163] A particular kind of subject identity may get constructed in specific contexts but the subject's essential attributes are predetermined.[164] Human agents and social structures are theoretically interdependent or mutually implicating entities: agents and social structures are both relevant to explanations of social behaviour.[165]

Critical theory/constructivism and discourse analysis (not only in IR but also in social sciences in general) are concerned with the social production of 'reality'. Although there is considerable diversity within and between these two, concerns over signification (meaning) and its materiality, ability to construct and structure our social reality are central to both.

Discursive constructivism as a combined approach bringing together discourse analysis and the radical strand of constructivism is adopted here through a focus on the role of identity in the process of, and constitution of, interests and action and the mutual constitution of agents and structures.[166] This approach offers analysts a framework for the analysis of the social construction of regions. By applying this approach to the case of the Mediterranean region, it is hoped that readers can find this combined theoretical programme/methodology a useful step for the advancement of regional studies within the field of IR.

In sum, the different approaches to regionalism can be depicted as a continuum of approaches (see Figure 2.1).[167]

Theoretical application. The study of the Mediterranean 'region'

We will now proceed by taking this process-based theoretical framework to the study of regions and apply it to the Mediterranean as a case study. This section will present some existing approaches to the study of regionality in the Mediterranean. This will be followed by a tentative theoretical outline for the Mediterranean based on the process-based framework presented above.

Differing academic works continue to characterise the Mediterranean as a holistic 'region'. The following analysis introduces some of these perspectives, which apply the underlying assumptions of regionalism as indicated above.

Sea-based perceptions. The Mediterranean as a unified area

Braudel's two volumes entitled *The Mediterranean and the Mediterranean World in the Age of Philip II*[168] bring to his readers, despite their complexities, a thorough reflection upon the societies, economies, politics and personalities of the Mediterranean world in the second half of the sixteenth century.[169] In the first volume, Braudel gives an account of the physical elements that shaped and influenced the Mediterranean and the influence of geography and environment in shaping its history. The second volume describes the political and military confrontations of the Spanish and Ottoman empires and their role in the early modern Mediterranean. Braudel rejects a narrow specialised approach, such as diplomacy, politics or economics, in his study on the Mediterranean and instead reconstructs a multidisciplinary approach, which surveys the Mediterranean as a whole way of life.

One issue, which Braudel seems to bypass, is the way the very term 'Mediterranean' came about. Moreover, in his two volumes, Braudel is not

Strands of actor-based	Strands of structure-based	Strands of process-based
Neo-realism/neo-liberalism Traditional Regional governance	Neo-Marxism/world-systems	Critical theories Contructivism
Language as passive		Language as active/constitutive of social reality

Figure 2.1 Continuum of approaches to regionalism studies

consistent with and uses the term 'region' very loosely to refer both to the holistic notion of the Mediterranean countries scattered around the Mediterranean Sea but also to the divisions within countries in this geographical space, for example the different regions within France.[170] Thus, he does not distinguish between macro and micro regions.[171]

Although Braudel himself mentions the difficulty in drawing a precise boundary around the countries bordering the Sea,[172] one must take this issue a step further in terms of the constant change in boundary drawing across time and space. The Mediterranean of today has changed somewhat since the time that Braudel defined this area, and the Mediterranean of this decade is possibly different from what it is perceived of as being today.[173] Geographical barriers and borders are continuously being raised and broken in a variety of ways, for example, through civil wars. Moreover, due to economic reasons, emigration from the Mediterranean area towards Europe brings about an extension of the Mediterranean beyond its frontiers to such an extent that it becomes even more difficult to define and identify the littoral as a region.[174] Even Braudel's notions of what constitutes the centre and the periphery of the countries bordering the Mediterranean Sea have a different meaning today. For Braudel the centre refers to those areas closest to the Sea whilst the peripheral areas are the mountainous parts.

In relation to the study of regions, Braudel's work is an example of how a 'region' may be united through conflictual relations for example between Spanish versus French versus Ottoman interests. Such relations in turn define the Mediterranean as an object of contestation and disagreement.

Another similar approach to the Mediterranean is found in Mohammed El-Sayed Selim's work,[175] in which the author stresses the difficulty inherent in Egypt's attempts at balancing its role and capabilities in the conduct of its foreign policy due to the blurred Egyptian identity which is divided between an Arab and a European-'Mediterranean' orientation. This insecurity is in turn reflected in a continuous concern about the avoidance of duplication in Egypt's association within institutional arrangements, which place the country between Mediterranean and/or Middle Eastern/Maghreb/Arab groupings.[176]

A specific reflection on the Mediterranean appears in Fenech's study.[177] Whilst Braudel tackles the definition of the Mediterranean area mostly through fixed geographical and historical parameters, Fenech analyses this definition through a more recent political lens, thus building upon and offering a contemporary perception to the parameters used by Braudel. Fenech observes that because the political nature and boundaries of this area have changed since the period which Braudel's analysis accounted for, even perceptions of the area have, out of this necessity, changed.[178] So, whilst before one spoke of 'the Balkans, Asia Minor and the westernmost territories of Asia' as the 'Near East', these territories are now referred to as the 'Middle East', reflecting the intervention of big powers in these areas.[179] The drastic changes in the political map of the Mediterranean force us to rediscover and reconstruct our perceptions and notions of the Mediterranean area, especially in our contemplation of the prospects and implications of a holistic Mediter-ranean. Fenech makes a crucial distinction between objective perceptions (such as history, geography, etc.) and subjective views on factors, which determine a region – if one thinks of a Mediterranean 'region' then 'it becomes a region by virtue of the attention paid to it as such'.[180]

Fenech's observation therefore questions sharply the very notion of a Mediterranean 'region', which Braudel took for granted as a single unit in his works. Fenech remains dubious of any attempt at classifying the Mediter-ranean from 'outside' and labels such categorisations as 'either fictitious or irrelevant'.[181]

Another significant point, which emerges from Fenech's work, is his reference to the linkages between various disciplines when thinking about the Mediterranean. Moreover, he makes a positive contribution to this thinking when he describes how perceptions which emerge from the people of the Mediterranean themselves are determined by the circumstances they face at particular points in time.[182] In this manner, Fenech implies a shifting notion (through time) of perceptions about the Mediterranean label, which he terms a 'vacuum ... not a region'.[183] In the author's words, 'it does not always follow that what we think or hope we are is always what we really are'.[184] Fenech reads constructions of the Mediterranean as processes of identification; that is, identity formation in terms of relational connections.[185]

In another text, Fenech attempts to combine his knowledge of the history of the Mediterranean with contemporary implications of this basin for IR.[186] In this article, he speaks of the Mediterranean in terms of conflicts and confrontations across this littoral such as those between Christian and Islamic groups and in terms of struggles within Europe, such as the North–South divide. Fenech describes how historically, in terms of the East–West contest, the Mediterranean had 'assumed the character of a geostrategic region', that is, seen as a single unit, whilst contemporary North–South IR depict the area in terms of 'regional fragmentation', the experience of nationalism attesting to this division.[187]

However, Fenech postulates that despite this clearly divided Mediterranean, the necessity emerging from economic conditions depicts the Mediterranean as an interdependent sphere. According to Fenech, a holistic way of thinking about the Mediterranean depends on international actors acting as regional actors in their attempt to meet their economic, political and security objectives. Both Braudel and Fenech perceive the Mediterranean area as a space of communication processes, trade flows and interaction, and in this sense give a somewhat functionalistic perspective to the Mediterranean.

In another work on the Mediterranean, Calleya examines the history of the Mediterranean region, paying particular attention to initiatives by multilateral organisations to pull together the diverse and often opposing interests within the area.[188] Calleya looks, among other things, at the extent to which trade patterns and other forms of interaction will contribute to a sense of regional identity now that the superpower overlay has been lifted in the post-Cold War world. He argues that interaction is still lacking among Mediterranean countries and that the USA is likely to maintain its presence in the area due to its strategic and political commitment to Israel, the need to secure access to oil supplies and its strong ties with such important Arab countries as Egypt and Saudi Arabia. His take on Mediterranean regionalism does not conceptualise the Mediterranean in terms of geographical contiguity but rather in terms of purposeful economic, political, cultural, social inter-action among states which often – but not always – inhabit the same geographical space. The author's conclusion is that the Mediterranean will remain more of a frontier and boundary than a real region for co-operative relations.

Other authors argue for a better understanding of the conditions under which pluralistic integration may develop in the Mediterranean and the obstacles Mediterranean integration efforts continue to face.[189] Adler and Crawford argue that for the Mediterranean to develop into a security community, a minimum basis of shared collective understandings and trust is required – crucial but absent elements in an area of serious and protracted conflicts such as the Mediterranean. Despite these drawbacks, external actors have attempted to build secure communities in and around the Mediterranean, such as the EU's Barcelona Process that frames a potential Mediterranean security community around processes, institutions and practices.[190] What remains lacking is a shared understanding between European and Mediterra-nean parties of the concept of partnership and the substance of this.

George Joffé focuses on the inherently asymmetrical power relationship embodied in the economic dependency of Mediterranean countries on the EU. As will be shown in Chapter 3, EU member states are in a powerful position to impose their own interests and desires on their Mediterranean neighbours.[191] Moreover, the disparities brought about by globalisation processes express themselves markedly between southern European states and Israel on the one hand and the poor non-European Union Mediterranean partners on the other.[192]

Having said this, however, a common limitation, which seems to run through the works cited in this section, is that they do not give due attention to the processes and discursive practices of region-formation around the Mediterranean.[193] The exception is Adler's work which seems to be moving in this direction.[194]

A constructivist approach. The Mediterranean in the making

In his article entitled 'Authors in Search of a Character: Personhood, Agency and Identity in the Mediterranean', Paul Sant Cassia uses Pirandello's play 'Six Characters in Search of an Author' as a metaphor to examine the anthropology of the Mediterranean.[195] This analysis is instrumental in exposing the shifting notion of the Mediterranean and the construction of typical images of the Mediterranean as a way of characterising this area as a 'region'. Sant Cassia also explains the different constructions made by anthropologists and the people of the Mediterranean, thus implying external and internal perceptions. This seminal work focuses on the construction of identities within the Mediterranean through an anthropological perspective.

Sant Cassia has a valid observation on the importance of using a 'deeper' level of analysis when studying the Mediterranean so as to recognise differences as well as similarities – and to be aware of the acceptance of certain constructions about the Mediterranean which are socially, politically and economically arrived at.[196] The Mediterranean is a terrain which is continuously challenged and defined. This observation nicely captures the view underlying this book, which sees the Mediterranean as having multiple meanings.

Sant Cassia's work has a further important corollary to international politics/IR discourse which has a tendency to see the Mediterranean as a unified region from the perspective of unequal power relations between the North (usually Europe and/or the USA) and the South where the Mediterranean is marginalised by reference to some (so-called) inherent characteristics, either in its colonial past, or its conflictual internal relations or its diverse religions (that is, a region of conflicts from the perception/conception of the Powers).

However, Sant Cassia has a narrow definition of the Mediterranean which for him, in terms of 'politico-cultural discourse', is the 'residual ... geographical area after the southern European countries, now members of the EC, are taken out of the equation – which in effect means North Africa'.[197] Like Braudel and Fenech, Sant Cassia also introduces the concept of centre-periphery, the Mediterranean being perceived as the periphery of Europe. At this stage he seems to shift into a state-based and functionalistic thinking mode on the Mediterranean.

However, he makes a further critical contribution when he states that the question of what a region is should address the issue of whether a region is only ever a construct imposed by elites, or whether the region can be a community (or an identity network) that forms the everyday 'being-in-the-world' of those that dwell in the region. If the latter is the case, then the specific discourse networks that characterise a region rather than a state would need to be delineated.

Applying the alternative theoretical framework on regionality to the Mediterranean – the Mediterranean as socially constructed

Underlying the above works are different ways in which we tend to produce and reproduce the Mediterranean as an entity through social action. It is therefore important to examine actions, institutions and structures that together constitute the Mediterranean as an entity. The section below shall present a tentative outline of how we can operationalise a discursive-constructivist/process-based theoretical framework for the study of regions in the specific case of the Mediterranean.

I will start with the hypothesis of this book that has served as the basis for its reasoning and for the fieldwork investigations which have been carried out accordingly. This book suggests that in different societies conceptualised as Mediterranean, we find different ways of perceiving, thinking and acting about this area. This hypothesis is underlined by the polysemic nature of the Mediterranean, which like all concepts and social phenomena has many diverse interpretations. Therefore, we may say that there are different meanings attached to the concept Mediterranean, usually depending on what issue is being considered. The Mediterranean is a fluid concept and is socially constructed through discursive practices.

Taking the proposed theoretical framework presented above as the basis for a better understanding of the Mediterranean, the following sections will put forward suggested factors relating to the Mediterranean which may be regarded as actor-based, process-based and structural-based. Considering these features together we should be able to come to a more informed understanding of what we mean when we refer to the term Mediterranean 'region'. The first section will present the actor-based features, the second the process-based features and finally the structural features. All these characteristics should be seen as complementary and as processes or practices that bring about Mediterranean 'reality' and that give meaning to this area through discursive constructions.

Actor-based factors relating to the Mediterranean

The claim that regions are social productions derives from the recognition of the fact that actors 'act towards objects … on the basis of the *meanings* that the objects have for them'.[198] Thus, at the level of action, we need to examine how regions are defined in terms of speech acts and of other acts.[199] A radical constructivist approach investigates actors' interests (which they form and keep before their social interaction with other actors) where these are formulated, that is, in discourse.[200] In the case of the Mediterranean, the task here is to ask questions about what makes this area meaningful; that is, to uncover the work of language. Policies, discourses, practices of states, practices of civil societies, acts of violence, acts of co-operation such as technological transfers, acts of commerce, the formation of alliances, numerous utterances, specific practices/ occurrences such as a discussion on environmental problems and co-operative actions aimed at solving these issues – all these acts and networks make the Mediterranean meaningful (or non-meaningful). To make a simple analogy, we can imagine two researchers who decide to start discussing a specific issue on the Mediterranean, for example, the number of academic institutions that focus on this area. By the very fact that these actors have taken a conscious decision to discuss something they refer to as Mediterranean institutions, their very acts of discussing this object are constructing the Mediterranean as an entity. The idea of the Mediterranean is thus re-produced through engagement of actors at a level of action on behalf of this object. In some situations, however, discourses refute the idea of the Mediterranean and speak instead of the Maghreb or the Balkans or make references to the Black Sea area. These references thus exclude the Mediterranean and reject its potential meaningfulness and 'reality'. This framework can eventually move into process/institutional-based approaches as discussed below.

Process-based factors relating to the Mediterranean

As I referred to earlier, institutions here do not refer to institutions in the everyday sense of the term. These are broader phenomena, for example, Mediterranean co-operation seen as sets of practices or social action repeated in a similar and regular fashion over long periods of time, thus acquiring some sense of stability and durability. Within this context, one can examine the EMP. The latter can be seen to have moved from a low-institutional framework to an organised institution in the sense that it has now developed into a Mediterranean institutional framework in which action becomes meaningful and organised. The EMP in fact now has its own dynamics. These institutional factors constructing the Mediterranean are shaped by the interplay between the longstanding European domination and interest in the area, the geopolitical understanding of the Mediterranean as a region and the history of Mediterranean interaction, co-operation and conflict which can be identified as structural factors. Other such process-based factors include the nation state and the logic it entails; that is, sovereignty and interstate relations; European integration and its logic. To continue the simple analogy given earlier, the two researchers are now meeting and discussing the issue of Mediterranean universities every week with an agenda for each meeting. Thus, over a certain period of time, this Mediterranean discussion team acquires a sense of stability and durability. The temporal repetition of the act, and the temporal dimension of it, validates and legitimises the existence of a Mediterranean.

Structural factors relating to the Mediterranean

In the context of the Mediterranean, structures refer to the geopolitical and cultural imagination that sustains the meaningfulness (albeit vague) of the 'Mediterranean' as a region. These discursive practices include historical ties and interaction, conflicts over the domination of the area that have made it a meaningful entity such as colonialism, economic ties, etc. Structural factors also include imaginations, which deny the Mediterranean its specificity. Another range of structures is provided by the geopolitical and cultural dynamics that shape current thinking and policy in the region. For example, European domination, Arab and Islamic unity and southern European underdevelopment.

Such structures can then be seen as even longer *reproduced* sets of action, meaning and discourse that provide a frame for the operation of institutions as well as of action. If such structures are not repeated in a similar and regular fashion over long periods of time, thus acquiring a sense of stability and durability, they may be relegated to institutional factors relating to the Mediterranean. Turning to our analogy, the two researchers have now put together some funding for a project on their discussion topic and have set up a Mediterranean database of academic institutions dealing with Mediterranean topics. In such a structural framework of the Mediterranean everything is defined a priori. The structure constrains and enables the institutions to be called Mediterranean and enables actors to act within it and their acts to be regarded as related to the notion of a Mediterranean. Thus the structural factor here is the overarching principle that makes these researchers discuss the idea of the Mediterranean.

Conclusion

The approach to the study of regions offered in this chapter is not meant as an attempt to replace any other approaches discussed here. What is being suggested is an opening up of the debate on regions that takes as its guiding question the manner in which regions are socially constructed and imagined. In the specific case of the Mediterranean what is being suggested is that we need to examine the processes through which geopolitical and other imaginings of the Mediterranean 'region' sustain this concept. This framework for analysing the social construction of regions maintains that we need to move beyond traditional approaches to the study of regions that take these concepts for granted. The Mediterranean is a social construction as its existence depends on the acceptance of all the actors concerned that there is some meaning in the term. There are, however, discourses and practices that have existed and have been reproduced and repeated over long periods and have therefore become institutionalised. These might have been embedded in the imaginaries of Mediterranean societies and other actors and might be more influential in contrast to more recent discourses, or might be more difficult to challenge and dislodge. A discursive constructivist perspective to the study of regions therefore does not ask 'what is a region?' but 'how and why is a region defined in such and such a manner?' By so doing, such an approach highlights how the principal actors in the process of the construction of such an entity, construct a multiple definition of an area that changes over time and by issue. This is a very important consideration to take on board in our theoretical understanding of how regional identities are constructed. The reality of regions and region-formations is complex and our theoretical frameworks that study these entities and processes must be likewise. The Mediterranean as a (free-floating) political phenomenon is constituted in and by discourse and therefore needs a descriptive theory of the interplay of general meanings of this area. The meaning of the Mediterranean can therefore be analysed through processes or modes of discourse or through institutions (in the sociological sense). The focus of Chapters 4 and 5 will be on the meanings given to this area by the EU and the constructions of the Mediterranean in Malta, Morocco and Greece. The region project, however, is not composed merely of abstract demarcations, but instead consists of particular ways in which demarcations are expressed. We often hear of the underdevelopment of the Mediterranean and in order to contextualise and foreground EU practices on the Mediterranean, Chapter 3 codifies such demarcations through an analysis of the levels of economic development in Euro-Mediterranean countries. It will be argued that such demarcations give rise to the hegemony of the EU in the Mediterranean. The region project consists of a variety of principles, norms and practices which serve the EU to authorise actions taken in the name of the Mediterranean region and thus to demarcate a region of social life, a social space. The often-cited inter-dependence between Europe and its Mediterranean partners should be treated as a subjectless process which gives rise to new configurations of relations.

3 Understanding EU hegemony

Levels of economic development between North and South and the EU's Mediterranean policies

Before advancing to the discourses of the EU on the Mediterranean, it is important to contextualise and foreground these practices. This chapter will therefore take a snapshot of the levels of economic development of countries from the North (EU members, accession countries (at time of writing) and Turkey and Israel) and south (Arab partners) that give rise to the hegemony of the EU in the Mediterranean area. A good level of economic development of a country is here taken to refer to its citizens having a decent standard of living including living a long and healthy life, having political freedoms and enjoying an adequate education system. This definition is in line with the United Nation's understanding of the concept of development. This *reality check* of the economic, political and cultural challenges will provide an analysis of the structural conditions which bring about the often cited and often mentioned development gap between the North and South. This chapter thus serves as a context chapter on the Euro–Mediterranean Partnership prior to the empirical chapters. Thus it also discusses the problems and opportunities of the EMP and gives some updated data on the progress made as well as the main problems of project implementation.

Reality on the ground: economic, political and cultural challenges in the North and South

Although the EU member states and the Mediterranean partners share, to some extent, a common or at least a very interrelated history, as far as economic and social development is concerned, the Mediterranean countries, particularly the Arab partners, do not constitute a homogenous group. It is therefore often argued that one of the reasons for the hegemony of the EU *vis-à-vis* the Mediterranean area is related to the levels of economic development between North and South. With Europe being so well integrated and the South so divided, the gap in degrees of regional integration between the two areas is evident.[1] The EU is the largest provider of financial aid to some Mediterranean partners including Jordan and the Palestinian Territories (West Bank and Gaza Strip) while the other Mediterranean partners are also beneficiaries of financial aid from the EU. Morocco has been the leading recipient among the Mediterranean partners in terms of total funds received from the MEDA programme.[2] Malta and Cyprus benefit from pre-accession aid that is targeted at investment priorities, institution-building priorities and support in economic and social cohesion.[3] Pre-accession assistance for Turkey has been made available in 2002 via a specific regulation (reg. 2500/2001).

Moreover, as per Table 3.1, while the 15 EU member states have a high gross domestic product (GDP) per capita, attaining a maximum of US$53,780 in the case of Luxembourg, Arab countries have a low GDP per capita; for example, Morocco's GDP per capita is approximately one-fifteenth of Luxembourg's and one-ninth of Ireland's. This disparity is also reflected in the human development index (HDI) established by the United Nations Development Programme (UNDP).[4]

The current 15 EU member states as well as the accession countries Malta and Cyprus plus Israel fall within the *high* human development (HD) class: the Arab partners of the EMP including Libya – which has observer status – all fall within the *medium* HD class. Interestingly, Turkey, which is likely to join the EU in the near future, also falls within this category. From the Mediterranean partners of the Barcelona Process, Mauritania – which, like Libya, currently holds observer status – falls within the *low* HD class. Over the past 20 years, the UNDP reports that most areas of the world have steadily progressed in their HDI with Arab States exceeding the average increase for developing countries as a result of substantial growth stemming from efforts made mainly in the education sector.

The Arab Human Development Report of 2003 complements the HDR 2003 in that it underlines the importance of education and knowledge to Arab countries as a powerful driver of economic growth through higher productivity. The said report asserts that an Arab educated society can achieve improved economic development (and thus the objectives of justice, human freedoms and dignity and good governance) through appropriate training of its youthful, albeit large, capable labour pool. The remaining obstructions to development relate to defective structures, in particular political ones, but economic and social too.[5]

In fact, the whole Mediterranean suffers from a negative image about the economic, political and social stability in the area coupled with the costs related to, for example, corruption or inefficient administration systems that foreign investors have to face. With its shadow economy and a static register of its taxpayer base – despite a population growth of 30 per cent over the last 15 years – Turkey's HDI ranking can be partly explained through an understanding of its blatantly populist politicians, ineffective judiciary and widespread corruption. EU efforts in support of reform in the Mediterranean include conditions attached to its financial assistance package as it does for example with the Palestinian Authority. Most Mediterranean countries *are* thus faced with political, economic as well as cultural challenges with related consequences spreading from one area to the other.

Table 3.1 GDP/capita and HDI rank, Mediterranean partners and EU member states

Country	GDP/capita*	HDI rank	Country	GDP/capita*	HDI rank
Algeria	6,090	107	Austria	26,730	16
Cyprus	21,190	25	Belgium	25,520	6
Egypt	3,520	120	Denmark	29,000	11
Israel	19,790	22	France	23,990	17
Jordan	3,870	90	Finland	24,430	14
Lebanon	4,170	83	Germany	25,350	18
Libyan Arab Jamahiriya**	7,570	61	Greece	17,440	24
Malta	13,160	33	Ireland	32,410	12
Mauritania**	1,990	154	Italy	24,670	21
Morocco	3,600	126	Luxembourg	53,780	15
Palestinian Territories	2,788	98	Netherlands	27,190	5
Syrian Arab Republic	3,280	110	Portugal	18,150	23
Tunisia	6,390	91	Spain	20,150	19
Turkey	5,890	96	Sweden	24,180	3
			UK	24,160	13

Source: Human Development Report 2003. Available at: http:www.undp.org/hdr2003/pdf/hdr03_HDI.pdf (accessed 20 December 2003).

Notes

* 2001 (ppp US$), Jordan, Lebanon and Syria have actually experienced a *decrease* in their GDP per capita since 1995.

** Following the lifting of UN sanctions and the announcements made by Tony Blair and George W. Bush about Libya's agreement to give up hitherto undisclosed weapons of mass destruction ('Blair hails Libya deal on arms', *The Guardian*, Saturday 20 December 2003), it is expected that Libya will become a full member of the EMP. On 30 December 2003, Col. Gaddafi called European Commission President Romano Prodi and declared Libya's preparations for joining the Barcelona Process. Prodi extended an invitation to receive Gaddafi in Brussels. Mauritania could eventually join as a full partner of the EMP.

Cultural challenges

It is often argued that civil society is underdeveloped in the Mediterranean partner countries. Arab voices acknowledge, for example, that Arab civil societies have so far played a weak role during the course of the EMP's third basket's implementation process.[6] For example, although Lebanon signed up to several international agreements on human and civil rights including in 1997 the International Covention on the Rights of Women, it refrained from signing the Agreement against torture. Following the arrest of anti-Syrian demonstrators in Beirut in August 2001, the EU expressed concern on human rights issues, passing of death sentences and lengthy prison sentences on journalists in Lebanon. Closure of MTV in the second half of 2002 was the subject of an EU *démarche* in Beirut. In its Resolution adopted on 16 January 2003, the European Parliament drew attention to the situation regarding human rights and democracy in Lebanon.

In 2000 the UN Millennium Declaration affirmed the Millennium Development Goals which oblige governments and communities to take national ownership of the inadequate development in communities lacking education, clean water, health care, etc. The Goals aim to promote better engagement from populations of poor countries in order to ensure more action from their leaders. For the Arab States achieving the Goals by 2015 is deemed challenging but not impossible.[7] Although gaps persist, since 1970, many aspects of human development have improved thanks to high incomes. Yet, gender *in*equality remains an issue, despite narrowing gender gaps in enrolments. (In terms of gender equality in primary and secondary education, Mauritania led the group of poor countries through an increase in the ratio of girls to boys from 67 per cent to 93 per cent between 1990 and 1996.) For instance, in those Arab countries with parliaments, only 5 per cent of seats are held by women. In Jordan, while not perfect, the democratisation process has been regarded as one of the most advanced in the region. However, there are still problems with levels of participation in political life and women's representation in Parliament has always been insignificant. In terms of political and civil rights, only 4 of the area's 17 countries (providing data) had multiparty electoral systems (as at 1999). According to the UNHDR 2003, the constraints for development in Arab States is related to their failure to convert income into human development and progress towards the Goals – rather than to income. Illiteracy rates remain high in most Arab-Mediterranean countries as can be seen from Table 3.2.

Political challenges

Regular references to shaky and/or undemocratic political systems, 'poor' governance, bad human rights records, regional conflicts and political violence as the order of the day in Mediterranean countries are not lacking in international media discourses, international reports and everyday political

Table 3.2   Illiteracy in Mediterranean partner countries and selected EU member states

	Illiteracy (% of population age 15+ for 2002)
Mediterranean partners	
Algeria	31
Egypt	43
Israel	5
Jordan	9
Lebanon	13
Libya	18
Mauritania	59
Morocco	49
Syria	24
Tunisia	27
EU member states and acceding states	
Cyprus	3
France	N/A
Greece	3
Italy	1
Malta	7
Portugal	7
Spain	2
Turkey*	14

Source: The World Bank Group: http://www.worldbank.org/data/.

Note
* Turkey is awaiting the announcement for a date for accession negotiations to start (at time of writing). This announcement is expected towards the end of 2004. On 6 October 2004, the Commission's Regular Report on Turkey indicated an amber light for the start of accession negotiations. See also Pace, M., 2004d. 'EU–Turkey Relations'.

speeches. In 1997, the Islamic Action Front in Jordan boycotted that year's parliamentary elections. In August 2002, King Abdullah once again postponed the parliamentary elections (due in November 2001) to Spring 2003, without giving any new elements (other than the instability in the 'region') to explain the new postponement. There have been several government reshuffles since the election of Ali Abul Ragheb's government in June 2000. In fact the average life span of governments has been less than one year (since the country's existence) making this a destabilising element (although key ministers do keep their portfolios). Hence, a major constraint to political and economic reforms in Jordan has been the lack of continuity in governments. In Turkey, despite the country's potential for growth and development, obstacles still persist along its long-sought path to EU membership: lack of political steadfastness and cohesiveness, internal strife involving the Kurdish minority in eastern Turkey, human rights issues and a powerful, interventionist military remain elements to be addressed for the country to meet the EU's criteria for commencement of accession negotiations.[8] Algeria continues to be threatened by internal strife both from Islamic militants who have conducted a terror campaign since 1992 and the Berber minority in eastern Algeria that has resorted to violence in search of greater autonomy, and the military continue to exert power.

Economic challenges

According to the UN's Human Development Report of 2003, during the 1990s, despite general economic stagnation, Lebanon and Tunisia grew by more than 3 per cent per year while Egypt realised the largest reduction in under-5 mortality rates (from 10 per cent to 4 per cent). However, the list of *economic challenges* Mediterranean countries struggle with remains a long one and includes: state-controlled economies, underdeveloped infrastructures, small foreign direct investment (FDI), low competitiveness, falling percentage of EU and CEECs' imports, deficit of the balance of payments, weak economic growth, high dependence on the EU market, low incomes, highly unequal distribution of incomes within the Mediterranean, high population growth, deficit in basic social services, high (youth) unemployment, high (illegal) emigration and environmental problems. Since 1995, only Lebanon experienced a fall in its population figure. The population of the majority of Mediterranean countries is relatively young. Young people are in turn most affected by unemployment. Egypt is by far the most populous country in the Arab world and the rate at which the country's population is increasing remains quite high, at around 1.7 per cent annually. With an official unemployment rate of 9.5 per cent in 2002 (see Table 3.3),[9] the country faces a great challenge in providing sufficient employment for large groups of young people entering the workforce each year. Unemployment is fairly high in most of the Mediterranean Partner countries, with the exception of Malta and Cyprus. Although unemployment rates have fallen slowly in the Maghreb countries since 2000, they are still among the highest in the region. In fact, from 1995, the rate of unemployment in the Mediterranean has been generally increasing – only Lebanon, Morocco and Tunisia experienced a slight decrease in unemployment since 1995. With a young population and an estimated 27.5 per cent unemployment rate Algeria, like Egypt, urgently requires economic opportunities for its young. In Turkey, the government is facing a challenging test of its commitment to the reform programme of the agricultural sector that employs nearly 50 per cent of the workforce. With more than a quarter of the population already living below the poverty line, Turkey has yet to organise large scale corporate farming to compete with the world's agricultural powers.

Moreover, most Mediterranean partners have a trade deficit with the EU (see Table 3.4). Syria and Algeria are the only Mediterranean partners that regularly record a trade surplus with the EU. Algeria's resource base, its geographic location close to Europe and the latter's endeavours to reduce the environmental impact of burning heavy hydrocarbons for heating and power generation, make pipeline deliveries of gas to the European energy

Table 3.3 Structural conditions in the Mediterranean

Country	Total population (millions – mid year average) 2002	Unemployment rate (%) 2002	Population below poverty line (%)	Government type*
Algeria	32.277942	27.50	23 (1999)	Republic
Cyprus	0.767314	3.30	N/A	Republic
Egypt	73.312559	9.5	22.9 (FY95)	(Arab Constitutional) Republic
Israel	6.029529	10.3	18 (2001)	Parliamentary democracy
Jordan	5.30747	15.3	30 (2001)	Constitutional monarchy
Lebanon	3.67778	N/A for 2002. 9.9 (2000)	28 (1999)	Republic
Libya	5.368585	N/A Other estimates: 30 (2001)	N/A	Jamahiriya (a state of the masses) in theory, governed by the populace through local councils; in practice, (often described as) a military dictatorship
Malta	0.397499	5.2	N/A	Parliamentary democracy
Mauritania	2.828858	N/A Other estimates: 21 (1999)	50 (2001)	Republic
Morocco	31.167783	18.4	19 (1999)	Constitutional monarchy
Palestinian Territories				
Gaza Strip	1.274868	50–60 (both in Gaza Strip and West Bank)	60 (2002)	Palestinian Authority as the Executive
West Bank	2.237,194			
Syria	22.454239	5.2–11.7	15–25	Republic
Tunisia	9.815644	15.4	6 (2000)	Republic
Turkey	67.308928	7.90	>25	Republic

Source: Compilation of tables from *Statistics in Focus*, European Communities, 2003; the *World Fact Book* 2003; the Economist Intelligence Unit, 2003, updated country-by-country information sources.

Note: * These refer to commonly used labels and are subject to criticism. Some would argue for example that Morocco is not a constitutional monarchy (which implies that there are real limits on the King's power) since the King has complete power in many areas. These issues are open to debate but this is not the place for this discussion nor is such a debate relevant for this chapter. These are not my personal labels but I have used labels from country's own sources which describe their respective regimes.

Table 3.4 External debt, EU exports to and EU imports from Mediterranean countries, and export partners to and import partners from EU members and other Mediterranean countries

Country	Debt (external)	EU exports to Med countries by Med country	EU imports from Med countries by Med country	Export partners from EU members and other Med (clients)	Import partners from EU members and other Med (suppliers)
Algeria	US$21.6 billion (2002 est.)	EU supplies 58% of Algeria's imports	62.7% of Algeria's exports go to the EU Trade balance in Algeria's favour (€11,250m in 2000)	Italy 22.8%, France 14.6%, Spain 13.9% (2001)	France 37.3%, Italy 10.0%, Germany 7.6%, Spain 5.7% (2001)
Cyprus		52% of Cyprus' imports, 2002	54% of Cyprus' exports, 2002		
Greek Cypriot area	US$8 billion			EU 36% (UK 21%, Greece 9%), Syria 7%, Lebanon 5% (2000)	EU 52% (UK 11%, Italy 9%, Greece 9%, Germany 7%) (2000)
Turkish Cypriot area	US$NA (2002)			Turkey 36.3%, UK 26.5%, Middle East 7.0% (2001)	Turkey 65.1%, UK 10.4%, other EU 13.4% (2001)
Egypt	US$30.5 billion (2002 est.)	EU accounts for 30% of Egyptian imports, €4.2 billion, 2001	EU accounts for 31% of Egyptian exports, €1.5 billion, 2001	Italy 13.5%, UK 9.2%, France 4.0% (2002)	Germany 7.9%, Italy 6.5%, France 6.2% (2002)
Israel	US$42.8 billion (2001 est.)	€14,449 million, 2001; EU-15 share of Israeli imports = 41% (2002)	€9,568 million, 2001; EU-15 share of Israeli exports = 25% (2002)	Belgium, Germany, Italy, the Netherlands, UK and Switzerland	Belgium, Germany, Italy, the Netherlands, UK and Switzerland
Jordan	US$8.2 billion (2002 est.)	€1800 million; EU-15 share of Jordan imports, 28.8% (2002)	€160 million; EU-15 share of Jordan exports, 2.9% (2002)	Israel 3.7% (2000)	EU 28.4% (Germany 9.2%, France 3.8%, Italy 3.3%) (2001)

continued…

Table 3.4 External debt, continued

Country	Debt (external)	EU exports to Med countries by Med country	EU imports from Med countries by Med country	Export partners from EU members and other Med (clients)	Import partners from EU members and other Med (suppliers)
Lebanon	US$9.3 billion (2002 est.)	€3,423 million in 2001 (no stats for 2002)	€191 million in 2001 (no stats for 2002)	France 11%, (Switzerland 10%), Jordan 4%, Syria 3% (2001 est.)	Italy 11%, France 10%, Germany 9%, Syria 5% UK 5%, (2001 est.)
Libya	US$4.4 billion (2001 est.)	50% of Libya's total imports of manufactures, energy and food products and raw materials from Italy, Germany, UK and France	Italy, Germany, Spain, France and Greece absorb 70% of its manufactures, energy and food products and raw materials. EU accounts for 90% of Libya's oil exports	Italy 39.6%, Germany 15.5%, Spain 14%, Turkey 6.3%, France, Switzerland, Tunisia (2001)	Italy 28.5%, Germany 12.1%, UK 6.6%, Tunisia 6.0%, France, other (2001)
Malta	US$130 million (1997)	EU-15 share of Maltese imports 67.2% (2002)	EU-15 share of Maltese exports 45.9% (2002)	Germany 14.1%, France 10.2%, UK 8.8%, Italy 3.4% (2001)	Italy 19.9%, France 15.0%, UK 10.0%, Germany 8.7% (2001)
Mauritania	US$2.5 billion (2000)	No stats	No stats	Italy 15.0%, France 14.9%, Spain 12.4%, (2001)	France 23.0%, Benelux 8.0%, Spain 5.5%, Algeria 3.7%, Germany (2001)
Morocco	US$17.7 billion (2002 est.)	€7,624 million, 2002; EU-15 share of MA imports 54% (2001)	€6,265 million, 2002; EU-15 share of MA exports 72.4% (2001)	France 27%, Spain 13%, UK 8%, Germany 6%, Italy 6% (2001)	France 23%, Spain 11%, Italy 6%, Germany 5%, UK 5% (2001)

Palestinian Territories	US$108 million (includes West Bank) (1997 est.)	N/A	N/A		
For Gaza Strip				Israel, Egypt, West Bank	Israel, Egypt, West Bank
For West Bank				Israel, Jordan, Gaza Strip (2000)	Israel, Jordan, Gaza Strip (2000)
Syria	US$22 billion (2002 est.)	EU accounts for 33.1% of Syrian imports (2001); for first half of 2002 = 25.4%	EU accounts for 64.3% of Syrian exports (2001); for first half of 2002 = 60.5%	Germany 19%, Italy 16%, France 12%, Turkey 7%, Lebanon 5%, Spain 4%, Austria 3% (2001)	Italy 8%, Germany 7%, France 6%, Lebanon 5%, Turkey 5% (2001 est.)
Tunisia	US$13.6 billion (2003 est.)	EU provides 70.3% of Tunisia's imports (2002)	78.6% of Tunisia's exports go to the EU (2002)	France 28.8%, Italy 22.5%, Germany 12.5%, Spain 5%, Belgium 2.98% (2001)	France 28.0%, Italy 19.8%, Germany 10.4%, Spain 4.6%, Libya 3.88% (2001)
Turkey	US$118.3 billion (year end 2001)	EU-15 share of TR imports 45.5%, 2002	EU-15 share of TR exports 51.5%, 2002	Germany 17.2%, Italy 7.5%, UK 6.9%, France 6.0% (2000)	Germany 12.9%, Italy 8.4%, France 5.5%, UK 4.6% (2000)

Source: Compilation of table from European Communities, 2003

market a feasible and highly demanded project. However, though the country possesses some of the larger proven natural gas reserves in the world, it is still considered as relatively under-explored. Its natural gas reserves of 160–200 trillion cubic feet (*c.*5.5 trillion m³) put it in the world's top 10 gas resource holders.[10] Hence, Algeria should theoretically have a positive future in terms of its potential as a growing supplier of gas to European markets for many years to come! Yet, the danger lies in its dependence on the agricultural and petroleum sectors (Table 3.5). Although the EU is Israel's main trading partner in terms of overall trade (imports and exports), since 1997, Israel's deficit *vis-à-vis* the EU has been larger than its overall deficit (Israel imports far more than it exports to the EU). In Jordan, this trade deficit is partially offset by a surplus in services, mostly through tourism and remittances from Jordanians working abroad.

Critiques further argue that there is a lack of intra-Arab commercial trade. According to the Egyptian Businessmen's Association, there are a number of reasons attributing to the limited Arab intra-trade including the instability of political relations between Arab countries; the high trade costs; with regard to trade financing; transport and communications; the big differences in individual incomes between Arab countries; the differences between consumption and buying behaviour in Arab countries; the competitive commercial structures; the differences in monetary and commercial policies; and the fact that Arab producers are unable to compete with international ones in terms of price and quality, which makes it more attractive to import from non-Arab countries.[11]

Also uneven is the level of integration of the Mediterranean, mainly Arab, partners in the world economy.[12] Besides the differences in natural resources and potential, this gap reflects the disparities between the economic policies of European and Arab governments and within Arab states. Up until the 1980s (even the 1990s in some cases), import substitution was the norm in the Arab partner states. The high tariffs applied converted import duties into a source of revenue, that constituted a barrier to international trade. New export-oriented policies had to face up to the challenge of poorly diversified economies that relied heavily on oil exports. Morocco, Tunisia and to some extent Egypt were the exceptions while other Arab countries, like Jordan and Lebanon, made progress in services. Arab economies also encountered political difficulties, besides the economic ones. This led to a low inter-Arab economic integration. The Greater Arab Free Trade Area (GAFTA) is one of the most significant steps taken by the Arab countries themselves aiming at achieving a significant level of economic integration. The League of Arab States, created on 22 March 1945 by the then seven independent Arab states, has played a significant role in the political framework of Arab economic integration attempts. Besides political objectives, Arab co-operation has been aimed at developing economic, financial, social and cultural ties between the member states of the League now numbering 22 states. In 2002, Tunisia, Morocco, Egypt and Jordan decided to speed up the liberalisation of trade

Table 3.5 Exports, commodities of Mediterranean partners

Country	Exports, commodities
Algeria	petroleum, natural gas, and petroleum products 97%
Cyprus	
Greek Cypriot area	citrus, potatoes, pharmaceuticals, cement, clothing and cigarettes;
Turkish Cypriot area	citrus, potatoes, textiles
Egypt	crude oil and petroleum products, cotton, textiles, metal products, chemicals
Israel	cut diamonds, high-technology equipment, and agricultural products (fruits and vegetables) are the leading exports
Jordan	phosphates, fertilisers, potash, agricultural products, manufactures, pharmaceuticals
Lebanon	foodstuffs and tobacco, textiles, chemicals, precious stones, metal products, electrical products, jewellery, paper products
Libya	crude oil, refined petroleum products (1999)
Malta	machinery and transport equipment, manufactures
Mauritania	iron ore, fish and fish products, gold
Morocco	clothing, fish, inorganic chemicals, transistors, crude minerals, fertilisers (including phosphates), petroleum products, fruits, vegetables
Palestinian Territories	
Gaza Strip	citrus, flowers
West Bank	olives, fruit, vegetables, limestone
Syria	crude oil 70%, petroleum products 7%, fruits and vegetables 5%, cotton fibre 4%, clothing 3%, meat and live animals 2% (2000 est.)
Tunisia	textiles, mechanical goods, phosphates and chemicals, agricultural products, hydrocarbons
Turkey	apparel, foodstuffs, textiles, metal manufactures, transport equipment

between them through what was then the Agadir Initiative. The Agadir Agreement provides for free trade between these four countries by 2006 (and with the Commission of the European Union's provision of technical support for its implementation). Political differences between Arab leaders also affect Arab economic relations. In the political context, apart from the periodic crises the Arab world suffered during recent times, leaders frequently undermine the mutual confidence between Arab countries and, as a result, a turbulent political atmosphere prevails.[13]

Apart from the efforts within the framework of the Arab League, sub-regional efforts have also been attempted. The Arab Maghreb Union (AMU) was founded in 1987 and comprised Algeria, Libya, Mauritania, Morocco and Tunisia. Egypt and Jordan form part of the Arab Co-operation Council together with Yemen and Iraq. The achievement of expected goals has been mainly hindered by political problems (especially for the AMU) and the lack of progress in these unions highlights the economic limitations of small-scale groups when compared to larger ones.

The events of 9/11, the wars in Afghanistan and Iraq, the heightened tension in the Middle East and the declaration of the US-led war against terrorism have all had a negative impact on the major FDIs in the Mediterranean desperately needed to implement many reform and economic programmes.[14] FDI flows have therefore been highly volatile: in Egypt, for example, only about US$500 million was received in 2001 compared to as much as US$1.2 billion in the previous year. The situation is not any better because Egypt's bond and stock markets are at a relatively low level of development. As Geradin and Petit argue:

> In emerging economies, the importance of FDI is reinforced by the fact that taxes and stock exchanges and credit institutions are all the more rudimentary and inefficient. The Commission has taken the view that the absence of a transparent economic and legal framework largely effects investments by EC operators in the Med region.[15]

European investment flows in the MPC-12 countries fell overall since 2001 due to this less favourable investment climate. The tragic events mentioned above made foreign investors rethink their investment strategy for the Mediterranean. The main, large economies in the Mediterranean area, Turkey, Egypt and Israel, have particularly felt the negative effects of this turnaround in foreign investment strategies. The exceptions were Morocco and especially Turkey but also Tunisia where overall FDI increased in 2002 as a result of investment in the transport and telecommunications sectors.

As one interviewee argued, the potential for Mediterranean countries lies in the expansion of their services sector. The exception here is Israel which, with a high level of wealth (reflected in the structure of production), sets itself apart from the majority of the other Mediterranean partners. Its structure of production is very similar to that of EU member states and accession countries, characterised by a dominant service sector and the limited part played by agriculture in the total value added. However, a significant share of Israel's income from trade in services (foreign currency revenue, transport and travel-related activities, etc.) is generated by tourism activities that have been diminishing since 1995. By contrast Israel often records a surplus *vis-à-vis* the EU in the field of computer technology.[16]

Another challenge related to the North–South development gap is the often iterated lack of economic advancement in the South: besides the differences in natural resources and the disparities between the economic policies of (Arab) governments, most Mediterranean countries produce similar products (see Table 3.5) that limits sub-regional trade and contributes to the lack of economic independence and development in these countries. In general, most Mediterranean partner countries have poorly diversified economies with some relying heavily on oil exports. This constitutes an important challenge for the Arab partners with limited competitiveness of Arab goods. Jordan, for example, is a small and poor Arab country with inadequate supplies of water and, in contrast to neighbouring countries, a lack of hydrocarbon resources. Jordan remains heavily dependent on merchandise imports. Its imports, mainly oil, capital goods, consumer durables and food, outstrip exports, mainly phosphates, fertilisers, potash, agricultural products and manufactures. Trade with Persian Gulf countries and bilateral and regional trade liberalisation under the Greater Arab Free Trade Area have started to improve its economic situation.

Many analysts have long argued that another key problem relating to the North–South development gap is the foreign debt of a number of Mediterranean partners which, for a large part, is in the hands of EU member states.[17] Lebanon has, for the past few years, experienced sluggish growth recording rates of 2 per cent in 2001 and 2002. Its economy has consistently run large fiscal deficits and in the process a very large domestic and external debt burden has been accumulated. Some observers blame this on Lebanon's profligate politicians. The sale of every state asset, for example, must be passed by the parliament, where opposition from senior politicians having personal interests and power bases in the state companies is most likely.[18] Spending levels are quite high in Morocco too. As a net debtor nation, Morocco pays more in interest on its debt to foreigners than it receives from its own investments abroad. To counteract these minuses on their budget records, most Mediterranean countries rely heavily on aid transfers from abroad and remittances from their workers with jobs overseas. Private transfers of funds from abroad into Morocco, mainly remittances of Moroccans who are employed outside the country who send part of their earnings home, form a large contribution to the country's current account.[19] On average, in the past few years, such private transfers provided a net inflow of funds of more than US$3.5 billion per year. Under 'normal' political climates, tourism also has considerable input in Mediterranean governments' income accounts.

But, with the tourism sector badly hit since 9/11, Mediterranean countries have realised the importance on not relying too much on this sector as the main income source.

Due to these structural asymmetries and the heavy dependence of Mediterranean partners on EU member states, one can argue that EU–Mediterranean relations correspond to a 'soft form of hegemony'.[20] These structural conditions in most Mediterranean countries translate into an unfavourable power distribution, as detailed above. The next section of this chapter will therefore provide the contours of the Euro–Mediterranean 'Partnership' as well as evaluate its achievements so far and the challenges of policy implementation that still lie ahead.

The EU's Mediterranean policies

From its conception, the European integration process included the Mediterranean element within its framework. The Rome Treaty, which established the European Economic Community (EEC), left its doors open to other 'European' countries that wished to become members.[21] Greece and Spain did so (in 1981 and 1986 respectively).[22] Malta and Cyprus became members on 1 May 2004 while Turkey[23] hopes to join the EU in the near future. The Treaty also contained a section[24] which pertains to the association of 'non-European countries and territories which have special relations' with the founding members.[25] Article 237, however, leaves no possibility for these or any other countries from the Maghreb or the Mashreq to become full members, as Morocco found out.[26]

Prior to 1989, the EC addressed the Mediterranean only in the context of bilateral agreements.[27] Throughout the 1960s, the EC signed trade agreements with various Mediterranean countries granting their manufactured products free or preferential access to the EEC, and a limited access for some specified agricultural products. In the mid-1970s, the EC adopted its GMP and proceeded to sign co-operation and association agreements with various Mediterranean non-member countries (MNCs): Algeria, Morocco and Tunisia in 1976 and Egypt, Jordan, Lebanon and Syria in 1977. It is important to note that during the GMP period, the EC tended to regard Morocco, Tunisia and Algeria (the 'Maghreb')[28] as a grouping, differentiated from eastern Mediterranean countries such as Jordan. In addition to traditional trade provisions, the new agreements included a financial component in the form of five-year protocols designed to support the process of economic development in the recipient countries. From the mid-1980s onwards, the development of several important events had a direct or indirect impact on Euro–Mediterranean relations; Spain and Portugal became members of the European club, the Communist bloc disintegrated and the Berlin Wall fell. There was also a rise of social, political, and economic crises in several countries of the southern Mediterranean; as in the case of Algeria where increased activism by fundamentalist movements led to an overturning of the election results in

January 1992[29] with the resulting outbreak of a civil war and the outbreak of the Gulf war.

In response to some of these events, the EC felt the need to revise its policy towards the Mediterranean and eventually adopted its RMP.[30] In addition to the traditional financial protocols, a new facility was introduced to promote regional and decentralised co-operation through projects that involved two or more MNCs; several programmes were then set up to that effect including Med-Invest, Med-Campus and Med-Urbs.[31] Under the RMP there was an initial attempt to add a trans-regional approach to certain questions/issues,[32] but this initiative was badly underfunded. It took six years (from the date of the RMP, that is 1989) to commit the EU to a reinforced Mediterranean policy.

During 1992 and 1993 the Commission proposed that future relations with MNCs should go beyond the financial sector and economic sphere to include a political dialogue between the parties, the creation of a Euro-Mediterranean free-trade area and social, economic and cultural co-operation. These recommendations, initially looking just to a Euro–Maghrebi partnership, were approved at the Lisbon summit in June 1992 and confirmed at the Corfu summit in June 1994 (these summits are in fact European Council meetings). In the meantime, negotiations got underway with Tunisia, Morocco and Israel on the basis of mandates specifying these four basic elements.

The Med Forum

With a clear vocation to influence matters on the Euro-Mediterranean agenda, a joint Franco–Egyptian initiative, the Mediterranean Forum, was developed in 1994. In July of that year the Ministers of Foreign Affairs of ten Mediterranean countries met in Alexandria, Egypt for the first meeting of the Mediterranean Forum. The countries were Algeria, Morocco, Tunisia, Egypt, Portugal, Spain, France, Italy, Greece and Turkey. In the course of that first meeting, Malta was admitted as the eleventh member. This forum excludes parties to the Arab–Israeli conflict (that is, Israel, the Palestinian Authority, Syria, Lebanon and Jordan) and also excludes Libya and Cyprus. But this does not mean that it regards them as non-Mediterranean. The original intention of the forum was for the core group of 11 states to set up a regional organisation in which other Mediterranean states would gradually be admitted. It is run by a Presidency taken in turn by the membership.[33] When Susanna Agnelli succeeded Martino during the Dini government (which took office in January 1995) she wrote a joint article with the then Spanish foreign minister, claiming that the southern Mediterranean deserved equal attention to East-Central Europe. They further called for 'political dialogue' – especially through the Mediterranean Forum; economic assistance – through the gradual constitution of a Mediterranean free trade area and by financial transfers; and for the stimulation of a greater mutual understanding between European and Arab cultures (in effect, the basis for the three pillars of the Barcelona Declaration). In the course of Mediterranean Forum meetings, an in-depth discussion on the EuroMed Charter for Peace and Stability was carried out. Greek interviewees consulted in the late 1990s stated that the EMP, despite its shortcomings, is expected to offer a better opportunity (albeit still not enough) for the much-needed financial solutions to the Mediterranean 'problem' than the Mediterranean Forum (which has no funding).

With the coming into being in November 1995 of the EMP, the Mediterranean Forum has since survived more as a discussion forum. The most recent ministerial meeting of the Mediterranean Forum was held in Antalya, Turkey on 9 October 2003 for two days. The agenda included organised crimes, weapon smuggling, money laundering, the fight against terrorism and other regional and international issues. The Mediterranean Forum has continued to exist as a forum where EU and non-EU Med countries can deliberate informally over their problems and discuss initiatives that could be presented for EMP endorsement: a meeting point in the shadow of the EMP. Its only collective act was perhaps the adoption of a code of conduct on terrorism at the ninth session of the Mediterranean forum foreign ministers (Delos, 20 and 21 May 2002): the oral conclusions of the presidency adding that the forum was aiming at the code's inclusion in the new Action Plan adopted at the EuroMed Ministerial Conference in April 2002 in Valencia.[34] Commission officials argue that there is a sporadic spread of fora on Euro-Mediterranean matters. Mediterranean partners seem to agree and prefer less fora, less frequent meetings and more concentrated encounters.[35]

The Euro–Mediterranean Partnership

During the Essen summit of December 1994 a declaration was made of the EU's support for Spain's intention to convene a Euro-Mediterranean conference in the second half of 1995[36] to carry out an in-depth appraisal of all major political, economic, social and cultural issues of mutual interest and to work out a general framework for permanent and regular dialogue and co-operation in these areas. The Council adopted a document[37] which defined the EU's position and which was to be presented at the Cannes summit in June 1995.[38]

In order to achieve its stated objectives of immigration management, trade, prosperity and peace, the EU has adopted a strategy that it termed a 'Partnership' with the MNCs. According to its formulators, this approach seeks to provide a framework where the MNCs and the EU can work as full and equal partners towards achieving mutually beneficial goals. This partnership was defined and adopted by the Euro-Mediterranean Conference in Barcelona in November 1995. The EMP was introduced to complement and not replace existing or forthcoming bilateral agreements linking the EU to individual MNCs. Compared with previous association agreements, this was an innovation in that it expanded the range of content covered by new agreements (compared with previous AAs. Thus, new Generation Association Agreements were contemplated then enhanced).

The Conference of EU and Mediterranean Foreign Ministers in Barcelona (27–28 November 1995) culminated from the increasingly intensive bilateral trade and development co-operation between the EU and its Mediterranean partners. Some officials argue that the EMP is:

> the child of the early Middle East Peace Process of 1993/4 ... Barcelona would otherwise not have been possible in 1995. The peace process created a conceptual setting ... remember, this happened after the fall of the Soviet Union, the break up of the Eastern Bloc ... we thought, let's replicate the Helsinki approach ... our success there can be copied ...[39]

The final Barcelona Declaration is undoubtedly an ambitious document which will remain in the history books as the first attempt to create a strong bond between EU member states and their partners in the Mediterranean. The Barcelona Process or the EMP led to the creation of a new 'partnership' phase of the EU–Mediterranean relationship – to include bilateral, multilateral and regional co-operation.

EMP membership

The Euro–Mediterranean process brought together the then 15 EU countries plus 12 neighbouring states/entities in the Mediterranean (Algeria, Cyprus, Egypt, Israel, Jordan, Lebanon, Malta, Morocco, Syria, Tunisia, Turkey, the Palestinian Authority), so far excluding the Balkan countries and Libya.[40] (Other 'special guests' include the Arab League, the Arab Maghreb Union or UMA and Mauritania.) Libya could be included as a full partner in the EMP since the UN sanctions on Libya have been permanently lifted. (On 12 September 2003 the UN Security Council voted to lift sanctions against Libya.)[41] The end of sanctions has been quite symbolic and a signal of Libya's 'rehabilitation'. Moreover, in December 2003, Col. Gaddafi unexpectedly renounced all efforts to build weapons of mass destruction and claimed he was opening Libya's arms production facilities to inspection.[42] The structure of the EMP's membership seems to have been destined to arrive at this composition. In light of the 2004 EU enlargement (including Malta and Cyprus), and following this round the possible inclusion of Turkey too, many analysts argue that the EMP was anyway originally inaugurated as a forum for the EU and those countries in the Mediterranean that are actually ruled out of the possibility for EU membership (Neugart and Schumacher, 2004).

Formation of the EMP policy

The Barcelona Process or EMP includes three main 'baskets' for developing the main elements of a political and security partnership, an economic and financial partnership, and a partnership in social, cultural and human affairs. The Barcelona Declaration adopted at the Barcelona Conference on 27–28 November 1995, clearly states the key objectives of the EMP, and covers three main areas:

- *Political and security area*: The Mediterranean countries committed themselves to setting up a regular political dialogue in order to promote a common Euro-Mediterranean area of peace, stability and security. The dialogue was to be based on the respect of certain fundamental principles such as respect for human rights and democracy, non-interference in internal affairs, the use of peaceful means for the settlement of disputes, and the adoption of confidence-building measures. It would further seek to achieve specific objectives such as fighting organised crime, drug trafficking and terrorism (political and security partnership).

- *Economic and financial area*: The Partnership would promote sustainable and balanced economic and social development with the view to building an area of shared prosperity. In addition, co-operation and consultations would be undertaken in various fields such as investment, environmental protection, water conservation, energy, rural development and infrastructure. The EU would also supply financial aid to assist the implementation of the above objectives. The aim is to create an area of shared prosperity through the progressive establishment of a free-trade zone between the EU and its Partners (EMFTZ) by the year 2010[43] – the best known aspect of the Declaration – and among the Mediterranean Partners themselves, accompanied by substantial EU financial support for economic transition in the Partners and for the social and economic consequences of this reform process (economic and financial partnership). Obviously, the EU alone lacks the resources to underwrite all these objectives. (In fact, UN, World Bank and IMF resources also fund Mediterranean projects alongside EU funds). The main financial instrument for the EMP is the MEDA programme. From 1995 until 2001, MEDA committed over €5,071 million in joint, co-operation programmes (for example the North Africa–Europe gas pipeline), projects aiming at improving essential social services in Mediterranean partner countries (such as education and health) and other supporting activities (aimed at job creation, public services improvements – including water supplies, rural–urban gap reductions, environmental protection). The participation of Israel in the MEDA programme is restricted to regional co-operation activities since Israel is not eligible for EU-funded bilateral co-operation programmes as a result of its high GNP level per inhabitant.[44] Another important source of funding is the European Investment Bank that, since 1995, has lent €7,424 million for developing activities in the Euro–Mediterranean Partner countries.[45] The MEDA funded EuroMed Market Regional Programme aims to help the Med Partners prepare themselves for the future Euro-Mediterranean Free Trade Area. Clearly, the leverage of the EU is where the money is![46]

- *Social, cultural and human areas*: The EMP is founded on a recognition of diverse cultural traditions and appreciation of mutual roots. The general aim of the EMP's third basket is to develop human resources, increase knowledge of and promote understanding between cultures, and encourage rapprochement of the peoples in the Euro-Mediterranean area through exchanges and development of free and flourishing civil societies. These goals are addressed through a variety of regional activities aimed at improving educational and training systems, controlling demographic growth, reducing migratory pressures and fighting racism, xenophobia and intolerance (social, cultural and human partnership). Specific areas addressed include those on cultural heritage, audio-visual, youth, media and women. The Barcelona Work Programme includes two specific action headings which call for meetings in the cultural field to make specific proposals for action and in the religious field to address intolerance and another calling for closer media interaction.[47]

Practical implementation of the EMP

The EMP was introduced to complement and not replace existing or forth-coming bilateral agreements (including those signed under the New Neighbourhood Policy) linking the EU to individual Mediterranean countries. As an intergovernmental, albeit one-sided power, structure (at the EuroMed regional level), the Barcelona Process consists of periodic meetings of the Ministers for Foreign Affairs and meetings of the Euro-Mediterranean Committee for the Barcelona Process.

Barcelona was the first Euromed Foreign Ministers Conference held on 28 November 1995. This was followed by the second Malta conference (held on 16 April 1997) and the Palermo EuroMed ad hoc Ministerial Meeting of 3–4 June 1998. The latter was conceived as an additional, informal, ad hoc event, outside the normal cycle of the Ministerial conferences in order to review the progress achieved in the EMP since its launch three years earlier and to help prepare the ground for the next Ministerial Conference in Stuttgart. This third conference was held on 15–16 April 1999 and was followed by a think-tank type meeting in Lisbon in May 2000 which again served as a preparatory meeting for the fourth Euromed Foreign Ministers Conference in Marseilles (15–16 November 2000). Another conference was held in Brussels on 5–6 November 2001 while the fifth Euromed Foreign Ministers Conference took place in Valencia on 22–23 April 2002. A Euro-Mediterranean Mid-Term Meeting of Ministers of Foreign Affairs in Crete followed on 26–27 May 2003. The sixth Euro-Mediterranean Foreign Ministers' Meeting was held in Naples in December 2003. During the latter, Ireland proposed to host a mid-term Ministerial meeting during the first half of 2004 which was held on 5–6 May in Dublin while the Netherlands will host the next meeting of Ministers of Foreign Affairs in the Hague on 29–30 November 2004. The seventh Euro-Mediterranean Conference of the Ministers of Foreign Affairs will take place in the first half of 2005 under the Presidency of Luxembourg.

The Euro-Mediterranean Committee for the Barcelona Process consists of high officials of the EU-Troika (past, present and future Presidency) and one representative of each Mediterranean partner, and meets every three months to prepare meetings of the Ministers for Foreign Affairs and to evaluate the follow-up to the Barcelona Process. The European Commission prepares and manages the monitoring of all the partnership work. Activities are split into regional events (ministerial meetings and other meetings) and bilateral activities (association councils and other meetings). In this framework, every six months, on average, two Ministerial meetings (for example, a mid-term meeting of EuroMed Foreign Affairs ministers) and five meetings at expert level (for example, a senior officials meeting/a Euromed Committee meeting) take place. There is also preparatory work and follow-up of meetings, undertaken by the EU Commission departments, ad hoc thematic meetings (for example, a seminar of Government experts on economic transition, meeting for EuroMed Youth platform) and conferences involving government officials and civil society members (EuroMed audiovisual annual conference). Other meetings include parliamentarian and civil society fora, as well as networks such as economic institutes (including the network of foreign policy institutes – EuroMeSCo – and the Euro-Mediterranean Forum of Economic Institutes – FEMISE – seminars), industrial federations and the media. A Euro-Mediterranean Parliamentary Forum was set up in October 1998 and meets in plenary session four times and several times in the shape of working parties and includes MPs representing the parliaments of the Med partner countries of the Barcelona Process, the national parliaments of the Member States of the EU and the EP. In its resolution of 11 April 2002, the EP proposed that a EuroMed Parliamentary Assembly be established to institutionalise and strengthen the parliamentary dimension of the Barcelona Process. A working party on the conversion of the Forum into a EuroMed Parliamentary Assembly was set up for this purpose. The terms of the Assembly are based on a guarantee of North–South parity in terms of membership, etc.[48] The Assembly will hold responsibility for the monitoring of the application of the Euro–Mediterranean Association Agreements (see below).

The Euro–Mediterranean Partnership facilitates the better understanding between cultures and religions as well as offering an opportunity to bridge the socio-economic gap that exists between the shores of the Mediterranean Sea.[49] It is, however, clearly more oriented towards the economic component of the partnership, undermining its other components. Particularly because of the failure of an agreement on a Security Charter (in the early years of Barcelona), a series of activities to reinforce *all* areas of the Partnership are now in place. Association Agreements remain at the core of the Partnership.

The completion of the grid of Euro-Mediterranean Association Agreements awaits the conclusion of negotiations with Syria. These agreements bring economic benefits/preferential trade terms and 'political dialogue' with the aim of political reform and progress on human rights and other issues. Hence, although the Euro-Mediterranean Association Agreements are free-trade agreements, they function as instruments of conditionality since they have a wider scope and differ from one Partner to another. Some common features include political provisions (respect for human rights and democratic principles with a proviso that each Agreement can be suspended in the event of major human rights violations), free trade (in accordance with WTO rules with trade in agricultural products to be liberalised 'gradually' while trade in services is covered by the General Agreement on Tariffs in Services), other economic provisions (including high level of protection of intellectual property rights and provisions on the liberalisation of capital movements), financial co-operation (with the exception of Cyprus, Malta and Israel which agreements provide EU financial assistance for the Partners but no amounts are specified), social and cultural co-operation (provisions on workers' rights and re-admission of nationals and non-nationals illegally arriving on the territory of one party from the other, reflecting EU concerns on illegal migration) and institutional and final provisions (this explains the long delay between signature of an agreement and entry into force. The Agreements are of unlimited duration and may be denounced: after signature, an agreement has to be ratified by the EP, by each EU member state and the Med partner before it enters into force, see Table 3.6).[50]

Achievements of the EMP 1995–2004

'Political dialogue' is often accepted as one of the main instruments and features of the EU-15's achievements in their co-operation with third countries. The term dialogue, however, has not been used consistently in the past. In order to ratify this, the term is today used by the EU only in those situations where three conditions are met:

a)   a formal decision of the ministers has been made to engage in a 'dialogue';
b)   a formal agreement with third countries has been arranged (as with Association Agreements with Mediterranean countries);
c)   the agreement provides for regular, political contact (apart from normal diplomatic relations) at one or several levels. 'Dialogues' have thus become a specific form of contact with the Mediterranean partners.[51]

With the signing of the EU-Lebanon Association Agreement, eight of the nine non-candidate members of the EMP are now linked to the Union by an Association Agreement, highlighting the positive achievement of the objectives set out in the 1995 Barcelona Conference.

Table 3.6 Table of Association Agreements

Country	AA *negotiations*	Notes	AA *signed*	AA *in force*
Algeria	Exploratory talks finished in 1995; formal opening of negotiations February 1997; initialled/concluded on 19 December 2001	Algeria enjoys duty and quota free access to EU markets for its industrial exports	Signed on 22 April 2002	Not yet (ratification pending). Until then political dialogue takes place on an *ad hoc* basis through twice-yearly meetings at ministerial level
Cyprus	AA provides for customs union with EU	Negotiated entry to the EU. Negotiations formally opened March 1998 and concluded December 2002. EU member since 1 May 2004		
Egypt	Formal opening of negotiations May 1994; discussions began in 1995, negotiations ended on 11 June 1999		AA signed on 25 June 2001. AA ratified by Egyptian People's Assembly and parliaments of EU-15. EP ratified AA in November 2001. Interim Agreement is applicable pending the completion of ratification of the AA by EU member states*	Trade and trade-related provisions of the EU-Egypt AA have been in force since 1 January 2004 by virtue of an 'Interim Agreement' between the two sides which was approved by the EU Council of Ministers on 19 December 2003. Ratification process is well underway and may be completed by end 2004

Israel	AA negotiations ended in September 1995	1st economic dialogue under the AA on 5 December 2000	Signed on 20 November 1995. The territories occupied by Israel are not covered by the territorial scope of the EC–Israel AA (EU's position)	Yes. AA in force since 1 June 2000. AA basis for EU–Israel trade relations and political dialogue
Jordan	AA negotiations end 16 April 1997		Signed on 24 November 1997	Yes. Entry into force on 1 May 2002 (replaces the 1977 co-op agreement)
Lebanon	Negotiations concluded December 2001; initialled 10 January 2002	Interim Agreement signed on 17 June 2002 on immediate effect of economic and trade related provisions of AA and entered into force on 1 March 2003	Signed 17 June 2002. EP voted in favour of AA on 15 January 2003	Ratification of AA pending
Malta	AA provides for customs union with EU. Candidate member state of the EU. Negotiations suspended 1996, resumed 1998 and concluded December 2002	Negotiated entry to the EU. EU member since 1 May 2004		
Morocco	AA negotiations ended in November 1995	1st economic dialogue under this agreement took place on 6 December 2000	Signed on 26 February 1996	Yes. AA in force since 1 March 2000
Palestinian Authority	Interim AA: end negotiations in December 1996		Signed on 24 February 1997 with PLO	On an interim basis: came into effect on 1 July 1997

continued…

Table 3.6 Table of Association Agreements, continued

Country	AA negotiations	Notes	AA signed	AA in force
Syria**	Formal opening of negotiations May 1998			End of negotiations formally marked on 19 October 2004
Tunisia	Negotiations ended in June 1995		Signed on 17 July 1995	Yes. AA in force since 1 March 1998
Turkey	AA of 1963 includes a membership pledge and provides for customs union with EU (customs union entered into force on 31 December 1995. Customs union agreement of 1996)	Candidate for membership, recognition of its status in December 1999. Awaiting EU green light to start negotiations: decision to be taken in December 2004. Commission regular report of 6 October 2004 gives amber light		

Notes

* *EuroMed Synopsis* 8 January 2004. Issue No 254, 1.
** For updates on EU–Syria talks see http://europa.eu.int/comm/external_relations/syria/intro/index.htm.

Further achievements of the EMP

Since the establishment of the EMP in Barcelona, the Summits have been accompanied by Civil Forums in various forms. The events have in the course of time developed from an almost complementary, or subaltern role in relation to the official summits focused on the third chapter of the Barcelona Declaration towards a new arena for dialogue and political approaches with a stronger attention to the first chapter, thus creating a linkage between the first and third baskets. The recurrent themes of the fora include social and workers' rights, cultural dialogue and exchange as well as the main challenges Mediterranean countries are faced with (detailed in the first section of this chapter). Depending on the participating organisations and preparation committee, these topics have been subject to varied interpretations. Observers argue that at least the fora create possibilities and an environment for the exchange of views while critiques complain that these meetings provide a meeting place for a group of friends and nothing concrete in terms of policy substance ever emerges from such gatherings.

Within the second basket, MEDA payments reached a record of nearly €500 million in 2003 (€497.7 million) paid out, up from €454 million in 2002 and €317.8 million in 2001. The disbursement rate, or payment/commitment ratio, reached 82.9 per cent against 74.2 per cent in 2002 and 53 per cent in 2001. The Programme implementation phase seems well into an accelerating phase with the bulk of MEDA funds (€385.8 million) going to bilateral co-operation with Algeria, Egypt, Jordan, Lebanon, Morocco, Syria, Tunisia, West Bank and Gaza Strip and the remainder mainly used for regional programmes and projects involving all 12 Mediterranean partners.[52]

In the field of statistics, relations between the 27 partners have been boosted through the MEDSTAT regional programme for statistical co-operation. Through MEDA funds, the programme is technically supervised by EUROSTAT as a support mechanism for the statistical institutes in the 12 Mediterranean partner countries for the provision of their statistical information systems.[53] The logic that has driven this initiative may be found in the belief that statistics are important in particular with regards to EU policy-making in the Mediterranean area. As Gilles Rambaud-Chanoz, Head of Division with the Eurostat DG claims:

> Statistics have to be fitted into programming ... statistics are crucial to how correctly situations are understood, as well as to how programmes are defined, and how well their achievements and their impact are measured.[54]

The use of direct conditionality has, in the eyes of Europhiles, brought about some specific achievements for the EMP. In fact, the EU's efforts in support of reform in the Mediterranean partner countries have already produced a number of positive results such as some improvements in the public finance management system of the Palestinian Authority. During 2003, the EU also provided extensive support towards the organisation and holding of free and fair Palestinian elections.

Another achievement for the Barcelona initiative relates to the functioning of the offices of the Delegation of the European Commission in Mediterranean partner countries, most of which serve as extremely useful information sources which constantly feed back to Brussels the situation on the ground in the respective Mediterranean countries.

The Barcelona Process has come a long way from 1995 to 2005, having its ten-year anniversary in November 2005, and its achievements cannot be underestimated. The areas where success can be registered are connected to those areas where the EU has leverage, where its institutions have competence to act and where there is expertise reflecting lessons learnt from the past. It is to the EU's credit that it has put its weight where it deemed feasible and effective. There should be no surprise then that since the EU is still addressing its Common Foreign and Security Policy, the first basket has been limited in its achievements, although the EMP still remains the only environment where Israeli and Arab partners sit together around the same table, despite the tragic ongoing events in the Middle East conflict. It is also the only environment where the Israeli government accepts the EU's involvement in matters relating to security of the Middle East.[55] As an economic giant (albeit a political dwarf), the EU's success in the second basket of the EMP signals what the EU is best in, namely, classical development assistance programmes. Developments here have been important, not least the signing of almost all association agreements (except for Syria's), but more has to be achieved in terms of the situation on the ground. Given the patronage system in most Mediterranean countries some dilemmas remain as to the effects of opening up their economies to international trade, for instance will security and family be sacrificed for competition? Moreover, the image of most Mediterranean partner countries has been severely and negatively affected following the declaration of the war against terrorism and the wars in Afghanistan and Iraq. Much needs to be done in terms of rebuilding investors' confidence. Added to these external factors, internal matters relating to corrupt systems and bureaucratic administrations are things which need time to change in Mediterranean countries. Hence, FDI, economic growth and people's quality of life have yet to improve.[56] Many programmes have been set up under the third basket but, so far, the most successful has been the Euro-Mediterranean Youth Action Programme which was adopted at the end of 1998.[57] Other programmes related to culture, audiovisual and educational areas are criticised for being elite-oriented. Thus, challenges remain for such an ambitious project, and this is the subject of the next section of this chapter.

Main challenges of EMP project implementation

After the end of the Cold War, the EU, through the EMP, attempted to address new security threats by promoting democratisation and liberalisation. Such a strategy, assuming that democratisation and the liberal agenda serves the EU's strategic interests and enhances stability in the Mediterranean, has gone by largely unquestioned.

Moreover, although the EU has been increasingly constructive in its relations with Mediterranean partners, there remains a gap between its construction of a EurMed proximity policy and the EU's potential as a key, unified actor in the Mediterranean area.[58] The discrepancy arises from a number of facts: diverse interests among EU member states in the Mediterranean which prevent the EU from acting as one unitary actor; the high disparities in economic levels between Mediterranean partner countries resulting in asymmetric relations operating between them and with their EU partners (as the first section of this chapter showed), particularly in the field of agriculture and political instability arising from long-standing conflicts in much of the area paralyses the process of regional co-operation. Some officials argue that with a possible resolution to the Cyprus issue before 1 May 2004, the USA's recent re-engagement in the Israeli–Palestinian conflict and the Turkish–Greek *rapprochment* there is hope for 2004 in the Euro-Mediterranean area.[59] However, scepticism of the long-term future of the EMP remains.[60] The EU has carefully attempted to address economic discrepancies, political challenges and social realities in the Mediterranean realising their potential consequences for the Euro-Mediterranean region as a whole. In particular, during the Valencia conference, an *Action Plan* for implementation[61] was agreed by all participants and includes short- and medium-term initiatives aimed at reinforcing the three chapters of the Barcelona Process.

Under the Political and Security Chapter: In light of the events of 9/11, the global war against terrorism, the developments in the Middle East and the challenges of the EU's enlargement, the Action Plan adopted guidelines on political dialogue and co-operation in the fight against terrorism and in preparation for other structural changes in the international scene. This was the moment when the EU-15 noted the importance of joint-ownership of the EMP with Mediterranean partners thus ensuring a mutual commitment to the objectives set for this process. The depth of the EMP was marked as the way forward for all partners to work towards. The documents prepared ahead of and the drafts presented in Valencia were organised following extensive consultations with all partners including visits by the Presidency, jointly with the Commission and the Council General Secretariat to Mediterranean capitals. At the rhetorical level, the Action plan emphasised dialogue on international terrorism and human rights issues and drew up the main efforts required for Partnership Building measures. Ministers also recommended the creation of a EuroMed Parliamentary Assembly.[62]

Under the Economic and Financial Chapter: In terms of South–South trade and integration, the initialling of the Agadir Agreements providing for free trade between Morocco, Tunisia, Jordan and Egypt by 2006 has been welcomed as an important step in the development of sub-regional integration.

Ministers reiterated their strong support for similar sub-regional initiatives while the Presidency noted the strong support Mediterranean partners voiced for the setting up of a Euro-Mediterranean Bank.

Under the Social, Cultural and Human Partnership Chapter: at Valencia, the principle of creating a *Euro-Mediterranean Foundation* to promote a dialogue of cultures and civilisations was agreed. At the Naples EuroMed Foreign Ministers' meeting, partners did not come to an agreement as to where the exact location of this foundation will be but it seems likely that the final choice will fall on one European partner and one Mediterranean partner, most likely Rome and Alexandria.[63] The funding for the Euro-Mediterranean Foundation was another main subject for discussion during the recent Euro-Mediterranean Committee for the Barcelona Process held on 22 January 2004 in Brussels. With debates on each member state's share into the EU budget following its next enlargement in May 2004 being 'hot' issues, the topic of the Foundation's funding is no easy matter. In fact, the future of this initiative does not look too bright. Following interviews carried out in Brussels during January 2004, it transpired that issues relating to religions, principles of tribal law and Mediterranean cultures are still uncomfortable issues for many and, according to one interviewee, not the Europeans' 'cup of tea'. This, according to an interviewee, may go to highlight why the third basket of the EMP is the one lagging behind since Europeans cannot and many times fear approaching such issues hands on. In official circles one often hears mention of the importance of such matters but in practice these issues are sidelined for the more approachable economic, 'hands-on stuff'.

The Barcelona Process has so far survived, fostered contacts at various levels in the Euro-Mediterranean area, enhanced European knowledge of the Mediterranean partner countries which improved understanding of mutual expectations, transparency, and of the international environment. Barcelona has also created the momentum and incentives for partners to abide by agreements, taking responsibility, gaining credibility in the process and positioning each partner in a better negotiating place. Trust-building and patience remains key to the future outlook of this game.

> We are now in 2004 ... it's been nine years since Barcelona ... where were we after Helsinki in 1983 ... the height of the Soviet Union ... Afghanisatan ... after five years all this was over ... we basically need patience.[64]

Wider Europe and the future of the EMP

Without doubt the enlargement of the EU in May 2004 imposes challenges of momentous importance to the geo-strategic configuration of Europe, which one may compare to the end of the Cold War. These changes will not only affect existing EU member states and accession countries, but also countries located on the borders of the new Europe. As a result of this strategic realignment, patterns of economic exchange, trade and independence between 'insiders' and 'outsiders' will be transformed and new, different opportunities are arising for the EU to govern existing relations. The EU has been proactive to define this new 'bargaining space' through its recent policy originally called Wider Europe but now being referred to as the New Neighbourhood Policy, an original idea of Britain's Foreign Secretary Jack Straw.[65] The idea here is to construct the EU's relations with its so called 'ring of friends' and to carve out a new structure within which common norms and regimes will be negotiated. The EU's outsiders include not only the countries of Eastern Europe and the former Soviet Union, but also Mediterranean countries with which the EU contemplates close relations. One interviewee confessed that the EU still treats Mediterranean 'friends' as different, almost as a burden – unlike its other ring of friends from the former East:

> ... the Council decided to involve and integrate the Mediterranean partners to avoid tensions arising with too much focus on the Eastern enlargement and former Eastern European partners ... the Mediterranean was included in the New Neighbourhood Initiative despite stiff resistance from the Commission ...

The European Community's new 'neighbourhood' policy intends to promote intra-regional, sub-regional and cross-border co-operation. But how serious is the EU in this new endeavour? The logic of the EU's meddling with the Mediterranean and other countries and regions in close proximity to its borders, seems to reflect upon its identity – in particular in the context of the May 2004 enlargement. It could also underline the acceptance from the EU's side that the Mediterranean is made up of a number of sub-units which challenge – even refute – any unifying ideas and therefore any holistic policy approach. The EU seems to be carving out how far Europe goes (although one interviewee told me 'we are not creating new borders') and where it stops ('with enlargement the EU will have borders with Syria and other countries in the Middle East, and we therefore have to encourage good relations with partners from the Mediterranean'). How this new initiative will differ from the EMP for Mediterranean partners remains to be seen. Will it serve as an extension of the bilateral arrangements falling under the EMP and as a possible new space for more forceful conditionality from the EU's side, another effective tool for the second basket?

Furthermore, with enlargement, the EU faces ever increasing regional as well as global responsibilities which add to the value of 'dialogue' with third countries as a crucial instrument. For Mediterranean partners, from their part, dialogue with the Union signals a precious instrument for increasing international diplomatic prestige (Turkey) or paving the way for a general political rehabilitation. An example of the latter has been the recent resumption of the discussion on dialogue with Libya, which sent strong signals on the international stage.[66] The form in which such dialogues take place with Mediterranean partners requires careful structuring in order to ensure the maximum benefit from the EU's most successful element so far: its flexibility. As one interviewee expressed, it has been through such regular contacts that the EU members have learnt a lot about what is happening in the Mediterranean. Such dialogues also impact on the intense EU dialogue with the USA (a country of immense economic and military strength which the EU cannot ignore) where, for example, following the recent war in Iraq, EU officials stress that if the USA addresses the Middle East conflict, it could also solve the current crisis in post-war Iraq.[67] The Mediterranean partners seem to prefer more dialogues at fewer levels and with less frequent meetings.[68] In view of the ever increasing load in terms of organisation and time, this is a welcoming suggestion for EU actors.

Some analysts argue that through its principles of differentiation and positive conditionality, this recent framework is expected to strengthen the institutional and financial conditions of the Barcelona Process.[69] Whether the most recent EU initiative, still confusingly referred to as Wider Europe, European Neighbourhood Policy or Wider Europe New Neighbourhood Initiative (interchangeably!)[70] emerges as yet another prominent albeit weak discursive strategy to include the Mediterranean partners remains to be seen once the programme is put into action through the National Action Plans.

This brings us to the next chapter that analyses the EU's discursive framework.

4   EU foreign policy as a discursive practice of the Mediterranean

In the aftermath of 9/11, the reiteration and insistence on linking the Mediterranean/Arab World to terrorism continues to contribute to the negative image of the South. Some analysts have suggested that this re-emphasis is the expression of an interpretation of security in 'Westcentric'/ 'Eurocentric' terms, particularly evident in the media. The creation of an area of peace and stability in the Mediterranean area is thus seen as desirable for European security and related issues such as 'illegal' immigration, drug trafficking, Islamic radicalism and international terrorism, perceived as affecting European security. These are the issues highlighted in EU documentation and by the European press,[1] that link (in)security to Southern countries. Such readings, have encouraged this author to analyse such positions in-them-selves. In this chapter, I present some select results of my analysis of EU documentation and try to shed some light on the relations between the Mediterranean as a field of knowledge the EU partakes in the constitution of, and wider discursive practices of EU foreign policy. I do this by offering a discursive constructivist analysis of the field of the Mediterranean in the development/process of official articulations by EU actors and in the context of EU structures and institutions. This analysis leads me to suggest a complex pattern of continuity in EU practices on the Mediterranean field. The key thing about the Mediterranean case is the *regularity* of the markers used across EU discourses rather than the variation.

The discursive contructivist strategy adopted here draws on Michel Foucault's *Archaeology of Knowledge* where he adopts an analytical approach of linguistic utterances based on a 'line of attack' ('archaeology') of such utterances emanating from organisations in the domain of knowledge.[2] The way the EU employs, for instance, the terms 'Mediterranean' and 'South' has to be related to the organisation of the knowledges articulated by the EU. Thus, when I refer to the Mediterranean as a field of knowledge, I refer to the system of the production and formation of utterances about the Mediterranean. The Mediterranean *is* and *becomes* knowledge in the constitution of utterances about this area. It is therefore important to follow a number of statements and the regularities in the process of 'formation' of the Mediterranean in EU practices. The regularities refer to the systematic character of the formation of this area. The field of the Mediterranean covers both how the Mediterranean should be and how the Mediterranean is. What is important to observe is how these utterances about the Mediterranean are given and the way in which they are given. The regularity of statements on the Mediterranean as generalisations trace a pattern of utterances uttered over time. The analysis of regularity covered by material from 1995 up to the present concerns the working of EU statements on the Mediterranean and how these have been played out.

In mapping out the regularity of markers used across EU discourses, discursive constructivism sheds light on the complex body of judgements of fact and judgements of value inherent in EU doctrines on the Mediterranean. These markers are then played out in terms of a system of concepts and of general propositions on this area which can be critically examined and which construct the Mediterranean discursively in the EU's Mediterranean policy.[3]

This chapter has four parts. The first examines some EU member states' Mediterranean policies as ideas that have moved onto the agenda and into EU policy on the Mediterranean. The nature of the 'foreign' (Mediterranean) policy process in France, Spain and Italy is an important consideration in itself but more so in how the idea of the Mediterranean in these member states' policies found its way into various EU Mediterranean initiatives, in particular the EMP. The cases of France, Spain and Italy have been selected for analytical purposes. The following section will summarise the regular markers in and across the three member states' discursive practices on the Mediterranean and prepare the groundwork for the next section. This explicates the themes used and references made to the Mediterranean in EMP documentation and traces out a regular pattern across these discourses. By way of further analysis a summary table is presented highlighting this regularity in the 'Med' markers used across EU discourses. In concluding, this chapter argues that the EU's Mediterranean area is just one among many possible readings of the EU's system of governing 'regions' and 'neighbouring areas'.[4]

How EU member states' policies affect EU Mediterranean policy

This section seeks to address some of the discursive practices that brought about the EMP, as a relatively recent EU policy on the Mediterranean.[5] Since the EU is not a unified subject,[6] it is important to look at how some member states, more than others, have been informative of the EU debate on the Mediterranean. For this purpose, it is deemed important to look at the manner in which some of the major EU member states think and act *vis-à-vis* the Mediterranean.

Some of the members of the EU that are not 'Mediterranean' have minimal interest in the area – with some exceptions, like the Germans and the Swedes – and this interest only arises when it is deemed to affect them directly or indirectly, for example in the case of a perceived threat of immigration flows from the 'South'.[7] Although it is not geographically located in the Mediterranean area, Portugal has shown interest in Mediterranean affairs, particularly since the country's integration into the EU.[8] Greece, although deemed a Mediterranean state, maintains little contact with its southern neighbours (in fact the regional concept which looms or hovers over the minds of its elites is that of the Balkans or south-eastern Europe – more on this in Chapter 5).[9] Greece's EU membership has activated its relationship with the Middle East (eastern Mediterranean). Greece has been reactive in many foreign policy areas – letting other actors determine EU policy on the Mediterranean. It has had relations with Algeria and Libya (oil and gas (Greek) imports from these countries) and also with Egypt, Syria and the Palestinian Territories. Its EU membership also upgraded its relations with Israel. Furthermore, Greece's EU membership has been central in developing its policy in areas other than the Balkans even if it is more proactive in the Balkans – although there is a parochial view of Greece's Balkan foreign policy.[10] Greece becomes active in the Mediterranean when issues arise on Cyprus or Turkey.[11]

Northern EU partners have not been involved to a great extent in the Mediterranean[12] (although even Scandinavian countries have become more interested as a result of events in the Mediterranean, the EMP, the MEPP, etc.). Italy has a historical connection with Libya. Spain has historical and commercial links with the area and a fear of immigrants from the 'South'. France has a colonial history that ties it to the area. It is therefore important to see which members were involved in the development of the construction of the Mediterranean in EU policy. This issue is examined in the following section.

For analytical purposes, the cases of France, Spain and Italy have been selected and will be analysed below: the Mediterranean has been an area of traditional influence for France:[13] for Spain the Mediterranean has long been viewed as an area where it can have an important and active role as an international actor. In fact, Spain often emerges as one of the most important actors in the evolution of Euro–Mediterranean relations.[14] Italy's discourse on the Mediterranean is primarily an economic one.[15] (On the other hand, Germany is traditionally acknowledged as having the leading role in issues pertaining to Eastern Europe.)[16] What is important here is to see how each of these southern European EU member states attempts to ally its domestic interests (regarding the Mediterranean) with those of the EU through influencing the EU's Mediterranean policy. By so doing, this analysis will map out the various discourses that are uncovered here through this inquiry, which will in turn illustrate the thematics, regularities, objects and speaking 'subjects' across these discourses.

France

French policy towards 'the Mediterranean' during the Gaullist period was known as *la politique arabe de la France* (France's Arab policy) whilst in

1995 it became *la politique méditerranéenne de la France* (France's Mediterranean policy) and involved four key elements:

- a shared concern with Italy, Spain and to some extent Greece, to balance the EU's Central European focus by paying more attention to the Mediterranean area;[17]
- French realisation that it had more clout in the region as a leading member of the EU[18] (power interests);
- recognition that following the first Gulf War, the Arab world had become more complex;
- French appreciation that its European influence in the Mediterranean was possible through its role in the Maghreb.[19]

Moreover, France's presidency of the EU during January until June 1995 pushed for a coherent EU policy towards the Mediterranean (thus reflecting its own interests). France also faced American pressure for dialogue with the countries in the area. During 8–9 April 1995 France hosted the second meeting of the Mediterranean Forum. The forum was important for a clarification to all the parties concerned of the 'three baskets', which were to form part of the Barcelona Conference and highlighted the French role in defining a coherent EU Mediterranean policy. French discourses about the Mediterranean area shifted from discourses of 'non-intervention' (security, state-centred discourse, especially in the case of Algeria) and 'economic *aid*' (to the area) to an emphasis on the 'need for cultural dialogue, negotiation (partnership) and elections (democracy) (which later entered EU discourses on the Med)'.[20] This change most probably came about not directly as a consequence of shifts in France but more due to the result of internal developments in countries like Algeria that included the election of President Zeroual. Moreover, during the Cannes summit in June, President Chirac attempted to transfer the Algerian 'problem' to a European forum, recognising that France was limited in its efforts to influence events there (not enough military power, hard security language/concerns).[21] Moreover, he shifted French foreign policy priorities to Morocco as France's privileged partner (economically) in the southern Mediterranean. President Chirac's intentions through this policy decision included the aim of emphasising the role of France as the main European partner of Morocco (also a term which entered EU discourse). He also made some diplomatic visits to Tunisia, thus attempting to widen French influence in the Maghreb. In this manner, France aimed at shifting European Mediterranean policy towards the Maghreb (a preoccupation which it shares with Spain) – an area where it dominated not least economically (France being the main EU partner in trade relations with the Maghreb).[22]

Thus, French practices seeped through to the EU level. France managed to refocus EU policy towards the Mediterranean – a diplomatic success which France shared with Spain by this time and which was reflected in the EU Council meetings in Corfu (March 1994), Essen (December 1994) and Cannes

(June 1995). During the Barcelona Conference, France managed to help in creating a single all-encompassing forum for relations between all the members of the EU and the countries of the Mediterranean (which were selected for this process). France thus established the importance of the Mediterranean being regarded as one indivisible entity.[23] On the other hand, it managed to bring the Mediterranean countries closer to the EU institutions and arena.[24] Of course French interests lay at the heart of all these initiatives – mainly the diffusion of the Algerian 'problem' by subsuming it under a regional security framework. This was the main reason why France pushed for an EU security partnership with the Mediterranean countries (which would also enhance the French role in the EU's CFSP and mark its position within the EU in terms of power relations). France tried to deny the USA access to the Barcelona Conference, but Spain insisted on the USA being allowed observer status.[25] These discursive practices and action reflect French ambitions to retain power in the Mediterranean area (albeit in the EU context. This cannot be compared with US power in the area but the French are keen to establish themselves as a key power within the EU and *vis-à-vis* the US on the world stage).[26]

Spain

Spain's relatively long period of domestic political stability under the Socialist Party (pre-Aznar), its national economic prosperity, its representatives' pro-active Mediterranean policy and the domestic unity behind its government's European policy brought about its crucial role in the EU's reformulation of its Mediterranean policy. Spain has been involved with the Mediterranean through its concerns with Morocco and Algeria and its membership of the EU has also brought about a new Spanish interest in the eastern Mediterranean.

Since the early 1980s, Spain's Mediterranean policy has been subject to a refocus of its foreign policy as well as its domestic policy.[27] The need for a North African policy encouraged its policy to include a multilateral dimension.[28] Moreover, after Franco's era, Spain emerged from its international isolation and became more involved in the European arena (to mark its post-dictatorship, modernisation process). The agenda setting of the EU's Mediterranean policy can be attributed in large part to Spanish efforts to commit EU members to collective action in the Mediterranean area. Its national background and commitment justify its influence in EU decision making in the area.

It is important to examine Spain's influence on EU discursive practices of the 'problems' emanating from its Mediterranean flank. Spanish concerns about Mediterranean security issues date back to the long Muslim presence on the Iberian peninsula prior to 1492. These collective memories conjure up images of Spain having been historically attacked from the South. This discursive practice has now extended to include fears of immigrants and Islamist radicals (mainly the former: the latter have not been very active in

Spain over the last decade, when for example compared to France: discourses which entered the EU discourse and became frequent markers across time and across discourses).[29] In the nineteenth and early twentieth centuries, Spain acquired territories in North Africa that it had to relinquish to Morocco from the 1950s.[30] Spain's territorial presence in the Maghreb is now restricted to Ceuta and Melilla (still subject to Moroccan claims).[31] Under pressure from Morocco, Spain had to withdraw from its Western Sahara colony in late 1975 through a tripartite agreement with Morocco and Mauritania. Just after the 1982 election and following Spain's entry into the EC, a more comprehensive Mediterranean policy was developed and based on Spain's national interests at that time, the international context during that period and its historical legacy in the area. Spain's policy, however, still remained mostly targeted on the western part of the Mediterranean area. It was not until the presentation in 1990 of the Hispano-Italian proposal for a CSCM, that Spain's discourse on the Mediterranean experienced the adoption of a wider perspective.[32] During 1991, Spain was the selected venue for the Madrid Peace Conference[33] that served as a thematic in Spanish discursive practices and efforts to bring the Mediterranean on to the EU (as well as NATO's) agenda. During the early 1990s, Spain felt in an advantaged position, *vis-à-vis* the other southern EU member states, to strengthen its influence in the Mediterranean. This was due to its domestic stability – having had the same political party in office since 1982. In contrast, Italy experienced acute political instability at this time and was forced to redirect its attention away from the Mediterranean. Due to its preoccupation with Turkey, Greece did not attempt to strengthen the EC's Mediterranean policy as it feared this would benefit its rival (Turkey). France found itself in an awkward position due to its deeper colonial involvement in the area and its criticisms of Morocco's political life were perceived as neo-colonial disapproval and caused hostile reactions.[34] It was, however, during this time that Spain got closer to France with regards to the EC's Mediterranean policy.[35] The EU was alarmed by the crisis in Algeria. Spain realised that no country alone could 'manage' the crisis. This challenge to governance led to a redirected emphasis of the EU's strategy on the Mediterranean. The measures taken included Spain's negotiations with Germany for financial support to the Mediterranean countries in return for its support towards the Central and Eastern European countries: thus ensuring a balancing of power within the EU. Furthermore, Spaniards, in one capacity or another – including EU commissioners – were leading protagonists in the drafting of the EU documents that led to the adoption of the EMP and in the negotiations on the wording of the Barcelona Declaration of 1995.

Although Spain claims that the main problems of the Mediterranean are social and economic, the European market has not offered greater market access to North African major exports – because these are the same exports that Spain and other EU Mediterranean countries trade with the rest of their European partners.[36] This situation has, however, brought about increased EU financial aid to compensate the non-member Mediterranean countries.

Moreover, Spain utilises the European Mediterranean policy as a lobby arena within the EU for its own national interests. The Mediterranean area thus offers Spain an opportunity to act within the EU arena as a leading European country. The leadership role which the discursive practices of the Mediterranean offered Spain in Europe seems to be a common thematic underlying not only Spain's discourse on the Mediterranean but also that of France and Italy.

Spain's discourse on the Mediterranean, based on a foreign policy model established in the mid-1980s, has primarily focused on the Maghreb. This discourse has been shaped by a concurrence of complementary interests and visions. The thematics of this discursive practice stem from geographical, historical and cultural associations and the traditional (albeit not adequately developed) relations with all the countries bordering the Mediterranean Sea, including Israel since 1986.[37] The objects of this discourse lie in Spain's attempts to be seen as a bridge between Europe and North Africa and as the country that seeks to solve the 'problems' in the Mediterranean area. Its diplomats, as the main speaking 'subjects', have led Spain's discursive practices on the Mediterranean. Its bilateral and multilateral relations with the Maghreb have been characterised by creative activism up to the period that led to the EMP in 1995. In fact, Spain's discourse on the Mediterranean during this period shifted from being primarily economic-commercial to include political, economic-financial, social and cultural discourses too. The objects of this wider Spanish discourse on the Mediterranean include Spain's defence of its own interests and the conversion of the area into a zone of political and social stability and economic prosperity (which entered EU discourses). In effect, the former is no more than the means of achieving the latter and thus safeguarding Spain's specific interests in the area, concentrated especially in the western part.[38] However, Spain's discursive practices on the Mediterranean seem to have dried up since Barcelona although the focus on the Maghreb – rather than the Mediterranean as a whole – is maintained (thus, Spain lacks a global framework of Mediterranean relations). The election of the Aznar government marked an important speaking subject in the period of hibernation in Spain's focus on the Mediterranean.[39] This change in Spain's discursive practice of the Mediterranean continued to be one of the few options Spain had for having a degree of international protagonism. Spain's discourse on the Mediterranean has therefore been an inconsistent one (reflecting the absence of consistent practices for an area that is important for Spanish interests). There may in future, however, be a shift in Spain's discourse on the Mediterranean owing to the challenges currently found in both the Maghreb and the Middle East.[40]

Italy

Since the days of Enrico Mattei at least, Italy's official Mediterranean policy has been mostly commercially geared to protect the interests of its business communities.[41] During its Presidency (July–December 2003), Italy focused on the organisation of a number of trade conferences clearly reflecting where its interests in the Mediterranean lie.[42] Italy's domestic politics have always encroached upon its foreign policy. During the mid-1980s Italy experienced three major events that caused a change in its Mediterranean policy. First, Italy clashed with the USA upon Italy's release of Abu Abbas, the mastermind of the October 1985 hijacking of the cruise ship *Achille Lauro* (during which an American citizen was killed). Second, the massacre at Rome airport in December 1985 proved to be evidence that the secret accord that Italy held with the PLO to spare it from terrorism was no longer paying off since the PLO seemed to have lost control over the latest actions of the Middle East terrorist groups. Third, in early 1986, when the USA bombed Libyan cities, Colonel Gaddafi responded by launching Scud missiles at the Italian island of Lampedusa, the effect of which was to remind Italy that it still depended on the USA for protection.[43]

These events caused Italy to search for closer European relations.[44] Its economic concentration on its neighbours in the south and the east of the Mediterranean seemed unjustified, despite the fact that the key to Italian prosperity lay in the Mediterranean. Following the end of the Cold War, Italy's then Foreign Minister, De Michelis, sought to exploit new openings in the Mediterranean. During December 1989 he proposed the extension of the Helsinki rationale to the Mediterranean, at a ministerial session of the Euro-Arab dialogue in Paris.[45] De Michelis also proposed the CSCM in September 1990 in Palma de Mallorca.[46] Italy made great efforts to make this proposal a reality and Spain also sponsored the idea. France was rather indifferent to the proposal.[47] The idea was put on hold at the end of 1991. Since 1992, Italian policy towards the Mediterranean has been silent, even difficult to detect at times.[48] Italy was presented as best acting in and through the EU. During the Berlusconi government of 1994, its foreign minister Martino claimed that '(C)ontinental security cannot be separated from that of the Mediterranean area (a discourse which is clearly encompassed in EU discourse)'[49] – in effect a discursive practice on the area which is security related. When Susanna Agnelli succeeded Martino during the Dini govern-ment (which took office in January 1995) she wrote a joint article with the then Spanish foreign minister, claiming that the southern Mediterranean deserved equal attention to East-Central Europe. They further called for political dialogue – especially through the Mediterranean Forum; economic assistance – through the gradual constitution of a Mediterranean free trade area and by financial transfers; and for the stimulation of a greater mutual understanding between European and Arab cultures (in effect, the basis for the three baskets of the Barcelona Declaration).

Thus, since 1992, Italy's strategy of securing its interests *vis-à-vis* perceived problems emanating from the Mediterranean area has been through the EU. Its diplomats claim that Italy played a crucial role in bringing the EU's southern frontier to its attention.[50] Since the mid-1980s, Italy has been sharing and discussing Mediterranean issues with Spain. Similar relations with France have been cooler and more reserved. However, in 1992, through the Western European Union (WEU), a series of tripartite military procedures were designed between France, Spain and Italy, in effect a shared (hard) security discourse on the Mediterranean as a securitising object. In May 1995, during a WEU ministerial meeting, these countries together with Portugal agreed to the formation of two multinational forces via the establishment of Euromarfor and Eurofor[51] for the Mediterranean.[52] A series of security practices/discourses thus emanated partly from Italy. In this vein, Italy also sought NATO's attention to the Mediterranean, although the NATO Mediterranean Dialogue was proposed by Spain. Moreover, when Italy chaired the December 1994 summit of the OSCE, it ensured that this organisation started a process of discussions with non-European Mediterranean countries.

Italy's Mediterranean policy is thus based on political co-operation within an institutional framework linked mostly to the EU's foreign and security policy. A study on Mediterranean co-operation conducted by the Istituto Affari Internazionali (commissioned by the Italian foreign ministry) during the Andreatta period, possibly served as a sound basis for the Barcelona Declaration.[53] The study comprised the work of three working groups on political and security matters, economics and culture.[54] Italy has also put forward the idea of a Mediterranean bank (reflecting its economic interests and which is being reiterated more recently).

At this stage, one can note that Italy's interests today are distinguishably European and it concerns itself more with Eastern European issues than with southern ones. However, one can still detect an Italian Mediterranean policy – although this is mainly one developed through the EU and to a certain extent through NATO. What seems to maintain Italy's interests in the Mediterranean is its concern with its relatively large imports of natural gas from Algeria, Libyan energy and recent human migration issues.[55] The latter can be traced back to Italy's Balkan preoccupations in the 1990s. War in Bosnia and Kosovo, neo-authoritarianism in Croatia (with its substantial Italian minority) and economic breakdown in Albania presented special problems for Italy since they were taking place in Italy's 'backyard' and have since presented Italian governments with dramatic policy challenges. What would Italy do if Albania imploded and the thousands of migrants seeking work and security in Italy suddenly become millions? These are some of the thematics of Italy's discursive practices on the Mediterranean, having as their speaking 'subjects' Italian policy-makers who confront such questions on a day-to-day basis (and who are highly influenced by the Italian media). Italy's discourse on the Mediterranean has as its object an efficient and effective diplomatic intervention in these situations that will meet Italy's political and economic interests. The premise is that political stability will have positive results on Italy's investment and commercial activity in the Balkans (wider Mediterranean). Subsumed under this discursive practice there is, however, yet another Italian discourse – on Eastern Europe. The Balkans may well have been the theatre for a systemic attempt by Italy to challenge Germany for a leadership role in this area and to shake off Italy's reputation as the 'toy' of the USA. By blocking air strikes from American airbases in Italy, the Italian government would have been able to put a spoke in the wheel of an aggressive policy against Yugoslavia. But such a policy would have implied that Italy was going to put *realpolitik* before internationalism and defend Serbian actions to maintain the precarious Yugoslav republic even when these led to massacres and the oppression of ethnic minorities in Kosovo and elsewhere. In such circumstances, Italy had no choice but to join the anti-Serb crusade.[56] Thus, Italy attempts to maintain a leadership role in the Mediterranean primarily through economic discursive practices while reassuring its security interests through US intervention in the area.

Member states'/domestic discourses enter EU discourses on the Mediterranean – and the regularity of markers

As shown above, the role of the individual EU member countries in influencing EU Mediterranean policy is a very complex issue and the conclusions reached by the authors cited seem rather conflicting.

The colonial past/historical legacy of countries such as France has had a particular impact on their desire to focus more energy on developments in the southern Mediterranean. France has in fact been, historically, more influential than other EU member states in influencing EU Mediterranean policy, at least up to the early 1990s. The literature on French involvement in this area might appear to be less evident – perhaps due to the fact that the French presence and involvement in the area has been taken for granted whilst the case with Italy and Spain is slightly different. France comes across as a confident player and a natural leader in Mediterranean affairs.[57] Spain and Italy take a somewhat cautious approach and have to prove their involvement in the area – they have to continuously build a relationship with the Mediterranean and justify their presence.[58] During the period 1992–5, Spain joined France as a *leading protagonist in this area of influence*. However, Spain's leading role has been receding since then.[59] (As far as Greece is concerned, it has mostly tended to react to Mediterranean issues raised within the EU. As Ioakimidis explains 'Greek foreign policy pursuits have been described as 'irrational', 'parochial', 'incomprehensible', 'aggressive', even 'crazy'.[60] According to Ioakimidis, such an attitude underlies the absence of a systemic institutional framework of foreign policy-making in Greece).[61] Italy was active in the Mediterranean for a while under De Michelis but its interests turned more towards Europe following its preoccupations with the Balkans, especially Albania. However, although Europe is fundamentally important for all these EU members, none of them can regard Europe without also considering 'unstable' peripheral areas.[62]

One issue, which arises from this analysis of domestic discourses on the Mediterranean and how these enter EU discourses, is whether these southern member states actually constitute a 'bloc' or set of discursive practices on the Mediterranean. According to an interviewee, the initial propaganda about the EMP being influenced by Spain and France is not really true. He insisted that, at least, it is no longer true that the Partnership is advocated or more influenced by these countries (which some nine/ten years ago claimed to be the real 'fathers' of the process). The same interviewee agrees that Spain is now much less active in the Mediterranean than it was before and new countries such as Sweden are becoming more involved in Mediterranean issues.[63] The balance of interests is constantly shifting in accordance with a lot of criteria that create the 'vitality' of the process. This shift depends on which type of discourses are more powerful than others at specific periods in time (thus context is also crucial for tracing the regularity of markers across discourses). The interviewee in question emphasised that the Partnership has to be perceived as a learning process. Other officials from the Commission agreed on this aspect – according to these sources, Sweden and Germany are becoming more interested in the Mediterranean. In fact, the discursive practices of northern European states on the Mediterranean are, more recently, becoming clearer especially those relating to third basket issues on Euro-Mediterranean dialogue and understanding.[64] The role of the Swedish Institute opened in Alexandria in 2000 (and strategically located in the 'heart' of the southern Mediterranean area where the Maghreb and Mashreq meet), and the key role Sweden has played among all the current EMP-27 in developing the cultural dimension of Barcelona since the mid-1990s became more explicit at the Valencia conference where Sweden contributed an important part in shaping the third basket agenda. The close relationship between Sweden and Egypt in the making was clearly marked when Egypt proposed (at the meeting of the Euro-Mediterranean Committee in Brussels on 25 September 2003) that the Euro-Mediterranean Foundation (to promote a dialogue of cultures and civilisations and to increase the visibility of the Barcelona Process) be called 'The Anna Lindh Euro-Mediterranean Foundation for Dialogue between Cultures'.[65] Germany has also been trying to play a role in the area: The Minister-President of the *Land* Baden-Württemberg, Erwin Teufel, shared these views during the Stuttgart conference. The Minister claimed that:

> ... this is the first time ... that the foreign ministers are meeting at a location that is not within sight of the Mediterranean. It is ... a highly symbolic occasion: the European-Mediterranean partnership is not something that only concerns those states immediately bordering the Mediterranean – it is a partnership that affects the entire EU. So to that extent one could say that Baden-Württemberg – and the city of Stuttgart – are themselves Mediterranean ... I am convinced that we should no longer just see geographical proximity as the crucial element for co-operation. To my mind it is more important to establish where our common interests lie – for example in the economy, culture, education or the environment.[66]

This is a good example of a symbolic construction of the Mediterranean through which Germany, although not being in the Mediterranean geographically, is constructed as being of the Mediterranean, that is having links with this area. This discourse is made meaningful through economic utterances and practices.

Moreover, the then President of the Council of the EU,[67] Federal Minister Joschka Fischer, stated that:

> for Germany the close partnership between the EU and the South is an *essential counterpart* of EU enlargement to the East. We therefore attached great importance to the fact that the course for the policy on the Mediterranean was set during our last Presidency, at the Essen European Council in 1994 (own emphasis).[68]

This is another thematic behind Germany's discourse on the Mediterranean. Germany's need to *balance* the attention it is perceived as giving to the Central and Eastern European Countries (CEECs) with that it gives to the Mediterranean. Such a discursive practice is aimed at avoiding labelling Germany as having any bias in favour of the CEECs (in effect, a *Realpolitik* balance speak).[69]

Clearly what marks the regularity across EU discourses on the Mediterranean is the role played out by member states of the EU.

Commission references to the 'Mediterranean'

By way of analysis of the selected member states' discourses and how these entered into the EU's Mediterranean discourses and policies, one observes that there is a regular *uncertainty* (marker) in the way in which the EU refers to the Mediterranean: this regularity plays itself out in terms of which countries are included and which are excluded as Mediterranean in the various EU statements. In fact, one can find several references to this area. References to the 'myth' of the Mediterranean idea as the cradle of civilisation, the birthplace of three religions: Christianity, Islam and Judaism and as an area where several cultures have interacted for a very long time often mark this area as a field of knowledge in EU practices.[70] There is also a frequent attempt in Commission documents to classify the Mediterranean – which marks EU attempts at breaking this area into sub-component parts. In its explanatory memorandum[71] the Commission states that:

> The beneficiaries (referred to as Mediterranean partners) under the proposed Regulation are the Maghreb and Mashrek countries and territories as well as Turkey, Cyprus and Malta.

In another document,[72] the Commission says that:

> It deals primarily with relations with the Maghreb and Mashreq countries and Israel, while noting the importance of the Community's particular

relations with Turkey, as well as those with Cyprus and Malta in the perspective of their accession to the Community.

In its conclusions on the EMP the Commission refers to:

> The Community's long-term strategy of creating a EMP, comprising a zone of peace and stability embracing the Union, Central and Eastern Europe and the southern and eastern Mediterranean ...

Such references emphasise a particular understanding of security in Europe – here encompassing the EU member states and accession countries from the former Eastern 'bloc' – which is played out as a mirror security image at Europe's periphery, that is, at its southern and eastern neighbours in the Mediterranean.

Further on in the same document,[73] the Commission makes reference to:

> All the Mediterranean countries, that is, those bordering the Mediterranean Sea, plus Jordan ...

whilst in the Annex to this same document[74] which provides tables illustrating interdependent relations between the EC and the Mediterranean countries (and also countries of Central and Eastern Europe), the Mediterranean is classified in a footnote as including 'Morocco, Algeria, Tunisia, Libya (even though at that time the EU had no official/formal relations with Libya due to UN sanctions), Egypt, Israel, Jordan, Lebanon, Syria, Turkey' while no reference is made to Malta, Cyprus and the Palestinian Territories in this definition.

Moreover, in this text[75] it is stated that 'The Community should also promote increased co-operation with the Gulf countries (underlying a security focus and a wider Middle East focus) in its activities in the Middle East ...' Here one can observe a 'widening' of the Commission's reference to the Mediterranean which emphasises the demarcation ground for Europe's security to include the wider Mediterranean.[76]

In fact, following the war in Iraq of 2003, the EU deemed it fit to:

> develop a new regional strategy that embraces Iraq, Iran and Syria. Only this kind of approach can lay the foundations for lasting stability and security ...[77]

in effect widening the field of the Mediterranean to include Iraq and Iran into a wider Middle East definition.[78]

It is also important to note the different views about the Mediterranean emanating from the Mediterranean partners of the EMP. The Minister of Foreign Affairs of Syria, for example, said that 'We also hope that Mauritania will join the Barcelona Process' after having welcomed a Libyan observer to the EMP Stuttgart conference.[79]

The regularity of EU markers of the Mediterranean thus become important for partners from this area to refer to and reiterate this discourse (and become embedded in the Med partners' own discourses). This side of this statement hints that in order to work upon terms like 'peace' and 'stability', the EU's remit must necessarily extend beyond the countries identified earlier above. It is interesting to see that Libya nowadays figures out more prominently in EU discourses on the future of the EMP, as we shall see shortly.

Another important regular marker of the Mediterranean used across EU discourses is the reference to dialogue between North and South. In a 1995 Bulletin,[80] references to the Mediterranean are said to involve 'initiatives under the first pillar [including] a dialogue with countries in the Arab-Muslim world, and with other countries [and] between Europe and its neighbours in the southern and eastern Mediterranean[81] … the Mediterranean rim countries …'.[82]

Although this term is used across several EMP documents and often taken as one of the main instruments of the EU-15's co-operation on the international stage, its meaning is nowhere clarified or distinguished from regular, institutionalised contact between two parties.[83]

In another document[84] reference is made to '… the establishment of a free trade area between the European Community and Mediterranean non-member countries and territories as well as the associated applicant countries Cyprus and Malta and a customs union with Turkey', while the Stuttgart proceedings[85] state that '… it is also important from a political standpoint that we extend the Barcelona Process beyond the riparian States of the Mediterranean into the centre of Europe'. Once again there is little debate in EU documentation as to what 'free' implies and free trade in what precisely is not clarified. Critiques argue that leaving the agriculture sector practically out of the free trade agenda serves to highlight the EU's privileged position in its relations with the Mediterranean partners and covers the Europeans' protectionist system.[86]

Another example of a sporadic reference of the EU's Mediterranean partners stipulates that:[87]

> The Community must make clear its wish to see the countries in question enter into similar negotiations with each other [that is through sub-regional integration] and with European countries which are not [yet] members of the Community (EFTA, Central and Eastern Europe, Cyprus, Malta and Turkey).

This implies a definition of who is considered as European which includes the latter three 'partners' of the EMP.

Before one can proceed with any further analysis of the EU's Barcelona declaration and other EU documentation on the Mediterranean, one must appreciate that the term Euro-Mediterranean is clearly a political and social construct, which does not necessarily reflect geographical or other less concrete features or characteristics. Although the term 'Europe' often refers to the EU, the membership of this international body is based on a predetermined selection of countries that are legitimately European.[88] Therefore, EU membership is not only about who belongs – one needs to assess the assumptions that exist about common goals. As Bretherton and Vogler[89] state, notions of the EU's presence and resulting actorness (EU identity) derive from shared internal beliefs about the Union. One also needs to reflect on how EU documentation refers to Europe and its relationship with the Mediterranean (as the analysis above attempted to investigate). Thus, European membership represents assumptions, forms and the personality of each EU member. Thus, EU membership is not about membership only, that is, who belongs to the EU. It is about identity, that is identification processes and processes of self-understanding. Identity is about what in legal terminology is called personality. The issue of identity is not only about who belongs but what this belonging does – whoever belongs participates in the construction of an identity. When one refers to the EU, there is a certain implied coherence of this actor and like any other actor in IR, it is a constructed one.[90]

The term 'Mediterranean', on the other hand, groups together a group of countries chosen on the basis of criteria sufficiently diverse and incoherent to be qualified as political. Thus, this group includes Jordan but on occasion excludes Libya[91] – although the latter was admitted as an observer to the Stuttgart conference. This group also excludes former Yugoslavia and Albania (for political and historical reasons[92]) which are perceived as more appropriately lumped with the group of CEEC since they do not qualify as either European or Mediterranean in terms of the EU's criteria for these categories.[93] However, German foreign minister Joschka Fischer did not hesitate to include Kosovo in the EU's discursive practice of the Mediterranean when during the Stuttgart Conference he claimed that:

> The Kosovo conflict … should encourage us to put our all into further developing the instruments of the Barcelona Process for peace and prosperity and thereby make the greatest possible contribution to resolving existing conflicts in the region.[94]

No matter how each group is composed, none of them is as cohesive or homogenous as they might be made to appear. The Mediterranean group includes non-European countries that extend from Morocco to Syria. These countries constitute half the membership of the League of Arab States and are part of what is often collectively referred to as the 'Arab world'. However, despite the fact that this area shares a common language (in written form at least), a common religion[95] (in terms of basic precepts) and a common heritage (depending on how one defines the term), it has rarely if ever constituted a homogenous entity. Adhering to the strict distinction that is sometimes made by academics, diplomats and politicians, requires a differentiation between the Maghreb and the Mashreq[96] or between North Africa and the Middle East. The latter includes Egypt and all the 'Arab' countries located to its east.[97] The former includes the five countries that are members of the Union of the Arab Maghreb,[98] namely, Algeria, Libya, Mauritania, Morocco and Tunisia. Differences can be found not only between the Maghreb and the Mashreq groups (relating to such factors as political orientations, political regimes, alliance systems, economic status, among other things) but also within members of a given group.[99] The EU often sets aside such differences when circumstances so require. Such EU practices mark regularities across its discourses through homogenising techniques.

Such categorisations as the 'Mediterranean region' may be useful as an intellectual abstract or as a convenient way of referring to a certain area of the globe but it is quite a contentious concept when referred to as a target for foreign policy decisions.[100] In the economic field, trade between and within the Mediterranean is very limited. In fact, horizontal exchange of goods, capital and human resources (or intraregional trade) accounts for only 5 per cent of the trade volume of the 12 Mediterranean partners of the EMP.[101] As Lewis and Wigen observe, it is important 'to make the case that concepts of global geography matter, not merely for how they influence discourse about the world, but for how they guide policy as well'.[102] This can be seen for example in another Commission document[103] that declares that:

> One of Europe's priorities is to consolidate peace and stability in the (Mediterranean) region. This challenging task would involve: ... promoting economic and social reform in such a way as to produce sustained growth (to create jobs) and an increase in standards of living, with the aim of stemming violence and easing migratory pressure.[104]
>
> The Ministers noted that the Commission's recent policy proposals on a 'Wider Europe' ... will encourage reform, especially in the services sector, that can give a strong boost to economic growth and competitiveness.[105]

Clearly, as one analyst puts it, European Political Co-operation in general and the Common Foreign and Security Policy in particular, were created to prevent international problems from disrupting the Community, not to help Europe solve international problems.[106] More specifically, the markers across EU discourses on the Mediterranean highlight where EU interests lie rather than where the Mediterranean partners needs are most urgent.

Furthermore, the construction of the Mediterranean by some of the EU member states, as presented in the first section of this chapter, may be interpreted as a post-colonial reading of the 'region'. Former colonies are perceived as being such weak states that they must be guided/governed, presumably by a stronger EU. 'Postcolonial' here refers to the ongoing practices of constituting the Mediterranean as less than European and thus constitutes a central position in European discourses as it supports what Europe is not (what the Mediterranean is). During a recent meeting in Brussels between Romano Prodi – President of the European Commission, Javier Solana – the High Representative for the Common Foreign and Security Policy and Aicha Belarbi – head of Morocco's Representation at the EU, Morocco's key role within the EMP was highlighted 'as part of the shared objective of building a region of peace, prosperity and dialogue, in which Rabat is seen as a potential pole of democracy and modernity'.[107]

Such a reading enables us to situate the EMP as an instance of the production of difference and 'otherness' as highlighted in EU contexts. If we observe member states and EU discourses critically we see how they construe the Med partners as learners or adopters of European norms.[108] The Med becomes one of the generalised 'others' necessary for Europe's self-image.[109] While normality is ascribed to the EU members, the Med other have to measure themselves against this in the process of learning European ways of being and doing. The EU is conceived as a model, a value-system for Med partners to follow and this is very clear through regular markers referring to the Med as developing, in need of development, etc. This framework of teaching and learning underlines the EU's alleged 'vision' of regional co-operation. For example, the Common Strategy on the Mediterranean is cited as an example of such EuroMed co-operation: under the title of 'Vision of the EU for the Mediterranean Region' this strategy claims that:

> The Mediterranean region is of strategic importance to the EU. A prosperous, democratic, stable and secure region, *with an open perspective towards Europe*, is in the best interests of the EU and Europe as a whole [own emphasis]; and:

> The EU will … encourage the *alignment* of policies relating to the EU Single Market [own emphasis]; and

> The EU will: take measures to persuade all Mediterranean Partners to abolish the death penalty *in accordance with agreed EU guidelines*.[110]

At a conference at the Université Catholique de Louvain-la-Neuve on 26 November 2002, Romano Prodi emphasised that:

> The Agadir initiative – the decision by Tunisia, Morocco, Egypt, and Jordan to speed up the liberalisation of trade between them – must be seen as a very positive step [of them becoming more like us],[111]

and on a separate occasion he reiterated that 'the network of association agreements … can be used to promote modernisation in our Mediterranean partners, which has been rendered more urgent and necessary by globalisation'.[112]

This can also be seen in the New Neighbourhood Policy (NNP) where partners who do not oblige to EU terms are framed as not yet up to European standards, even archaic at times:[113]

> ... the EU wishes to define an ambitious new range of policies towards its neighbours based on *shared values* such as liberty, democracy, respect for human rights and fundamental freedoms, and the rule of law [own emphasis] ... to work with the partners to reduce poverty and create an area of *shared* prosperity and values based on free trade, deeper economic integration, intensified political and cultural relations, enhanced cross-border co-operation and shared responsibility for conflict prevention and conflict resolution ... The EU's approach ... [is] based on ... perspectives for participating *progressively* in the EU's Internal Market.[114]

As one interviewee put it, although the Neighbourhood policy is very much in its preliminary stages (at the time of writing) its *finalité* is very important.

> We are clear where we want to go, but the direction depends on our partners ... *if they want to progress* this should be an attractive option ... the idea behind this initiative is for us *to take each partner country by the hand* towards joint ownership of this project ... the Council decided to integrate the Mediterranean in order to avoid tensions arising about the EU focusing only on Eastern countries ... the Med was included against stiff resistance from the Commission. The original label of Wider Europe albeit vague would surely not include North Africa – which is not Europe ... there was fear that Mediterranean countries would argue that this is an imperialist approach ... So we shifted the idea to New Neighbourhood Policy ... This policy creates a competitive environment [read as a neoliberal model] ... for the Free Trade Area to become a reality in 2010 ... what we need is a bilateral relationship so that those who can advance quicker will not have to wait for the slow movers (as in EMP context) ...[115]

In effect, the European Neighbourhood Policy (ENP) is not very different from the Barcelona Process, in that it frames a neo-liberal project meant to incorporate Med countries into a European-led economic region.[116] This raises questions of *who* defines shared standards, *who* says that the best system is the neo-liberal global system for all – perhaps a discursive framework marking an instance of EU attempts to socialise the Med into a pre-structured mould in its making? Just to give one example, perceptions of what constitutes a security threat in Arab partner countries are different from security threat perceptions in Europe.[117] EU markers of the field of the Med are, therefore, not always 'shared' markers among Arab partners. Moreover, narratives of a peaceful zone of prosperity and stability in the Med serve to reify the very world that EU members seek to overcome and which they see as a burden!

Italy, Spain, France and the UK maintained or continue to maintain a colonial presence in North Africa, which may help to justify their continued interest in the area.[118] France can be considered as the only EU member to have had a continuous substantial presence and interest in the non-European part of the Mediterranean. This presence can be traced to at least 1830 when France occupied Algiers and then proceeded to colonise the rest of Algeria and some other parts of North Africa. In the Mashreq, its influence was limited to the inter-war period when France was granted a mandate over Lebanon and Syria. This post-colonial reading of the area carries with it specific conceptions of the Mediterranean. In France, for example, the Mediterranean is a Latin lake of a former colonial empire.[119] The notion of the Mediterranean thereby carries with it elements of power and security and of cultural hegemony for France. The Mediterranean is thus constructed as a securitising object.[120] This post-colonial reading of the Mediterranean thus carries with it different interpretations of interests and of old ties with the area. The issue that arises in this context is about what makes insecurity. The portrayed instability in the Mediterranean is perceived as a source of insecurity for Europe. In a speech delivered recently in Bologna, Prodi emphasised that the construction of a 'new' Europe *necessitates* a strategy that tackles a number of issues within the Mediterranean particularly long-running conflicts that 'divide the region'.[121]

Differences between Europe and the Mediterranean are conceived not only as differences but as distances in space and time. In terms of symbolic theories of culture such differences rest on temporal distancing between the decoding subject and the encoded object. Therefore, EU markers of the Med can be read as differences in representation, exchange and meaning. Europe is symbolised as the signifying subject, the here and now, the form and structure where meaning is given, the knower and thus the decoding subject. The Mediterranean is the signified, the 'there and then', the content, function or event, symbol or icon, the known and thus the encoded subject.[122] The assertiveness of this visual-spatial representation and the EU's authoritative role in the transmission of the field of knowledge of the Med is expressed through the rhetoric of 'vision' where the EU presents its object primarily as seen, observed and as represented. Derrida's work on the use of binary divisions can be very insightful here. The hierarchical division which the EU has created *vis-à-vis* its southern partners always portrays the European partners as superior and the Mediterranean partners as inferior. Thus, security discourses separate the alleged (assumed) victim of insecurity and the cause of insecurity that is Europe and the Mediterranean respectively. The Mediterranean is thereby constructed as a breeding ground for uncivilised people. Discourses on immigration emanating, for example, from France (about the Mediterranean) are primarily presented through a security prism. Immigration is thus expressed as an economic and security problem and a problem of ungovernability (in the Foucauldian sense).[123] During the Stuttgart conference, the Minister of Foreign Affairs of Cyprus stated that:

> If we manage to join forces in the fight against exploitation of human beings by traffickers, by working together on a continuous basis, we will direct our efforts towards *perceiving immigration as less of a threat* and more as a cause of enrichment of our societies.[124]

Moreover, one notes that during the conclusions of the EuroMed Experts Meeting on 'Migration and Human Exchanges' held in The Hague on 1–2 March 1999 it was stated that:

> An integrated and balanced approach is necessary to deal with the phenomenon of migration and human exchanges which *concerns the three chapters of the Euro–Med Partnership* [my emphasis].

Such practices underpin the EMP's role as an important instrument for the EU but to an extent, to ensure a common European voice is heard in international affairs (especially with regards to issues such as migration which often pop up as crucial in international events). This also sheds light on the EU's identity: having no one single actor to speak on its behalf, the importance of addressing crucial, common 'issues' becomes pivotal.

It is therefore clear that the Mediterranean becomes more 'real' on the EU agenda when issues are conceived as a threat to Europe's security,[125] for example, immigration, fundamentalism and terrorism or when the EU has to decide on an issue that affects one of its members, for instance, the granting of import quotas to third countries or when a member of the 'southern' EU members presides over the Union and succeeds in carrying the rest of the members along a Mediterranean track.[126] This can also be seen in the EMP Commission document[127] which clearly states in the introduction that:

> One of Europe's priorities is … supporting political reform and defending human rights and freedom of expression as a means of containing extremism.

Thus, what unifies the Mediterranean in European eyes and what makes discursive practices of the Mediterranean 'effective' (to the extent that these are effective) are security issues, etc. (issues raised above). Through the prism of the EU as a security community, the Mediterranean states are made *equivalent*, that is a mirror reference point. As Laclau and Mouffe state, when we have a bipolar political field, or what Derrida calls binary divisions, the two poles are homogenised.[128] The EU can thus portray its understanding of the Mediterranean countries through the prism of its own concerns (mainly security). This does not imply that the EU does not discriminate between NMCs. In fact, during the Stuttgart conference:

> The issue of sub-regionality was discussed. It was agreed that in many cases a series of activities each involving only a few of the Partners, within the overall framework of a regional programme ('cluster' approach) is appropriate: this has proved to be a fruitful model for co-operation in several fields and its use in others was encouraged.[129]

The Agadir process as well as the NNP may well be the outcomes of this thinking which started in Stuttgart. Thus, we need to analyse not only *who* constructs policy but *how* policies are constructed: in the context of the EMP we are therefore interested in not only who has constructed the EMP but how the EMP has been constructed. The pattern/regularity of the EU discourse on the Mediterranean includes a section about what the EMP *is not*:

> ... the EMP ... Differs fundamentally from the peace process in the Middle East. The partnership is not a new forum for resolving other objectives, it can help to promote its success ... Nor is the EMP intended to replace the other activities and initiatives pursued in the interest of the peace, stability and development of the region ...[130]

The manner in which the Middle East (conflict) is presented in EU documentation reinforces the negative impact of the South. (It goes without saying that the media plays a role in the way it forms public opinion and in the way it affects decision-makers' perceptions.) These regular markers in EU discourses also mark important gaps between EU interests and member states' interests on the one hand, and EU policies and national policies on the other.

This discourse changed in the Common Strategy on the Mediterranean which stipulates that:

> The EU's Mediterranean policy ... will work with its Mediterranean Partners ... by contributing to the creation of a peaceful environment in the Middle East ... The EU is convinced that the successful conclusion of the Middle East Peace Process on all its tracks, and the resolution of other conflicts in the region, are important prerequisites for peace and stability in the Mediterranean ...

Although in a later section it stipulates that:

> this Common Strategy will cover the EU's contribution to the consolidation of peace in the Middle East once a comprehensive peace settlement has been achieved(!)

The cautious tone in this EU discourse may be read as an attempt to avoid allegations of neo-colonial influence in the area. Yet, the Middle East is given a very prominent discourse in the Common Strategy, a discourse which was communicated during a positive climate in the Middle East, prior to the second intifada.[131]

One notes that when the MEPP was coming close to a solution (summer 2000) the EU wanted to be affiliated with the success story in the possible conflict resolution but disassociates itself from the very same conflict when events turn very negative.

Discourse analysis (as a method) highlights the importance of these regularities in political documents. The following section attempts to offer a more in-depth discourse analysis of how the EU's EMP frames its object, that is, the Mediterranean. This analysis highlights how the EU's categorisation of this area is just one 'truth' held in place by language and power.

Evaluating the regularity of concepts/markers across EU discourses

These markers across EU discourses on the Mediterranean draw heavily albeit implicitly on modernisation theory. Situating these markers in postmodernist critiques of modernisation theory will help us examine the familiar categories of what makes Europe, democracy, the market economy, etc., and display European willingness to transform these categories onto the Mediterranean area.[132] It emerges that the EU treats the Mediterranean as an entity that is developing along the same time-line as itself, and is even a former instantiation of itself (ancient Greece, the Roman empire etc.). Reading EU markers of the Mediterranean in terms of postmodernist critiques illustrates how the intent of the EU to act on behalf of the Med, what observers refer to as 'trusteeship', has been a powerful force in the formation of doctrines/practices of development which accompany capitalism.[133] Europe's colonial legacy in the Mediterranean may help us understand why North African and Middle Eastern partners in particular view the EU's neo-liberal model as a new form of colonialism/trusteeship.[134] These critiques shed further light on how the EU's perception of the Med as an area which needs 'help' does not question the desirability of development. Rather, as can be analysed through the language in the EU's documentation on the Med, this conceptualisation is in effect a process of discursive constructivism in ways which homogenise and systematise the Med which in turn empower Western discourses. The EU tends to force the Med partners into certain categories that its members can literally 'manage'. By producing the Mediterranean in and across its discourses and through practices of 'regionalism' (since their inception in the 1960s), the 'region' has achieved the status of a certainty in the social imaginary of EU members.[135]

Thus, the construction of the Mediterranean, which has been constituted so far in the EU's policies towards the area, reads in terms of security discourses, discourses of social stability, strategic discourses and economic discourses.[136] There is a cultural discourse too but this is rather romantic and flimsy. From various Commission documents it is possible to identify these various discourses:

Security discourses: discourses on the threat of 'immigrant flow from the south into the European borders' – the EU's objective is to manage this flow and at the same time to check the 'drug traffic'.[137] The current debate centres on what kind of immigration is essential for the EU.[138] Other such discourses include those on 'fundamentalism'. Here, the EU seeks to prevent Muslim fundamentalists from gaining power in a Mediterranean country and setting up regimes that would be hostile to Western interests. On 13 April 1999, the then President-designate of the Commission, Romano Prodi stated (in front of the EP) that in his view the future relations of the EU with the Islamic countries are a question of life and death for the EU – which according to one interviewee may seem a little exaggerated but it does indicate that 'we have to do with vital interests and not only with, let's say, marginal economic or trade or whatever interests'.[139]

The marker of threat in this speech act became even more pronounced in the context of and following the events of 9/11 and 11 March 2004.

Hence, the debate about the 'Mediterranean' is primarily focused on a security appeal by Western Europe on behalf of an imagined community.[140] The discourse of the Mediterranean does not carry the negative loading a discourse of Arab does in European eyes.[141] Therefore, this is the case of how specific carriers/speaking 'subjects' of discourses – statesmen/policy officials/diplomats for one group, are able to change the framing of one particular discourse in what they consider to be an advantageous direction.[142]

It is important to note that in these descriptions of the Mediterranean, regardless of the specific threat treated (that is, an instance of securitisation through regular markers across discourses on fundamentalism, terrorism, drug trafficking, illegal migration etc.), the concept of security is employed in the same very particular way whenever its referent object is Europe. Security is always presented as being concerned with having a stable, peaceful area in and around Europe sufficient to act out the principles of European interests. This requires the EU advocating important financial contributions via its MEDA spending (to ensure democracy, peace and security according to the EU's logic). The shaping of a EuroMed area of peace and stability amounts to a policy in agreement with what Europe *is*, a policy that unites its member states and associated partners through shared principles. The content of the term 'European principles' is most often left implicit in EU articulations. The statement is not limited to these precise terms. It regularly covers a number of other concepts such as 'values' but sometimes also in similar ways concepts such as 'interests'. Such 'European principles' is another concept used in many arguments. The statement that works upon this concept and combines it with the concept of 'interests' is an important discourse to observe as it often hides one concept behind the other. Similar terms are always articulated in a way that implies that an understanding of them belongs to the taken-for-granted as in references to 'democracy', 'free markets', 'human rights', 'justice'. These terms are often said to be universal principles and universal values embodied by Europeans. These markers in EU discourses with reference to what the Mediterranean partners should ameliorate, combine with the idea that the EU represents an image of a 'good' regional organisation/global actor expressed through the principles it upholds.

Another often reiterated term is the concept of 'development aid' that is often employed in articulations about development in the Mediterranean. Hence, particular markers are regularly invoked as those with which EU interests are concerned, and thus with what a EU foreign policy in harmony with what the EU is and in line with what EU interests and principles amount to.

In terms of economic and trade discourses, EU member states aim to secure oil and gas supplies on which Europe is dependent.[143] Moreover, in the long term, the MNCs are a large potential market for European goods. The EU has committed itself:

> to the creation of the Euro-Mediterranean economic area, namely the establishment of free trade, reforms for economic transition and promotion of private investment [thus aiming at] creating a Euro-Mediterranean economic area of shared prosperity ...[144]

In the area of investments, the *Financial Times* in March 2000 announced that the countries of the southern and eastern Mediterranean face growing marginalisation from the global economy with a share of global foreign direct investment (FDI) of just above 1 per cent, despite attempts over the past decade or so (including those of the EMP) to increase FDI through investor protection and privatisation, which have so far failed.[145] Furthermore, it is interesting to note that the MENA (Middle East and North Africa) area 'risks becoming increasingly specialised in energy exports and in labour intensive, low-skilled manufactures' which seems to confirm where EU member states' interests lie. What is still missing is a 'regional' regulatory and rules structure despite the existence of 140 bilateral trade agreements between Arab countries and the existing agreements between the EU and most of the EMP Mediterranean partners. Moreover, as Professor Mohamed Lahouel of Tunis University claimed, 'Competition laws are necessary to achieve trade liberalisation. What is needed in the MENA region is a multilateral competition framework containing a minimum set of rules and principles'.[146] Trade liberalisation is not just about ameliorating the European model but about bringing in place the mechanisms for such a framework to be worked out in the context of the Mediterranean.

Clearly, the voices of the Mediterranean partners need to be heard, especially in this respect, within the EMP. What could emerge from the frustrations of many of the Mediterranean partners is the creation of an (in)formal contact group to co-ordinate their trade issues.[147] However, some of the administrators at the Commission may disagree with such a proposal as they would deem it more important to set up some kind of Mediterranean group on political issues. If the internal governance of the EU retains exclusionary features as it does in the area of Common Agricultural Policy (CAP), the Mediterranean partners will soon be pushed to address these issues.

Prosperity discourse: the EU seeks to improve standards of living in Mediterranean countries so as to ensure social and political stability in the area and indirectly in Europe. According to one interviewee, the most important role of the EU in this process is perhaps not the one of providing finance to the Partnership but rather to act as a catalyst to bring these Mediterranean partners closer together. The Barcelona Declaration has made it easier for these partners to co-operate amongst themselves due to the fact that it enshrines some basic principles including economic principles, principles of respect for human rights and democracy – which all these countries have agreed to adhere to (in principle at least). This does not mean that they implement them but at least there is a kind of consensus on basic principles.[148] The Commission emphasises the need for 'promoting understanding between *them* and improving *their* perception of each other'[149] but does not deal directly with the European side in this respect within the Partnership.

Peace discourses: the EU aims to prevent internal and interregional conflicts that may make European intervention necessary.[150] According to an official at the European Commission, the Kosovo crisis definitely had an impact on what the EU has been doing with the Mediterranean and resulted in a further encouragement to look into the region and to try economically, politically and also, if possible, through cultural means to develop links through dialogue and to stabilise the region.

All these discourses are somewhat interrelated. The EMP encourages economic development, promotes the rule of law, seeks the protection of human rights and supports the growth of democratic institutions – all of which objectives are increasingly being recognised as regular discursive practices/discourse markers (security policies) of the EU. This can be seen, for example, in the Community document[151] where it is stated that:

> The Community and its partners in the Mediterranean are interdependent in many respects. Europe's interests in the region are many and varied, including as they do the environment, energy supplies, migration, trade and investment. The drug problem … is one which all the countries involved will have to tackle together. Instability in the region cannot fail to have negative consequences for all the countries of the European Community.

One surely cannot challenge the EU for defending its interests – yet, one can and should evaluate the approach used to define those interests and the methods applied to achieve them.[152]

For example, the discourse of 'dialogue' has become increasingly marked more forcefully through regular references to the Foundation and the Civil Fora (which run parallel to the Meetings of Foreign Ministers and which 'constituted a platform of dialogue') and have become established regularities in the expressions of EU concerns on the Med.[153] But as one interviewee put it, the discourse on dialogue goes beyond what at face value appears as a 'talk-shop' and uncovers hidden anxieties and fears that EU actors feel when having to deal with sensitive issues such as 'religion, particularly Islam and religious freedom, homosexuality, women's role etc. which EU actors shy away from and prefer not to deal with'.[154]

Moreover, the term European–Mediterranean 'Partnership' has several problematic connotations, one of which is the concept of 'European' – this prefix extends to encompassing in the 2004 enlargement new Union members to the East as well as to the North and South – the latter of which could be countries designated in the 'Mediterranean' part of the term (like Malta). The latter thus involves the EU in further line drawing exercises over time.

In fact, European line drawing still defines the primary borders of EU identification processes. On the one hand, the persistence of national discourses on Europe may well prevent the construction of a European collective political identity (as does EU enlargement) that is necessary for an effective European foreign policy.[155] However, it may be argued that national discourses can exist as long as they are subsumed under the heading of a common threat. On the other hand, the EU has its own dynamics. Discourses are thus marked by continuities, regularities. Perhaps, in this case, this is why a European foreign policy is important which implies that this is also why boundaries are important markers of EU discourses. EU discourses and national discourses can exist together and what is important is the manner in which they are articulated. The EU claims to be developing a Common Foreign Policy and a Common Security Policy – the CFSP[156] – two discourses subsumed under a threat. Therefore, national discourses may well possibly be complementary to EU discourses. The manner in which the Mediterranean is conceived of within national discourses (as discussed in the first section above) as well as at the EU level implies that the EU can claim to have both a Mediterranean (that is Foreign) Policy as well as a Security Policy. This process of articulation shows that there is nothing that can be neutralised in discourse. The articulation of a discourse makes it a discourse.

Understanding the ways in which policy is formulated is crucial, in particular the relationship between knowledge, power and ideas, and the process whereby ideas are translated into policy proposals and move onto the policy agenda. Discourse analysis creates the possibility of standing detached from the Mediterranean discourses/markers, bracketing their familiarity, in order to analyse the theoretical and practical context with which they have been associated. In this context, Mediterraneanism as a Western style for dominating, restructuring and having authority over an area, requires an analysis of regionalism as a regime of representation. These representations, in turn, implicitly assume Western standards as the benchmark against which to measure the situation in the Mediterranean. The deployment of such a discourse in a world system in which the West has a certain dominance over the 'Third World' has profound political, economic and cultural effects that must be explored.[157] Thus, in line with the discourse analysis methodology adopted in this book, policy implementation can be assessed through this process. An assumption about the relationship between ideas, interest formation and agenda setting is crucial to the formulation of policy and ultimately to policy outcomes/implementation. Both interests and identities are essentially constructed by, or are endogenous to, processes of social interaction.[158] In sum, what is necessary is a more effective linkage between FPA and other approaches to the study of policy-making at the domestic and international levels.[159]

The EMP has successfully deployed a regime of EU government over the Med, a space for 'subject peoples' that ensures a certain control over it. In the late Said's terminology, this space is a geopolitical space and for some this will to spatial power is implicit in expressions such as North and South. This pattern of practices formulates the Med as a discursive formation, giving rise to an efficient apparatus, that systematically relates forms of knowledge (the Med) and techniques of power (EU).

This chapter has presented Mediterraneanism as a discursive field. It has paid close attention to the deployment of the EU discourses through practices and showed how discourses result in concrete practices of thinking and acting through which the Med is produced. EU markers of the Med take place at many levels – economic, political and cultural (in effect the three baskets of the EMP). Interventions in the Med are accompanied by goals such as those of promoting democracy. Attitudes of superiority convince EU members that they have an obligation and responsibility to intervene politically in what they perceive as needy partners in the Med.

Conclusion

In its various initiatives, the EU has vacillated in its conceptualisation of Mediterranean 'otherness', exposing the limits of its representation: ideas of a European missionary purpose to civilise and democratise the (Arab) world is one example. This instance of securitisation has been made even more urgent through the various discursive practices on the Arab world post 9/11. While understandings of the Mediterranean shifted, and European imaginings of the foreign grew to include many other countries, one thing does not change: the Mediterranean (I would say Arab as a thematic object of the EU discourse on the Mediterranean) 'otherness' remains the continuous object of European foreign policy.[160] It is important here to stress that as Borneman states, 'a conceptual framework or model is a perceptual orientation for political action; it is intellectual labour and distinct from the labours of (those) who themselves (work) as administrators in the carrying out of foreign … policy'.[161] Many administrators rely on the work of academicians in order to orient policy. This gives us more reason to engage ourselves in a critical approach to foreign policy analysis and the construction of what is 'foreign' that it entails.[162] Such an approach has the potential of generating positive policy ideas, not least in the cultural, rather than political, dialogue element of the EMP.

The EU's notion of the Mediterranean consists of individual member states' discursive practices. These range from Spain's and France's discourse as being primarily a fixation on the Maghreb to Italy's (and Greece's) focus on the Balkans (and Eastern Europe). The Balkans is not included in the EU (as a whole group)'s discourse on the Mediterranean. What unites these discursive practices on the Mediterranean is the common securitisation/discursive practice about the Mediterranean (as a security threat) – which the individual member states cannot attend to alone and this vindicates their interest in drawing the attention of the EU to the Mediterranean. This is how the attempts of Spain, Italy, France and Portugal (and Greece, albeit to a very limited extent) to ensure the inclusion of the Mediterranean in the EU's foreign policy agenda should be analysed. One may speculate that, in an area where EU members have particular interests and potential influence, the EU (as a whole) feels the need to frequently resort to a continuous self-assessment of how it is playing out in international affairs as a global actor, in particular in the development of its Mediterranean initiatives such as the EMP.[163] The EMP still suffers from a clear definition of the *type* of Mediterranean the EU is trying to deal with (in effect a lack of defining the aims and instruments that need to be utilised to achieve security in the Mediterranean and thereby security in Europe). EU member states still regard the defence of their interests as requiring the identification of an 'adversary', an 'other', who could endanger them (and the drawing up of a defensive strategy). With its focus on security in the Mediterranean, the EU has failed to mobilise sufficient resources within its EMP to fulfil its policy aims.[164] Nor does the EU's security discourse on the Mediterranean justify the predominance of its members' commercial and corporate interests, whose discourse is echoed by senior officials responsible for these areas, together with entrepreneurs and agricultural and fishing interests.[165] The interests of EU member states are represented by those who argue for the development of the non-EU Mediterranean countries, but action is lacking in this direction so far. Among other things, the EU needs to contribute decisively to the development of the productive sectors of the Mediterranean partners that are labour intensive (such as agriculture, tourism and textiles), act to reduce the burden of their foreign debt (60 per cent of which is owed to EU countries), apply a free trade regime to Mediterranean agricultural exports and establish a less restrictive immigration policy.[166]

As Borneman points out:

> The foreign is not something that has meaning in and of itself, nor is it territorially fixed. It is an unstable counter concept, opposed to the

native and constitutive of the human. Our task is to situate ourselves more clearly in relation to the foreign and to justify our positions more rigorously. Such positions ... provide the grounds on which foreign policy is made and on which distinctions between us and them are drawn.[167]

Therefore, it follows that the division between Europe and the Mediterranean is not necessary but contingent. The EU's Mediterranean area is just one among many possible readings of the EU system of governing the Mediterranean. It is such EU constructions that the speech acts discussed in this chapter were about: that is, the Mediterranean is not a neutral reality but a 'contested concept', the meaning of which is not fixed but fluid. There are numerous ways to construct such an area (in content, nature and scope). Fieldwork offers an additional check on textual analysis as well as a privileged insight into the conditions of possibility of discourses and processes by which the Mediterranean takes on form and meaning. Moreover, the personality and individuality of each Mediterranean partner is an important object for analysis. The next chapter will thereby analyse some of the subjugated discourses of the Mediterranean as they have been investigated in Malta, Greece and Morocco and will present a comparative investigation of these discourses. With this insight, I wish to challenge the notion of the Med partners' learning process by examining the rhetorical strategies employed by Med elites to discursively locate their countries in Europe while othering other Med neighbours. Readers may be surprised that, while recognising the unequal power relationships between the EU and the Med partners, the latter do not always internalise western assumptions about them.

Box 4.1 The EU's othering of the Mediterranean

Europe	*Mediterranean*
civilised	uncivilised
developed	developing/underdeveloped
industrialised	industrialising
postmodern	premodern/modern
stable	unstable
peaceful	conflictual
signifier	signified
subject	object
independent	dependent
coloniser	colonised
centre	periphery
forward looking	backward

This chapter has focused on the fact that although there is not one 'real' Mediterranean, some references to the area may be more close to the everyday and the practices of the people than others (that is, some discourses are more 'powerful' than others). The social construction of the Mediterranean via discourse, therefore, does not imply that all discourses are equally powerful and meaningful. This matter is looked into in some more detail in Chapter 5 which deals with three case studies. Moreover, the Mediterranean region is rather an ambiguous term because discourses are not 'pure' but are always involved in processes of articulation and confrontation. Whereas there may be a shared reference to the Mediterranean by many actors, the concept of the Mediterranean and the 'reality' it is seen to represent are subject to such processes whereby EU member Mediterranean states may articulate the Mediterranean to their overall EU policies, interests, etc. or Mediterranean partners might introduce Mediterranean-ness as a parameter in their regional and global discourses, policies and practices. Other actors may develop different discourses which might not be in a position to accommodate notions such as that of the Mediterranean – we can, for example, observe references to the Black Sea area or the Maghreb that might exclude the Mediterranean and reject its potential meaningfulness and 'reality'.

Table 4.1 offers an attempt, in summary form, at a collection of the regularity of markers of the Mediterranean across EU discourses, including those arising from member states' practices which have made their way through into EU discourses: these regularities are divided into those of a general nature and into those which pertain to either of the three baskets of the EMP.

Summary of the main arguments in this chapter

Regular markers in EU discourses on the Mediterranean

- Power: all member states arguing that there needs to be a balance within EU between focus on CEECs and Med (N+S in EU and CEECs and South/Med).
- Security: linkage between 'Continental/European' security and Mediterranean security (Martino, Italy).
- Threat/risk markers: historical narratives mark regularity in discourse (e.g. references to Kosovo and former Yugoslavia as shedding light on need to focus on Med). Also a marker showing EU spreading its security net wider, for example, through its NNP (lessons learnt from Kosovo, applied by encompassing neighbouring areas, possible 'conflict areas' reasoning).
- Med constituting a homogenous entity. Homogenising techniques include the use of the same references – as in Table 4.1 – often repeated terms which become synonymous with the Med, e.g. FTA, aid, dialogue, etc. and become a homogenising policy instrument.

Table 4.1 Mapping out regularity of Med markers across EU discourses in EMP texts

Discursive markers	France	Italy	Spain	EU	EMP basket	Source
Leadership role in Mediterranean (as an area of influence) – power marker	∧	∧	∧	∧	all	Various
Zone/area of peace and political and social stability, peace and shared economic prosperity ... through a FTA by 2010 ... linked to security				∧	all	Bulletin 2/95 very important marker. EU and the Med: Towards Integration 2003.*
Euro–Mediterranean Charter for Peace and Stability				∧	1st	Various
Sense of ownership, visibility				∧	all	Commission, 2002. 5th EuroMed Conference of Ministers for Foreign Affairs. Valencia Action Plan.
New institutional structures/democracy/ human rights				∧	1st	Commission, 2002. The Barcelona Process, 2001 Review.
Migration, immigration	∧	∧	∧	∧	1st & 3rd	With Morocco, talks around its AA hovered around the issue of migration, as the main EU concern
Security/Eurofor/Euromarfor/linkage between Continental and Med security/security partnership		∧	∧	∧ ∧	1st	Various/1990 Proposal for a CSCM (Italy/Spain)
Sub-regional (intra-) integration/ EuroMed (inter-) integration/ regional integration/create a South-Med market (economic integration, e.g. Agadir)/bilateral? (New Neighbourhood Policy)				∧	2nd	Brussels ministerial 5th Conference of EuroMed Foreign Ministers, Confindustria, March 2003, Presidency Conclusions Crete May 2003

Table 4.1 continued

Discursive markers	France	Italy	Spain	EU	EMP basket	Source
FEMIP, Facility for Euro-Mediterranean Investment and Partnership launched in October 2002 with an endowment of €918 million for 2003–6				>	2nd	Various
Free trade area/trade		>		>	2nd	Various
Interdependence	>	>		>	2nd	Various
Promotion of increased co-operation		>		>	2nd	Various
Economic interests: energy sources, natural gas, oil/national interests		>		>	2nd	Various
Development/reduction of development gap				>	2nd	Various
Liberalisation		>		>	2nd	Various
Reform of economic and social structures				>	2nd & 3rd	Various
Dialogue (political, cultural)	>			>	3rd	Chris Patten, 2002. Commission. The Barcelona Process – the European Mediterranean Partnership, 2001 review. Luxembourg: Office of the Official Publications of the European Communities. Valencia Presidency conclusions 2002
Dialogue among civilisations and among the young						
'Management' of South/Med				>		Various
Bridge	>	>	>	>	3rd	Various
Financial and economic aid				>	2nd	Various

Note
* Commission of the European Communities, 2003c. *European Union and the Mediterranean: Towards Integration*. Final conference of the 'UNIMED Business Network' project. CONFINDUSTRIA, Rome, 11 March. Accessed through the EuroMed Calendar.

- EU-speak of 'assistance' for Med partners.
- Markers provide EU with an identity of who 'we are not'.
- Markers of Med give EU meaning.
- Markers highlight how EMP is framed by the dichotomy of Europe versus the Mediterranean and how the EMP process simultaneously transforms this dichotomy. This policy is underpinned by a broadly orientalist reading that assumes essential differences between Europe and the Mediterranean partners and frames Mediterranean differences from EU member states as a distance from and a lack of European-ness. (Further research on the Mediterranean is required to expose this re-inscription of otherness: postcolonial theory holds a more direct and sustained instrument for carrying out this exercise.) Consequently, the implication of the Med as inferior stems from construing the Med as essentially different from Europe and not yet fully European.
- These markers highlight both the internal consistencies (regularities) within the EU's discourse of the Mediterranean as well as the fluidity and flexibility of this discourse.
- Markers frame the Med in terms of distance from an 'idealised' Europe, that is, Europe as a model to emulate. EU discursive markers channel various representations into a framework – the gradation of Europe – within which it is possible to discuss the Med in terms of proximity to, or likenesss of, Europe. Greece has made it, Malta about to, Morocco still on the lower side of the scale. Turkey is still questionable. Europe is mapped out as the site of specific values. Some Med partners are still marked as lacking these values. The ENP is about encouraging neighbours to align themselves with the 'right' side (framings used through power markers. This is important as to how different kinds and degrees of *otherness* function in the construction of Europe, even today!).
- The concept of 'nesting orientalism' in the case of the Med underscores that the Med is never a fixed location but a characteristic (Mediterranean-ness) attributed differently in different circumstances.[168]
- The Med is an intellectual and political project in EU discursive frameworks that functions to shift 'otherness' further south and provides a platform from which to make appeals for EU assistance and to enhance the EU's role as a 'good' global actor (almost missionary towards the Med or what may be termed as the EU's civilising mission).
- Integration logic theme running through the three EMP baskets: political integration, economic integration and human dimension of integration in the EuroMed region.

5 Discursive practices of the Mediterranean from Greece, Malta and Morocco

A comparative analysis

Having applied a discursive constructivist theoretical framework to EU discourses on the Mediterranean, this chapter will focus on the regular markers across discursive practices in Greece, Malta and Morocco on the Mediterranean and on Europe. It aims to do this by presenting historical background sections on each case study as the doxic backdrop to ongoing debates in these case study countries on the Mediterranean and on Europe: in effect, presenting the past as part of the present discourses. By doing so, this chapter will excavate some overarching generalisations on how the respective nation-building processes involved inform contemporary national discourses on the Mediterranean and on Europe. Hence, it will map out prominent themes, dissonances, incoherencies or coherences in these discourses. These case studies were selected on the basis that, at the time of writing, they are at different stages in their relations with the EU and can therefore offer some varied insights. The question then becomes one of to what extent a particular collective (such as the three cases here) is ready to tear itself away from 'the Mediterranean' and into 'Europe'. The chapter will therefore be divided as follows: the first section will look into the social-historical background of Malta, Greece and Morocco in order to construct the parameters/context of interpretation and understanding responses (prepared from textual analysis and analysed in light of fieldwork carried out in the three countries), and the overall attitudes reflected in them. Then, by adopting a hermeneutic standpoint this chapter will attempt a comparative analysis of elite discourses on issues including the Mediterranean and Europe (the EU and the EMP). This analysis will then be linked to the historical background presented in the first part of the chapter and to the political situation (context) in the cases at the time of writing. This will reveal the historical (past) or cultural background on which some of these discourses are based and which may also be tied up with more contemporary discursive practices (present). Discourses often carry with them embedded cultures or they may reflect the current political situation in the particular context or they may even contain specific conjunctions (discourses that connect other discourses). Culture is here taken to refer to the 'social heritage' of a community: the total body of material artefacts (tools, weapons, houses, places of work, worship, government, recreation, works of art, etc.), of collective mental and spiritual 'artefacts' (systems of symbols, ideas, beliefs, aesthetic perceptions, values, etc.), and of distinctive forms of behaviour (institutions, groupings, rituals, modes of organisation, etc.), created by a people (sometimes deliberately, sometimes through unforeseen interconnections and consequences) in their ongoing activities within their particular life-conditions, and (through undergoing various kinds and degrees of change) transmitted from generation to generation.[1] It is the purpose of this chapter to uncover some workings of elite discourses on the Mediterranean and Europe in Greece, Malta and Morocco. The aim of this chapter is not to neglect any fundamental and fairly obvious differences that exist between the societies under consideration by fitting them into a procrustean bed of structural similarities. The objective is rather to show that those features they have in common provide a basis for a systematic comparison and explanation of their differences. In any case, the present chapter does not claim to offer any definite or final solutions to the empirical and theoretical issues it raises: it merely presents a number of tentative ideas which may stimulate further empirical research and advance the more abstract debates on some basic themes and concepts on the Mediterranean.

A social-historical background: the case of Malta

A deconstruction of history texts of the Maltese Islands helps to uncover regular markers across discourses in Malta on the Mediterranean and Europe and link these to the resilience and adaptability of the Maltese people through history and up to contemporary times. These texts depict an interesting discourse about the permanence of Malta and the Maltese people in the Mediterranean.

Historical narratives link the religion of the first settlers on the islands of Malta and Gozo with Sicily. With its strategic location in the middle of the Mediterranean Sea and the mildness of its climate, Malta was an ideal place for conquerors throughout the ages: Phoenicians, Carthaginians, Romans, Vandals and Goths, Byzantines, Muslim Arabs, Sicilians, Germans, French, feudal lords, Knights Hospitallers of St John of Jerusalem and British. The Turks also raised a siege but were unsuccessful in their attempts: a victory for the Maltese, which is still celebrated as a 'historical event' every year during carnival celebrations.

In spite of its Arabic influence, Malta has always been directed away from Islam and from an Arab culture and instead always considered itself Christian and European. In other words, through these historical, colonial periods Malta has had not only Arab influences but also links with Europe. Yet, the Muslim-Arab influence on the Maltese language and culture of the islands – especially in the popular way of thinking which includes the belief in the will of God: of *Allah* for the faithful Muslim and the will of *Alla* for the Christian Maltese – in its Semitic roots has been accepted.

Narratives of the past 40 years also trace issues of independence and identification processes of the Maltese people. Historical stories give details of the period when proposals were made for Malta's independence and when a new Constitution led to the formation of the 'State of Malta' in 1962. Malta became an independent nation in 1964. Malta's independence led to its links with international organisations (it was already a member of the Commonwealth)[2] including an Association Agreement signed (by the then Nationalist party, or PN (Partit Nazzjonalista), in government) with the EC in 1970. The first general election after independence was held in 1966 and in 1974 the Constitution was revised and Malta became a republic with its first president (Sir Anthony Mamo). The Maltese islands were still dependent, however, on a foreign presence in Malta – they were leased to NATO as a military base and Great Britain was still present militarily. The same movement that clamoured for independence, procured the withdrawal of British forces from the islands. This agreement came into effect in 1979 (popularly known as 'freedom day'). In 1987 Malta was declared a neutral state and non-aligned, without a military base or foreign interference. Now an independent nation, Malta vowed to work for peace, particularly in the Mediterranean basin.

An interesting point lies in the fact that Malta still celebrates independence day *and* freedom day as separate public holidays. Depending on whether one is a Nationalist or a Labourite (the two main political movements in Malta),[3] one will have different perspectives as to when the modern era for Malta began. The Nationalists hold that this occurred on 21 September 1964. This day is observed by this segment of Maltese as Independence Day. However, Malta's still strong alliance with Western powers after 1964 was considered by the Malta Labour Party (MLP) as constituting a strong economic and political dependence on a foreign power. Hence, in contrast to the Nationalists, the Labourites hold that true independence for Malta came when Malta negotiated the withdrawal from the islands (*kicked out* is the term used at times) of all British troops. Thus, according to the MLP, true emancipation from the foreigner was achieved on 31 March 1979 and this date is staunchly observed as Freedom Day. Since this little contest between the two major political parties is difficult to resolve, both dates have been enshrined as national holidays in the Malta calendar.[4]

This division in opinion can also be traced in Malta's relations with Europe at least up until the end of 2003. The MLP has for a long time emphasised the importance of maintaining friendly relations with Malta's Mediterranean neighbours whilst emphasising a close link between security in Europe and security in the Mediterranean in the spirit of the Conference on Security and Co-operation in Europe (CSCE). This political party favoured joining an EFTA-type association. The main argument for this choice was that for a small country like Malta, joining the EU will mean playing second class to big nations like Germany, France and Britain. Thus, Malta's hard-won independence from 'the foreigner' would soon be lost to all the various directives issued from Brussels. In contrast, the PN has always preferred Malta's full membership of the EU. These views on Malta's joining the EU were eventually worked out through the will of the majority of the population via a recent national referendum. (Arguably, referenda can be divisive. In fact, their nature is to divide opinion rather than build a consensus. This is why the will of the majority determines the outcome.) A clear tension/contradiction was observed across Maltese discourses on the EU. Unofficially (following an interview with a prominent Maltese official) the position of the MLP and the PN regarding the EU was quite similar – eventual EU membership for Malta.[5] The difference in these two party positions on this issue was the timing of this process and *how* to get 'there'. The MLP had hoped to take Malta's relations with the EU along a step-by-step, process-based approach, with an-EFTA type of arrangement first and a long run full membership as the ultimate objective for these relations. The PN wanted a quick, 'as soon as possible', 'jump' into EU membership. The official discourses of the two parties were hyped up and differences highlighted especially through media discourses in Malta that play a very important role in influencing people's political attitudes and beliefs.[6]

Malta had originally submitted its EU membership application in July 1990 (under a Nationalist government. The European Commission issued a favourable Opinion Report in 1993). In October 1996 the leader of the MLP, Alfred Sant, came into power and 'froze' Malta's EU application.[7] During the freezing of this application, the EU opened negotiations with other candidates including the Czech Republic, Poland, Hungary, Cyprus, Slovenia and Estonia as the six 'fast-track applicants'. The Labour administration led by Sant adopted a 'step-by-step' foreign policy agenda. The country needed more convincing as to its national interest for a re-activation of its EU application or until geo-strategic realities in Europe and the Mediterranean changed in such a way as to make EU membership a more attractive option. Sant preferred to negotiate a free trade agreement with the EU instead of pursuing the full membership option.

Malta's EU relationship, however, was destined to go through a re-activation. In the (early) election of 1998, the Fenech Adami government was awarded a five-seat majority[8] – clearly a strong political platform for its pursuit of full EU membership negotiations in the shortest possible time frame. A few days after the election, Malta reactivated its EU membership application and managed to catch up with the other nine candidate countries.[9] Despite the opposite extremes along the Maltese political spectrum, a positive result for EU membership was obtained during the referendum on membership held on 8 March 2003 that was followed by a general election on 12 April 2003. The intensity of debates on EU membership can be compared to three historical debates that the Maltese 'polis' experienced after the Second World War, namely the debate on the integration of Malta with the United Kingdom (1955–8), the quest for independence (1962–4) and the crisis over majority rule (1981–7).[10] Moreover, the discursive events around the issue of EU membership have been internalised by the Labour party which underwent a thorough internal debate on its EU policy. Respecting the democratic will of the majority of the Maltese people, the position of the Maltese Labour party turned around and changed its historical anti-EU policy. Although this change occurred in just a few months, the turnaround in the Malta Labour Party's policy on the EU can be compared to that which the Greek Panellino Socialistiko Kinima (or Pan Hellenic Socialist Movement, PASOK) experienced, albeit after a longer time span.[11] The Party of European Socialists unanimously accepted the MLP as a full member on 14 November 2003 and marked a crucial step for the MLP to prepare the party for the European Parliamentary elections of June 2004.

With the return in 1998 of Fenech Adami's pro-EU government, Malta also continued its proactive constructive role in the Euro-Mediterranean process that was launched in Barcelona in November 1995. This included furthering the association and partnership roles developed within the framework of the EMP process. In April 1997 Malta hosted the second Euro-Mediterranean ministerial meeting. Malta has also been promoting the idea of a stability pact for the Mediterranean.[12] Although it claimed to have adopted a 'EuroMed' balanced foreign policy agenda, the main priority for Fenech Adami's government has been Malta's full EU membership. Current popular and political narratives might ignore any references to history and connection with the Phoenicians and Arabs due to the negative loading of the terms Arab, Middle Eastern or North African: the Maltese people are a Mediterranean people having a Mediterranean presence which can be traced throughout the history of the islands. In other words, history and geography have placed Malta in a Mediterranean context[13] – yet, despite some Arab influence, Christianity reigned and therefore the Maltese are not Muslims. As already mentioned, this identity statement is also reflected in the way in which Turks are portrayed as the 'other', the 'enemy' and the 'bad and evil' party in carnival rituals every year in contrast to the good and friendly Knights. This ritual commemorates the March 1565 appearance of the Turkish armada off Fort St Elmo. The 'Mediterranean' feeling is still strongly reflected within the ambit of Maltese and Gozitan village feasts, festivals, fairs, carnivals and *souks* (markets). These quintessentially Mediterranean rituals and rites reflect the islanders' sense of celebration, the importance accorded to such practices and the persistence of pre-industrial forms of social togetherness. In such cases relating to Maltese identity, a gap appears between the operative discourse and action on the one hand and what 'ought to be said and done' on the other (that is, between what the Maltese are not – Turks, Muslims or Arabs – and what the Maltese are – Europeans). This trait can be depicted as a set of concentric circles emphasising how identity is fluid and flexible at the same time as it is a core aspect of collective 'selfhood', a fundamental, deep, basic, abiding and foundational condition of social being.[14]

Maltese identity is also reflected in the people's tradition of struggling for independence and pride in independence. In Foucauldian terms, when these practices are repeated thereafter in a regular fashion and in a similar manner over long periods of time, they then acquire a sense of durability and stability.

EU membership has been a thorny issue between the two main political parties because it impinges on Malta's sovereignty and independence from any form of foreign rule. The new MLP policy on the EU has been opposed by a former prime minister of Malta and former leader of the MLP, Karmenu Mifsud Bonnici, who had founded the Campaign for National Independence (CNI) to campaign against Malta's membership after EU membership negotiations were started. Bonnici later joined Dom Mintoff (Maltese prime minister 1955–8, 1971–85) at the head of a new organisation, the Front Maltin Iqumu (Maltese Arise! Front). The very title of the organisation echoes embedded feelings against any new form of colonisation and a call for the Maltese people to join hands in their struggle against oppressors and arise once again to the occasion: an important event which marks past historical experiences as part of the present discourses. The Maltese elite discourses that will be analysed below have to be reflected upon in the light of these historical issues. These embedded feelings also find their way into discourses on the EMP. In general terms, Nationalist supporters reinforced the possibility of Malta's enhanced position within the EU in a post-colonial world. The Labourites, on the other hand, emphasised Malta's loss of independence, its loss of sovereignty and the loss of its unique language and identity once it joined the EU.[15] This anti-imperialist stance held that after having stood against so many foreign forces through the years, Maltese identity had to be restored.[16] These different positions are reflected in the responses given by Maltese elites as regards to their identity and affiliations and on EU-EMP issues – issues which one may trace back to the days of struggle for independence and freedom day. The MLP's turnaround in its policy on Europe has not only transformed the duopoly/competitive nature of Maltese politics but also underscores the dual nature of Maltese nationalism. As a long-time colonised people, the Maltese have long struggled for independence and Maltese nationalism has thus been historically defined by this necessity. At the same time, the small size of the islands has encouraged Maltese governments to have some form of relationship with Europe in order to be tacked onto the European mainstream and avoid isolation. This dual nature in Maltese nationalism was recently reflected in the membership negotiations where the Maltese language was accepted as an official EU language, a crucial symbol for Maltese nationalism.

A social-historical background: the case of Greece

The official history of Greece to date traces a strong tradition in seeing the Greek nation as a continuous line of inheritance from classical antiquity to modern Greece.[17] Since medieval times and in the modern era, the main threat for the Greek people were the 'Latins' – that is, anybody from the West. Much effort was dedicated to promote a certain self-understanding of Greekness in opposition to other competing alternatives. Through processes of identification, Greek national identity was mapped out in terms of what *is* part of the national self and what *is not*.[18] One can uncover such efforts through the relationality established between the Greek Orthodox Church (East) and the (Latin) Catholic and Protestant churches (West).[19] The Greek Church has always felt closer to its Slav neighbours in this respect and to Islam. Islam has not been a threat since it has historically acted as a guarantor of the Greeks' existence (during the period when Islam fought against the (Christian Latins).[20] The pro- and anti-Europe positions in Greece can be traced back to this ecclesiastical view. The two main traditions in thinking can be split into one group that emphasises Eastern Orthodoxy and differences and is quite ambivalent (but not entirely negative and is similar to the case in Malta) on EU membership,[21] and a second group that argues for a European orientation for Greece.[22]

European intellectuals from the time of the Enlightenment and since, have posited Greece as the cradle of European civilisation. Greece was at these times configured as a Western European culture and was associated with modern democracies. The Greek enlightenment movement accepted this stance and pushed for the Westernisation of their country. Another aspect of Greek culture links Greece with the Orient, North Africa, Egypt, Syria and Lebanon. This school of thought created cultures of resistance against the West and vernacular groups in Greece. Hence, Greece has always been defined in two ways: on the one hand, the Enlightenment way – that is, the non-Orient way; some Greeks speak of themselves as 'Romioi', that is, Roman and thereby educated according to Western Enlightenment and of how modern Greece can be seen as a purified kind of Greece.[23] On the other hand, the vernacular/resistance way, which emphasises Mediterranean/Balkan elements. This school of thought is supported by the Greek Orthodox Church. It is possible to trace elements of this view in the day-to-day culture of Greece, for example in music and food that are very similar to those found in the 'Orient'. The split and ambivalent identity in Greece and Malta between European and Mediterranean (or Balkan in Greece) elements marks a regular discourse across these cases. Moreover, the respective nation-building processes inform present discourses on the Mediterranean and Europe in both cases.

It was during the early 1800s that the notion of the Greek state and Greek-ness emerged. The period between 1833 and 1913 was one of independence from Ottoman rule, nation building and irredentism.[24] Since many Greeks still remained under alien rule, this fact had a profound influence on the policies, both domestic and foreign, of the independent state. The educational system of the new state was based on French and German models and institutional structures were moulded in accordance with a conservative European model. A lot of emphasis was placed on the study of the classics of ancient Greek literature and on knowledge of a 'purified' form of the language (depicting what is *ours*, what *Greekness* is about). The Greek Church was declared to be independent but firmly subordinated to the state. The large Greek populations who were still under Ottoman rule had little consciousness of being Greek, in particular the Turkish-speaking Greeks of Anatolia, and the irredentist aspirations of the Greeks had little effect on them. On the other hand, many Ottoman Greeks, particularly those in the large and prosperous communities of the coastal cities of the empire, with their excellent and richly endowed schools, were fully conscious of their Greek heritage. During the financial collapse of December 1893, the Greek economy was in dire straits. This gave impetus to emigration, an important safety valve in times of economic distress. Between 1890 and 1914 about 350,000 Greeks (approximately one-sixth of the entire population) migrated to the USA. (A similar flux of Maltese migrated to Canada, the USA, Australia and the UK after the Second World War.) The remittances they sent to their families in Greece were important for the Greek balance of payments. (The expatriate Moroccan community has also sent similar remittances from savings to their relatives in Morocco. Such remittances have been the prime source of income of the Moroccan state for two–three decades.)[25] Some Greeks also emigrated to Egypt.[26]

In the 1920s, there was a massive influx of refugees that placed enormous strains on the cohesion of Greek society. In 1936, the radicalisation of the working-class movement reached its peak with a massive strike of tobacco workers in Macedonia. This led to the death of 22 strikers. A subsequent general strike was initiated. One day before the launching of a second general strike, John Metaxas stepped in and established a dictatorial regime that put an abrupt end to parliamentary politics and trade-union autonomy in interwar Greece.[27] An outright civil war broke out between 1946 and 1949. The communists who had taken the lead in resistance against the Axis occupiers tried an unsuccessful armed bid for power. When George Papandreou replaced Venizelos, he enjoyed British support as he was anti-communist and determined to prevent a communist assumption of power. In fact, a government led by Papandreou landed in Greece on 18 October 1944. For much of the twentieth century the issue of monarchy versus republic was a vital topic. A constitutional monarchy type of government was rejected by referendum on 8 December 1974.[28]

A highly politicised army has frequently intervened in Greek politics. This led to the Colonels' dictatorship of 1967–74.[29] During and following the fall of the dictatorship of the Colonels, the Greeks sought to restore democracy in Greece until their country became a modern nation. (Approximately the same time as the Maltese 'kicked out' the British.) There was some opposition and resistance to the Greek dictatorship during its final years in particular.[30] Since 1974, the Greek political party scene has been dominated by two main parties: the socialist PASOK and the conservative Nea Demokratia (ND). (These two main parties are similar to the MLP and the PN in Malta respectively. PASOK also had a strong populist tradition (which differentiates it from the MLP).)[31]

As regards the Cyprus issue, Greeks maintain an anti-imperialist position.[32] Greeks blame the British and the Americans for this problem that underpins

Greek animosity toward Turkey.[33] The constitution drafted on 16 August 1960, which proclaimed Cyprus to be an independent state, is believed to have been the source of problems on the issue.[34] This matter is a balance of power game between Greece and Turkey but security and stability in the Balkans remain Greece's primary (security/political/foreign policy) concerns.

Greek suspicions have been underlying its regional identity that has fluctuated in accordance with the political environment at the time in Greece and the ability of political parties to use this to their advantage.[35] Upon deeper analysis, one can trace a degree of localism/nationalism in Greek historical discourses as well as more contemporary discourses. (A degree of localism/ nationalism can also be traced in the history of Malta especially during Mintoff's era. Just before the end of each and every political mass (popular) meeting he held, Mintoff would always finish with the words 'Għax Malta tal-Maltin u tiġi l-ewwel u qabel kollox' [because Malta belongs to the Maltese and it will always be the first priority before anything else]. This may be interpreted as quite a nationalistic discourse and uncovers/reveals the historical struggle for independence and freedom from foreign rule. Mintoff also emphasised Malta's good neighbourly relations with Libya and is famous for the controversy he raised in Malta when he stated that the Maltese and the Libyans were 'blood brothers'. His emphasis on Malta having a say went as far as declaring that Malta would have its best international standing as a leader of the North African states rather than as a little island in the big European ocean where Malta would have no say at all.)[36] The discourse of Balkan/south-eastern Europe in Greece is an important one and depicts a similar regular marker of nationalist discourses in Malta and Greece.[37] Within this latter discourse, a whole society abandons its Mediterranean identity and invests all its political and cultural energies in this 'region' it is constructing for its own survival. As mentioned earlier, Greeks feel that they have more in common with their Slav neighbours. The Mediterranean still seems far away for Greeks, unless a political discourse incorporates this area. When a political discourse such as that of a Balkan/south-eastern European identity emerges, it works to eliminate a Mediterranean 'feeling' among the Greeks: this is reinforced externally by the EC's/EU's division between the Balkans and the Mediterranean. Moreover, as Foucault states, when discourses are institutionalised (by political parties) they tend to have more durability even though they are the products of a construct. Greece today has a European orientation yet it has its own Balkan/eastern Mediterranean concerns that relate to security and identity issues (the Greeks are *for* Europe but they will keep their differences).[38]

Modern Greece and nationalism in Greece are, to a substantial degree, premised on opposition to Turkish rule. Turkey and occasionally the West are portrayed as the 'other' of Greece. Greece may occasionally perceive the Mediterranean through its 'eastern' Mediterranean prism or it does not conceive of it at all.[39] In fact, Greece sees its EMP partners as being far away from the 'realities' it faces, be they political or otherwise. Relations between

Greece and Turkey have warmed since both countries suffered earthquakes during 1999 and offered each other practical help. This will be dealt with in more detail below, in the analysis of Greek elite discourses.

In summary, Greece has its religious anti-European elements that hold that Greek interests are in the East (especially spiritually). On the other hand, Greece has had its anti-dictatorship and pro-European movement.[40] Andreas Papandreou's PASOK came to power on an anti-imperialist ticket in 1980 and promised the closure of NATO bases.[41] In 1981, PASOK flagged its pride in EU membership and highlighted Greece's eventual membership of the EMU.[42] With Papandreou's resignation in 1996 (due to old age), Kostas Simitis was chosen as PASOK's leader. He called general elections early in September 1996 and PASOK secured a victory over ND (Nea Demokratia). Simitis was far more pro-European than his predecessor and managed to get the Greek economy in sufficiently good shape to meet the criteria for monetary union. (Greece joined the EMU in January 2001.) However, on the domestic front, Simitis failed to solve unemployment problems, corruption scandals and bureaucratic hurdles that deter foreign investors. Early in 2004, he announced an early general election on 7 March and made way for George Papandreou who took over the leadership of PASOK. The Greeks' desire for more economic security and better services in areas like education and healthcare led to the downfall of the Greek socialists and the coming into power of Costas Karamanlis of the ND. These events reflect some of the key parameters of the political culture in modern Greece.[43]

A social-historical background: the case of Morocco

The history of Morocco reveals the orientation Morocco has had to Mediterranean European countries, especially France and Spain and Mediterranean Arab countries, and Morocco's relations with the USA.

Before the European colonial powers began carving up Morocco, it was mostly under Berber rule. These medieval dynasties were an important force in the formulation of Morocco's identity. With an outdated and medieval form of government (by European standards) and virtual bankruptcy, Morocco could do little to resist European domination. It actually found itself locked in European rivalry. The first pressures came from the French who occupied Algiers in 1830. During the reign of Mohammed III (1859–73), the Spanish occupied Tetouan.[44]

In 1904, France and Spain reached a secret agreement on how they were going to divide Morocco. Colonial occupation began in 1907. In 1912 with the Treaty of Fez, the French were given the right to 'protect'[45] Morocco and represent it abroad. A similar document was signed with Spain. The colonial divisions of Morocco were very artificial.[46] The French *'mission civilisatrice'* meant that France intended to extend the benefits of French culture and language to all corners of its colonies and protectorates.[47] There were several revolts including the important one against the French in 1912. An armed revolt arose when the Spanish tried to extend their control into the Rif mountains of the interior. Faced with the Spanish troops the Berber tribes of the region united under the leadership of Abd El-Krim (around 1920). After the rebellion was crushed,[48] the route to Moroccan independence changed from armed revolt to evolving middle-class resistance to the colonial rulers. The educated classes of Rabat and Fez were the first to demand reforms from the French that would give greater rights to Moroccans. When the government failed to respond, the demand for reforms escalated into demands for total independence. In 1943 the Independence party of Morocco called for complete separation from France. Morocco gained full independence from France and Spain in 1956. On independence, Sultan Mohammed V changed his title to that of king, and paved the path to a constitutional monarchy.[49] As leader of the Muslim faith and the figurehead of independence, he commanded huge support and influence in Morocco as a whole. It is also important to note here the importance of the *Makhzan*. This word refers to:

> the centuries-old apparatus of government and political influence that is under the exclusive control of the Palace, and through which the monarchy still exercises much of its authority. The *Makhzan* consists of a nation-wide network of influential individuals and families that share three main attributes: their influence at the local level or within a particular segment of the Moroccan population, their intimate knowledge of their own sphere of influence, and their allegiance to the throne. Unlike the institutions around which the formal political system is built (the monarchy, the cabinet, the legislature, the judiciary, and local government), the *Makhzan* and its prerogatives are not discussed in the constitution. Moreover, unlike the modern state – with its clearly visible pyramid of government bureaucracies and elected bodies that reach from the local to the national level – the *Makhzan* operates under the surface, and is run directly from the Palace by (the) King ... and his inner circle.[50]

In 1963, Morocco had its first parliamentary elections. In party politics, two main parties emerged following independence: the Mouvement Populaire (MP), a moderate party set up to represent the Berbers,[51] and the Union Nationale des Forces Populaires (UNFP), a left-wing party. ('Berber' no longer seems to signify the unspoken dirty word that it once used to. Conceptually it has come to occupy the historical and sociological backbone of the Moroccan nation.) A tendency towards parties dividing within and among themselves has been apparent in Moroccan politics ever since (similar to Maltese and Greek political parties, especially the MLP and PASOK respectively) – which helps to maintain the primal role of the Palace in the political arena.[52] The king built links with the army – with the help of Crown Prince Hassan (who was the army's commander-in-chief) – and with the police.

The French and Spanish interventions in Morocco, however, penetrated its society and left an important mark on Moroccan identity that is still visible today (past as part of the present discourse in Morocco).[53] Morocco is a North African country but retains strong links with Europe. Morocco's first association agreement with the EEC, to run for five years, was signed in Rabat on 31 March 1969. This was a partial agreement limited to trade and excluded any economic assistance.

During the 1980s, Morocco approached the EU for full EU membership – an overture which was turned down. Morocco's economic relations with the EU from the late 1970s to the early 1990s were not without difficulties and shortcomings. EU financial aid in its absolute level was quite modest in relation to Morocco's development needs.[54] In December 1992, following evolving EU efforts to prioritise the Mediterranean basin, the European Commission adopted a 'Negotiation Instructions Draft' for a future association agreement between the EU and Morocco. In 1994 the EU offered an agricultural proposal to Morocco.[55] In January 1995, Morocco's negotiations with the EU to adapt the 1976 co-operation agreement came to an end. Inconclusive discussions on the gradual opening of the European market to Moroccan agricultural products were held and proved very difficult. Apart from the difficulty in resolving various issues,[56] progress in negotiating an association agreement became closely tied to negotiations for a new Moroccan–EU fisheries agreement.[57] The two sides wanted the opposite sequence of events: Morocco wanted to conclude a new association agreement and then follow it with a new fisheries agreement while the EU wanted the reverse.[58]

During King Hassan's reign – which represented the longest period of stability in the country's troubled history – Morocco experienced a huge population explosion and there are now some 30 million Moroccans – most of whom are very young.[59] Graduate unemployment is almost 80 per cent (while the overall unemployment rate is 18.4 per cent according to 2002 estimates).[60] Hassan II was considered to be a very modern monarch but he was also careful to maintain his status as traditional ruler. Hassan II used traditions based on the days of the Sultanate to underpin his modern monarchy and they seem to have served him well. The king[61] also played a central role in government. At times there have been some violent incidents in the kingdom's universities, where the student movement is linked to Morocco's biggest party, the Union Socialiste des Forces Populaires (USFP). Mention can also be made of the growing appeal of the Islamists. USFP was established through its linkage with UNFP. USFPists wanted to enter government, become social democrats and abandon 'revolutionary' alternatives. The violence in universities has been caused by clashes between government forces (police, military) and Marxist/Socialist groups (not USFP). From the 1960s to the mid-1980s, clashes occurred between different political movements in the universities through the whole period.[62] Since the mid-1980s Islamist movements have been the dominant political opposition in Morocco. The violence against these has been organised by the state apparatus.

In economic, political and civil society terms Morocco is still perceived as a developing country. However, this does not necessarily mean that Morocco is developing towards a Western type of state: first of all, it does not have a multi-party democracy and a lot depends on the monarchy and the clan system. Moreover, the country has not yet developed a number of differentiated institutions that the 'West' recognises as modern liberal ones.[63] The king emphasises how tradition is very strong in the Maghreb, and that Morocco is built around tolerance. He also states that Morocco needs its own model for democracy and that his main challenges are Morocco's poverty, misery and illiteracy. He further reveals that he does not want Europe to help Morocco but to treat Morocco as a partner. (It may be argued that this is an issue of self-respect.) He also calls for the eradication of European misunderstandings of Moroccans. This has become more challenging after the Madrid 11 March 2004 bombings after which a number of Moroccans were arrested. Thus, the king faces a number of diverse challenges.[64] First of all he has the Western Sahara issue. This issue accounts for the strained relations between Morocco and Algeria. While Morocco still claims the territory, Algeria supports the independence-seeking Polisario front. The young king has been attempting to reinvigorate the Arab Maghreb Union which includes Morocco, Algeria, Libya, Mauritania and Tunisia [65] and to return his kingdom to the Organisation of African Unity which it left in 1984 over the admission of the Saharawi Arab Democratic Republic (SADR). Since Morocco is affected by northward migration, Mohammed VI constantly calls for the alleviation of suffering of Africans, particularly those living south of the Sahara who are confronted with fratricidal wars, the burden of external debt[66] and the lack of infrastructures.

Another diplomatic challenge for the king has been the strengthening of Morocco's economic partnership with the EU.[67] In 1995, Rabat rejected the possibility of renewing its fishing agreement that expired on 30 November 1999. However, there is now movement and a modest agreement is expected fairly soon.[68]

Recently, an agricultural trade liberalisation agreement was signed between the EU and Morocco and entered into force on 1 January 2004 after being approved by the EU Council of Ministers on 22 December 2003 and by the relevant Moroccan authorities. This Agreement takes the form of an exchange of letters between the EU and the Moroccan government. It replaces the Protocol to the AA with the EU regarding reciprocal agricultural trade. The said Agreement provides for liberalisation of reciprocal agricultural trade across a wide spectrum, including fruit, vegetables, meat and flowers, and opening in particular new opportunities for Moroccan exports of tomatoes to the EU. The provision on tomato quotas have been in force since 1 October 2003 as an exception to take into account the start of the marketing year for tomatoes and to avoid market disturbance.

Despite difficulties in EU–Moroccan relations on the fisheries issue, Morocco has established a reputation as a very skilled negotiating partner with a very articulate position. The EMP offers Morocco an environment in which it can negotiate its position in this regard.[69] In its other relations with

Europe, Morocco also chose dialogue for the settlement of the thorny issue of Ceuta and Melilla, currently occupied by Spain.[70] On the Arab front, Mohammed VI will strive to preserve the constructive role his country has so far played in the peaceful settlement of the Middle East crisis. On the domestic front, issues of human rights, unemployment and social inequality remain to be addressed. Since his ascendancy to the throne, the king has been expected to take concrete steps in these directions.[71] So far, his popular progressive policies have indeed brought about political and social changes. In early 2004, women's rights improved under government initiatives to eliminate polygamy, raise the legal marriage age from 15 to 18, and grant divorced women rights to 50 per cent of the couple's assets.[72] Muhammad also decided to free almost 3,000 political prisoners connected with Polisario and the Western Sahara conflict, and in 2002, he announced his intention to make some form of self-rule possible for the occupied Western Sahara.

Comparison of the social-historical backgrounds of the case studies

As a summary of the above, this section attempts to highlight the common or diverse aspects that these three case studies share in their social-historical backgrounds, particularly highlighting the respective nation-building processes in each case and how these inform national discourses on the Mediterranean and on Europe. What can be observed are the attempts that were made in each case to recontextualise the links of the country with the Mediterranean or the Orient or Europe and how each case recasts these links as unique aspects of the respective country.

To begin with, it is clear that through their nation-building processes, the three countries have had a strong movement that resisted foreign rule and struggled for the country's independence. A poem at the time of the Greek national movement for independence ends with 'an exhortation to the Greeks not to place any faith in foreign powers as potential liberators as they were only interested in furthering their own interests'.[73] Greece emerges as the oldest country in this sense[74] since it gained its independence in 1832, followed by Morocco which regained its independence in 1956 and Malta in 1964. However, the 'modern' era[75] is said to have started in Greece as late as after 1974 when the dictatorship collapsed and the country sought to restore democracy and to make Greece a modern nation. In Malta, this issue is a controversial one between the two main political parties. For the – rather outdatedly named – PN, the start of the modern era for Malta came on 21 September 1964 but for the Labour Party it is 31 March 1979 when the last British fleets were seen out of the grand harbour. As for Morocco, one can state that it is characterised by a rather late rendezvous with the modern era.[76] In terms of regimes, Morocco is the only case with a monarchy[77] and where the king is both the state figurehead as well as the spiritual leader of the people. Malta and Greece are both parliamentary democracies.

The experiences of these countries with independence have a lot to uncover about their identities. Identity boundaries of these regional groupings, in fact, have their own historical depth. Moroccans have an interesting orientation with an identity that oscillates between a North African, a Maghrebian and an Arab one with some affinity to the Middle East.[78] This fluid identity has been strongly influenced by the Berbers.[79] Morocco also has a Mediterranean-European orientation especially towards France and Spain (but, arguably, proximity to Europe also comes into it). This is shared with Malta although recently there has been much more emphasis on Malta's European identity particularly during the phase of Malta's EU accession negotiations. By emphasising their European credentials the Maltese sought to shift the discursive boundaries between Europe and the Med further south and to thereby move themselves into Europe.[80] Morocco claims to have strong links with Europe. Morocco has also had an Atlantic link to the USA developed during the Cold War. Due mainly to its security concerns and to the centrality of religion to national identity (historically), Greece orients its (ambivalent) identity more towards the Balkans and south-eastern Europe rather than the Mediterranean.[81] An eastern Mediterranean identity is as far as Greeks may go with regards to a Mediterranean identity.[82] As to their very vague European identity, it is still not uncommon to hear a Greek say 'I am going to Europe', when travelling to London or Paris![83] Greece and Malta have both experienced Turkish, Arab and Islamic confrontations and the (identity) discourse of these as an 'other' who ought to be kept at bay remains up to this day. The historical addressivity in each case situates the meaning and referent of national identity as an expression of a 'people', a 'nation', expressed in relation to a temporal continuum: the present discourse uttering past and shared historical experiences, which are never really fixed by time.[84]

As to language, the Maltese and the Greeks are both very proud of their Maltese and Greek respectively. In Morocco, although Arabic is the national language, spoken as the first language by around 55 per cent of the population, Berber is the first language of the remainder. Moreover, Morocco still carries its French influence through the French language that is widely spoken (Morocco has not yet had the kind of language battle that Algeria has had).[85] Language is an important mark on these countries' identities. The regularity in these markers across discourses in Greece, Malta and Morocco define the necessary relation and dependence of present to/on the past (nation-building processes, nationalism, etc.) and how identity is an element/continuous flow in the making through multiple processes.

In terms of religion, as an important marker along a country's nation-building process, Morocco is the only Muslim country of the three. Malta is mostly Catholic and Greece Orthodox. The Maltese and Greek attitudes *vis-à-vis* Islam are quite similar. Both state that they have been very close to yet not overrun by Islamic rule. Yet, Christianity persevered in Malta and Greece respectively. In Malta, however, Orthodoxy has been perceived as Oriental, that is, different from Malta's religious affiliation. In this respect, Greece has often been placed in the same category as an Oriental in the eyes of the Maltese.[86] These specific discursive practices/cartographic mappings, however, often have to do with specific geographies that are drawn by Europe:[87] borders delineating who is 'in' and who is 'out'. For Malta, Greece lies to the East. This clearly emerged during discussions with Maltese interviewees on discourses of the Mediterranean where the said interviewees categorised the Mediterranean into a number of subregions, one of which was that of Greece/ Turkey/Cyprus which they claimed 'had affinities towards the East' (the East as being 'out there'). Islam and Greek Orthodoxy are often both seen as equally barbaric in Malta. In fact, some Maltese interviewees share a discourse about Greek Orthodoxy according to which it is not 'really' Western/European (this seems to echo Greek ambivalence over European identity, although this has recently changed) – due to the Christian (in the eyes of the Maltese particularly Catholic and Protestant) label that Europe carries with it. It is important to note here the relation between the state and the Church in Malta and Greece. In both cases the Church is officially independent and firmly subordinated to the state. However, the Church has historically had a strong influence on state matters. For instance, the Church was seen as a major obstacle to the rise in the cultural level of compatriots, especially the intellectuals, many of whom rejected the corruption of the Church as an institution.

In terms of geographic discourses in these countries, Malta and Greece present themselves at the fringe and border of Europe and therefore as bridges: the concept of the 'bridge' emerged as a clear regular marker across discourses in Greece, Malta and Morocco:[88] Malta as a bridge between Europe and North Africa and Greece as a bridge between the Middle East and Europe. Greek interviewees claimed that this gives Greece a kind of Mediterranean role. These are examples of local frameworks for understanding Maltese and Greek identity discourses. Upon deeper analysis, one may of course discover some cultural or political bias in these contexts.[89] Morocco also stresses its critical position as an ideal intermediary between the Arab (North Africa/Maghreb) and the Western world (Europe). But in the background of these discursive practices (present) lurk historical communications (past) – especially trade-related communications, the sea-faring experiences of Maltese and Greek life – which these countries shared across and around the Mediterranean Sea.[90] (This observation includes the traditional African trade routes of Morocco.) The result of this was a geopolitical and geocultural immersion of these countries in the Mediterranean. For Morocco, however, the Maghreb is a more appropriate place for it to be involved in – in contemporary times. An interesting ambiguity can be traced in this Moroccan discourse. Morocco has been involved in the AMU, but for dealings with the EU it prefers separate dealings and a special relationship. A Spanish source claimed that Moroccans preferred NATO's Mediterranean dialogue (19 + 1) to the EMP (currently 15 + 12) for this reason.[91] Malta, on the other hand, still has good relations with Italy and Libya while Greece has been orienting its relations more towards the eastern Mediterranean – when it was part of the Ottoman empire its (political, economic and cultural) discourses could stretch as far as Egypt: hence its more vivid modern discourses of the 'Near East' and the Balkans. These concepts of bridges and borders show how geography is manipulated. Malta and Greece have Christian borders between the Islamic and the European worlds and emphasise their countries as meeting points of multi-religious gatherings.

As regards the three countries' discourses on Europe, the EU and the EMP, there are some important common elements and differences too. For instance, the Socialist parties in Malta and Greece, the MLP and PASOK held an anti-imperialist and anti-European discourse in respect of EU membership.[92] PASOK and more recently the MLP have, however, become more pro-European officially although there are still divisions within these parties on this issue. On the other hand, the Maltese PN and the Greek ND have similarly shared a very pro-European stance. Malta and Morocco are both quite active within the EMP. The PN has striven hard for full membership of the EU by stressing Malta's European identity. Greece has felt threatened historically by the West and still has problems in affiliating with Europe. It feels quite distant from its Mediterranean partners of the EMP too.

Since it may be argued that the EU helps in shaping national discourses, it is important to end this section with a brief mention of the EU's policy towards the sub-regional areas to which each case country is normally attached. As regards Malta, the EU has clearly accepted this country as a European candidate from the initial stage of Malta's submission of its EU application. Clearly, Malta is treated differently from North African countries like Morocco since the Commission announced that Malta was eligible for accession negotiations for the 2004 enlargement of the EU. Malta has been treated as a country in the entry hall of Brussels. There is no constitutional problem with Malta whilst there seems to be with the case of Turkey.[93] Hence, the EU considers Malta as European but not North African – such as Algeria or Morocco – for example. This, as stated above, was not the case for Morocco which the EU treats as a partner – albeit one of its most important partners in the Maghreb with its rich offshore fishing grounds.[94] The EU often also gives a lot of attention to Morocco due to issues that have been persistently problematic between this country and Spain. Apart from the fishing waters off Morocco, the agricultural products of Spain that are directly competitive with those of Morocco are among the issues on the EU–Morocco agenda. These issues place the EU as an intermediary[95] between one of its member states and one of its EMP partners. Morocco has another thorny issue – that of the Western Sahara – which causes friction with one of its close Maghrebian neighbours, Algeria. However, the EU still managed to bring the two countries within the EMP process and the Western Sahara issue does not seem to impede progress in common Mediterranean concerns (as the MEPP does for instance).[96] As regards Greece, the EU treats this state as a crucial member in its south-east European stability programme. (Also a result of Greece's sympathies for Serbia, which have affected sanctions against Belgrade.) Greece has often been a stumbling bloc for the EU whenever issues relating to Turkey have arisen within the Brussels corridors with Greece often threatening to use its veto power.[97]

These are different identity issues that relate to how the EU perceives Malta, Morocco and Greece. From the EU's side, these may be said to reflect specific cultural biases or specific local frameworks of understanding these countries and how they are constructed as (specific frameworks) fields of knowledge and the underlying *meaning* of the Mediterranean that ensues from these processes. Meaning is therefore never entirely fixed in time but rather a continuous flow. As different *problématiques* emerge from the Mediterranean area through time, they continuously reactivate a variety of meaning-labels attached particularly from 'external' powers.[98] Some aspects of these countries' relations with the other Mediterranean partners of the EMP may relate to a long experience of participation in Mediterranean affairs. For example, a common historical sea-faring tradition. One may argue, however, that these are still marked by huge differences. They may also have their own local frameworks where interviewees place the Mediterranean as, for instance, a secondary priority on their foreign policy agenda. These issues will be analysed further below.

As the second section of this chapter will attempt to show, there is a 'Europe' consciousness in each case country but there is a specific treatment of each country and its surrounding area from the EU's side. The next chapter of this book will try to speculate about whether this has always been the case.

Having established the socio-historical background to the case countries of this book, this chapter now moves to identify contemporary elite discourses from these societies on the Mediterranean, the EU and the EMP. The formation of these discourses will be examined in the light of their historical and contemporary contexts.

Local frameworks for understanding the Mediterranean: an interpretation of the Mediterranean 'identity/identities nexus'

It cannot be denied that any attempt at defining the Mediterranean as an empirical entity is quite a complex task. Such definitions depend on the political, economic and societal commitments of those who undertake such an endeavour. Moreover, when a Mediterranean is identified, or rather, when various 'Mediterraneans' are identified, these can vary between a Mediterranean of the imagination, particularly associated with the Roman Empire at its peak, and a 'Romantic' Mediterranean and a 'scholarly' Mediterranean – chiefly the product of northern European travellers and intellectuals.[99] Historic Mediterranean discourses uncover a whole history of the relationship between people and their environments in and around the Mediterranean and their relations with the wider world and offer us frameworks through which we can use the present to elucidate the past. Associated with these meanings are the notions of Mediterranean 'identities' as *une trame du monde*, a weave of the world's surface. The Mediterranean's unity yet fragmentation, its interconnected local places, its web of microenvironments make up a set of loci of contact that overlap and in which political, economic, social and ecological change are bound up with each other – a necessary understanding of a complex space like the Mediterranean. Mediterranean agricultural systems and processes have, for example, throughout the years, played a crucial role in inducing economic stability at times and, in some circumstances, instability. Nowadays the immobility of Mediterranean peasantry no longer holds: local continuities over many generations of rural life are not expected. Many ethnographic studies also highlight the role of religion in the Mediterranean as a rich and multi-layered canvas of spiritual occasions and places and sites of boundaries and belongingness: interlocking historical processes operating at different timescales amidst this rich and mostly shifting mosaic of peoples and places therefore offers us the possibility of detecting underlying themes in contemporary discourses on the Mediterranean. Taking particular Mediterranean societies today and reflecting on their recent and not so recent past allows us to uncover how none of these cases are isolated from their contemporary worlds nor are they frozen-in-aspic lifeways of antiquity. Indeed, the one observation of the Mediterranean people which strikes any observer has been their readiness to shift along a spectrum of possibilities.[100]

This section will identify the main themes and attitudes that emanated from the fieldwork trips carried out in Malta, Morocco and Greece. The main themes which will be analysed here are discursive practices (read discourses and practices) from these case countries on the Mediterranean, Europe, the EU and the EMP.[101] The analysis hopes to reveal interviewees' emotional attachments which were intertwined with the political and pragmatic views they expressed in their responses to these discourses.

This analysis will thus attempt to show how interviewees adopt instrumental views in their discursive practices. It will also reveal how (present) discourses reflect a historical reference point (past) or more contemporary political tactics – the path back to history or an orientation of the Mediterranean. For example, some aspects of these discourses draw upon the historical position of Malta or the eastern concerns of Greece. These discourses also trace personal communications of interviewees.

Attitudes towards and discourses of the Mediterranean

There seems to be a lack of discursive practices of the Mediterranean in Greece. As the only female interviewee in Greece pointed out, the Mediterranean is thought of as a flexible notion.[102] Moreover, Greek interviewees doubted the existence of any Mediterranean identification.

Or when they referred to such identification, they stated that the Greek Mediterranean identity is part of the Greek identity, meaning that it is subsumed under a more 'holistic' Greek identity. The latter is said to be a combination of Mediterranean identity, ancient culture (thus making historical connections and tracing back Greek heritage to Hellenic and Byzantine periods), Balkan culture and Ottoman culture. Greeks do not believe that a Mediterranean identity has any deeply rooted cultural traits – perhaps some touristic ones (constructed ones) – whereas Balkan and European identities are perceived to have such cultural and traditional traits and roots. It is also important to note here that one Maltese interviewee claimed that a typical Mediterranean is a Greek. Greek discourses varied from an 'ambience' to 'méditerranité feeling' or from a number of common elements to 'the olive-tree zone' and 'despite the mistrust in this area there is a strange Mediterranean solidarity but also a number of differences'. It may be stated that the Mediterranean 'is a periphery of Southern Europe' for Greece. In general, Greek cultural identity is an ambivalent one between a Greek and a European identity. One interviewee stated '*We* must see *them* as partners – *our* interests as much as *theirs*' referring to 'third Mediterranean countries'.[103] The local framework for thinking about the Mediterranean emerged when reference was made to Turkey's EU membership application (the context for Greece's Mediterranean thereby being the 'other') that according to the Greek interviewees is an identity issue. For Greeks, Turkey will change the EU completely.[104] Academics stated that it would be best for the EU to consider such applications using similar criteria for all applicants.[105] If Europe is truly a multicultural phenomenon it should not be reserved for Christians only – all elements can coexist.[106] For Greek interviewees there are multiple identities (reflecting especially those of Greece within!) that can coexist as in the case of the Greek identity (but no mention was made of Greece as Mediterranean).[107] Interviewees were strongly against a civilisational definition and ranking (that is, contrary to Huntington's claim). According to one interviewee, Mediterranean identity is part of a European identity[108] in a cohesive sense but, another interviewee stated:

> Do we know who we are? There is no European identity and there cannot be a Mediterranean identity. What is a European identity first of all? What does it mean to be European? Does a Mediterranean identity exist? ... I am not able to see a community in today's Mediterranean. Even a common European identity is doubtful. It does not mean that I favour drawing lines between North and South Mediterranean ... No, it does not exist ... they do not ... have a common ground to discover this common identity.

This is an interesting utterance that refutes any figurations of otherness. Greek interviewees, however, agreed that it is important not to alienate the

North African area from the rest of the European architecture. This discourse has become even more prominent following the events of 9/11 and the Madrid bombings of 11 March 2004 in particular.

On the question of the classification of the Mediterranean territorial states, it is important to note that Greek interviewees were clearly drawn to the classification of Cyprus (as Aegean) which shows how important this issue is in Greece. These interviewees emphasised that 'Cyprus is part of the Mediterranean and will be part of Europe, ... actually more part of Western Europe *even though* it has relations with the Middle East'.[109] As regards Malta, Greek interviewees stated that Malta is thought of as either being in the EU or as a North African country. This reflects poor knowledge on the part of some EU members about EU politics, in particular in Greece.[110] What clearly emerged from this question is the Greek pro-Arab stance. In fact, Greek interviewees clearly included Libya in their discourse of the Mediterranean – they also included and widened their mental mappings of the Mediterranean to Iran and Iraq.[111] These mappings have recently entered the EU's discursive framework on its New Neighbourhood Initiative. Greeks clearly included the Balkans in their discursive practices of the Mediterranean – perhaps due to the close geographic proximity but also to historical (mostly religious) links between Greece and 'the Balkans'. These Greek interviewees also made a distinction between the 'haves' (European partners) and the 'have nots' (Mediterranean partners) – that is, the rich in the North and the poor in the South respectively.[112] The label of South Mediterranean states or Southern Mediterranean countries was often used to refer to the Mediterranean partners – thus distinguishing these from the implied North Mediterranean partners of Spain, Italy, Portugal and perhaps even France, with Greece indirectly placed in this category. The latter group were also referred to as the Southern European Mediterranean states. Greece clearly emerged as a Balkan and South European Mediterranean state in this question.[113] One can speculate here whether these are different categories/mappings (double-hatting). It may be argued that these are two different labels but one country can be categorised under both.[114]

Having reflected on the classification offered for the Mediterranean, the Greek interviewees, especially academics, were critical and strong in their opinion about the fictitious nature of such a classification, stating that this cannot serve as a formal, fixed categorisation but should be considered as flexible over time. Referring to an old French concept of the term Mediterranean as *le prochain Orient*, Greek interviewees claimed that this phrase summarises what the Mediterranean is all about:[115] that this term requires the immediate interdependence between states for an area (such as the Mediterranean) *to exist*. This discourse emphasises the constructed nature of the Mediterranean 'region'. One interviewee stated that 'If I had to opt for a narrow definition (of the Mediterranean), I would say the countries on the periphery that have an impact on each other'. However, Greek interviewees did refer to the Mediterranean partners of the EMP as 'third' countries![116] These discourses link to the discourses of the Mediterranean as a securitising object that were examined in Chapter 2.

For Moroccan interviewees, Mediterranean identity is about values, linking past and present experiences.[117] Moroccans do feel Mediterranean and as one interviewee said:

> Morocco surely has a Mediterranean perspective. We have no problem with our identity.[118] I understood Europe when it *naturally* said that Morocco is not European. Europe has its history, its religion and its culture. Morocco is an old civilisation, with its old monarchy/dynasty and it is an ancient place[119] – it existed [as a 'state'] before France[120] [that is Europe in Moroccan mappings]. We are coherent with ourselves, we have no superiority or inferiority complex. We have our music and gastronomy and a population which is naturally tolerant and which has lived amongst Jews and Berbers.[121]

This is an important discourse that shows that Moroccan identity is based on its religious Islamic faith (its version of Islam differs from certain other strands in this regard) – especially with regards to the importance of values and tolerance.

For Moroccan interviewees, 'the perception in the EU of the Mediterranean is just a tool to develop its financial package' – a view that might be interpreted as reflecting Morocco's local framework of needs. 'Europe knows that it is not even a political union itself. If the Mediterranean had one vision of Europe together they would be stronger as a group to do business with Europe'. This reflects Moroccan cynicism towards the EU's instrumental attitude to the Mediterranean.

Even in Morocco, however, there were tensions in discourses on the Mediterranean. One critical Moroccan interviewee stated that:

> I cannot think that there can be a Mediterranean identity ... This is a silly concept for those days when people communicated with boats ... Today we cannot speak of a geographic region – what does it mean? One can create what I shall call a bouquet – one can weed out an association – a bouquet of something that might work out without the need for common borders but with the facilities for exchange that can be created with modern technology. A geographic 'bloc' thinking comes from history. We must do away with the notion of regional identity and instead create norms and a European constitution. The Mediterranean needs objectives and rules, not sentiments.

This is an interesting instance of how a discourse from one context and one voice (Morocco) connects to another discourse (EU debates on its constitution).

The question of the Mediterranean is an important one for Morocco albeit a difficult one. Another interviewee claimed that:

> A Mediterranean identity fits and accommodates Morocco best. We are not European and will never be. We are African but there are always some differences. We are Arab but again there are different types of Arabs. We are Muslim but our Muslim religion is not like that in Indonesia for example. The Mediterranean represents the strongest coefficient of coherence.[122]

Here there is an implicit reference to a common collective identity arrived at through the lowest common denominator principle as a point of convergence to accommodate diversities.

It was noted that in accordance with Islamic religion, most interviewees claimed that what is needed (for a more Mediterranean feeling) is more tolerance of differences when it comes to issues of identity. Moroccan interviewees pointed out that what is important is that all partners have an agreement on universal principles.[123] One interviewee even mentioned how:

> in Morocco a distinction is made between the Occident and the Orient, the former being the Maghreb and the latter the Mashrek and Middle East countries. We all need an identity as a point of convergence not divergence: basically, a flexible understanding of identities as systems of values – systems that need an evolution over time. I don't like to make a contrast but to emphasise tolerance, of accepting otherness ... I see a difference but it is this that makes identities rich. They are two identities that can live together in a positive way. I do not see it as a Mediterranean identity against a European identity. All partners need to be self-assured.

This Moroccan academic, who is also involved in politics, included Mauritania within the North African category in his discourse of the Mediterranean.[124] Another interviewee referred to Spain and Portugal as Latin Europe. This 'Latin' label for Europe echoes Greek historical references to the West or Europe as the Latins, and Spanish- or Ibero-America as Latin America (originally a French term).

Like their Greek and Moroccan counterparts, Maltese interviewees consider the question of a Mediterranean region from a critical position as an idea rather than a 'real' notion. According to these Maltese interviewees, any classification of the Mediterranean varies – it is a sea between three continents so the Mediterranean is sometimes classified as part of Europe (by the UN for example), other times as Africa or the Middle East or the Arab world. As to the question on the classification of the Mediterranean, the Maltese interviewees had quite a wide classificatory discourse of the area which they divided into the Balkans, South/West Europe (Spain, Italy and France), Greece/Turkey/Cyprus, the Arab World, Israel, the Maghreb, Libya (classified on its own which shows the historically important links of Malta with this country but also Libya's up-to-recent isolation), the Middle East, North–South and East–West. However, like their counterparts in Greece and Morocco, the Maltese interviewees emphasised that such classifications of the Mediterranean are problematic and should be used only as simplifications for analytical and research purposes. Nevertheless, it was noted that underlying this discourse on problematic 'mapping cut-offs', there was a deeper sense of nationalistic discourses which reflect Malta's historical struggle for independence and freedom when one interviewee argued that 'Who draws the map (of the Mediterranean)? ... forces of globalisation ... *erosion of national values* ... these are problematic', in effect a regular marker across case study discourses.[125]

Maltese interviewees emphasised how identities cannot be seen as differences:

> Identities cannot be defined in terms of how different two groups are from one another ... it is important to find common areas too. For instance, religious diversity must be allowed and articulated. Identity has two sides ... how we see ourselves and how we see ourselves through contact with others. Identity must be outward looking. We cannot create stereotypes of identities. We need to cultivate and build and express our different forms of identity ... identities are often built in response to external threats, in contact with others. We need to change our concepts. We can be both at the same time ... why should we differ? Any talk of a division between the Mediterranean and Europe goes against the idea of the EMP. One should not have a single identity. There must be space left for cultural diversity within a diverse Euro-Mediterranean region.[126]

Another interviewee stated that 'I would rather see this (the Euro-Mediterranean area) as two concentric circles which cross each other around a common area – Mediterranean/European'. These views (present) reflect the historical resilience of the Maltese (past) and their tolerance towards different religions and, moreover, their more contemporary concerns with the EMP as a meeting ground for dialogue between diverse partners (and support for a dialogic relationship).[127]

On the specific question of which priority they would give to their identity/ies, the Maltese and the Greek interviewees showed that the country/nation is the primary context in which people define their identity: reflecting past struggles for the Maltese and the pride of the Greeks in their Hellenic heritage. In the case of Malta this might be said to be particularly strong as it is a small island state and in the case of Greece this could be a result of the fact that most Greeks (there might be a generational dimension to this) feel isolated from Europe and therefore hold on stronger to their Greek identity. The responses to this question also reflect the struggle for independence and freedom in both Greece and Malta.[128] Moroccan interviewees stated that 'we all have our own national identities and we need to respect them all', reflecting Morocco's strong religious influence upon these views.

A summary comparison of the discursive practices of the Mediterranean from the case studies

It was observed that both Maltese and Moroccan interviewees related to a Mediterranean feeling but this was not the case with the Greek interviewees. This is interesting as the Maltese and Greeks can be said to share a sea-faring tradition across and around the Mediterranean while Morocco has hardly had a navy.[129] Greece and Malta have a tradition of shipbuilding and are now established as cruise centres, Greece even more so. Greece feels closer to its eastern Balkan neighbours and the Mediterranean is, at least currently, far away from the mental mappings of interviewees. Moreover, Maltese and Moroccan interviewees seemed more self-assured than Greeks *vis-à-vis* their identity (that is their self-understanding and identification processes).[130] Moreover, Maltese and Greek interviewees emphasised the importance of making a distinction between 'old' concepts and meanings of the Mediterranean and more contemporary ones – the latter being a more flexible notion based on exchanges and relations between countries which makes the Mediterranean 'an emergent entity'; that is, 'an entity in the making'.

It was noted that there were official as well as unofficial Greek discourses on the Mediterranean. Although officially Greeks include the Balkans in their discourse of the Mediterranean, a few interviewees stated that it would be doubtful as to which parts of former Yugoslavia they would perceive as Mediterranean since the frontiers created within this area are not real (other Greek interviewees explicitly stated that former Yugoslavia must be included in a classification of the Mediterranean). Some interviewees even included (the long-time enemy) Turkey as part of the Mediterranean (Turkey is in the EMP, after all).[131] Greeks also included 'the end part of Gibraltar' with this classification. Greek interviewees also mentioned the flexibility of the concept of the Mediterranean according to the issue being considered.[132] Maltese interviewees excluded Portugal, Mauritania, Jordan, (even the Vatican and San Marino) from their classification of the Mediterranean (after taking a sea-based approach) and stated that these countries are included only by extension.

Another interesting discourse which was observed in Greece was that, on the one hand, Greek interviewees stated that what 'make' the Mediterranean an 'area' are trade and co-operative initiatives, while on the other hand they stated that nowadays issues of identity and national interests are more important in the making of this area than issues of trade and movements (of goods, capital, services and people) – perhaps what they actually referred to in the former is the old notion of the Mediterranean as a trading post. One Greek interviewee claimed that there is a difference between Greek and Turkish perspectives on the Mediterranean that he claimed is due to the Asian character of the Turkish people. 'What we signify as Mediterranean is different from what they signify'. It was observed that when interviewees expressed strong feelings these had to be contrasted with those of their Turkish counterparts. For the said interviewee, 'the Mediterranean is an empty signifier ... I put a description to it because you asked me to. I do not think about it'.

Moroccan interviewees, like their Greek counterparts, pointed to the exclusion of Turkey from the interview guidelines and also included the Balkans in their discourse of the Mediterranean. It seems that both groups thought it was not right to exclude Turkey from the classification of the Mediterranean.[133]

Reflecting Malta's more recent political scenario and its European aspirations, Maltese interviewees stated that the Mediterranean is not a homogenous structure like Europe and that it is more complex to make reference to someone coming from the Mediterranean than to someone coming from Europe – the latter having a more predictable pattern of (identity) characteristics. This Maltese discourse divided the northern Christian European states from the southern, Islamic ones[134] and made a cross reference to historical discourses (that is, to the past) on the clashes and collaboration between these two communities. This discourse contrasts with more contemporary discourses where Maltese interviewees speak of the importance of multiple identities and the need for respect of differences.

Attitudes towards and discourses of the EU[135]

Greeks oscillated between talking of Greece as external to the EU – in terms of 'them' and 'we' and sometimes including Greece with the EU. This ambiguity with regards to references to Greece and the EU seems to underline an identity vacuum as to where Greece stands *vis-à-vis* the EU.[136] Greece and Greek European identity 'credentials' seem very unstable in these situations.[137] This can be seen as, at times, a vague discourse of Greek ambivalent identity that seems to oscillate not between but around a European and a Mediterranean consciousness/identification/self-understanding (hence the ambivalence). Moreover, Greek interviewees suggested that things are not clear (and too bureaucratic) at the EU level as to how procedures work.[138] Sometimes interviewees included Greece with the Mediterranean partners as when they said 'it will be a victory if we have the same amount of money as the previous MEDA programme' when talking of the MEDA II negotiations (which have been recently resolved).[139] Such discourses reflect the ambivalent Mediterranean and European identities pertaining to Greece (as in Malta). When reference was made of deficiencies of EU members, Greeks were quick to clearly detach themselves from this group: 'They need to talk about where they are and to define where they want to go'. According to Greek interviewees, the EU is not focused enough on its relations with the Mediterranean countries since its EMP strategy is (inevitably) entangled with the MEPP. They also mentioned the need for EU member states to change their attitude and discursive practices which see the Mediterranean as a threat and as a danger (de-securitisation) – seemingly excluding Greece from such views.

Greek interviewees stated that the EU has *created*, that is constructed, a holistic, Mediterranean regional approach in its policy for a purpose (instrumental reasons). Although they acknowledge that the making of such a 'region' is an ambitious aim, with each country having its own characteristics, Greek interviewees agree that the EU needs a Common Foreign Policy and a Common Economic Policy.[140] In the words of Greek interviewees, although Turkey is different from Israel which is different from Tunisia etc., in our era of globalisation the EU as an international institution needs an integrated approach *vis-à-vis* all its neighbours and it therefore groups common areas such as the Mediterranean for policy-making purposes.[141]

Here it is important to note that different views emerged on this issue between Greek academics and Greek officials who work in institutions like the Ministry of Foreign Affairs (MFA).[142] In academic circles there seems to be an agreement that ideally the EU should have an holistic approach to the Mediterranean since this encourages countries in the area to a higher propensity to work together. According to one interviewee, an holistic view is better than one of boundaries or fences: 'Yes, we need to *think* holistic, not as a boundary or a fence'.[143] However, Greek MFA representatives claim that the Eastern Mediterranean is different from the Western Mediterranean.[144] This is a very important discourse since Greece is an EU member.[145] Since Greek interviewees clearly stated that Greece has its own priorities, it seems that the EU as a whole perceives the Mediterranean from a different angle to individual member states like Greece. In other words, it seems that the 'total' EU discourse of the Mediterranean is not equivalent to the sum of the discourses of its individual member states – more perhaps to the lowest common denominator discourse.

In the words of Moroccan interviewees, EU member states need to join forces *vis-à-vis* their Mediterranean initiatives. They particularly referred to their historical 'protector' France (past) which, according to interviewees, needs to join forces with Germany in their joint efforts towards the Mediterranean and the Central and Eastern European countries (present). They also made reference to Spain, Italy and Portugal which, according to them, should join France in pushing the EU for more Euro-Mediterranean interdependence. These discourses show that Morocco considers these European Mediterranean member states as positive allies within the EU to push for their concerns[146] – an historical link with countries Morocco has experienced. For Moroccans, the EU (particularly during 1998–9) is preoccupied mostly with its own internal affairs including the then Commission crisis, its budget, its institutional reforms and Kosovo on the international front and more recently with the debate on the EU constitution and the war against terrorism.[147] One interviewee was quite pessimistic about the possible improvements that Europe could implement in the Mediterranean. He said that there is:

a lot of rhetoric repeated in most Euro-Mediterranean meetings which I attend. Europe does not have anything grand to offer the Mediterranean since it will not engage in, for example, Morocco's debt issues and it will not alter matters in the agricultural field because of its CAP politics. The EU will not change the course of events on the cultural and social side either.[148]

For Moroccans:

Europe *dictates* what is Mediterranean ... Europe proposes the same package to the Mediterranean as it does to Latin America, Asia ... A homogenising strategy, a pigeon-hole strategy ... Europe generalises its model of liberal, commercial and economic exchange ... Europe is searching to give this region an identity ... This is how Europe has a vision of a region – a multilateral agreement for the globalisation of its economic relations ... The EU is less coherent than the Mediterranean but the latter lacks the institutional set-up of the EU.[149]

Like their Moroccan counterparts, Maltese interviewees reiterated the need for more EU political vision and more attention and importance to be given to the Mediterranean – in terms of more finance and better co-ordination between EU members over Mediterranean affairs. These interviewees called for smaller projects to be planned for the Mediterranean by Brussels and for decentralisation in its structure.[150]

For Maltese interviewees, the EU needs a manner of organising its external relations and to perceive the Mediterranean as a whole is an advantage. One interviewee stated that the EU's depiction of the Mediterranean is 'an umbrella statement for an area which lacks a cohesive culture – a region with a difference or as Braudel calls it "the liquid continent"'.[151] However, they questioned whether the EU is clear on this concept of the Mediterranean and emphasised the need for the EU to question the purpose of its use of the term. In other words, although the EU addresses its partners all together, it needs to be clearer in its own mind as to what it is actually addressing. (In fact, in the recently launched New Neighbourhood Policy, there is a noted change of term from Mediterranean to 'our neighbours in the South'). Policy-wise, however, the EU's discourse of the Mediterranean is an improvement (perhaps because it makes Malta more central) on the US approach that does not recognise the area as one whole region – but refers to either South Europe or the Middle East or North Africa. This reflects the balance of power realistic thinking (realpolitik) of Maltese interviewees (who also compared the EU's role in the Mediterranean with that of the USA). The EU's view of the Mediterranean is understood to be a sea-centred one not a land-centred one.

Attitudes towards and discourses of the EMP

The above ambivalence in some of interviewees' discourses of the Mediterranean and the EU has repercussions on their views and attitudes to the EMP. Moreover, the flexible and multiple meanings given by interviewees for the 'Mediterranean' and 'Europe', also have a bearing on the meaning of the EMP for the same sample group. The EMP has emerged from these interviews as, on the one hand, a tool for further Mediterranean integration with Europe – the talk of those who speak of 'regions' and what many may consider as an idealist perspective. On the other hand, the EMP is perceived by others as an opportunity for member states and Mediterranean partners to extract every financial opportunity from the Partnership as possible – which may be referred to as the pragmatic perspective.

For example, Greeks look at Europe in terms of any interests that Greece might have and will similarly look at any initiative for the Mediterranean when the country can gain something out of its involvement in such initiatives.[152] According to Greek interviewees, the EU has introduced the EMP as a way of securing the flow of, and access to, oil and the potential of the Mediterranean markets.[153] Moreover, although Greeks have been ambivalent about their European identity, they did mention the fear of refugees arriving in Europe from the Balkans, even though the latter countries are not included in the EMP. This reflects the concerns of Greece that were quite evident during the early phase of the fieldwork period. A deeper analysis of this issue shows that Greece relates to immigration issues as these affect it directly. Therefore, although the EU is portrayed as being involved in the Mediterranean for reasons of immigration problems (amongst its primary concerns), these reasons are also Greece's for its interest in the Mediterranean.[154] In Greek eyes the Partnership provides the appropriate mechanisms for enhanced security in the Balkan area. The MEPP was mentioned as the main obstacle to any substantial improvements in the EMP programmes. It was also mentioned that the officials who drafted the EMP wanted to make it clear that the Partnership was not to form any part of the MEPP. Greek interviewees stated that the EMP, despite its shortcomings, is expected to offer a better opportunity (albeit still not enough) for the much-needed financial solutions to the Mediterranean 'problem' than the Mediterranean Forum (which has no funding).

Moroccan interviewees look at the EMP as just one of the many zones of EU co-operation programmes (that is, as an EU policy, not a real partnership). They claim that this Mediterranean programme came about as a result of globalisation. Like their Greek counterparts, Moroccan interviewees perceive the EMP as a process aimed at (de-)securitising and stabilising the Mediterranean – an area of great development gaps between North and South. This actually reflects one key contemporary area of concern for Morocco: economic development (which matches the EU's discourse on the Med). Other Moroccan concerns include a young Mediterranean population and poverty areas that are incorporated into a strong security syndrome (securitisation of the Med through discursive practices about young population 'explosion' and poverty setting off flows of immigrants towards Europe). Like their Greek counterparts (in general, but in particular academics and diplomats), Moroccan interviewees also see the EMP as a potential framework to address these Mediterranean problems. Again, like the Greeks, the Moroccans also mentioned the key European interests in the Mediterranean, perhaps reflecting their own protectorate experiences with France and Spain. They acknowledged that the Mediterranean is a very important market for Europe especially with regards to oil and gas supplies.[155] Thus, the EMP is a European process aimed at securing enough supplies of these products for Europe.[156] Moroccan interviewees also raised their concern about the 'conflict' behind the EMP process – the EU describes it as a Euro–'Mediterranean' Partnership when in effect it refers to the Middle East and North Africa.[157] Moroccan interviewees believe that the Maghreb is especially important for Europe. They also acknowledge the innovative global vision of the EMP in that it encompasses three baskets. However, reflecting Moroccan concerns, interviewees claimed that the EU should aim for commercial reciprocity especially in terms of preferential agreements and its objective of an FTA by the year 2010.[158] They also acknowledged, however, that 'the EMP is not innovative in its recognition of how much it needs to understand the "South". Although Europe wishes well for the Mediterranean it has too much on its own agenda and it would perhaps improve its EMP by simplifying the process through the introduction of norms'.[159] This discourse connects to the recent debates on the EU's constitution.

Moroccan interviewees also noted the difference between the 'declared objectives' of the EMP and the 'reality' of the Mediterranean area. For Moroccans it is important that the EMP creates the necessary base for economic, political and cultural relations in this 'uncertain region where disequilibriums and conflicts are very complex' – in effect, a Mediterranean security discourse.

It is important to note that Moroccan interviewees claimed that Morocco sees its relations with the EU as a Euro–Moroccan partnership and differentiate this from Morocco's relations with Mediterranean countries. This might reflect the importance given to Morocco by the EU in its dealings with this partner. Still, they added that Morocco does perceive the EMP as a possible framework (context) for it to develop both sets of relations. One important matter that was noted by Moroccan interviewees is that the EMP has been built on a negative discourse of the Mediterranean – more specifically around the issue of immigration 'flows' from the 'South' (in parallel with the EU's preoccupation with its energy requirements). Moreover, according to these interviewees, the EMP lacks a real strategy for development in the Mediterranean countries – which was proven at the Malta conference that was taken over by the MEPP (in effect, the EU had to change its agenda).

It was also noted that for Moroccan interviewees the aspect of the EMP which came up most often in their views on this process was the economic area which reflects the aspect which concerns Morocco's interests most.[160] Finally for Moroccan interviewees the EMP has to address its heavily bureaucratic procedures so that projects relating to the Mediterranean area do not get blocked.[161] It was also mentioned that the EMP requires a more effective follow-up system for projects and decisions or resolutions taken on behalf of

Mediterranean partners. Overall, Moroccan interviewees called for both sides of the Partnership to understand each other since even EU states have their own internal difficulties, while Mediterranean partners should be more self-critical. As examined above, these Moroccan discourses reflect Morocco's local frameworks of concerns.

For Maltese interviewees, the EMP has a dual aim: that of addressing the issue of immigration from the South (a notion which seems common in all three cases) and a more strategic vision of balancing its power to counteract the major influence which the USA has over the area (a former-colony speech act). These interviewees also mentioned the aim for a free trade and co-operation area between the European and Mediterranean partners. The issue of security was also mentioned especially in relation to the stabilisation of the North African and Middle Eastern areas. It is important here to note that Maltese interviewees separated Malta from these latter concerns, implicitly emphasising that Malta is neither North African nor Middle Eastern but European (that is, inside Europe and not 'outside') and therefore belongs to the stable partners. Like their Greek and Moroccan counterparts, Maltese interviewees recognise the EMP as a process that needs to address the investment needs of the area rather than just give aid. It was also mentioned that it is an innovative idea when compared to previous EU Mediterranean initiatives.

One observes that these case countries' discourses on the EMP are announced on the basis of each local framework for the concerns of the particular country and that, on the one hand, discourses carry historical baggages, while on the other hand, they reflect present concerns.[162] In the case of Morocco the only framework for its relations with the EU is the EMP, whilst for Malta the EMP offered an environment where it could lobby for its full membership of the EU.[163] Interviewees from these two countries were found to be more versed, more critical and more reflexive on EMP matters at the time of the fieldwork in each case country. Having said this, however, it is important to note that during the fieldtrip to Greece, this country was being perceived as the 'California of the Balkans'[164] in that many immigrants were seeking shelter in Greece – a very important concern which was implicitly in the minds of Greek interviewees during the interviews. Greek interviewees felt that this concern was not shared with them by their EU partners.[165] This observation seems to contradict the importance given within the EMP to this very issue of immigration. Another important observation from the fieldwork is that interviewees tend to discuss with more enthusiasm those issues they happen to be focusing on at the time of the interviews (rather than past experiences).

Concluding remarks

During the initial phase of the fieldwork carried out in these three case countries, each case was overshadowed by a specific external context that might have affected the views expressed by the interviewees of this research.

Greece was experiencing the Öcalan crisis as well as the process of Greece seeking to qualify for the single European currency. Although these issues appeared to be the most important items on the Greek foreign policy agenda[166] during February and March 1999, there were other underlying issues. The Cyprus issue and the related Greek security concerns *vis-à-vis* Turkey reflect the constant (current/present discourses) threat felt by Greece from Turkey, which in turn reflects historical struggles (past experiences) as analysed in earlier sections of this chapter. However, it must be stated that the 1999 earthquakes in both Turkey and Greece have brought these two countries closer together and kicked off a process of 'earthquake diplomacy' – following the aid they gave each other in these catastrophic occurrences. Moreover, more contemporary discourses in Greece speak of the fact that it would be more advantageous for Greece if Turkey were to have better and closer relations with the EU. (For the moment, at least, Greece has dropped its veto.)[167] Greek diplomats were also concerned with improving relations with the Balkan states which are perceived as investment/financial opportunity areas for Greece (Greeks focus on investment opportunities in countries surrounding Greece and a lot of activity and efforts are directed towards this objective) – and not only as trouble-spot areas with the potential of refugee flows to Greek land perceived as a space opened for immigration (Greece as the California of the Balkans).[168] These political security challenges were of course issues on the Greek foreign policy agenda at the time of the interviews but not the most important ones. Although the subject of the EMP was discussed during the interviews, and although theoretically this issue is supposed to be one of the priorities on the Greek foreign policy agenda, it became evident during the said interviews that in practice this is not the case. Even during the Greek Presidency (January–June 2003) the Mediterranean was not on the top of the Greeks' priority list.[169]

The fieldwork results in Greece reflect the opening of the Balkans for Greece both as a fruitful investment and financial opportunity and a security problem. Greece has geographical borders with Albania with the ensuing problems of drug trafficking but also with the constant fear that parts of Greek territory might be claimed – as with the case of FYROM.[170] These discourses formed part of media discourses too and were dominant in Greece at the time of the interviews. Approximately 15 per cent of the Greek population is made up of migrants.[171] By way of a residual acceptance, Greeks recognise the Mediterranean as a meaningful place but it emerged that in contemporary times, Greeks are interested in something else other than the Mediterranean.

The interviews held in Malta followed the early election of September 1998. With a change of government to the pro-EU PN, the air was overtaken by the issue of Malta's unfreezing and resubmission of its EU application – a political bias one may note. On its top priority foreign policy list, Malta's EMP involvement gave way to its strong European aspirations. Still, the debate in Malta today places Malta in the Mediterranean through its historical influences – as a sort of fact which has to be taken for granted and which lies in the background of any discussion about Malta and the Mediterranean. What this reflects is the theme of its permanence that places the Maltese (and the story of the people of Malta) as having been 'there' in the Mediterranean, as having taken and absorbed lots of influences and survived through the years by means of their adaptable attitude: in other words, a Mediterranean people have been there and soaked up many influences from their conquerors. The anti-imperialist issues raised by the MLP, however, have been crucial throughout the formation processes of Maltese identity. The fieldtrip to Morocco was held at the end of March and beginning of April of 1999. King Hassan was still reigning during this period. Some other interviews were held in April 2002 during fieldwork carried out for a MEDA democracy project.

Common issues

In all three cases, but especially in Greece and Morocco, there was a shared view that the EMP should be a common space of free trade areas. Interviewees emphasised that Europe needs to buy Mediterranean products too[172] and thus open its market to the Mediterranean partners (that is, Europe to move from a 'one-stop shop' mentality). Moreover, it is interesting to note here the underlying ambivalent Greek European identity which some analysts argue has recently shown signs of changing through a Europeanisation process.[173]

As to a common Mediterranean identity, Greece, Malta and Morocco have all been observed to utilise a Mediterranean policy as a tactical tool in their relations with Europe. Even though Greece is an EU member, it emphasises its Mediterranean connections every time its interests call for such an approach – even though, in Greece, there has not been any coherent strain of Greek thinking regarding the Mediterranean. (Some would say Greece has no Mediterranean policy.) Any Mediterranean discourse in Greece comes along as a by-product, not as a result of some strategic thinking. Morocco uses its Mediterranean strategy as a way of communicating with its European partners. With its current pro-EU government, Malta also flags a Mediterranean connection as a way of getting closer relations with Europe and as having a contribution to make to Europe. It did emerge, however, as the case with the longest embedded engagement in the Mediterranean. As regards their religious identity, it was noted that the Greek Orthodox Church[174] and the Maltese Catholic Church[175] are both officially subordinated to the state – yet both are unofficially historical influences in popular thinking on the countries' relations with external partners. It is important to note that Greece is the only European country that imposed, until recently, the declaration of religion on its identity cards – a reflection of strong Orthodox identity and influence on state affairs.[176] In Morocco, the king is both the spiritual representative of his people and their leader. With divisions common within political parties in Morocco, the king is left with a lot of space to manoeuvre in the political arena. As to cultural biases, the interviews in Greece, Malta and Morocco uncovered unofficial discourses about the common practice of clientelistic politics[177] and the high black/underground economy[178] in all three cases.

In the contemporary political arena, Morocco emerged as being more interested in the western Mediterranean area while Greece seems more concerned with establishing relations with the eastern Mediterranean countries. Malta, due to its particular geopolitical position, continues to strengthen its relations with all its Mediterranean partners. There are local issues that affect these discourses. These were analysed throughout the chapter but, in sum, Morocco orients itself more towards its Maghreb neighbours than its Mashreq partners of the EMP. Greek interviewees perceive Greece as having more in common with its 'Balkan' neighbours and also distinguish between the Eastern and the Western Mediterranean whilst Maltese interviewees had a less North–South and West–East division discourse of the Mediterranean which could be reflected back to Malta's history in the Mediterranean area (past-present discursive practices).

In all three cases, however, a reflection was observed on the way in which the Mediterranean carries different meanings between peaceful periods and war periods. As this chapter has tried to analyse, regular discursive markers can be mapped out (through both coherences and incoherences) across elite discursive practices in Malta, Greece and Morocco on the Mediterranean, the EU and the EMP. In fact, there is still a *discourse* on the Mediterranean in all three case studies. By using references to embedded (historical narratives) notions such as their heritage, climate, sea, etc., interviewees indicated that the Mediterranean is as much a concept shrouded in myth as a geographical entity hit by the shores of the Mediterranean Sea. These outcomes seem to reflect regular oscillations and ambivalence in the EU's conceptualisation of the Mediterranean that were analysed in Chapter 4. Thus a comparison of the EU's discursive practices of the Mediterranean with those discourses from the case studies has important implications for policy-making addressing this important area. This will be the main objective of the next chapter.

6 Which 'Mediterranean'?

A comparison of discursive practices from the EU and the case studies

Chapter 4 presented an analysis of the struggle of the EU to define the Mediterranean through its policies addressed at this area. The aim here was to critically evaluate EU Mediterranean policy as a discursive practice and in so doing to reveal the vague EU representations of this area that is here understood as an area continuously in the making. As a contribution to the explanation and critique of such international practices, Chapter 5 attempted to draw out some of the subjugated knowledges and alternative discourses on the Mediterranean that have been excluded or silenced by the EU's hegemonic discourse. This was carried out through an examination of the discourses about the Mediterranean and Europe emanating from Greece, Malta and Morocco. It was observed that these alternative discourses on the Mediterranean often work in resistance to the dominant EU knowledge/power nexus (created through its discourse on the area). While the EU struggles to fix meaning to the Mediterranean area, the cases revealed practices of questioning this flexible concept. Moreover, the discourse emerging from the EU about the Mediterranean has been noted to be complicit with its structures of domination in certain sectors as shown in Chapter 3. The EU clearly possesses a degree of control in the economic field. (In contrast to this, the EU lacks military clout that leaves it dependent on the USA, as in the case, for example, of the Middle East.) In this manner, EU discourses have served as systems and structures of signification that construct Mediterranean social realities.

In order to tie up these research results with the theoretical framework adopted in this book, this chapter seeks to summarise and compare the predications/'truth statements' of the Mediterranean in EU discourses and practices (statements and texts) and discourses/practices of the Mediterranean in Greece, Morocco and Malta.

The first section of this chapter will present and discuss a schematic outline of some of the various types of *Mediterraneans* that emerged from the discursive practices investigated through EU texts/practices and through the textual analysis and interviews carried out in Brussels, Greece, Morocco and Malta.

The following section will investigate how these different discourses/ practices of the Mediterranean reflect upon the deficiencies of the EMP.

This will include an analysis of the implications of these diverse discourses on the Mediterranean for policy-making, which are here termed the *effects* of discourses on the Mediterranean. This section will present some ways in which the European Mediterranean policy can be re-analysed from a discursive-constructivist angle and in light of the findings of this research on discourses of the Mediterranean. The concluding section will rethink the reality and re-presentation of the Mediterranean in light of this research.

The various types of Mediterraneans – mapping out the various discourses uncovered through this inquiry

This book has been inspired by critical constructivist, discourse analysis and foreign policy writings in its investigation of the resulting essences and meanings of the Mediterranean from discursive practices of this area. In particular, the EU's construction of the Mediterranean rests on a struggle to classify, organise and structure this area on the basis of some characteristics or contents that make the Mediterranean,[1] as a community, meaningful and manageable for the EU. This representation of the Mediterranean echoes Foucault's work that looks at how a domain can be organised and socially constructed through discursive practices and how such discourses contain a plurality of meanings.[2] The outline presented below sketches out some of the contents or characters of the Mediterranean (not in any order of importance) that emerged from the discursive practices investigated here.

Content/'substance' of the Mediterranean (set 1)

- Economic market.
- Securising object.
- Myth of Med: common/cradle of civilisation.
- Contact/networks/communications: cultural, people-to-people Med.
- Political sphere/arena of influence.
- A multi-religious area.
- Historical trade route.
- Countries on the periphery that have an impact on each other.
- A unified area in terms of its immigration 'problem'.
- Identities.

Through the above contents of the Mediterranean, EU action is expressed as a need to code its experience with its Mediterranean partners and to see this area as a representation. In other words, the EU needs to simplify the Mediterranean 'reality' – and in the process distorts the area – in order to act towards this object/field of knowledge of the Mediterranean. EU practices of the Mediterranean include discourses of this area as an economic market, a securitising object, a political area of influence, a multi-religious sphere, a historical trading route, a communications arena and a unified area in terms of immigration problems. EU discourses also include references to the myth[3] of the Mediterranean as the cradle of civilisation, Mediterranean identity/ies and the impact that the countries around the Mediterranean Sea have on each other.

As a reflection of what the Mediterranean is all about, one interviewee claimed that: 'the term requires the immediate interdependence between states for such an area to exist'. Moreover, the diverse references to the Mediterranean concept reflect the constructed nature of such an area. For instance, when the Mediterranean partners of the EMP are referred to as 'third countries' this certainly reflects part of the ordained Euro speak of the EU (which is not only applied to the Mediterranean). When contrasting EU discourses of the Mediterranean with those of Greece, Malta and Morocco, a perennial struggle emerges between these different discourses about the definition (and meaning) of the Mediterranean phenomenon. A deeper reading of EU documents and case study materials which have been analysed show that apart from this recorded material, the Mediterranean is also continuously undergoing a process, an unbroken process of semantic choices, a movement through a network of potential meaning, where each set of choices creates an environment for action on the Mediterranean.[4] These issues all deal with questions of EU positioning, self-understanding, signification and identification – in other words, issues of identity.[5] In its discourses on the Mediterranean, the EU depicts this area as having 'different' problems and 'different' regimes and any references to the Mediterranean are rather vague and confusing. Underlying this confusion is a power notion of who these 'other' are when compared to the European 'self'. The challenges marked out by the EU with regards to the Mediterranean and which differentiate the EU from the Mediterranean include: a cultural divide (Christian/ Islam mainly); an economic divide (rich EU/poor Mediterranean); social divide (demographic trends, nutrition, housing, health care, literacy, etc.); political divide (democracy versus authoritarian or quasi-authoritarian regimes); irregular and not intense patterns of interaction as well as the absence of regional identity and 'we' feeling in the Mediterranean.

Consequently, the context in which the EU recognises this 'Mediterranean' entity is fear or risk stemming from 'insecurity' and 'instability' emanating from this area (that is through processes of securitisation). In fact, the EU discourse on the Mediterranean as a securitising object emerged as a very powerful discourse, even more so before the events of 9/11 and 11 March 2004.[6] It has been noted that the EU's securitisation of the Mediterranean is prominent (the EU seems to be almost obsessed with Mediterranean security issues). Linked to this discourse is another powerful discourse on the risk of immigration/terrorists from the area entering into the borders of Europe (securitisation of issues such as migration, drugs and crime also brings in the inter-regional level).[7] Through these discursive practices the EU extends the boundaries of the Mediterranean into its own borders. There has been a discussion on an EU common migration policy but not all member states accept the communitisation of migration policy.[8] An analysis of these discourses reveals, on the one hand, economies of hope and aspirations of migrants and would-be migrants and, on the other hand, economic relations of exploitation through which the EU member states plan to grant permission of stay to migrants who can fill the gap in areas of employment in demand in EU states, like education, health and information technology. In this manner, EU discourses on the Mediterranean show that there are no concrete geographies of the Mediterranean, but power relations that are constructed through the discursive practices of the EU. In this fluidity of its discourses on the Mediterranean, the EU has created policies and programmes of development and co-operation, aid programmes for the economic restructuring of countries in this basin and plans to facilitate trade with these countries/partners in an effort to build confidence and security measures, to promote 'development' and to 'stabilise' southern economies – a Stability Pact for the Mediterranean. The EMP has been specifically analysed in this book as one of the EU's most recent discursive practices of the Mediterranean. What clearly emerged is that the Mediterranean *is* important for European identification. The process of identification needs others, plenty of others – security-wise, in terms of economic requirements, political reasons, etc. The Mediterranean is thus one external space in the political practice of forging a European Self.[9]

Hence, the Mediterranean is an important factor in the 'otherness' of Europe – but not necessary since there are many 'others' (of Europe). The Mediterranean is one of Europe's 'others' but not the only 'other'. In short, Europe has many 'others' and 'otherness' is a factor in the EU's identification processes – the Mediterranean being one of these others. Therefore, as concluded in Chapter 4, the EU's making of the Mediterranean is a need – a must for the EU's political action and a construction of what the EU's 'foreign' or one of its 'other' entails. Moreover, the ensuing division between what is 'Europe' and what is 'Mediterranean' is contingent. The EU's Mediterranean (or any other Mediterranean for that matter) is an unstable counter concept often in opposition to what should be familiar – as in 'Europe' that is often taken for granted. Thus, Mediterranean 'otherness' is necessary for the EU but remains almost entirely impossible to point at – the EU's Mediterranean in effect is a process of interdependent yet unsettling units. The regular markers across EU discourses of the Mediterranean are reflected in its policies (practices) addressing this area.

Moreover, it has been observed that some aspects of identification may not be necessarily purposeful but rather *resourceful*. As noted above, the EU, for example, seeks to understand the Mediterranean in order to manage it. Accordingly, it creates a framework of understanding and acting towards its object/field of knowledge, that is, the Mediterranean. Thus, not every discourse from the EU on the Mediterranean has a purpose to do something to the Mediterranean partners but could be a recourse to manage the complexity of the Mediterranean. Discourses may have a purpose – for example, as shown in Chapter 4, the text for 'stability', 'peace', 'prosperity', etc. – but it is rather the dynamics of constructing and defining a specific Mediterranean that are present within these discourses. This EU framework of constructing and conceptualising the Mediterranean has the Mediterranean as a tool not as a purpose: a tool to construct the subaltern Mediterranean that works as a dynamic with an *effect* but not a purpose (otherwise the discourse would be an instrumentalist – serving as a means to – one which defines its object).

It is worth recalling that discourses have unintended effects. It is thereby important to reiterate the affectivity and effect of discourses on the Mediterranean and not just the purpose of such a discourse. Social constructs have effects and this is why it is important to observe and examine the availability of such an EU framework for the Mediterranean through which European self-understanding/identity can be asserted. This emerges as an unfocused process and, at the same time, as an unintentional process but it has an effect – the formation of a stronger European identity (especially in security matters). One can thus speak of the reflexes of discourse. Libya can be said to have been invited as an observer for the Stuttgart conference for a purpose – the EU has had the will and wanted to normalise its relations with Libya (which seem to be bearing fruit recently) but this also has an effect in the definition of who 'we' (European) are and who the Mediterranean are. (The recent discourse of Mauritania's inclusion in the EMP may be read as having a similar effect).[10] Therefore, it is crucial to stress that what is important is not what parts of the Mediterranean the EU addresses but what *types*, what kinds of Mediterranean the EU deals with (in terms of issues, contents and characteristics of the Mediterranean). The EU looks through 'eyes'/'lenses' that try to eliminate factors of complexity.[11] The EU overlooks the concerns of countries for underdevelopment and it presents them as equals but they are not. As one interviewee in Morocco stated:

> Partnership (referring to the EMP) means you are equal somehow and obviously we are not. The strength (especially economic) of the EU is felt within the EMP. Even within the Mediterranean (itself), some countries are weaker than others. It is therefore difficult to talk of a partnership.[12]

Discursive constructivism as a community of theory/research programme has therefore been useful in showing the way in which discourses contain multiple meanings.[13] In the case of the discourses on the Mediterranean, it has revealed underlying interviewees' feelings of frustration, anger and feelings of being let down or feelings of hope of interviewees in the Mediterranean countries investigated that are part of the EMP.

Furthermore, the EU can be said to be emphasising its European self-understanding forcefully in a way through its discourses of the Mediterranean. The same can be observed in discourses emanating from NATO. It has been stated that all European countries will be part of NATO – implying that NATO is in part European.[14] Some institutions thus try to privilege Europeanness as a quintessential element of being a part of this club. The EU in fact identifies itself as European par excellence.[15] The EU has been trying to construct and give meaning to Europe through cultural values, religious values, etc. which are distinguished from those values of 'others',[16] even though some member states have taken multiculturalism on board (officially at least).

Thus, these characteristics of the Mediterranean that make up this socially constructed area for the EU can be said to persist for a long time through processes of inertia and institutionalisation of discourses. This illustrates why some discourses are more powerful than other discourses and why some discourses become embedded in structures.

Chapter 4 examined the meaning of the Mediterranean emanating from EU sources; that is, meaning where it arises, namely in EU language itself. Language is here understood as a social system that also follows its own logic and this is the logic that produces the Mediterranean 'reality' for the EU. Thus, EU language on the Mediterranean is said to be relational and a system of relations. Chapter 4 also mapped out the EU–Mediterranean relational system that is latent and examined how the actual patterns of social interaction between the two parties look. This relation was found to be an asymmetrical one. As Bakhtin states, language only lives through the dialogical intercourse between those who use it[17] (or what Shapiro and Der Derian call intersubjectivity and intertextuality).[18] This may clarify why EU officials adopt instrumental views in their discourses on the Mediterranean. The EU's language on/references to the Mediterranean create an impression that the EU–Mediterranean relation is an active and developed one. The EU's Mediterranean is clearly shifting through time and space too.

What is important to observe is the context in which this discourse has been developed and the power lying behind such discourses – in other words, what Foucault terms the signification (or characteristics) of discourse. Foucault is concerned with showing 'that the analysis of discursive formations really is centred on a description of the statement in its specificity ... that they really are the proper dimensions of the statement that are at work in the mapping of discursive formations'.[19] It is thus crucial to question this discourse and to analyse the systems that make possible new discourses on the Mediterranean. The EU's current reiteration 'for Mauritania to be able to participate as a full member in the political dialogue of the Barcelona Process'[20] may be examined in light of Foucault's work. Firstly, this discursive practice reveals a widening of the EU's discourse on the Mediterranean to include Mauritania, which had so far been excluded from the Partnership (as well as the more recent EU initiative on the Greater Middle East that includes the Gulf states).[21] This statement thus shows how the EU's Mediterranean is a fluid concept, continuously in the making and it also shows how the EU persistently struggles to define the Mediterranean and to fix meaning and delineate borders around this area. Beneath this statement, however, lies the question of whether France has somehow been involved in this recent inclusion of Mauritania. At times when Britain and Germany work at enhancing their dual nexus and when France seems to loose its own nexus with Germany, France's leadership role within the EU appears in flux.[22] One may therefore speculate that France has attempted to influence the EU's discourse on the Mediterranean by going back to its historical links with Mauritania and the role it has had in North Africa in order to reiterate its role within the EU.[23] In light of this analysis the current EU discourse on the Mediterranean can be said to be a power discourse emanating from France.

This observation leads to the next set of Mediterranean*s* that emerged from the nation-state imaginings investigated through the documentation analysis and empirical work carried out for this book. The outline presented below must be analysed as an extension of the first set of Mediterranean*s* presented above and not as separate types of Mediterranean*s*. This separation in terms of analytic presentation is here made in order to show that distinctions of the Mediterranean can be made through various discourses: on the one hand, through the 'contents' of the Mediterranean as described above (for example, security or economic issues) and, on the other hand, in terms of national imaginings which may contain specific contents of the Mediterranean. Therefore, as Foucault claims, discourses may overlap which means we can trace the regularity of markers across discourses. This second set or *types* of Mediterranean are mainly geographically determined and are presented below.

Nation-state imaginings of the Mediterranean (set 2)

- French Mediterranean.
- Spanish Mediterranean.
- Italian Mediterranean.
- Maltese Mediterranean.
- Moroccan Mediterranean.
- Greek Mediterranean.

France, Spain and Italy's Mediterranean

It may be argued that, because of its established (even taken-for-granted) leading role within the EU, France's discourse may appear to fix a specific meaning to its Mediterranean. However, upon further analysis it seems that its discursive practices show that they are subject to change whenever its political influence is put to question. Spanish and Italian constructions of the Mediterranean appear to be more flexible, in accordance with external events and these countries' particular interests at certain periods. One may speculate that these discourses reflect the challenge Spain and Italy still have to establish themselves as important and influential EU members. Having analysed these discourses, however, it appears that French, Spanish and Italian discursive practices on the Mediterranean reiterate and reflect the more important discourses on Europe for these countries.[24] Therefore, it follows that the argument that southern European EU member states such as France, Italy and Spain act as a 'bloc' in their discursive practices on the Mediterranean is currently not a powerful discourse. Northern European countries, especially Sweden and Germany,[25] have been emerging with their own discourses on the Mediterranean that they deem as a very important area of influence and which therefore construct the Mediterranean in terms of its content. As one interviewee put it:

> The EMP cannot be influenced by Spain and France only. This is merely propaganda. Spain is now much less active in the Mediterranean than it used to be. New countries are showing interest in the Mediterranean now, Sweden being one of these. The balance of interests in the Mediter-ranean area shifts according to different criteria at specific time periods. This reflects the vitality of the Barcelona process.[26]

This discourse reflects how the EMP as a discursive practice on the Mediterranean constructs this area through different discourses stemming from diverse EU member states. It thereby emerges that the EU's Mediter-ranean is shifting not only in time but also in accordance with varied EU member states' national discourses (through their foreign policies as discursive practices).

It is interesting to note that there currently seems to be less of a discourse on the Mediterranean in the South European members of the EU – Italy, Spain and Portugal (and Greece too). These countries have been the most 'backward' European countries prior to their integration into the EU process. When they joined the EU, it seems that their national discourses on the Mediterranean faded and they only participated in discursive practices on the Mediterranean through official EU discourses. Yet, as the EU becomes more integrated with the entry of new members, southern European countries may develop more active discourses on the Mediterranean that in turn may influence EU practices on the area.[27] However, such more recent discourses on the Mediterranean reflect a different Spain, a different Italy and a different Portugal: these countries' discourses on the Mediterranean now reflect a certain distance in the positions and practices of these EU member states as compared to their earlier discourses on the Mediterranean as non-EU member states.[28]

This analysis confirms the work of critical political geographers[29] who state that geography supports increasingly uncertain socio-cultural and political spheres. In such dubious environments (post-9/11, 11 March),[30] geographical imaginings are constructed as an attempt to denote territory as well as identity concretely. Modern geography grew out of a support discipline for military campaigns. EU geographic imaginings (especially some specific nation-state imaginings like those of France) of the Mediterranean still reflect this origin. Furthermore, as noted by Neumann, 'the geographer's concept of "region" stems from the Latin term *regere*, to rule. The original region was thus what one today would call a theatre of war'.[31] The term Mediterranean is also essentially Latin and means 'in the middle of the lands'.[32] Thus the prevalent meaning of the Mediterranean region may be read as the middle of the lands as the theatre of war. Although it is not clear whether all Europeans would make this connection, the Mediterranean is often imagined as a conflict zone. It is no surprise then that the most regular marker across EU discourses on the Mediterranean is the securitisation of the area. Such geographical views fail to be conscious of the historicity of an area.[33]

Malta, Greece and Morocco's Mediterranean

Malta, Greece and Morocco can be said to be geopolitically and geoculturally engaged in the Mediterranean. Morocco is more involved with the Maghreb (but also with the EU, especially France and Spain, as well as with the USA); Malta is more involved with Italy and Libya and the EU ;and Greece more with the eastern Mediterranean (Israel, Egypt, Turkey, Cyprus, etc.), 'Near East' and the Balkans. Maltese and Moroccan interviewees related to the Mediterranean feeling but Greeks did not relate to this as much. Moreover, the discourses on the Mediterranean in Greece, Malta and Morocco seem to reflect some common practices of the fluidity of this concept. In fact, in all three cases the Mediterranean emerged as a fragmented area through the use of the bridge notion. It is also interesting to observe that the Mediterranean which emerged in the nation-state imaginings of France, Spain, Italy, Malta, Greece and Morocco underlines a particular reference to the Arab countries, these being referred to as either the Maghreb (in French and Moroccan discourses) or the Western Mediterranean (in Spanish discourses) or North Africa (in Maltese and Moroccan discourses) or the Middle East (in Greek discourses). These discourses can throw some light on the EMP as it is constructed in the partners' discourses. One may speculate whether it may be the case that all partners to the EMP unofficially treat this policy as an EU discursive practice of its relations with its Arab partners (rather than all the Mediterranean countries). After all, Malta and Cyprus joined the EU in May 2004, Turkey awaits its final verdict in October 2005 and Israel has special relations with the EU. The speaking 'subjects' of these discourses – that is those who can utter and make meaningful utterances about the Mediterranean – are the elites interviewed for this research. The thematics of these discourses, that is, their object/field of knowledge is the Mediterranean as a socially constructed area. Moreover, even within countries delineated as Mediterranean, it is important to distinguish between old concepts and meanings of the Mediterranean and more contemporary ones. The latter refer to more flexible notions of the content of the Mediterranean based on exchanges and relations between countries that make the area an emergent entity; that is, an entity in the making. Old concepts of the Mediterranean in these case studies refer to trade and co-operation initiatives and movements – in other words, the old notion of the Mediterranean as a trading post that 'makes' the 'area'. More contemporary discourses of the Mediterranean in Greece, Malta and Morocco still refer to specific but different characteristics of the area, namely to identity issues (broadly defined), cultural exchanges, educational and economic/business networks, contacts and national interests. This contrasts sharply with the resulting fixed meaning of the Mediterranean within EU discourses – which construct the area as a holistic group of similar countries that the EU must 'deal' with and 'manage'.[34]

Before investigating how these different discourses on the Mediterranean reflect upon the deficiencies of the EMP (as these have been presented in Chapter 3), it is worth mentioning a third set of *Mediterraneans* underlying discourses on this area. These are outlined below as common discourses of the Mediterranean:

Common discourses of the Mediterranean (set 3)

- Sea.
- Sun.
- Cuisine.
- Ambiance.
- Feeling.
- Olive-tree zone.

The meaning of an area like the Mediterranean has been strongly influenced by the writings of travellers and traders who have imposed specific meanings on this space over time. Among the common discourses on the Mediterranean are references to the sea, the sun, the Mediterranean cuisine, the Mediterranean ambiance, the Mediterranean feeling and the area as the olive-tree zone. These common discourses were frequently noted when nation-state imaginings of the Mediterranean were observed and also when the Mediterranean is socially constructed through specific contents or characteristics. Thus, for example, when the Mediterranean was constructed in terms of people-to-people relations and exchanges (set 1 – content of Med), statements about the Mediterranean also mentioned that such interpersonal relations are usually experienced in a Mediterranean environment. Interviewees cited conferences they attended on the Mediterranean in Greece, Spain, Italy or southern France for example. The context of these conferences thus reflects the agenda of the discussions on the Mediterranean. For instance, the Halki international seminars on themes related to the Mediterranean are conducted on a yearly basis on the island of Halki in Greece. As a participant during these conferences I observe many other participants referring to the 'appropriate' ambiance offered by Halki for such a conference. Therefore, although these types of Mediterraneans have been presented as three different sets, these are often overlapping discourses that contain elements of all three broad outlines. Hence, geography and politics contribute to each other's construction.[35] Certain groups of metaphors about the Mediterranean – especially the spatial ones – are built into the way people think of the Mediterranean and are impossible to escape. Certain embedded metaphors and ways of thinking about the Mediterranean are therefore difficult to remove but may be reflected upon. In sum, language is metaphorical and each text on the Mediterranean is influenced by its preceding text (if known) – be this a common discourse, or specific characteristics of the Mediterranean or geographical determinants. The following section will look at some of the deficiencies in the EMP as the most recent EU discursive practice of the Mediterranean – which attempts to address the Mediterranean through a policy.

Some deficiencies in the EMP as a discursive practice

As a reflection of EU discourses/representations of the Mediterranean, Chapter Four analysed the EMP as a discursive strategy. Although this policy suggests relations between European and Mediterranean partners, the Mediterranean that emerged in the nation-state imaginings of France, Spain, Italy, Malta, Greece and Morocco underlines a particular reference to Arab partners. These discourses suggest that the EMP is in effect about European–Arab relations, at least in the manner in which the EMP is constructed in some of the partners' discourses. This observation is in line with Foucault's analysis of statements in which he claims that:

> The enunciative level is neutralized each time: either it is defined only as a representative sample that enables one to free endlessly applicable structures; or it disappears into a pure appearance behind which the truth of words is revealed; or it acts as a neutral substance that serves as a support for formal relations ... In considering statements in themselves ... We shall try to render visible, and analysable, that immediate transparency that constitutes the element of their possibility.[36]

The analysis of the discursive formations of the Mediterranean in EU policy that has been carried out throughout this book has attempted to analyse EU statements on the Mediterranean. In so doing, it has exposed the constraints and resources of such statements and the regularity across markers in EU discourses. It has also revealed that what made these discursive practices possible included the colonial legacy of European countries (along the thinking developed in new development theories) and their economic power (as a form of hegemony) for effective action. This section will now endeavour to present some of the lessons that can be learned from adopting a discursive constructivist approach to the study of European-Mediterranean policies. This analysis is not meant as a direct prescription of how the EMP can emerge as a successful policy. Rather, it seeks to scrutinise the implications of how the EU defines the Mediterranean and the manner in which its discourses on this area govern its relations with Mediterranean partners. By uncovering the discursive formations of the Mediterranean in the EMP, this book hopes to offer some tools for understanding the way in which EU discourses on the Mediterranean have become institutionalised and how this area has been constructed as an element of EU strategy.

In its first pillar of the EMP, EU discourses on the Mediterranean offer ideas and directions for 'political dialogue' between the two partners to cover the rule of law, human rights and democracy. It may be argued that the effect of this discourse leaves much to be desired since the EMP pays 'little more than lip-service to democracy and the rule of law, and it still contains only few concrete steps towards a political implementation of the goals set'. Moreover, its 'success ... can hardly be assessed in any serious way as yet'.[37] During President Prodi's visit to Jordan, Lebanon and Syria in 2001, the implementation of these ideas was attempted through a public address by Prodi at Damascus University.[38] The EU is seeking ways to look into these issues through such public practices or through the use of institutional means to promote human rights.[39] The discursive practices analysed in this research, however, point to the vagueness in EU discourses on such issues that seem to remain at the level of rhetoric. EU definitions of the Mediterranean in terms of the 'common' problem of immigration is an example of such an EU practice at the level of rhetoric. The EU does not show enough political will to go beyond its strategy of controlling immigration. Perhaps it attempts to do so through the Schengen agreement and the support it offers for border guards, but it has not seriously dealt with this issue so far.[40] Thus, this is an example of a regular marker across EU discourses on the Mediterranean, if one sticks to the level of rhetoric. Even elites from its member states, Italy and France, note that not much has been done regarding this issue area. In short, the EU is not dealing with the issue of immigration. Therefore, one may observe that although the EU identifies the Mediterranean as an area where immigration is a unifying factor – an 'identity' aspect (broadly defined), this is another instance of a gap between EU rhetoric on the Mediterranean and its action towards the implemented goals in EU Mediterranean policies.[41]

This is also the case in the second pillar of the EMP that 'is less (about) poverty eradication as an objective in its own right, (and) rather the cushioning of adverse social effects which liberal reforms invariably bring about ...'. The third pillar also 'presents a somewhat ambiguous picture'.[42] This latter pillar reflects a lack of EU understanding of the Mediterranean countries it deals with within the context of the EMP.[43]

Moreover, it seems that the EU has its own priority list in its (EMP) Mediterranean policy. The struggle for 'stability' – which reflects the EU's securitisation discourse on the Mediterranean – has priority over 'democracy' (for the EU in its Mediterranean policy). This EU priority list is also reflected in the unbalanced distribution of funds between the different baskets. It seems quite obvious that the EU prioritises economic reform processes in its

Mediterranean partner states. This is a sector that allows for an impression that EU–Mediterranean relations are active and developed. Economics is the sector that authorises the EU to govern its relations with the Mediterranean partners since it has more clout in this field. In fact, the EU tends to marginalise the political component of its stated policy objectives since this is the field where Mediterranean reality and complexity lies. EU involvement or attempts at involvement in this area would therefore not reflect well on EU credentials: because of the EU's lack of political (especially military) clout within the political pillar, this pillar does not reflect well on the success of the EMP and thereby on EU–Mediterranean relations. It cannot be denied that the EU is in the process of establishing itself as an international actor still.[44] If the EU allowed issues/voices (that is a space for utterances from within the Mediterranean) to emerge from the Mediterranean, it might be incompetent to address them. Therefore, it sets the agenda and responses for questions it can give on the Mediterranean – questions it can solve and issues that give credence to the reasons for its very existence.

There is no doubt that the Mediterranean gives Europe and specifically the EU some *materiality*.[45] The EU deals with many countries as one group in order to reduce its variables, thus increasing the manageability of a regional system. This is an important insight derived from discourse analysis that differs from many other social scientific approaches that tend to define parts of the world as unproblematic. By freezing reality in this manner (of controlling these variables), the EU can say something about the Mediterranean other than about those issues which it cannot deal with or which would reflect negatively on it as an international actor, albeit in the making. The EU, for example, is unprepared to deal with so many complex issues such as the Middle East crisis[46] – it has too much of a straightjacket in dealing with its regional groupings: even though the EMP and the MEPP are interrelated.[47] These are the variables that are relevant when dealing with the Mediterranean – an effort from the EU's side to manage, make more easily controllable the international reality that is surrounding it (a strategy of bringing/selecting common denominators). In defence of the EU as an international actor, the EU therefore shuts out parts of the Mediterranean and reduces the rest to clearly ordered categories. Thus, the EU only senses part of the Mediterranean and adapts the countries selected as its Mediterranean to pre-stored regional models.

> Cognitive consistence theory makes this insight the starting point for the study of the social, by studying (a) 'the framing problem': what frame one chooses to interpret something within, and (b) how expectations about what can be found inside the frame determine what one observes.[48]

The EU sees what its members want to see of the Mediterranean. The Mediterranean has to therefore be put forward in EU discourses time and again. Yet, there is no 'true' or 'correct' discourse of the Mediterranean. From the EU's side, one can agree with Schlumberger that:

> (t)he EU is ... no homogenous actor. In many policy areas, the southern member states' interests differ significantly from the northern members, and overlapping institutional responsibilities and competencies further complicate the formulation of coherent policies.[49]

Practical implications for EU Mediterranean Policy

This observation fits with the results of the documentation analysis and fieldwork of this research in terms of the ambiguous EU discourses of the Mediterranean that challenge the EU's international actorness. As a Maltese interviewee stated, unless EU Mediterranean policy attempts to be attractive to all parties in terms of responding to their individual interests and needs,[50] it is unlikely that any EU Mediterranean policy will succeed. EU practices of the Mediterranean cannot be grounded in a holistic view of all its Mediterranean partners as one group: they are different, with their own specific needs, requirements and priorities. The adoption of such a flexible EU Mediterranean practice can bring about improvements in EU–Mediterranean relations in terms of better communications and understanding between partners.[51] Whenever possible, EU partners can act through a sensitive approach to the specificity of each Mediterranean partner. The Mediterranean is a plural area in terms of (broadly defined) identities, cultures, development stages, economic performance, etc.[52] The discursive constructivist framework adopted in this book sheds light on the nature of dialogue which is a fundamental building block in EU–Mediterranean relations. When one enters into a dialogic relationship, one cannot assume that one partner is superior and the other inferior:[53] such a relationship assumes that other partners are equal and the relationship is based on premises of exchange between the two partners. In such a dialogue, it follows that the EU does not only enter into a relationship with its Mediterranean partners through regular meetings and a furtherance of understanding but also the determination to deconstruct the EU's sense of 'holiness'.[54] As Prodi said recently:

> The only way to express ourselves in the new world is by being together. I don't like to be a colony. If we do not get together, we will disappear from world history.[55]

If the EU's Mediterranean policy is to be revisited, almost ten years since its inception, these reflections point to the need of the EU to strengthen the social component within the EMP. The EU has to do without its neo- or post-colonial discourses/practices in order to avoid the impression that its institutions and elites are all about political interference in the Mediterranean partner countries. Instead, the EU could aim to fulfil the objectives set for the social and human 'basket' of its Mediterranean policies. In practice, this means addressing the fears of Mediterranean partners about the EU's neo-colonial project, that is the suspicion of Western attempts to impose a European agenda. This will require a building process of shared norms and institutions that create mutual understanding. The envisaged Foundation for the Dialogue of Cultures could be seen as a positive step in this direction and could be the 'catalyst for all initiatives aimed at increasing dialogue and common understanding'.[56] This effort could balance the pressure and strong concentration on the purely technical-economic aspects of Euro–Mediterranean relations. It is commonly recognised that strong social safety nets are essential to ensure the success of transitional processes in developing societies. It will also be useful if the EU tries to involve its Mediterranean partners in a truly dialogic relationship before any strategy is 'commonly' agreed upon.[57] This could ensure that any strategy respects the fears, anxieties, interests of both the Mediterranean partner governments and those of the EU partners. In this manner, the EU could be presented as a context, an 'action system',[58] rather than as *the* centre of action.

Discourse analysis and foreign policy

Discourse theory can thus inform EU–Mediterranean relations through its focus on the intersubjectivity of communication processes.[59] In the case of EU–Mediterranean relations these can flow through both the parliamentary bodies and the informal networks of the public sphere.[60] The recent mention of Mauritania's potential inclusion in the EMP (within a parliamentarians' environment) shows that the European Parliament and parliamentarians in Mediterranean countries can have an important and effective role in enhancing EU–Mediterranean relations and understandings. It may be argued that the discourse of parliamentarians on the Mediterranean is more flexible than that of Commission officials as a result of the nature of their tasks: the latter deal with Mediterranean issues in a more direct manner while parliamentarians operate more at the strategic level. However, the Commission delegations in Mediterranean partner countries can play a crucial role in reinforcing and implementing the EMP's partnership building instruments. This can be further facilitated through the recently established Euro-Mediterranean Parliamentary body. This author supports the continuation of the dialogue environment created in Barcelona between the partners in the EMP as a means of clearing up misunderstandings and to foster the approximation of discursive practices and perceptions and to make it possible to strengthen confidence and trust amongst all the EMP partners.[61] Rather than attempting the symbolic ordering of Mediterranean social relations, European partners have to understand their Mediterranean partners better. Likewise, Mediterranean partners have to enhance their understanding of their European colleagues.[62]

Therefore, when applied to this work, discursive constructivism points to the importance of the third pillar of the EMP and the meaning of the Mediterraneans that emerge from informal networks of communications and exchanges.[63] The Mediterranean is a set of complex societies rather than one holistic and homogenous society: the EU *cannot* therefore be effective in the area through its presuppositions and rhetoric of these societies as one holistic group. When dealing with this area, the EU has to accept its Mediterranean politics as continuous, ceaseless and endless, a process that the EU needs to work on too and not expect things to happen from the Mediterranean partners' side alone. The EU has been conceived in this book as the marker of a Mediterranean certainty that characterises the specific form of social symbolic power that is at the core of EU 'democracy'. It has to do away with the specific kind of politics which the development of the modern state in Western industrial societies created – that is, it has to do away with the politics of domestication, containment and boundary-drawing. The alternative for the EU lies in a non-state centred vision of the political.[64]

Conclusion

This book has focused on the Mediterranean and on the manner in which this 'region' is integrated in EU policy discourses and practices. Thus, a central concept in this book has been that of 'region' and a central process that of 'region-formation'. The literature on the Mediterranean commonly offers two different representations of this area: the Mediterranean as a region with sub-regions and/or the Mediterranean as an interface between coherent regions.[1] Upon evaluation of this literature, it was revealed that there seems to be a systemic deficiency in the manner in which the Mediterranean is treated – namely, as a fixed, taken-for-granted entity. This book has sought to question such conventional conceptions of the Mediterranean by problematising the concept of regionality and rethinking the Mediterranean in an open, relational context. In so doing, it aimed at bringing to the fore, the particular specificities of Mediterranean countries.

On this basis, this book adopted a language approach and explored Mediterranean and EU perceptions on the Mediterranean and the EU's policy on this area. This language framework takes a radical constructivist approach and combines it with discourse analysis where discourse is taken as praxis (the study of practices) and where structures within discourse condition possible policies.[2] This theoretical framework espouses a conceptualisation of regions as socially constructed and looks into the processes of region making through the practice of foreign policy and identity politics. This involves agents that classify 'regions' in specific contexts. This was carried out through a discourse analysis of the EU's most recent Mediterranean policy, the Euro–Mediterranean Partnership (EMP) and the 'region' as these are explicated in EU documentation and through interviews carried out with a sample of elite interviewees in Brussels and Greece, Malta and Morocco. Some examples of the limits of rationalist approaches and the advantages of a discourse analysis approach can be seen in how the chapter on Greece, Malta and Morrocco depicts these countries' ambivalent attitudes to the EU's policy on the Mediterranean. In these countries, the EU's EMP initiative was portrayed as another attempt to manipulate the Med partners through false calls for reform and historical references to the colonial era, the EU was constructed as an imperial power, motivated by its member states' own self-interests and not by the interests of Med partners. Even more radical accounts saw the EMP initiative as part of a new guardianship, a return to the colonial era. The identification of the EU as a partner reached an all-time low with accusations of EU member states working to maximise their individual interests through the Greater Middle East Initiative and against the interests of the Med region. This methodology helped to codify the effects of the EU's discourse on the Mediterranean through the EMP, that is to codify the actions, processes and structures that forge an idea of the Mediterranean (both at the Commission level and within the partner countries). The aim was to tease out attitudes towards the Partnership and to examine whether the Mediterranean is perceived as a comprehensive political, economic and cultural space, and to contrast the nature of these perceptions on each side of the Partnership. The conceptions gathered from Brussels were then compared with those from the other cases in order to assess any differences, contradictions or similarities across discourses and, by doing so, to understand what action or thought structures and processes bring about such regular markers of discourse. This methodology was adopted since awareness of the partnership is largely confined to officials, researchers and the political elite in general. It was concluded that contexts, knowledgeable practices and embedded notions about the Mediterranean are what make any discourse on the Mediterranean 'real' and meaningful.

Now that Malta, Cyprus, and possibly Turkey in the future, are helping to determine the EU's future, an understanding of Mediterranean attitudes and positions becomes progressively more important. An appreciation of their complex and varied (or similar) reactions to the EMP and the more recent ENP shows how the future prospects of the EU's foreign policy are to be increasingly shaped by opinions and preferences of Mediterranean countries. Mediterranean countries thus offer a rich field for the analysis of discourses on European issues, especially on EU foreign policy (on the wider Mediterranean in particular). This book has focused on how three different Mediterranean countries perceive the idea of the Mediterranean and on their conceptions of the EMP. The evidence from the case studies' historical development produced a conceptual constellation of each country's complex political and cultural identity. This helps us to understand, for example, Greece's ambivalent relationship to Europe, Malta's eventual acceptance to integrate into 'Europe' (in a political sense) and Morocco's happy acceptance of being a partner of the EU (but not a member). Malta's case showed how identity negotiations addressed fears of the European integration project which threatened the nation's cultural identity. This was a case where the EU membership referendum result was a close one and this may be partly appreciated by a mind-set in which the Maltese state and nation are closely intertwined, so that pooling political sovereignty with Europe – for almost half of the island's population – meant a threat to the nation's very identity. A further critical dimension – particularly in the cases of Greece and Malta – is the persuasive power of the *people* who hold on to and are called upon to defend their birthright against the 'elitist project' of European integration. This book hopes to add to the existing literature but also to shed some further light on the fuzzy aspects of the interactions between the EU and (Med) civil society. By adopting an application of discourse analysis in the context of studying EU policy-making processes on the Med, it has sought to show *how* perceptions of (national, regional, cultural, political) identity can and do influence specific EU foreign policy decisions. The next section will therefore present some policy implications of this theoretical approach for the three baskets of the EMP.

Policy implications

The analysis throughout this book points at the need for the development of both theoretical and practical suggestions as to how to promote a convergence of perceptions around the EU-Mediterranean space. The emerging literature on regionalism moves away from conceptualising regions in terms of geographical contiguity and rather emphasises the political, economic, cultural and social interaction processes among states and nations which do not necessarily inhabit the same geographical space. A convergence of perceptions can help towards constituting policies which enable people in EU countries as well as Mediterranean countries feel and talk more positively about the 'other' through a better understanding of the 'other'. The documents analysed for this research, as well as the general view from the people interviewed for this purpose, seem receptive towards regional integration forums, particularly the EMP. In fact, it seems that the EMP is the best framework for regional integration in the EU-Med zone. Although Arab regionalism is a preferred option for the Arab partners of the EMP, the EMP still emerges as a good alternative in the view of officials, academics and other professionals interviewed, in terms of its potential positive impact on Med national economies. Arab regionalist frameworks such as the Agadir[3] process (within the context of the EMP) are considered as positive schemes for Arab economies and welfare and the EMP remains the most viable and credible regionalist process to drive such initiatives. Despite a broad ambivalent attitude towards the EMP and economic liberalisation in Med partner countries, regional economic integration is viewed as a positive step in the development of EU–Med relations. The development of a stable, peaceful, prosperous Mediterranean may require a process of learned trust and collective understandings both within the Med and in Europe. The instruments required for this process already exist within the Barcelona Process. The EU has a reasonably clear agenda outlined in its EMP, broadly based on its members' collective interests and sense of 'responsibility' towards the southern and eastern Mediterranean area. The idea of building a peaceful neighbour at the EU's periphery can come to reality through the implementation of the structures, processes, institutions and practices contained within the EMP. This can be kicked off with the application of the concept of Partnership in terms of shared understandings which can be developed through a 'bottom-up' process of purposeful social communication between networks and the wider civil societies in EU countries and the Mediterranean partner states. The EU-Med partnership as a form of interaction that has thrived since 1995 is a relationship that has to be based on mutual trust and a sense of interdependence. Although the contractual aspects of the EMP are important, the cognitive and psychological aspects of the partnership and the EU's institutional modes of operation tend to be critical in this complex relationship. In theory, a partnership is ideal and should be balanced with a positive-sum interaction capacity which generates positive effects for all parties involved and where the gains of one actor are not attained at the expense of others.[4] A successful partnership requires certain policy imperatives to address the needs and concerns of partners involved. Each actor must have the same rights, duties and vested interests. In an ideal partnership, interdependence assumes harmony in partners' interactions. The EMP, almost a decade after its launching, constitutes a deviation from the partnership ideal: it remains coloured by unresolved apprehensions and misperceptions. The southern partners' vision of the EMP are at times contradictory to the vision of the EMP in Brussels. The EMP is thus still in formation. Most of the association agreements between the EU and the Mediterranean partners were characterised by prolonged and complex processes of negotiations. Moreover, the EU has been reluctant to take the partnership beyond the economic sphere. Although the EMP has a high level of credibility, it still lacks clarity of where it is going (that is, detailed objectives). Consequently, cost–benefit assessments are little debated beyond officials and the elite classes directly involved. Although, in general, the public in Mediterranean countries is supportive of the economic programmes of the EMP, it remains ignorant of the overall debate on all baskets of the partnership.[5] Ambiguous attitudes remain in particular towards the 'elitist' nature of the EMP.

The economic basket of the EMP

Criticism of the EMP has been most intense in what are perceived as vulnerable economic sectors, particularly agricultural production and domestic industries (food industries, engineering industries and textiles). Critical voices echo deep apprehensions about the trade imbalance that remains between the EU and the Med partner countries. Mediterranean industrial exports remain uncompetitive, agricultural exports struggle to have a comparative advantage, while increases in the Med agricultural export quotas are permitted only for marginal crops, rather than major commercial ones.[6] Expectations of increased foreign direct investment (FDI) from the EU have not materialised. The need for modernisation in Med partner countries is not confined to technical modernisation alone, but also to procedural, managerial and legislative requirements. The EU is called upon to work more consistently with local Med business communities to encourage Med governments to ease their bureaucratic hold and to create an atmosphere supportive for industrial competitiveness. The EU, on its part, is considered too protectionist through its quotas, 'protectionist measures', 'exaggerated entry conditions' and extreme quality control standards. Despite these differences in the evaluation of the EMP between European and Mediterranean partners, there seems to be an underlying consensus that the EMP is a good process to deal with the challenges of globalisation and as a preparatory phase from regional integration towards global integration. It is also expected to stimulate administrative and legal reforms in Med countries, much needed for the achievement of the multifaceted task of modernisation, including an extensive R&D programme, marketing research and training (in addition to the more structural aspects of bureaucratic and legislative reforms).

The future legitimacy of the EMP hangs on the balance between the sponsored free trade and progress in the unfinished task of industrial modernisation in Med partner countries. There have been increasing concerns and fears among Med partner countries that, with the May 2004 enlargement, Eastern European countries will be favoured by EU economic assistance and direct investment policies at the expense of the Med partners. However, there has also been an optimistic view from Med countries on the economic impact of the EU's recent enlargement relating to the vast European market and the existence of special relationships with some of the newcomers – particularly Malta. However, the new members do not constitute traditional export markets for Med partners, so that their agricultural export quotas will have to be redistributed among the 25 members, while new members will enjoy full access to the Med partners' markets. Still, the general perception is one of the EMP as a model for further Arab regionalism. With the Agadir initiative, it is argued that Arab integration within the EMP has an added-value to the EMP by facilitating inter-Arab co-operation and balancing Euro–Arab relations, creating a relationship between balanced blocs rather than between a unified EU bloc on the one side and individual Arab countries on the other. Official discourses have compared the Agadir process to European integration which started as an economic enterprise and is expanding into political integration.[7] The Med partners' bargaining power *vis-à-vis* the EU is thus expected to improve through inter-Arab sub-regional frameworks (like the Agadir initiative).

The political basket of the EMP

Med perceptions of the EMP as, mainly, an economic enterprise have arguably had a negative impact on its political profile. For (most of) the Mediterranean partners, their view of the world and their foreign relations are particularly defined by the Arab–Israeli conflict. In fact, the political basket of the EMP has been having added resonance in the Arab partner countries since the second Palestinian *intifada*. Although the original, intentional separation of the Barcelona Process and the Israeli–Palestinian conflict is echoed in many documents (from 1995), this is an artificial separation. At the latest Euro-Med conferences (Marseilles in 2000, Valencia in 2002, the informal meeting in Crete and Naples in 2003, Dublin and The Hague in 2004) the situation in the Middle East conflict was reviewed on each occasion and Presidency Conclusions from each meeting included lengthy analyses of the crisis. The analysis of these EU documents seems to imply that the EMP *cannot* and *should not* abandon its efforts to deal with what is the most important political challenge in the region in a multilateral way. In line with the EU's own discourse on political security equated to economic security which is in turn equated to societal security, Arab partners (of the EMP) look up to the EU as a symbol of successful integration and peaceful coexistence. The EMP is thus perceived as an ideal forum for discussing the Middle East conflict (and when the time comes the peace) in a regional framework. The EU's contribution to solving the Middle East conflict and its role in the Barcelona Process are perceived, in the Arab partners' viewpoint, as complementary. A reformed Barcelona Process constitutes the EU's long-term framework for its relationship with the Med, whereas measures required for resolution of the conflict will in principle be of a limited duration (albeit a long-term impact). Ideally, resolution of the Israel–Palestine conflict will give the Barcelona Process a central role in the region.[8] For the EU, this involvement would boost its political image in the region and its role as a global actor. For Mediterranean Arab partners of the EMP, such a resolution would be viewed as a way to further Arab interests by diminishing US hegemony and influence in the region.

The social basket of the EMP

Although the future of the EMP's cultural aspects are less clear, the dramatic events of 9/11 have forcefully brought the cultural aspects of the partnership to the fore. The debate, however, has been treated as an extension of existing EU–Med relations but not as an important part of the EMP. The visibility of the cultural aspects of the EMP must be increased and a transparent dialogue on sensitive issues initiated. The general perception in Mediterranean partner countries is that EU partners deny the Mediterranean partners a 'consciousness of themselves' – and that by doing so the Europeans settle any qualms of conscience as to the EU's right to be involved in the Mediterranean space. As long as Europeans believe that Mediterranean partner countries are like pets or small children, Europeans can remain involved to 'guide them' and help them 'develop'. But if Europeans perceive that Mediterranean partner countries are as fully conscious of themselves and their place in the world as Europeans are, then the third basket of the EMP can offer the EU a functional and advisory role in political, economic *and* social matters – which Mediterranean partners would not resist. At a time when the perception of the irreconcilable nature of cultures is growing, it is important to take the concept of dialogue between European and Mediterranean cultures seriously.[9]

The EU has long been acknowledged, not least in the Mediterranean, for its role in the world through half a century of uninterrupted, traditional and multilateral diplomacy. Through its various Mediterranean policies, particularly the EMP, the EU has created a number of forums on dialogue with Mediterranean partners. For a true dialogic relationship, the focus has to be on a *set* of relations: rather than having a dialogue, what is crucial is what dialogue converges to. Hence, for a plurality of inter-cultural consciousness to blossom, a dialectic understanding of dialogue is crucial.[10] Euro–Mediterranean partners need to find the space for critical self-reflection. Moving away from relations of domination, critical dialogue entails an overlap of the Self and the Other. Self-identity always owes a debt to difference, and the Other always exists within as a source of internal difference. The future effectiveness of the EMP rests on the partners' ability to 'read' each other's worlds. By understanding the Other, we are more likely to share with our partners local or global visions and to anticipate behaviours and reactions of our partners. This means some hard realities: Europeans have to face their colonial past and Europe's colonial legacy, while Med partners have to engage in more self-criticisms. The recognition of one's own participation in another's *language* can create a bridge and a common horizon for dialogic interactions, or a co-presence with the Other.[11] True dialogue and participation entail a recognition of one's particularities as a step towards realisations of the particularities of Others. Euro–Mediterranean dialogic relations must work towards establishing this overlap.

Conclusion

The language approach adopted in this book highlights the importance of language to an understanding of issues of political, economic and social concerns for EU–Med relations and the future development of this relation. In terms of practical relevance, it helps in our understanding of the ways we communicate both influence and are influenced by the structures and forces of contemporary political, economic and social institutions. Discourse analysis as a method furthers our knowledge on: how language functions in maintaining and changing power relations in modern and post-modern societies; the ways in which we can analyse language and which can reveal these processes and on how people can become more conscious of themselves and more able to resist and change power relations. The question of language and power remains important and urgent today, and with the substantial changes in the international context in the past three years or so, the nature of unequal power relationships has been particularly challenging. The agenda for a critical study of international relations through language is much called for.

Although it focuses on EU–Med relations, this book extends beyond this subject and reaches out to a much broader audience interested in issues of IR theory and foreign policy analysis more generally. The theoretical approach laid out, which built on previous works within the IR field, elaborates a discourse analysis theory of foreign policy.[12] Through this language approach, this theory identifies problems with rationalist accounts and approaches to foreign policy analysis. In this respect, it highlights how rationalist explanations of foreign policy analysis (FPA) fail to capture the significance of identity-based arguments in understanding EU policy on the Mediterranean. These insights do not just affect how we should understand particular countries' attitudes to the EU but also indicate a need to rethink predominant understandings of the EU more generally. What is presented is not simply another advocation of the importance of the politics of identity, but a systematically adapted and developed theory of foreign policy from a post-structuralist discourse analysis perspective. In particular, a specific attempt is made to show how discourses frame political, economic and social environments, thereby structuring options for EU action within Med bounds. It has been highlighted that while all discourses have structuring effects, some are more important than others (dominant or embedded discourses). The idea of structural depth suggests that some discourses should be understood as rather deeply embedded in the discursive field at particular times and are relatively immune to change.[13] Other discourses, in contrast, are nearer the surface level, and are thus open to much greater contestation. This book makes an important contribution by showing the way in which the idea of the 'Mediterranean' has been and is variously conceptualised in EU discourses and in Mediterranean countries. The chapters focus on these different discourses and how these have impacted on the EU's policy on the Mediterranean. Taken together, these chapters illustrate the difficulties of treating the Mediterranean countries as an undifferentiated group. The fact that the case studies illustrate that multiple competing 'Mediterraneans' exist within different national debates both in Europe as well as in the Med further highlights the difficulties facing EU Mediterranean policies. The Union and the Med partners are aware of these challenges and should use all the instruments at their disposal within the EMP framework to develop their relations. The more recent European Neighbourhood Policy (ENP) offers new opportunities for both partners. Efforts within the ENP context should:

- encourage public discussion on the impact of the EU on the democratisation processes of its southern neighbours;
- which will in turn influence decision makers in the EU to adopt mutually motivating action plans concerning each southern country that is included in the ENP;
- improve the willingness and ability of NGOs from the EU and its southern neighbours to co-operate in implementing the ENP;
- develop networks between EU and southern neighbours and support new co-operation projects, particularly those which impact on the local populations;
- address obstacles for development in the South particularly those deriving from different political and institutional systems (as well as value-systems);

- develop tailor-made external policies or action plans to meet the internal political conditions of any given southern country since progress towards reform depends largely on the latter. Therefore, rather than adopting a one-size-fits-all list of reform priorities, the Action Plans should take into account the specificities of each southern neighbour.

The General Affairs and External Relations Council conclusions have highlighted the need for jointly devised Action Plans which set out realistic and limited objectives, based on a set of shared principles.[14] This is a positive step forward in addressing past accusations of the EU's imposition of its value systems on the southern partners. These are the keys which can open possibilities for future EU–Med neighbourly relations, on a more equal footing. The ENP needs to be accompanied by political conditionality strategies for those southern partners who are not willing to comply or co-operate according to predefined and pre-agreed structures. The value of a single framework for relations with a number of diversified neighbours is an opportunity not to be missed!

Notes

1 Introduction

1 This book aims to investigate the study of macro – that is, transnational regions rather than micro or sub-national – regions.
2 There is no incompatibility between regarding the Mediterranean as a region and then saying that it is composed of sub-regions – the two views are compatible.
3 Mauritania is often considered a marginal state although it has been mentioned as a potential future partner in the Euro–Mediterranean Partnership (EMP). See *EuroMed Report*. 'Final Declaration of the Second Session of the Euro-Mediterranean Parliamentary Forum', Issue 25, 9 February 2001. Brussels, 8–9 February, 3.
4 In many ways, it may be argued that it makes sense to include Egypt under the Levant sub-region, even if it also features as part of North Africa.
5 There is a reluctance to include the Balkans (as a Mediterranean sub-region), which instead is seen as a separate region ('Balkans' or 'south-east Europe').
6 Most of these studies focus on security issues in the Mediterranean. See, amongst others, Aliboni, Roberto (ed.) 1992. *Southern European Security in the 1990s*. London: Pinter Publishers; Latter, Richard, 1992. *Mediterranean Security*. London: HMSO, Wilton Park papers, 48; Kinacioglu, Muge, 2000. 'From East–West Rivalry to North–South Division: Redefining the Mediterranean Security Agenda', *International Relations*, 15(2), August, 27–39.
7 The understanding of 'identity' in this book has been influenced by the seminal work of Brubaker and Cooper who opt for three alternative terms for 'identity' arguing that the latter is confusing as a term and that it is overburdened with multiple meanings and multiple functions. Hence, they opt for identification and categorisation, self-understanding and commonality/connectedness/groupness. See Brubaker, Rogers and Cooper, Frederick, 2000. 'Beyond "Identity"', *Theory and Society*, 29, 1–47.
8 This discussion gains from debates on multiple identities in the European Union (supranational, national, regional and local). See Smith, Michael E., 2004a. 'Institutionalization, Policy Adaptation and European Foreign Policy Cooperation', *European Journal of International Relations*, 10(1), 95–136.
9 Pace, Michelle, 2004a. 'Collective Identity: The Greek Case', in W. Carlnaes, H. Sjursen and B. White (eds) *Contemporary European Foreign Policy*. London: Sage Publications, 227–38.
10 Al-Mani, Saleh A., 1983. *The Euro–Arab Dialogue. A Study in Associative Diplomacy*. London: Frances Pinter, 12–13.
11 Ibid., 36.
12 Ibid., 61. It should come as no surprise that the Euro–Arab dialogue did not succeed since any EC/EU political policy is usually clothed in trade clothes, for most European attempts at political/regional unification have functional, instrumental goals. This will be developed later in the book.
13 Disparities between 'North' and 'South' are analysed in Chapter 3.
14 For the literature on 'securitization' see Wæver, Ole, 1995. 'Securitization and Desecuritization', in R.D. Lipschutz (ed.) *On Security*. New York: Columbia University Press, 46–86; and Wæver, Ole, 2003. 'Securitization: Taking Stock of a Research

Programme in Security Studies'. Draft paper discussed at a PIPES (Program on International Politics, Economics and Security) seminar at The University of Chicago, 24 February.

15   Although the theory reviewed – both briefly in this introductory chapter but in more detail in the Chapter 2 of this book – may initially seem odd – since most of it does not address regionalism explicitly – I draw upon these works and connect them with the analysis of regions through the common underlying theme in these works, that is, identity politics.

16   See, for example, the work of Buzan, Barry, 1991. *People, States and Fear: An Agenda for International Security Studies in the Post-Cold War Era*, 2nd edn. Hemel Hempstead: Harvester; on regional security complex theory or one of the standard textbooks in the area: Lake, David A. and Morgan, Patrick M. (eds) 1997. *Regional Orders: Building Security in a New World*. University Park, PA: Pennsylvania State University Press. The most recent work is that of Buzan, Barry and Wæver, Ole, 2003. *Regions and Powers: The Structure of International Security*. Cambridge: Cambridge University Press.

17   See, for example, Neumann, Iver B., 1994. 'A Region-Building Approach to Northern Europe', *Review of International Studies*, 20(1), 53–74; Larsen, H., 1997. *Foreign Policy and Discourse Analysis: France, Britain and Europe*. London: Routledge.

18   Pervin, David J. in Lake and Morgan, 1997, 272.

19   Lake and Morgan, 1997, 12.

20   A similar work is that of Cantori, Louis J. and Spiegel, Steven L., 1970. *The International Politics of Regions. A Comparative Approach*. Englewood Cliffs, NJ: Prentice-Hall.

21   Lake and Morgan, 1997, 59.

22   Buzan, 1991, 188.

23   Ibid., 190.

24   Deutsch, K. *et al.*, 1957. *Political Community and the North Atlantic Area: International Organisation in the Light of Historical Experience*. Princeton, NJ: Princeton University Press.

25   Buzan, 1991, 218.

26   For an interesting analysis of the impact of EU integration on Nordic states see Hansen, Lene and Wæver, Ole, 2002. *European Integration and National Identity. The Challenge of the Nordic States*. London: Routledge.

27   Wæver, Ole *et al.*, 1993. *Identity, Migration and the New Security Agenda in Europe*. London: Pinter. In a more recent piece, Wæver argues that 'Methodologically, discourses are the source of understanding ... discourses. Methodologically, the major clue is to stick to *discourse* as interesting in itself. We do not ask for something inaccessible and then make do with substitutes and indicators. Rather, we study something openly accessible and think about exactly how *it* works, and what it can explain' (author's own emphasis). In other words, discourse can be understood as praxis (action or practices). Wæver, Ole, 2004a. 'European Intergration and Security: Analysing French and German Discourses on State, Nation and Europe'. Paper presented at a Conference on Security and Integration, 6–7 February. Article downloaded from the author's website: http://www.polsci.ku.dk/people/Faculty/Waever_Ole.htm.

28   Giddens, Anthony, 1989. *Sociology*. Cambridge: Polity Press, 32. The understanding of culture employed in this book follows the proposed definition of culture by critiques of holistic ethnographic representations that they associate with the essentialising and totalising tendencies of earlier anthropologists. They propose a more discursive theory of 'culture' that focuses on discontent, contest and negotiation rather than consensus and harmony. This approach is adopted here and rather than focusing on, for example, Greek/Maltese/Moroccan culture as a deterministic system, I investigate Greek/Maltese/Moroccan elites' debates and arguments *about* culture. For a fascinating example of how culture can be explored in this way see Mitchell, Jon P., 2002. *Ambivalent Europeans: Ritual, Memory and the Public Sphere in Malta*. London: Routledge.

29   Wæver *et al.*, 1993, 26.

30   Carr, Fergus (ed.), 1998. *Europe: The Cold Divide*. Basingstoke: Macmillan.

31   Wæver *et al.*, 1993, 20.

32   Buzan, Barry *et al.*, 1998. *Security: A New Framework for Analysis*. London: Lynne Rienner Publishers.

33   Wæver, 1995, 54–5; Buzan *et al.*, 1998, 21–6.

34   Huysmans, Jef, 1998. 'Security! What Do You Mean? From Concept to Thick Signifier', *European Journal of International Relations*, 4(2), 226–55.

35 Ibid.
36 Ibid., 232.
37 Bicchi, Federica, 2003. 'European Foreign Policy Making Towards the Mediterranean Non Member Countries'. Unpublished PhD thesis, European University Institute, Florence.
38 Wæver developed a (tree) metaphor for the multilayered nature of discourse where we can think of surface layer discourses as the branches and twigs of a tree, the deeper structures as its trunk and roots. His point is that change can occur within continuity, that change is not always an either/or question. His insight also shows that marginalised and opposing discourses and groups will often only be in disagreement with the dominant position 'at the level of manifest politics', near the surface of the discursive structure. See Wæver, Ole, 2002. 'Identity, Communities and Foreign Policy: Discourse Analysis as Foreign Policy Theory', in Hansen and Wæver, 2002, 31.
39 Bagge Laustsen, Carsten and Wæver, Ole, 2000. 'In Defence of Religion: Sacred Referent Objects for Securitization', *Millennium: Journal of International Studies*, 29(3), 705–39.
40 McSweeney, Bill, 1996. 'Identity and Security: Buzan and the Copenhagen School', *Review of International Studies*, 22(1), November, 81–93. See also Brubaker and Cooper, 2000.
41 For instance, because the EU constructs a security threat from the Mediterranean, its identity becomes, as an effect, threatened. This and similar analysis will be developed later in this book.
42 See Hansen and Wæver, 2002; Larsen, 1997; Wæver, 2004a.
43 Brubaker and Cooper, 2000. For an interesting overview of the different strands of social constructivist works see Smith, Steve, 1999. 'Social Constructivisms and European Studies: a Reflectivist Critique', *Journal of European Public Policy*, 6(4), Special Issue, 682–91.
44 Smith, 1999.
45 Ibid., 682.
46 Foucault, Michel, 1973. *The Order of Things*. New York: Pantheon, xiv.
47 See, for example, Neumann, Iver B., 1996a. 'European Identity, EU Expansion and the Integration/Exclusion Nexus'. Paper presented at the conference: Defining and Projecting Europe's Identity: Issues and Trade-Offs. Institut Universaire de Hautes Etudes Internationales, Geneva, 21–22 March.
48 Wendt, Alexander, 1999. *Social Theory of International Politics*. Cambridge: Cambridge University Press.
49 For example, what makes 'us' European. These themes will be explored in a later chapter.
50 Waltz, Kenneth N., 1979. *Theory of International Politics*. Reading, MA: Addison-Wesley.
51 In effect, this is what the EU does with the 'regions' it co-operates with: it homogenises them in order to develop a European (EU) collective identity. Smith is critical of Wendt's constructivist strand, arguing that Wendt seems to alter his view on the relationship between the material and the ideational. See Smith, Steve, 2000. 'Wendt's World', *Review of International Studies*, 26, 151–63.
52 Wendt, 1999, 94.
53 The process-based theoretical framework adopted here has broadly benefited from debates in sociology, philosophy and international relations (IR) on substantialist and relationalist approaches to the study of change in global politics. See Emirbayer, Mustafa, 1997. 'Manifesto for a Relational Sociology', *American Journal of Sociology*, 103(2), September, 281–317; Jackson, Patrick Thaddeus and Nexon, Daniel H., 1999. 'Relations Before States: Substance, Process and the Study of World Politics', *European Journal of International Relations*, 5(3), 291–332. See also Larsen, Henrik, 1997.
54 See, for example, Diez, Thomas, 2001. 'Europe as a Discursive Battleground: Discourse Analysis and European Integration Studies', *Cooperation and Conflict*, 36(1), 5–38.
55 Available at: http://europa.eu.int/comm/europeaid/projects/med/index_en.htm; http://europa.eu.int/comm/external_relations/euromed/publication.htm; http://europa.eu.int/comm/europeaid/index_en.htm.
56 The analysis was carried out prior to the EU's 1 May 2004 enlargement.
57 A dual methodology is employed here to enhance reliability and avoid bias. Each method acts as a counter-check of the other.
58 For a meticulous analysis of how to do discourse analysis see Wæver, 2004a.
59 Malta signed the treaty of accession on 16 April 2003 and became a full member of the EU on 1 May 2004.
60 Quoted in Neumann, Iver B., 2001. 'From Meta to Method: The Materiality of Discourse'. Paper presented at ISA 2001.

61 Wæver, 2004a.
62 Ibid.
63 Larsen, 1997.
64 Ibid. This term was coined by Keohane in 1989 to describe a group of theorists who 'emphasize the importance of human reflection for the nature of institutions and ultimately for the character of world politics': the term is widely used to refer to post-structuralists, critical theorists and feminists. Keohane, R.O., 1989. *International Institutions and State Power: Essays in International Relations Theory*. Boulder, CO: Westview. The lack of empirical studies drawing on a reflectivist approach is often seen, by mainstream scholars, as a weakness of the reflectivist argument. This work is interested in the meaning of concepts like 'Mediterranean' and 'region' for explicating foreign policy.
65 Neumann, Shapiro, Milliken, and Wæver, amongst others. Neumann, 2001; Shapiro, Michael J., 1981. *Language and Political Understanding: The Politics of Discursive Practices*. New Haven, CT: Yale University Press; Milliken, Jennifer, 1999a. 'The Study of Discourse in IR: A Critique of Research and Methods', *European Journal of International Relations*, 5(2), 234; Wæver, 2004a.
66 See also Wæver, 2004a.
67 See Milliken, 1999a for more on this.
68 For an interesting discussion on this topic see Browning, Christopher Stephen, 2001. 'Constructing Finnish National Identity and Foreign Policy, 1809–2000'. Unpublished PhD dissertation, University of Wales, Aberystwyth.
69 See, for example, Buzan *et al.*, 1998; Larsen, 1997; Larsen, Henrik, 1999. 'British and Danish European Policies in the 1990s: A Discourse Approach', *European Journal of International Relations*, 5(4), 451–83; Wæver, 2004a, 2004b. 'Discursive Approaches', in Antje Wiener and Thomas Diez (eds) *European Integration Theory*. Oxford: Oxford University Press, 197–214.
70 It is important to mention here the tension between the EU efforts, on the one hand, to create an EMP and the plans, on the other hand and as part of this, to develop horizontal co-operation in the Mediterranean – that is, implicitly, to relaunch the Mediterranean region. It is not clear whether the EU originally intended to focus more on the partnership or on assisting Mediterranean countries in the development of their economies. The partnership's economic objectives seem to dominate EU documentation. There is an underlying presumption that free trade is good for stability – in this manner EU texts contain an association of politics served through economics, even though the discourse is one of economics (where discourse of economic development (primarily free trade) is linked to stability which is in turn associated with security).
71 On the concept of constellation see Wæver, 2002, 20–49.

2 Regionalism in IR

1 See, for example, Wæver, 2002.
2 In his 1975 book *Foreign Policy Analysis*. Toronto and London: Lexington Books, 1, Richard L. Merritt claims that the core concerns for both those who formulate foreign policies and those who analyse the policies developed include: what the nation-state's capabilities are and how they are perceived, how decision makers mobilise these capabilities, who the individuals and groups that play significant roles are, what their patterns of interactions are, what they perceive their valued goals to be, how they seek to implement them, what international constraints foreclose some options and make the selection of others more likely. All these questions include discursive practices which construct identity boundaries and a shared meaning of who the self is and who the 'other' is. For this type of analysis see Neumann, Iver B., 1996b. 'Collective Identity Formation: Self and Other in International Relations', *European Journal of International Relations*, 2(2), 139–74; Neumann, Iver B., 1996c. *Russia and the Idea of Europe: A Study in Identity and International Relations*. London: Routledge.
3 Buzan and Wæver, 2003.
4 See, for example, Buzan *et al.*, 1998; Larsen, 1997; Larsen, Henrik, 1999. 'British and Danish European Policies in the 1990s: A Discourse Approach', *European Journal of International Relations*, 5(4), 451–83; Wæver, Ole, 2004a. Wæver, Ole, 2004b. 'Discursive Approaches', in Wiener and Diez.

5 See Wæver, 2002.
6 This does not imply in any way any sort of IR monopoly on the analysis of foreign policy.
7 Eliassen, K.A. (ed.), 1998. *Foreign and Security Policy in the EU*. London: Sage, 1.
8 This was of course also the case in the context of the wars in Yugoslavia.
9 Examples of the literature include Bretherton, Charlotte and Vogler, John, 1999. *The EU as a Global Actor*. London: Routledge; Hill, Christopher, 1993. 'The Capability–Expectations Gap, or Conceptualising Europe's International Role', *Journal of Common Market Studies*, 31(3), 305–28; Holland, Martin (ed.), 1997. *Common Foreign and Security Policy: The Record and Reforms*. London: Pinter; Jørgensen, Knud Erik (ed.), 1997. *European Approaches to Crisis Management*. London: Kluwer; Nuttall, Simon, 1992. *European Political Cooperation*. Oxford: Clarendon Press; Peterson, John and Sjursen, Helene (eds), 1998. *A Common Foreign Policy for Europe? Competing Visions of the CFSP*. London: Routledge; Piening, Christopher, 1997. *Global Europe: The EU in World Affairs*. Boulder, CO: Lynne Rienner; Regelsberger, Elfriede *et al.* (eds), 1997. *Foreign Policy of the EU: From EPC to CFSP and Beyond*. Boulder, CO: Lynne Rienner; Smith, Karen E., 1999. *The Making of EU Foreign Policy*. Basingstoke: Macmillan; Wessels, Wolfgang, 1982. 'European Political Cooperation: A New Approach to European Foreign Policy', in David Allen *et al.* (eds) *European Political Cooperation: Towards a Foreign Policy for Western Europe*. London: Butterworths, 1–20. Recent additions to this debate include Smith, Michael E., 2004b. *Europe's Foreign and Security Policy: The Institutionalization of Cooperation*. Cambridge: Cambridge University Press; Carlnaes, W. *et al.* (eds), 2004. *Contemporary European Foreign Policy*. London: Sage Publications.
10 Allen and Cameron in Peterson and Sjursen, 1998; Eliassen, 1998.
11 Jørgensen, 1997; Piening, 1997; and Smith, 1999.
12 Hill, 1993. Hill defines EU foreign policy as being the 'sum of what the EU and its Member States do in IR' (p. 18). Analysts are thus left free to assess the extent to which the Union succeeds in measuring up to a 'normal' foreign policy standard.
13 Klaus Hänsch in his foreword in Piening, 1997, ix.
14 See, in particular, Carlnaes *et al.*, 2004 and Smith, M.E., 2004a. See also Larsen, H., 1997; and Hansen and Wæver, 2002.
15 Tonra, Ben, 2000. 'Mapping EU Foreign Policy Studies', *Journal of European Public Policy*, 7(1), March, 163–9; Buzan and Wæver, 2003. 'The Europes', *Regions and Power*, 343–76; and Pace, M., 2004a.
16 Europe documents, 1995: *Council Report on Relations Between the EU and the Mediterranean Countries*, in preparation for the conference on 27–28 November in Barcelona: No. 1930/31, 27 April (own emphasis).
17 White, Brian, 1999. 'The European Challenge to Foreign Policy Analysis', *European Journal of International Relations*, 5(1), 37–66.
18 These country groups include the African Caribbean and Pacific (ACP) countries, Russia and the Commonwealth of Independent States (CIS) and the Association of Southeast Asian Nations (ASEAN), amongst others. Pace, M., 2004b. 'The Euro–Mediterranean *Partnership* and the *Common* Mediterranean Strategy? European Union Policy from a Discursive Perspective', *Geopolitics*, 9(2), 292–309.
19 Kuus, Merje, 2004. 'Europe's Eastern Expansion and the Re-inscription of Otherness in East-Central Europe', *Progress in Human Geography*, 4(1), August, 472–89; and Pace, M., 2002. 'The Ugly Duckling of Europe: The Mediterranean in the Foreign Policy of the European Union', *Journal of European Area Studies*, 10(2), 189–209.
20 White, 1999.
21 This is not to say that structures in the form of institutions (as the latter are commonly understood, and not in the sociological sense) are not important. In fact, different Ministries of Foreign Affairs manage Mediterranean issues in different ways – which practices 'speak' volumes about their notions of the Mediterranean. The volume of institutional resources also helps shape foreign policy.
22 Hansen and Wæver, 2002.
23 Larsen, 1997, 14.
24 Ibid., 32.
25 Foucault also speaks about the 'interior hierarchies within enunciative regularities' (Foucault, M., 1989. *Archaeology of Knowledge*. London: Routledge, 146), where concepts are related in a hierarchical way, like a tree with roots, trunks and branches (Foucault, 1989, 147).

26 Browning, 2001.
27 Some may argue that, none the less, the efforts of the EU to evolve common policies and strategies do invite considerations of the EU as an actor, even if it is unique.
28 Lister, Marjorie, 1997. *The EU and the South: Relations with Developing Countries.* London: Routledge/UACES, 6.
29 Monar, Jörg, 1998. 'Institutional Constraints of the EU's Mediterranean Policy', *Mediterranean Politics*, 3(2), Autumn, 39. See also Hill, 1993.
30 Monar, 1998, 39.
31 Interviews in Brussels, January 2004. See Pace, M., 2004c. 'Governing Border Conflicts: When Can the EU be an Effective Mediator'. Paper presented at the International Studies Association convention, Montreal, 17–20 March.
32 See Larsen, 1997; Hansen and Wæver, 2002.
33 Whitaker, Brian, 2004. 'Egypt rebuffs US over regional reform', *The Guardian*, 8 March 2004, 15.
34 In terms of Foucault's definitions of discourse. See Larsen, 1997; Wæver 2004b in Wiener and Diez.
35 Kuus, M., 2004.
36 Barber, James and Smith, Michael (eds), 1974. *The Nature of Foreign Policy: A Reader.* Milton Keynes: The Open University Press; Smith, M.E., 2004a, 2004b.
37 Campbell, D., 1992. *Writing Security: United States Foreign Policy and the Politics of Identity.* Minneapolis, MN: University of Minnesota Press.
38 Attinà, Fulvio, 1996. 'Regional Cooperation in Global Perspective: The Case of the "Mediterranean" Regions', Jean Monnet Working Papers in Comparative and International Politics, 6 April.
39 Joenniemi, Pertti and Wæver, Ole, 1992. *Regionalization Around The Baltic Rim: Notions on Baltic Sea Politics.* Prepared for the Presidium of the Nordic Council for the 2nd Parliamentary Conference on Co-operation in the Baltic Sea Area, Oslo, 22–24 April. One may argue that following this thinking there seems to be a kind of systemic/functionalist logic behind mainstream theorisations on regionalism that draws upon systemic/functionalistic political theory along the lines of Pye, L., 1962. *Politics, Personality and Nation Building: Burma's Search for Identity.* New Haven, CT: Yale University Press; Almond, Mundt R.A. and Verba, S., 1963. *The Civic Culture.* Boston, MA: Little Brown. In this context, regionalism is therefore open to criticisms usually addressed to these theories (in terms of their underlying assumptions) as well as their offshoot political development theories of the 1960s and later.
40 Giddens, Anthony, 1984. *The Constitution of Society: Outline of the Theory of Structuration.* Cambridge: Polity Press.
41 Berger, Peter L. and Luckmann, Thomas, 1966. *The Social Construction of Reality: A Treatise in the Sociology of Knowledge.* New York: Penguin Books.
42 More on this point in Chapter 4.
43 Giddens, Anthony, 1976. *New Rules of Sociological Method: A Positive Critique of Interpretative Sociologies.* London: Hutchinson.
44 Pace, Michelle, 2000. 'Regionalism in International Relations: The Mediterranean as a Social Construct', *Agora Without Frontiers*, 5(3), 207–19 (translated into Greek). Athens: Institute of International Economic Relations.
45 Müftüler-Bac, Meltem, 1997. *Turkey's Relations With a Changing Europe.* Manchester and New York: Manchester University Press, 6–7.
46 Grugel, Jean and Hout, Wil (eds), 1999. *Regionalism Across the North-South Divide: State Strategies and Globalization.* Routledge: London, 15.
47 Waltz, K., 1979; Buzan, B., 1991; Grieco, Joseph, 1990. *Cooperation Among Nations: Europe, America and Non-Tariff Barriers to Trade.* Ithaca, NY: Cornell University Press; Gilpin, Robert, 1975. *U.S. Power and the Multinational Corporation.* New York: Basic Books.
48 Neo-realists have a substantialist conception of power at work – as something that someone uses or holds.
49 Hasenclever, A., Mayer, P. and Rittberger, V., 2000. 'Integrating Theories of International Regimes', *Review of International Studies*, 26(1), 3–33.
50 Ashley, Richard K., 1984. 'The Poverty of Neorealism', *International Organization*, 38(2), Spring, 225–86. Cox, Robert, 1981. 'Social Forces, States and World Orders: Beyond IR Theory', *Millennium: Journal of International Studies*, 10(2), 126–55; Cox, Robert, 1987.

Production, Power and World Order: Social Forces in the Making of History. New York: Columbia University Press. Also see Cox, Robert and Sinclair, Timothy J., 1996. *Approaches to World Order*. Cambridge: Cambridge University Press.

51 Haas, Ernst B., 1980. 'Why Collaborate? Issue-linkage and International Regimes', *World Politics*, 32, 357–405; Moravcsik, Andrew, 1998. *Centralization or Fragmentation? Europe Facing the Challenges of Deepening, Diversity and Democracy*. New York: Council on Foreign Relations.

52 Hasenclever *et al.*, 2000.

53 Neo-liberals share a substantialist conception of power (as neo-realists do).

54 Müftüler-Bac, 1997. Turkey has recently adopted a number of crucial reforms in anticipation of the Council's December 2004 decision with regards to its potential and future EU membership. See also, Rumelili, Bahar, 2004a. 'The European Union's Impact on the Greek–Turkish Conflict. A Review of the Literature'. EUBorderConf project working papers series, No. 6. Available at: http://www.euborderconf.bham.ac.uk/ publications/files/WP6GreeceTurkey.pdf; Rumelili, Bahar, 2004b. 'The Talkers and the Silent Ones: The European Union and Change in Greek–Turkish Relations'. EUBorderConf project working papers series, number 10, October. Available at: http:// www.euborderconf.bham.ac.uk/publications/files/GreeceTurkey2.pdf; and Pace, Michelle, 2004d. 'EU–Turkey Relations', presented at Britain and Greece: 5th Annual Bilateral Conference. Hydra, Greece, 8–10 October. Available at: http://www.euborderconf.bham. ac.uk/publications/files/EU-TurkishrelationsHydra.pdf.

55 Grugel and Hout, 1999.

56 One should stress here that realists tend to focus, broadly speaking, on military security issues whereas liberals on issues of political economy. Therefore, they see different prospects for co-operation within the different issue areas, which feeds into their regional level analysis.

57 Galtung, Johan, 1971. 'A Structural Theory of Imperialism', *Journal of Peace Research*, 2, 81–98.

58 Grugel and Hout, 1999, 20. This could be one reason why Mediterranean sub-regionalism is still in its infancy.

59 Hence, power understood in a substantialist way.

60 For example, the claim that they are all structurally disadvantaged by a capitalist system managed by the imperial powers.

61 In early 2001, a target date was set for the launch of the FTAA (Free Trade Area of the Americas) which would supersede NAFTA. See Martinson, Jane, 2001. 'Quebec Rioters Cry Foul, but Free Trade Deal is Done', *The Guardian*, 23 April, 12.

62 Laursen, F. (ed.) 2003. *Comparative Regional Integration: Theoretical Perspectives*. Aldershot: Ashgate.

63 Higgott, Richard A., 1983. *Political Development Theory: The Contemporary Debate*. London and Canberra: Croom Helm International.

64 Grugel and Hout, 1999.

65 Cantori, Louis J. and Spiegel, Steven L., 1970. *The International Politics of Regions. A Comparative Approach*. Englewood Cliffs, NJ: Prentice-Hall.

66 Ibid., 3.

67 See also Knudsen, Olav F. and Neumann, Iver B., 1995. *Subregional Security Cooperation in the Baltic Sea Area: An Exploratory Study*. Oslo: Norsk Utenrikspolitisk Institutt. Also Buzan and Wæver, 2003.

68 Wallerstein, Immanuel, 1979. *The Capitalist World Economy*. Cambridge: Cambridge University Press; Chase-Dunn, Christopher, 1981. 'Interstate System and Capitalist World-Economy: One Logic or Two?', in W. Ladd Hollist and James N. Rosenau (eds) *World System Structure: Continuity and Change*. Beverly Hills, CA: Sage Publications, 1981. In their recent work, Buzan and Wæver, 2003 also reify the nature of regions.

69 See, for example, the work of Cox, R., 1981; Cox and Sinclair, 1996; Gill, Stephen (ed.) 1993. *Gramsci, Historical Materialism and International Relations*. Cambridge: Cambridge University Press, Cambridge Studies in International Relations, 26.

70 Apart from Cox see also Gamble, Andrew and Payne, Anthony, 1996. *Regionalism and World Order*. Basingstoke: Macmillan.

71 Cox, R., 1981; Cox and Sinclair, 1996.

72 Some would, however, argue that this is far more 'realistic' than the material pre-ponderance that realists and liberals use.

73 Burchill, Scott and Linklater, Andrew, 1996. *Theories of IR*. London and New York: Macmillan Press.
74 This debate is a complex one. There is a definition of hegemony to do with those values that come to resemble commonsense knowledge among the dominant social forces and which are kept in place through mechanisms of both coercion and consent. The debate on whether Gramsci's notion of hegemony can be translated to the international or global level has been the subject of further debate – for a supportive view see Augelli, Enrico and Murphy, Craig, 1988. *America's Quest For Supremacy and the Third World: A Gramscian Analysis*. London: Pinter; and for a critical view see Germain, Randall and Kenny, Michael, 1998. 'International Relations Theory and the New Gramscians', *Review of International Studies*, 24(1), January, 3–21.
75 Ohmae, Kenichi, 1995a. *The Evolving Global Economy: Making Sense of the New World Order*. Boston, MA: Harvard Business School. See also Ohmae, Kenichi, 1990. *The Borderless World: Power and Strategy in the Interlinked Economy*. London: Collins; Ohmae, Kenichi, 1995b. *End of the Nation State: the Rise of Regional Economies*. London: HarperCollins.
76 Kofman, Eleonore and Youngs, Gillian, 1996. *Globalisation: Theory and Practice*. London: Pinter.
77 Agnew, John and Corbridge, Stuart, 1995. *Mastering Space: Hegemony, Territory and International Political Economy*. London: Routledge.
78 Falk, Richard, 1986. *Reviving the World Court*. Charlottesville, VA: University of Virginia Press; Falk, Richard, 1987. *The Promise of World Order*. Philadelphia, PA: Temple University Press. Also see Hirst, Francis W., 1998. *Liberalism and the Empire: Three Essays*. London: Routledge.
79 Grugel and Hout, 1999.
80 Richard Higgott argues otherwise. He states that 'State policies towards regional cooperation, in either the economic or the security domain are not ... exercises in the "pooling of sovereignty". Underpinning Asian and European approaches to the question of regionalism is a different approach to the relationship between sovereignty and territory. Asian conceptions of sovereignty are much more territorially contingent than those in Europe', 1994. 'Ideas, Identity and Policy Coordination in the Asia-Pacific'. *The Pacific Review*, 7(4), 375.
81 Although Gramscians are not as economically reductionist as Marxists.
82 Mingst, Karen, 1999. *Essentials of IR*. New York and London: W. W. Norton.
83 Actor-based theories refer to a fixed sense of perceiving the international environment (neorealists/structural realists recognise actors and their constrained room for manoeuvre at the international level, heavily constrained by structure) and should be distinguished from action processes that refer to flexible ways of viewing the world.
84 It is acknowledged that Gramsci, for example, went into great detail to discuss the power of individual intellectuals and groups within civil society to change political structures. But my reading/understanding of power in terms of relationships is different from this substantialist conception of power as something that someone uses or holds. See Emirbayer, 1997.
85 Pace, 2000. The exception here is the position of neo-Gramscians who make explicit their awareness of the reflexive nature of theorising and who have adopted an epistemological position that rejects naturalist approaches. This is why it is suggested here that neo-Gramscian thought is a good step into critical thinking on regions.
86 Static in the sense that they reify regions. History is crucial to neo-Marxist variants (world systems) and Gramscians as these orders have developed alongside capitalism and imperialism. In Cox's work, for example, the fit between ideas, states and social forces is constantly in flux. Also, hegemony is by definition never static but is in a constant process of construction and reconstruction. Elements of these approaches can be detected in a process-based framework such as the one suggested here.
87 The language of neo-Marxists, for example on praxis, suggests they take the reciprocal relationship between ideas and practice seriously.
88 There are thus, strands of actor-based approaches, strands of structure-based approaches and strands of process-based approaches.
89 Gamble and Payne, 1996, 2.

90   Doty, Roxanne Lynn, 1993. 'Foreign Policy as Social Construction: A Post-Positivist Analysis of US Counterinsurgency in the Philippines', *International Studies Quarterly*, 37, 304.
91   Laffey, Mark and Jutta, Weldes, 1997. 'Beyond Belief: Ideas and Symbolic Technologies in the Study of IR', *European Journal of International Relations*, 3(2), 208.
92   Searle, John R., 1995. *The Construction of Social Reality*. London: Penguin Books, 66–71.
93   See Doty, 1993, 304–5.
94   Foucault, 1973.
95   Foucault has a broad conception of discourse. See, in particular, Foucault, 1972 and 1977. *Discipline and Punish*. London: Allen Lane. For example, in his *History of Sexuality*, Foucault argues that the idea of sexuality as something meaningful, with some social significance, became possible when people started 'talking' about something called 'sexuality' in the Victorian era. Foucault is here actually talking about discourse and the construction of social reality. See Foucault, Michel, 1979–86. *The History of Sexuality* (3 volumes). London: Allen Lane.
96   See Foucault's *Archaeology of Knowledge* for more on this.
97   Power as relationships.
98   The relation between actor and structure and how these reproduce each other has been thoroughly developed by Anthony Giddens in his theory of structuration. According to this theory, '(t)he basic domain of study of the social sciences ... is neither the experience of the individual actor, nor the existence of any form of societal totality, but social practices ordered across time and space', in effect, actors acting in a language world. Giddens, 1984, 2.
99   Thompson, John B., 1984. *Studies in the Theory of Ideology*. Cambridge: Polity Press and Oxford: Basil Blackwell.
100 Emirbayer, 1997; Jackson and Nexon, 1999.
101 Giddens, 1976, 121.
102 Ibid.
103 Ibid.
104 The recursive ordering of social practices involves a reflexive form of the knowledgeability of human agents. Continuity of practices presumes reflexivity that in turn is possible only because of the continuity of practices that makes them distinctively 'the same' across space and time. Reflexivity here refers to 'the monitored character of the ongoing flow of social life' and not just 'self-consciousness'. See Cassell, Philip (ed.), 1993. *The Giddens Reader*. Basingstoke: Macmillan.
105 Thompson, 1984. This refers to what was earlier defined as *institutions* or sets of practices or social action repeated in a similar and regular fashion over long periods of time, thus acquiring a sense of stability and durability, regardless of whether the outcome is intended by the agent concerned. Giddens ascribes to institutions a different sense from the common one as he does also to the concept of structure.
106 Thompson, 1984.
107 Giddens, 1976, 127.
108 Here I refer to my previous definition of structure in the introduction to this chapter – long reproduced sets of action, meaning and discourse that provide a frame for the operation of institutions as well as of action. See also Thompson, 1984.
109 Craib, Ian, 1992. *Modern Social Theory: From Parsons To Habermas*. London: Harvester Wheatsheaf, 117.
110 By ontology I here refer to a theory of what really exists, as opposed to that which appears to exist but does not, or to that which can properly be said to exist but only if conceived as some complex whose constituents are the things that really exist. Some ontologists have argued that many things exist that are not commonly acknowledged to do so, such as abstract *entities*. See Bullock, Alan, Stallybrass, Oliver and Trombley, Stephen, 1977. *The Fontana Dictionary of Modern Thought*. London: Fontana Press, 605 for an interesting discussion on this. For example, how deeply does an author's own context – where she is physically situated and the timing of her writing – that is, her 'spatial socialization' (explained later in the text) into a specific society and history, inform and influence her argumentation on regions?
111 Neumann, 1994; Neumann, Iver B., 1998. *Uses of the Other: The 'East' in European Identity Formation*. Minneapolis, MN: University of Minnesota Press; Todorov, Tzvetan,

1984. *Mikhail Bakhtin: The Dialogical Principle*. Trans. by Wlad Godzich. Minneapolis, MN: University of Minnesota Press; Der Derian, James and Shapiro, Michael J., 1989. *International/Intertextual Relations: Postmodern Readings of World Politics*. Lexington, MA: Lexington Books; Shapiro, Michael J., 1994. 'Moral Geographies and the Ethics of Post-Sovereignty', *Public Culture*, 6, 479–502. See also Shapiro, Michael J. and Hayward R. Alker (eds), 1996. *Challenging Boundaries: Global Flows, Territorial Identities*. Minneapolis, MN and London: University of Minnesota Press. Borderlines, 2; Campbell, David, 1998. 'MetaBosnia: A Review of Narratives of the Bosnian War', *Review of International Studies*, 24(2), 261–81; Wendt, Alexander E., 1987. 'The Agent-Structure Problem in IR Theory', *International Organization*, 41(3), Summer, 335–70; Barth, Fredrik (ed.), 1969. *Ethnic Groups and Boundaries – The Social Organization of Culture Difference*. Oslo: Universitetsforlaget.

112 Shields, Rob, 1990. *Places on the Margin: Alternative Geographies of Modernity*. London: Routledge.

113 Paasi, Anssi, 1996. *Territories, Boundaries and Consciousness: The Changing Geographies of the Finnish-Russian Border*. Chichester: Wiley.

114 Connolly, William E., 1991. *Identity/Difference: Democratic Negotiations of Political Paradox*. New York: Cornell University Press, 64.

115 Weldes, Jutta *et al.*, 1999. *Cultures of Insecurity: States, Communities and the Production of Danger*. Minneapolis, MN: University of Minnesota Press. Borderlines, 11, 14.

116 For this argumentation see Said, Edward W., 1993. *Culture and Imperialism*. London: Vintage. See also his 1978. *Orientalism. Western Conceptions Of the Orient*. London: Penguin Books.

117 See, for example, Cohler, Anne M., Miller, Basia Carolyn and Stone, Harold Samuel (eds), 1989. *Montesquieu. The Spirit of the Laws*. Cambridge: Cambridge University Press; Cowen, Michael P. and Shenton, Robert W., 1995. *Doctrines of Development*. London: Routledge; Escobar, Arturo, 1995. *Encountering Development: The Making and Unmaking of the Third World*. Princeton, NJ: Princeton University Press; Fabian, Johannes, 1983. *Time and the Other: How Anthropology Makes Its Object*. New York: Columbia University Press; Ferguson, James, 1990. *The Anti-Politics Machine: 'Development', Depoliticization and Bureaucratic Power in Lesotho*. Cambridge: Cambridge University Press.

118 Said, E.W., 1993, 120.

119 Buzan and Wæver, 2003, 73, 86–7 where the authors develop the idea of securitisation as a means of mapping regional variations.

120 Said, E.W., 1993, 120 (power as non-substantialist).

121 Hall, Stuart, Held, David and McGrew, Tony 1992. *Modernity and its Futures*. Oxford: Polity Press; Appadurai, Arjun, 1996. *Modernity at Large. Cultural Dimensions of Globalization*. Minneapolis, MN: University of Minnesota Press.

122 One can assume that these observations have similar implications for sub-national identities.

123 Appadurai, 1996, 9.

124 We therefore need analytic and explanatory models of the social sciences to adjust to the reality of the modern and postmodern, rapidly developing world with its continuously and extensive transformations – not to be misunderstood as an attempt at representing reality 'out there', rather to understand societies and regions as processes of overlapping dimensions, each with its own patterns of change and development. In other words, we need to redraw political and cultural maps of our period. Jameson, Frederic, 1981. *The Political Unconscious: Narrative as a Socially Symbolic Act*. London: Metheun.

125 Connolly, William E., 1995. *The Ethos of Pluralization*. Minneapolis, MN: University of Minnesota Press, 202–3.

126 Shapiro, Michael J., 1997. *Violent Cartographies: Mapping Cultures of War*. Minneapolis, MN: University of Minnesota Press.

127 Ibid., ix.

128 See Derrida, Jacques, 1976. *Of Grammatology*. Baltimore, MD: Johns Hopkins University Press.

129 Shapiro, 1997, xi.

130 Hall *et al.*, 1992, 9.

131 Pace, 2000.

132 Theory and method are combined here since discourse analysts often analyse theory and method as closely related concerns, referred to as 'analysis strategy'. Constructivism has been variously subdivided into 'conventional' and 'critical'; 'neoclassical', 'postmodernist' and 'naturalistic'; 'thick' and 'thin'; 'weak' and 'strong'. I situate myself within the radical/ reflectivist/postmodern strand of constructivism. For a thorough analysis of the various strands of constructivism see Smith, S., 1999.

133 Jackson and Nexon, 1999, 301. The authors' approach focuses around four key concepts developed in scholarship on processes and relations, namely, processes, configurations, projects and yoking.

134 Such authority is embedded in other power centres. Walker, R.B.J., 1993. *Inside/Outside: International Relations as Political Theory*. Cambridge: Cambridge University Press. See also Thomson, Janice, 1995. 'State Sovereignty in International Relations', *International Studies Quarterly*, 39, 213–33, particularly 225.

135 Jackson and Nexon, 1999, 314–15.

136 Pace, 2000.

137 Smith, S., 1999.

138 Milliken, 1999a; Shapiro, 1981. See Richardson, John T.E. (ed.), 1996. *Handbook of Qualitative Research Methods for Psychology and the Social Sciences*. Leicester: The British Psychological Society, 127; Neumann, 2001, 2002. Wæver, Ole, 2002 in Hansen and Wæver; Wæver, 2004b in Wiener and Diez; Larsen, 1997; Diez, 2001.

139 Craib, 1992.

140 Ibid.

141 Price, Richard and Reus-Smit, Christian, 1998. 'Dangerous Liaisons? Critical International Theory and Constructivism', *European Journal of International Relations*, 4(3), 259–94.

142 Wendt, Alexander, 1992. 'Anarchy is What States Make of It: The Social Construction of Power Politics', *International Organization*, 46(2), 398.

143 Wendt, Alexander and Duvall, Raymond, 1989. 'Institutions and International Order', in Ernst-Otto Czempiel and James N. Rosenau (eds) *Global Changes and Theoretical Challenges: Approaches to World Politics for the 1990s*. Lexington, MA: Lexington Books, 60.

144 Smith, S., 1999.

145 Ibid.

146 Cited by Neumann, 2001.

147 Derrida, 1976.

148 Doty, Roxanne Lynn, 1997. 'Aporia: A Critical Exploration of the Agent-Structure Problematique in IR Theory', *European Journal of International Relations*, 3(3), 378.

149 Milliken, 1999a, 231.

150 Richardson, 1996.

151 See, for example, Larsen, 1997.

152 George, Jim, 1994. *Discourses of Global Politics: A Critical (Re) Introduction to IR*. Boulder, CO: Lynne Rienner, 16, 204, 210.

153 Larsen, 1997, 14.

154 Ibid., 32.

155 Hansen and Wæver, 2002; Diez, 2001; Larsen, 1997.

156 Giddens, 1984; Neumann, 2001.

157 Foucault, Michel, 1980. *Power/Knowledge: Selected Interviews and Other Writings, 1972–1977*. Gordon, Colin (ed.), New York: Pantheon Books.

158 Ibid, 27. Foucault, 1977, 1980, 1991. 'Governmentality', in G. Burchell, C. Gordon and P. Miller (eds) *The Foucault Effect: Studies in Governmentality*. Chicago, IL: University of Chicago Press, 1991, 87–104.

159 Escobar, 1995; Woods, Clyde, 1998. *Development Arrested: The Blues and Plantation Power in the Mississippi Delta*. London: Verso; Ó Tuathail, G., 1996. *Critical Geopolitics: The Politics of Writing Global Space*. Minneapolis, MN: University of Minnesota Press. Borderlines Series 6.

160 Lyotard, Jean-François, 1984. *The Postmodern Condition: A Report on Knowledge*. Manchester: Manchester University Press.

161 Giddens, 1984.

162 Milliken, 1999a.

163 Doty, 1997.

164 Shapiro, Michael J., 1992. *Reading the Postmodern Polity*. Minneapolis, MN: University of Minnesota Press.

165 Wendt follows Thrift's structuration theory which he deems as more inclusive as a term than Giddens'. See Wendt, 1987.

166 I am indebted to the article of Laffey and Weldes, 1997 and articles by various members of the 'Copenhagen School', in particular Larsen, 1997; Hansen and Wæver, 2002, for being sources of enlightenment.

167 A recent study which takes a similar approach to the one adopted here is the work of Tassinari, Fabrizio, 2004. '*Mare Europaeum*: Baltic Sea Region Security and Cooperation from post-Wall to post-Enlargement Europe', Copenhagen: Department of Political Science, University of Copenhagen, PhD dissertation.

168 Braudel, F., 1972. *The Mediterranean and the Mediterranean World in the Age of Philip II, Volumes I & II*. London: Collins.

169 This was roughly around the same time that the Mediterranean was thought of as 'the centre of the world'. See Mingolo, Walter D., 1998. *The Darker Side of the Renaissance: Literacy, Territoriality, and Colonization*. Ann Arbor, MI: University of Michigan Press.

170 Braudel, 1972, vol. I, 45; vol. II, 670.

171 I do appreciate that many of those who feel that there can be some valid geographical connotations to the term Mediterranean 'region' would disagree with the inconsistent use of the Mediterranean in a holistic sense and in relation to parts of countries. Although this may be perceived as splitting hairs, I feel that for analytical purposes acknowledging this distinction between macro and micro regions is important.

172 Braudel, 1972, vol. I, 32.

173 Following the war in Iraq, analysts are looking at the wider Middle East rather than the Mediterranean. See Neugart, F. and Schumacher, Tobias, 2004. 'Thinking about the EU's Future Neighbourhood Policy in the Middle East: From the Euro–Mediterranean Partnership to "Barcelona plus"', in Christian-Peter Hanelt, Giacomo Luciani and Felix Neugart (eds) *Regime Change in Iraq, 2003*. Florence: EUI-RSCAS, 169–99.

174 This point was developed earlier in the section drawing from critical approaches. Braudel developed a notion of 'world economies' built around a central city which tells us a lot about the processes constructing regionalisms such as New York, Tokyo, Frankfurt, Hong Kong, Johannesburg, etc.

175 El-Sayed Selim, Mohammed, 1995. 'Mediterraneanism: A New Dimension in Egypt's Foreign Policy'. *Kurasat Istratijiya*, Strategic Papers, 27.

176 These problems are inherent in the case of Egypt individually, let alone when reference is made to the whole area! Thus, a blurred construction or representation of an area often results in problematic policy planning and making.

177 Fenech, Dominic, 1991. 'Mediterranean Regionality', in S. Fiorini and V. Mallia-Milanes (eds) *Malta: A Case Study in International Cross-Currents*. Malta: Malta University Publications, 267–77.

178 Thus, as time changes, space changes too.

179 Fenech, 1991, 268.

180 Ibid.

181 Fenech seems to retreat back to a 'subjective' view of the Mediterranean. His position reflects the difficulty and the inevitable oscillation experienced when an observer attempts to investigate the concept of the Mediterranean. Fenech, 1991, 270.

182 Thinking about the Mediterranean is very context specific.

183 A vacuum in the sense of no a priori classifications of what should constitute a region. Fenech, 1991, 273.

184 Ibid.

185 This statement is in line with the literature in the field of identity politics in terms of identity notions of the 'signifier' and the 'signified'. See Lacan, Jacques, 1977. *Écrits: A Selection*. Transl. Alan Sheridan. New York: W.W. Norton on this. It also suggests the nature of multiple identities within the Mediterranean.

186 Fenech, Dominic, 1993. 'East–West to North–South in the Mediterranean', *GeoJournal*, 31(2), 129–40.

187 Ibid., 129. For a historicised analysis of the North–South perspective see Montesquieu and his juxtaposition of the Mediterranean/South/culture and the Teutonic/North/nature. One important aspect of Montesquieu's work is that there is a limit to how far one can go to mould peoples and institutions and ignore the culture they are embedded in –

basically one cannot ignore culture altogether. IR thus reproduces political history by foregrounding the North and bracketing the South/the Mediterranean. Montesquieu, Charles de Secondat, 1989. *The Spirit of the Laws*. Cambridge: Cambridge University Press. Translated and edited by Anne M. Cohler, Basia Carolyn Miller and Harold Samuel Stone.

188 Calleya, Stephen C., 1997. *Navigating Regional Dynamics in the Post-Cold War World: Patterns of Relations in the Mediterranean Area*. Brookfield, VT: Dartmouth Publishing Company.

189 Adler, Emanuel and Crawford, Beverly, 2002. 'Constructing a Mediterranean Region: A Cultural Approach'. Paper presented at the conference on The Convergence of Civilizations? Constructing a Mediterranean Region, Arrábida Monastery, Fundação Oriente, Lisbon, Portugal, 6–9 June.

190 Ibid., 13.

191 Joffé, George, 2001. 'European Union and the Mediterranean', in Mario Tele (ed.) *The European Union and the New Regionalism*. Burlington, VT: Ashgate, 207–25. See also Tovias, Alfred, 1997. 'The Economic Impact of the Euro-Mediterranean Free Trade Area on Mediterranean Non-Member Countries', *Mediterranean Politics*, 2(1), 113–28; Tovias, Alfred, 2001. 'On the External Relations of the EU 21: The Case of the Mediterranean Periphery', *European Foreign Affairs Review*, 6, 375–94.

192 Joffé, George, 2000. 'Europe and the Mediterranean: The Barcelona Process Five Years On', RIIA Briefing Paper number 16.

193 Pace, 2000.

194 Steve Smith includes Adler with the work of 'thin' or 'soft' constructivists.

195 Sant Cassia, Paul, 1991. 'Authors In Search of a Character: Personhood, Agency and Identity in the Mediterranean', *Journal of Mediterranean Studies*, 1(1), 1–17.

196 In cultural theory, such a construction is said to be polysemic. While many writers argue that most texts contain a preferred reading, they also contain several other meanings that may be less powerful. It is almost impossible to produce a single, unified meaning for a text and many writers deliberately aim for multiple meanings, that is, an arbitrary character of classifications.

197 Sant Cassia, 1991, 5.

198 Wendt, 1992, emphasis added.

199 Shapiro, Michael, 1981.

200 Neumann, 1998, 116.

3 Understanding EU hegemony

1 Moré, Iñigo, 2004. 'The Economic Step Between Neighbours: The Case of Spain–Morocco', *Mediterranean Politics*, 9(2), 165–200. A preliminary version was published in Spanish by the Real Instituto Elcano de Estudios Internacionales y Estratégicos and can be accessed at: http://www.realinstitutoelcano.org/documentos/44.asp.

2 MEDA is the acronym for *mesures d'accompagnement financiers et techniques à la réforme des structures économiques et socials dans le cadre du partenariat euro-méditerranéen*.

3 Malta and Cyprus joined the EU on 1 May 2004.

4 According to the latter, the HDI is: 'a simple summary measure of three dimensions of the human development concept: living a long and healthy life, being educated and having a decent standard of living'. Human Development Report 2003, 60. According to World Bank figures, there are about 85 million people in the South Mediterranean countries trying to survive on US$2 a day or less. In drawing up the tables in this chapter an effort was made to check several sources including the Economist Intelligence Unit country reviews available at: http://www.economist.com/countries; the World Bank Group available at: http://www.worldbank.org/data/; European Union reports and sources available at: http//europa.eu.int/ and UN sources. As is commonly acknowledged, statistics and their reliability have to be treated with great caution: the power of digits has to be kept in mind.

5 http://www.undp.org/rbas/ahdr/english2003.html.

6 Fouad Ammor and Ambassador Shalaby, Sayyed Amin, Alexandria conference, October 2003. Pace, Michelle and Schumacher, Tobias, 2004. 'Report: Culture and Community

in the Euro-Mediterranean Partnership: A Roundtable on the Third Basket, Alexandria, 5–7 October 2003', *Mediterranean Politics*, 9(1), 122–6.

7 Human Development Report 2003.

8 Some analysts refer to the 'deep state' in Turkey. These issues have started to be addressed already, at time of writing. In his speech delivered on the 14 January 2004 at the Turkish Grand National Assembly in Ankara, Romano Prodi, President of the European Commision, acknowledged that '[T]he question of full democratic control of the [Turkish] military, including full parliamentary authority over the defence budget, is [also] being addressed'. In its November 2003 Report, the Commission had highlighted those areas where more progress is needed including the full alignment of civil–military relations on EU standards. See Strategy Paper and Report of the European Commission on the Progress Towards Accession by Bulgaria, Romania and Turkey, November 2003a. Especially Section entitled 'Turkey In The Enlargement Process – Progress and Challenges'. Prodi's speech and the Commission's Strategy Paper on Turkey outlining the Conclusions of the Commission's Regular Report of November 2003 on Turkey are available at the Centre for European Policy Studies (CEPS) Bulletin, *Turkey in Europe* Monitor Issue 1, January 2004. For an update see also the Commission's Regular Report on Turkey of 6 October 2004.

9 Unofficial estimates are that actual unemployment is about twice that level.

10 Economist Intelligence Unit, 2003. 'Algeria Review'.

11 Egyptian Businessmen Association, 2000. 'The World Trade Organisation and the Arab countries'. Communication to the 4th forum of Arab Businessmen Society, Kuwait, May, 6.

12 Escribano, Gonzalo and Jordán, Josep María, 1998. 'Subregional Integration in the Southern Shore of the Mediterranean and the Euro-Mediterranean Free Trade Area'. Paper presented at the Valencia Forum on the Euro-Mediterranean Free Trade Area, organised by the Centro Español de Relaciones Internacionales, 20–21 November.

13 Discussions with an interviewee, Alexandria, October 2003. See Pace and Schumacher, 2004.

14 Although this may suggest that FDI is linked to reform and economic progress, it is important to clarify here that investment is in reform and that investment has an indirect relationship to reform.

15 Geradin, Damien and Petit, Nicolas, 2003. 'Competition Policy and the Euro-Med Partnership', *European Foreign Affairs Review*, 8, 153–80, 172 footnote 77.

16 Source: European Communities, 2003. 'The Israeli Economy and the European Union'. Statistics in Focus (Stéphane Quefelec). Also available at: http://www. europa.eu.int/comm/eurostat/.

17 Philippart, Eric, 2003. 'The Euro-Mediterranean Partnership: A Critical Evaluation of an Ambitious Scheme', *European Foreign Affairs Review*, 8(2), Summer, 216.

18 Economist Intelligence Unit, country overview, 2003.

19 Morocco's informal economy, especially its drug trade, also forms an important part of its economy.

20 Philippart, 2003, 11.

21 Article 237. On the other hand, there is some vagueness here. Non-European countries (whatever these may be!) are not specifically excluded. The phrase in Art. 237 is: 'any European nation can apply', quoted in Croft, Stuart *et al.*, 1999. *The Enlargement of Europe*. Manchester: Manchester University Press, 61.

22 Spain and Portugal signed up in June 1985 but only became members from 1 January 1986.

23 Turkey was granted candidate status at the December 1999 Helsinki Summit. See *European Voice*, 9–15 March 2000 for more on this issue. See also, Sofos, Spyros, 2001. 'Reluctant Europeans? European Integration and the Transformation of Turkish Politics', in Kevin Featherstone and George Kazamias (eds) *Europeanization and the Southern European Periphery*. London: Frank Cass. Originally appeared in *South European Society and Politics*, 2000, 5(2) (Autumn), special issue on Europeanization and the Southern Periphery. Following the announcement at Helsinki, Turkey embarked upon constitutional and legislative reforms that have been acknowledged in the European Commission's successive reports. In its November 2003 Report, the Commission highlighted those areas where more progress is needed for Turkey to fully satisfy the criteria for accession. The European Council has made it clear that when Turkey meets the Copenhagen political criteria, accession negotiations will be opened. See Strategy Paper and Report of the European Commission on the

Progress Towards Accession by Bulgaria, Romania and Turkey, November 2003. 'Turkey In The Enlargement Process – Progress and Challenges', and Speech of Romano Prodi, The President of the European Commission, at the Turkish Grand National Assembly, Ankara, 14 January 2004 in *Turkey in Europe* monitor.

24 Articles 131–6.

25 The concept of 'association' with the EEC refers to a set of initiatives taken towards a multilateral dialogue and co-operation between European and southern Mediterranean countries.

26 Article 237 is actually quite ambiguous on whether countries have to be European or not to become members of the then EEC. This is why countries like Morocco and Turkey had to test this out over the years. In time the EU had to build a case law based on initiatives stemming from other countries that now makes it more clear. At the time of the Rome Treaty, European-ness was implicit but Europe was not defined. This is an interesting case of the making of Europe in the EU Treaties.

27 See, for example, Commission of the European Communities, 1993. *EEC Mediterranean Agreements*. Bureau D'Informations Européennes, Brussels.

28 This is not to imply that the EU established the dichotomy of Maghreb-Mashreq. This distinction emanates from Arab culture (the 'labels' are of Arab origin).

29 The first round of elections was held in December 1991 and gave a plurality to the FIS (Front Islamique du Salut), although only about one-quarter of the electorate voted FIS. The second round did not go ahead.

30 It is important to clarify that the RMP was approved in principle in 1989 but was not immediately implemented. Morocco rejected its funding at first owing to the European Parliament (EP) and French criticisms of Moroccan policies towards human rights and on the issue of the Western Sahara. (That is, Morocco 'rejected' assistance under the RMP but only because the EP had already 'vetoed' such aid to Morocco, pending improvements in respect for human rights, etc. The EP was, perhaps rightfully so, accused of this but this implies MEPs voted to stop aid. But during the session when this issue came up, the EP did not have the requisite quorum to approve the aid.)

31 Since suspended, although some programmes may be resuming. See Giammusso, Maurizio, 1999. 'Civil Society Initiatives and Prospects of Economic Development: The Euro-Mediterranean Decentralized Co-operation Networks', *Mediterranean Politics*, 4(1), Spring, 25–52.

32 See, for example, Commission of the European Communities, 1991. Communication from the Commission to the Council on *The Implementation Of Trade Arrangements Under The New Mediterranean Policy*. COM(91)179 final, 22 May and Commission of the European Communities, 1994a. Report from the Commission to the Council and the European Parliament on *The Implementation of Financial and Technical Cooperation with Mediterranean non-Member Countries and on Financial Cooperation with those Countries as a Group*. COM(94)384 final, 18 November 1994.

33 See Chérigui, Hayète, 1997. *La Politique Méditerranéenne de la France: entre diplomatie collective et leadership*. Paris: L'Harmattan, for more on the Mediterranean forum.

34 The code of conduct on terrorism was included in the Action Plan at Valencia.

35 Interviews held in Brussels, January 2004.

36 That is, during the Spanish presidency of the EU.

37 Commission of the European Communities, 1994b. *A Strategy for Euro-Mediterranean Partnership*. Essen: IP/94/1156, 06/12/94.

38 It is important to note here that the Mediterranean countries (the other party to the supposed dialogue), were not invited to submit a document of their own defining their position on what was to be discussed (although there were a few bilateral consultations). It may be argued that the Mediterranean countries did not have an organisation capable of articulating a common position (certainly not in the case of Israel and Syria, for example). However, for the sake of the EU's democratic structure, one would have at least expected the partners to be invited to give their views.

39 Interview at the European Commission, DG External Relations and Enlargement, Charlemagne Building, Brussels, January 2004.

40 The rationale was that agreements would be signed only with countries that already had agreements with the EU, although the door was left open for future partners. During this time, Libya did not have such an agreement. Currently, Libya has observer status in EMP fora.

41 Whitaker, Brian, 2003. 'British Firms set sights on Libya as Hopes Rise of an End to Sanctions', *The Guardian*, 2 September, 12.

42 During August 2003, Libya had agreed to pay US$2.7bn (£1.7bn) to the families of people who died in the bombing of a Pan Am airliner over Lockerbie in 1988. France insisted that it would block the move unless Libya increased its compensation – an initial US$34m settlement – for the bombing of a French UTA airliner which killed 170 people in 1989. On 9 January 2004 Libya signed a compensation accord with the families of 170 killed in the bombing of the French airliner, marking a further significant step in its efforts at ridding itself of its image as a 'rogue' state and its rapprochement with the West. The deal was made for US$170m (£92m), that is US$1m for each of the 170 people killed. Henley, Jon, 2004. 'Libya Agrees Payout for French Jet Bombing', *The Guardian*, 10 January, 14.

43 This has been revised. For example, the date envisaged in the latest association agreement with Morocco is 2012.

44 European Commission, External Relations, 2003.

45 Source: European Commission, 2002. *Euromed Information Notes*. 'Euro-Mediterranean Partnership and MEDA Regional Activities', June. Also available at: http://europa.eu.int/comm/europeaid/projects/med/regional_en.htm.

46 Interviews in Brussels, January 2004. See http://www.euromedmarket.org/.

47 *EuroMed Information Notes*, 2002.

48 See Annex to the final Conclusions of the 6th Euro-Mediterranean meeting of Foreign Ministers, Naples December 2003. 'Recommendation From the Euro-Mediterranean Parliamentary Forum to the Sixth Euro-Mediterranean Ministerial Conference on Setting Up a Euro-Mediterranean Parliamentary Assembly', 2 December, especially pp. 17–18.

49 Interviews in Brussels, January 2004.

50 *Euromed Information Notes*, 2002.

51 Monar, Jörg, 1997. 'Political Dialogue with Third Countries and Regional Political Groupings: The Fifteen as an Attractive Interlocutor', in Regelsberger *et al.*, *Foreign Policy of the EU. From EPC to CFSP and Beyond*. London: Lynne Rienner Publishers, 263–74; Pace, Michelle, 2004e. 'The Role of "Political Dialogue": A Dialogic Understanding of EU–Mediterranean Relations'. Paper presented at the ECPR Standing group on the European Union. 2nd Pan-European conference on EU Politics. 'Implications of a Wider Europe: Politics, Institutions and Diversity', held in Bologna, 25 June.

52 *EuroMed Synopsis*, 15 January 2004, Issue No. 255.

53 Quefelec, Stéphane, 2003. '2002 in the Mediterranean Countries: Selected Indicators', *Statistics in Focus*. European Communities.

54 *Euromed Special Feature* No. 30, 27 May 2002. Available at: http://www.deljor. cec.eu.int/en/images/special_features/special_features_30.htm.

55 Brussels interviews, January 2004. See also Philippart, 2003.

56 See Murphy, Emma (ed.), 2001. *Mediterranean Politics*, special issue on the state and the private sector in North Africa, (6)2, Summer. Also Murphy, Emma, 2002. 'Navigating the Economic Reform in the Arab World: Social Responses, Political Structures and Dilemmas for the European Union', in C.P. Hanelt, F. Neugart and M. Peitz (eds) *Europe's Emerging Foreign Policy and the Middle East Challenge*. Munich: Bertelsmann Foundation, 33–57.

57 See Pace and Schumacher, 2004. See also the evaluation report from the Commission entitled 'Mid-term Evaluation of the Euromed-Youth programme' ref. no. MEI/B7-4100/1B/0418, dated 24 August 2001.

58 Hill, 1993.

59 At time of writing. In hindsight, neither the result of the April 2004 referendum in Cyprus on the Annan Plan nor the Bush victory in the US elections of November 2004 bode well for the future of the EMP.

60 Interviews in Brussels, January 2004.

61 This has not been implemented in full.

62 http://europa.eu.int/comm/external_relations/euromed/conf/val/concl.pdf. Accessed on 27 August 2003.

63 Interviews held in Brussels, January 2004. See also the complete Action Plan of the Valencia Conference at: http://europa.eu.int/comm/external_relations/euromed/conf/val/action.pdf; and for the Naples Conclusions: http://europa.eu. int/comm/external_relations/euromed/publications.htm.

64 Interview in Brussels, January 2004.

65 Ibid.
66 On 14 October 2004 the EU Council adopted a Common Position and a Regulation lifting the restrictive measures and the arms embargo against Libya as a result of the Libyan Government's compliance with the relevant United Nations Security Council Resolutions, accepting the responsibility for actions of Libyan officials, payment of appropriate compensation and renunciation of terrorism. The decisions are part of an EU policy of engagement towards Libya. More on this at: http://europa.eu.int/news/index_en.htm.
67 Interviews held in Brussels at the European Commission, Charlemagne Building, January 2004.
68 Alexandria Roundtable on Culture and Community in the Euro-Mediterranean Partnership held in October 2003 in Alexandria, Egypt. For more information see Pace and Schumacher, 2004.
69 Meyer-Resende, Madalena, 2004. Paper presented at the panel on Europe and the Mediterranean, ECPR, Bologna, June.
70 *EuroMed Synopsis*, 29 January 2004, Issue No. 257.

4 EU foreign policy as a discursive practice of the Mediterranean

1 Sánchez Mateos, Elvira, 2003. 'European Perceptions of Southern Countries Security and Defence Issues: A Reflection on the European Press'. EuroMeSCo Paper 23. Lisboa: EuroMeSCo Secretariat at the IEEI.
2 This strategy also draws upon works within the radical strand of constructivism in IR, especially the work of authors who adopt a discourse analysis/foreign policy approach. See, for example, Larsen, 1997; Hansen and Wæver, 2002.
3 The analysis of systems of concepts is prominent in the work of Aron, Raymond, 1967. *Main Currents In Sociological Thought 2: Durkheim, Pareto, Weber*. Harmondsworth: Penguin Books. Translated by Richard Howard and Helen Weaver.
4 Prozorov, Sergei, 2004. 'Three Theses on Governance and the Political', *Journal of International Relations and Development*, 7(3), 267–93.
5 As already mentioned, more recently, in March 2003, a communication from the Commission to the Council and the European Parliament announced the 'Wider Europe – Neighbourhood' initiative which includes the EU's 'Southern Neighbours'. Commission of the European Communities, 2003b. *Wider Europe – Neighbourhood: A New Framework for Relations with our Eastern and Southern Neighbours*. Brussels, 11 March. COM(2003) 104 final.
6 No subject is really unified. In the EU case this is more clear than in the case of national actors.
7 It is important to note here that although the issue of immigration from the 'South' is often linked to the possible danger this would represent for Europe (the problem relates more to xenophobia creating instability by enabling extremist political forces to grow), that is, as a threat, this issue of immigration is placed under the third pillar of the EMP and not the first. The issue of immigration is one of the most ambiguous and remains a vague concept that the EU does not know how to deal with. It is interesting to note the current debate which emerged in Britain on this issue in the context of the 2004 enlargement and fears that Britain will be 'flooded' with immigrants from the former Eastern 'bloc', *The Guardian*, February 2004.
8 Faria, Fernanda, 1996. 'The Mediterranean: A New Priority in Portuguese Foreign Policy', *Mediterranean Politics*, special issue on Western Approaches to the Mediterranean, 1(2), Autumn, 212–30.
9 Greece continues to maintain contact both with northern EU states and with its southern neighbours but puts more energy into its relations with its Balkan neighbours.
10 Ioakimidis, P.C., 1993. 'Greece in the EC: Policies, Experiences and Prospects', in Harry J. Psomiadis and Stavros B. Thomadakis (eds) *Greece, The New Europe and The Changing International Order*. New York: Pella Publishing, 405–20.
11 Rozakis, Christos, 1986. 'Greek Foreign Policy 1974–85: Modernization and the International Role of a Small State', in A. Manessis *et al.* (eds) *Greece in Motion*. Athens:

Exandas (in Greek). According to interviewees in Brussels, Greece has had quite an impact on EU discourses when these relate to Cyprus or Turkey, January 2004.

12 Núñez Villaverde, Jesús A., 2000. 'The Mediterranean: A Firm Priority of Spanish Foreign Policy?', *Mediterranean Politics*, 5(2), Summer, 138. During the informal meeting of NATO defence ministers in Seville on 29 September 1994, the decision to establish a NATO Mediterranean Dialogue 'initiative was nothing more than a concession by the USA and most of the northern members in exchange for the support of countries like Spain and Italy for eastern European expansion', ibid., 141.

13 Meyrede, Laurent, 1999. 'France's Foreign Policy in the Mediterranean', in S. Stavridis *et al.* (eds), 70.

14 Echeverría, J.C., 1999. 'Spain and the Mediterranean', in S. Stavridis *et al.* (eds), 109.

15 Aliboni, Roberto, 1999. 'Italy and the Mediterranean in the 1990s', in S. Stavridis *et al.* (eds) *The Foreign Policies of the EU's Mediterranean States and Applicant Countries in the 1990s*. Basingstoke: Macmillan, 92.

16 Ibid., 94.

17 Greece lobbied very hard on Cyprus' accession to the EU. Interviews at the EP and Commissoin DG Enlargement, January 2004.

18 On France's leadership role see Chérigui, 1997.

19 Howorth, Jolyon, 1996. 'France and the Mediterranean in 1995: From Tactical Ambiguity to Inchoate Strategy', *Mediterranean Politics*, special issue on Western approaches to the Mediterranean, 1(2), Autumn, 157–8.

20 Howorth 1996, 162.

21 Chérigui offers an interesting account on *l'approche Française de la crise Algérienne* (p. 100).

22 See Chérigui, 1997.

23 Chérigui talks about *la Méditerranée occidentale comme espace international* (p. 109).

24 In fact, it established (albeit weak) Euro-Mediterranean institutions and processes.

25 Howorth, 1996.

26 Chérigui, 1997, 116–17. French discursive practices of the Mediterranean often depend on the approaches adopted which vary according to criteria such as the Mediterranean as a zone for cultural exchanges, a trading zone, a conflict zone, a risk zone (or an arc of crises) and a strategic zone. In other words, in terms of economic discourses, security discourses or political discourses on the Mediterranean.

27 The original interest in the Mediterranean can be seen as part of González's policy of seeking improved relations with all Spain's neighbours – France, Portugal and Morocco – and also in terms of developing ties of (economic) interdependence with Morocco so as to neutralise the Ceuta-Melilla issue. Morrocan immigration did not become a major issue for Spain until the late 1980s (and was therefore not the main motive for developing Spain's Mediterranean policy).

28 Gillespie, Richard, 1996. 'Spain and the Mediterranean: Southern Sensitivity, European Aspirations', *Mediterranean Politics*, special issue on Western approaches to the Mediterranean, 1(2), Autumn, 93–211.

29 This has changed since the events of 11 March 2004 in Madrid.

30 Gillespie, 1996.

31 Spain is the youngest Western European democracy and the only European country holding territory in North Africa (Gillespie, 1996).

32 Núñez Villaverde, 2000, 137.

33 It is important to note the special character of Spain's relations with the Palestinian Territories in the fields of politics and development co-operation (Núñez Villaverde, 2000, 139).

34 Gillespie, 1996.

35 Chérigui, 1997.

36 Spain is not the only protectionist force, however.

37 Rein, R. (ed.), 1999. *Spain and the Mediterranean Since 1898*. London and Portland, OR: Frank Cass.

38 The Mediterranean provides 72 per cent of Spain's gas and 17 per cent of its oil; 80 per cent of Spain's phosphates requirements come from Morocco and fish stocks from Morocco, the Sahara and Mauritania are highly valued by Spanish fishermen (Núñez Villaverde, 2000, 131).

39 It must be noted that Seville was the place which gave rise to NATO's discourse on the Mediterranean at an informal meeting of NATO defence ministers and which also gave rise to NATO's Mediterranean Dialogue. This discursive practice was aimed at bringing the 'reality' of the area closer to NATO as a defence organisation that seemed to need the identification of a new 'enemy' (an 'other') with which to justify its very existence (Núñez Villaverde, 2000, 141). Spain was an important speaking subject behind this NATO discourse on the Mediterranean. For an update on NATO's Mediterranean Dialogue see Dokos, Thanos, 2003. *NATO's Mediterranean Dialogue: Prospects and Policy Recommendations*. ELIAMEP Policy Paper No. 3. Athens: Hellenic Foundation for European and Foreign Policy (ELIAMEP).

40 Núñez Villaverde, 2000. Following the events in Madrid of 11 March 2004, the ensuing elections resulting in the defeat of Aznar's party and the withdrawal of Spanish troops from Iraq, the discursive practices on the wider Mediterranean in Spain have already undergone interesting changes (at time of writing).

41 Holmes, John W., 1996. 'Italy: In the Mediterranean, but *of* it?', *Mediterranean Politics*, special issue on Western approaches to the Mediterranean, 1(2), Autumn, 176–92.

42 Some examples: Proposal For Third Euro-Mediterranean Ministerial Trade Conference, held in Palermo, 7 July 2003; Proposal for the First Euro-Mediterranean Conference of the Ministers of Agriculture, Venice, 27 November, 2003; Proposal for the Euro-Mediterranean Ministerial Conference 'Towards a New Euro-Med Partnership on Investment Promotion, Infrastructure Financing and Energy Supply Security', Rome, 1–2 December, 2003. At the latter, emphasis was made on 'the energy field [of the Partnership which now] requires greater momentum'.

43 Holmes, 1996.

44 This is also the case following the 9/11 and 11 March 2004 events.

45 Chérigui, 1997, 30. The author talks *de l'alliance Franco–Italienne au clivage Latino–Grec*.

46 Here, he upset Spanish partners who had largely drafted the CSCM proposal.

47 France was threatened since it perceived a loss of protagonism. It also saw the CSCM as a grandiose project and preferred its 'own' 4+5 initiative.

48 The Balkan distraction is fundamental here: for historical, geopolitical and economic reasons, Italy's foreign policy-makers saw the emerging post-Cold War Balkans as an area deserving close attention.

49 Holmes, 1996, 185.

50 Martino claimed specific credit for the decision to give Cyprus and Malta priority consideration for accession to the EU.

51 Aliboni, 1999, 94.

52 Holmes, John W. (ed.), 1995. *Maelstrom, The United States, Southern Europe, and the Challenges of the Mediterranean*. Cambridge, MA: World Peace Foundation; Holmes 1996, 187. These multinational rapid deployment forces were established without prior notification to the Mediterranean partners. Arab governments expressed their disapproval arguing that the initiative was directed against the Arabs. This was a case of violence in a European discourse since these member states' actions resulted in a loss of trust of Arab states for European governments. See Attinà, Fulvio, 2003. 'The Euro-Mediterranean Partnership Assessed: The Realist and Liberal Views', *European Foreign Affairs Review*, 8, 181–99.

53 Holmes, 1996, 187–8. I have recently been advised that this speculation is not grounded in facts. I thank Waddah Saab at the European Commission for clarifying this for me.

54 This tripartite approach goes back to Helsinki.

55 Holmes, 1996.

56 For an interesting analysis on Italy's foreign policy see Carracciolo, Luciano and Korinman, Michel (eds), 1998. *Italy and the Balkans*. Washington, DC: The Center for Strategic and International Studies.

57 Chérigui, 1997.

58 The power of France is not as questionable as that of Italy or Spain in the Mediterranean – as an area of influence.

59 Núñez Villaverde, 2000.

60 Ioakimidis, P.C., 1999. 'The Model of Foreign Policy-Making in Greece: Personalities versus Institutions', in S. Stavridis *et al.* (eds), 140.

61 Greece as a case study will be dealt with more specifically in Chapter 5.

62 The New Neighbourhood Policy may be read as another instance of securitisation stemming from such threat perceptions.

63 Although Spain was of some importance as a partner for the USA and Britain in the recent second Gulf War in Iraq (before José Luis Rodríguez Zapatero's government came to power following the March 2004 elections). The present Spanish government is more committed to good relations with the Moroccan government.

64 Interviews at the European Commission, 18 May 1999.

65 Anna Lindh, the popular Swedish foreign minister, was murdered on 10 September 2003.

66 European Commission, 1999. 'Conclusions: Third Euro-Mediterranean Conference of Foreign Ministers', Stuttgart, 15–16 April 1999. Available at: http://europa.eu.int/comm/external_relations/euromed/conf/stutg/conc_en.htm. Accessed January 2001.

67 Member states only hold the presidency for a six-month term.

68 Stuttgart opening statement: see European Commission, 1999.

69 It is worth noting that Germany also has interests in the South – trade and investment; migration from Turkey and links with Balkan countries such as Croatia.

70 The late Mrs Lindh at the Stuttgart conference (held in Stuttgart 12–17 April 1999). See European Commission, 1999 where Lindh referred to culture and 'the three monotheistic religions' of the Mediterranean area. This was the third Euro-Mediterranean conference of foreign ministers, after the conferences held in Barcelona and Malta (Chapter 3).

71 Commission of the European Communities 1995a *Strengthening the Mediterranean Policy of the European Union: Proposals for Implementing a EMP*. COM(95)72 final, 8 March; and 1995b. *Proposal for a Council Regulation (EC) on Financial and Technical Measures to Support the Reform of Economic and Social Structures in Mediterranean non-Member Countries and Territories*. COM(95)204 final, 7 June.

72 Bulletin of the EU, Bulletin 2/95. *Strengthening the Mediterranean Policy of the EU: Establishing a EMP*, 10.

73 Ibid., 18.

74 Ibid., Annex 4, 25.

75 Ibid., 39.

76 This is also reflected in the EU's recent focus on a wider Middle East initiative, following the 9/11 and 11 March 2004 events.

77 European Commission. *EuroMed Report*, Issue No. 57, 22 May 2003.

78 Analysts argue that should Turkey join the EU, Iraq, Iran and Syria will become Europe's 'front garden'.

79 European Commission, 1999. Accessed January 2001.

80 Bulletin 2/95, 57.

81 Ibid., 58.

82 Ibid., 64.

83 For a very interesting debate on 'dialogue' see Monar, 1997.

84 Commission of the European Communities 1996. *Amended proposal for a Council Regulation (EC) on Financial and Technical Measures to Support the Reform of Economic and Social Structures in Mediterranean non-Member Countries and Territories*. COM(96)113 final, 25 March, 1c.

85 European Commission, 1999.

86 Attinà, 2003.

87 Bulletin 2/95, 34.

88 This is not just a question of current membership. Here I am referring to both current and potential EU members. In the past, for instance, most EU officials would have regarded former Czechoslovakia as European and thus a potential member.

89 Bretherton and Vogler, 1999.

90 Spatial changes carry time, that is, they have a historical dimension. When Greece joined the EU, for example, its Balkan dimension had an impact on European identity. This process of the construction and production of identity of this actor known as the EU is also about who does not belong, who does the belonging, who marks who's in and who's out (in terms of Foucault's power structures, governmentality etc.). An illustration of this is the debate on Turkish membership of the EU. See, for example, Taylor, Simon, 1999. 'Turkish Poll will do Little to Thaw Ice', *The European Voice*, 8–14 April, 12–13; Black, Ian, 2000. 'Aspirants Vow to Obey EU Code' (European Parliament Special Report), *The Guardian*, 16 February, 13; Hodge, Carl Cavanagh, 1999. 'Turkey and the Pale Light of European Democracy', *Mediterranean Politics*, 4(3), Autumn, 56–68; Neumann, Iver B.

and Welsh, Jennifer M., 1997. '"The Turk" as Europe's Other', in Peter J. Burgess (ed.) *Cultural Politics and Political Culture in Postmodern Europe*. Amsterdam and Atlanta, GA: Rodopi; Sofos, 2001. (It would have been interesting if there had been a similar debate on Morocco's membership of the EU.) Such debates clearly show that the EU is not a given but the product of conscious and even subconscious choices and embodies concepts of where the boundary of Europe starts and where it stops.

91 As mentioned in the Chapter 3, Libya at the time was subject to UN sanctions, after it was accused of being responsible for the terrorist bombs that caused the crash at Lockerbie and that of the UTA aeroplane (Faria, Fernanda, 1999. 'The Making of Portugal's Mediterranean Policy', in S. Stavridis *et al.* (eds), 113–39). Of course, EU members – especially Italy and Spain – do perceive Libya as Mediterranean (not only because they have energy interests there). It is Spain's intention to sign a similar Treaty to the one it has with Morocco (Treaty of Friendship, Good Neighbourliness and Co-operation) with Libya when circumstances allow (Núñez Villaverde, 2000, 135). As stated above, it is important to note here not only the composition of the membership of a group but also assumptions about that group. Up until recently, this group assumed a specific definition of Libya (and gives a negative image of Libya as a 'rogue' state).

92 See Commission of the European Communities, 1994c. *The European Union Relations with the Mediterranean*. MEMO/94/74, 06/12/94.

93 It may be argued that this is a result of political and historical processes, not a simple selection. In fact, these countries were so lumped, in this manner, during the Cold War, not just more recently.

94 European Commission, 1999. It is important to note that the EU has a common strategy on the Balkans. During June 2000, the European Council also adopted its common strategy on the Mediterranean that interestingly 'covers all the EU's relations with all its partners in the Barcelona Process, and with Libya', *Official Journal of the European Communities*, 2000. *Common Strategy of the European Council of 19 June 2000 on the Mediterranean Region*. Santa Maria da Feira, 1.

95 It is interesting to note that although a common Islamic religion is assumed, Europeans see this Islamic area or Arab Mediterranean with some exceptions, see Said, Edward W., 1981. *Covering Islam: How the Media and the Experts Determine How We See the Rest of the World*. New York: Pantheon Books (reprinted in 1997, New York: Vintage Books), for more on this issue. Two of the non-Arab partner countries in the EMP are treated with a certain preference (Israel and Turkey. So are Malta and Cyprus). It is therefore important to observe not only the membership of the non-EU Mediterranean countries but who they seem to be – are these partners seen as Arab and Islamic in a 'region' which poses challenges to the EU? More recently the EU seems to be changing its course and is taking a sub-regional approach without abandoning its EMP's purported 'global' approach. The New Neighbourhood Policy is for some officials a policy going back to bilateral relations (interviews in Brussels, January 2004). A colleague described this policy as simply an EU shift from its EMP to an ENP!

96 Significantly, as mentioned earlier, the derivation of these terms is Arabic.

97 Egypt is sometimes placed in both categories.

98 Historically, there have been various different notions of the extent of the Maghreb. (In fact, it has always been variously defined.)

99 For example, there is great rivalry within the Maghreb between Morocco and Algeria.

100 Chourou, Béchir, 1999. 'A Challenge For EU Mediterranean Policy: Upgrading Democracy From Threat to Risk'. Paper presented at The International Workshop on The Human Dimension of Security and the EMP. Malta, 14–15 May.

101 European Commission, 2000. *The Barcelona Process: Five Years On, 1995–2000*, Luxembourg: Office for Official Publications of the European Communities.

102 Lewis, Martin W. and Wigen, Kären E., 1997. *The Myth of Continents: A Critique of Metageography*. Berkeley, CA and London: University of California Press, preface, xii. Shapiro elaborates on this point by claiming that boundaries are not just borders or spaces – there is a whole social dimension attached to boundary delineation. He also cites Connolly for whom boundaries do not just secure protection from violence: they also constitute a form of violence. Connolly states that 'Boundaries form indispensable protections against violation and violence, but the divisions they sustain in doing so also carry cruelty and violence. *Boundaries provide preconditions of identity*, ... and collective action ...'. Connolly in Shapiro and Alker, 1996, 141, own emphasis.

103   Commission of the European Communities, 1995a.
104   This quotation neatly brings together the regular markers across EU discourses on the Mediterranean where the EU's logic equates welfare creation to a halt in violence that means less migration flows and in turn more stability and security.
105   *EuroMed Report*, Issue No. 59, 28 May 2003, Presidency Conclusions. Mid-Term Euro-Mediterranean Conference, Crete, 26–27 May.
106   Smith, M.E., 2004b.
107   EuroMeSCo, 2003. *European Security and Defence Policy – Latest News*. Available at: http://www.euromesco.net/euromesco/artigo.asp?cod_artigo= 88651. Accessed on 22 September 2003. See esp. Section on 'EU–Morocco: Positive Appraisal of the Partnership'.
108   Kuus, 2004.
109   Neumann, 1998. (The uses of the Other.)
110   European Council, 2000. *Common Strategy*. Thus, the EU is promoted as a value system for all Mediterranean partners to emulate.
111   *EuroMed Report*, Issue No. 52, 28 November 2002. Romano Prodi, President of the European Commission, *Europe and the Mediterranean: Time for Action*. Louvain-la-Neuve: Université Catholique de Louvain-la-Neuve, 26 November 2002.
112   *EuroMed Report*, Issue No. 57, 22 May 2003. In effect, the EU's modernisation discourse on the Mediterranean.
113   One may also argue that behind this New Neighbourhood Policy lies an implicit recognition by EU members that the Mediterranean partners are different and hence require a different approach which takes the EU back to its original EuroMed bilateral relations of the 1960s. Interviews held in Brussels, January 2004.
114   *EuroMed Report*, Issue No. 61, 18 June 2003. *Council Conclusions On Wider Europe – New Neighbourhood*. In effect, the EU's welfare discourse on the Mediterranean.
115   Interview at the European Commission, January 2004.
116   Attinà, F., 2003.
117   Interview in Alexandria, 2003.
118   Some officials believe that the EU interest in the Mediterranean area is not just a case of nostalgic issues of former colonial times or of marginal trade or economic interests but of a direct concern with one of the regions of vicinity (which echoes the recent New Neighbourhood Policy) – interviews held on the 18 May 1999.
119   I owe this insight to Dr Spyros Sofos.
120   Thus, the Mediterranean is perceived as a threat to European security.
121   Prodi, 2003. *Building a Euro-Mediterranean Area*, own emphasis.
122   For an interesting work on such interpretations see Fabian, 1983.
123   See section within text below for more detailed analysis of these issues.
124   My emphasis: see European Commission, 1999.
125   There is also a weaker level of concern in relation to 'risks' as opposed to 'threats'.
126   Chourou, 1999.
127   Commission of the European Communities, 1995a.
128   Derrida, Jacques, 1992. *The Other Heading: Reflections on Today's Europe*. Bloomington, IN: Indiana University Press; Laclau, Ernesto and Mouffe, Chantal, 1985. *Hegemony and Socialist Strategy: Towards a Radical Democratic Politics*. London and New York: Verso.
129   Euro-Mediterranean Conference on Regional Co-operation, 1999. Concluding statement by Von Ploetz.
130   Europe Documents, 1995, 2. In other words, the EU is not trying to tread on the toes of Washington!
131   Hence the importance of analysing the emergence of an utterance and discourse in its context.
132   Cowen and Shenton, 1996; Escobar, 1995; Fabian, 1983; Ferguson, 1990.
133   That is, the neo-liberalist agenda. See Cowen and Shenton, 1996.
134   Ibid.
135   Escobar, 1995.
136   The EMP as a discourse constructs priority areas for the partner countries.
137   When questioned about what the EMP is trying to achieve, one official at the European Commission referred to the question of migration under the third pillar of the 'coming together of people'. There therefore seems to be a positive EU sub-discourse on migration. This may also be interpreted as a contradictory discourse in that a negative discourse is

hidden behind a more positive one. Martín, Iván, 2004. 'Social consultation and the impact of the Euro-Mediterranean free trade areas and the MEDA programme on economic and social rights: A case for surpassing the division between the three baskets of the EMP'. Paper presented at an international workshop on the impact of European Union involvement in civil society structures in the Southern Mediterranean. Friedrich Ebert Stiftung, Rabat, Morocco, 4–5 December.

138 On immigration see King, Russell and Black, Richard, 1997. *Southern Europe and the New Immigrations.* Brighton: Sussex Academic Press. In the Tampere conclusions it was noted that halting immigration could be disastrous for the EU, especially for Italy and Spain. Italy has actually been contemplating a replacement migration strategy where migrants of a working age are invited to go to Italy to replace the lack of Italians in this age bracket (Italy has been experiencing, for the past years, a slow birth rate and a low death rate). The Tampere European Council, 15–16 October 1999, Presidency Conclusions may be found at: http://europa.eu.int/council/off/conclu/oct99/oct99_en.htm.

139 Interview at the European Commission, 18 May 1999.

140 The discourse of the Mediterranean is not that different though from applicant discourse generally – see Chapter 5.

141 Some may wish to argue that EU policy practitioners may well be more enlightened than Europeans in general, in terms of seeing benefits to be derived from allocating resources to a Mediterranean policy. Moreover, they are aware that such a policy is more easily 'sold' to tax payers/voters if presented as a Mediterranean policy, as opposed to an Arab, Jewish/Israeli or Middle East policy.

142 Morocco did this too: following its rejection as 'European' it flagged its 'Mediterranean' label in order to secure benefits other than EU membership.

143 Spain also imports phosphates from Morocco.

144 Commission of the European Communities, 1999. *Survey On Free Trade And Economic Transition in the Mediterranean.* DG1B/A/4, 1 April.

145 Huband, Mark, 2000. World News: Trade: 'Mediterranean Region Facing Marginalisation', *Financial Times*, 9 March, 16.

146 Ibid.

147 Ibid.

148 Interview, 18 May 1999.

149 My emphasis: Commission of the European Communities, 1995c. Barcelona Euro-Mediterranean Conference, 27–28 November, Declaration and Work Programme. DOC/95/7, 04/12/95. Also interview at the European Commission, January 2004.

150 It is important to note the EU's growing capacity to intervene as a result of the EU-WEU merger and the decision to create a rapid deployment force. Norton-Taylor, Richard, 2000. 'Comment and Analysis: "Analysis: Intelligence Test"'. Features. *The Guardian*, 20 December, 17.

151 Commission of the European Communities, 1995a, 2.

152 Chourou, 1999.

153 For example, the recent Tempus MEDA regional conference on higher education co-operation and intercultural dialogue across the Mediterranean held in Alexandria, Egypt between 13–14 October 2003. The most recent Euro-Mediterranean Civil Forum was held in Naples, 28–30 November 2003.

154 Interviews at the Commission, January 2004.

155 White, 1999.

156 CFSP is an outgrowth of other forms of European integration. See, for example, Eliassen, 1998. Since 1999, the EU also includes its Common European Security Defence Policy (CESDP). This is interesting considering the lack of a military threat to the EU.

157 Escobar, 1995.

158 Obviously, interests are also created by resource considerations.

159 Larsen, 1997; Hansen and Wæver, 2002.

160 It would be interesting to consider the status of Berbers in this context.

161 Borneman, John, 1995. 'American Anthropology as Foreign Policy', *American Anthropologist*, 97(4), December, 667.

162 Campbell, 1992.

163 Larsen, Henrik, 2002. 'The EU: A Global Military Actor?', *Co-operation and Conflict: Journal of the Nordic International Studies Association*, 37(3), 283–302.

164   One suspects that if this security concern did not exist, even less resources might be mobilised!
165   In terms of Buzan and Wæver's 2003 work, this may highlight the importance of the economic security sector for the EU in the Mediterranean.
166   Núñez Villaverde, 2000, 144–5. As long as member states retain veto rights on immigration issues and with the reactions from various European countries to the 2004 enlargement to the East, a less restrictive immigration policy is highly unlikely.
167   Borneman, 1995, 669.
168   See Bakic-Hayden, M., 1995. 'Nesting Orientalisms: The Case of Former Yugoslavia', *Slavic Review* 54(4), 917–31 (nested orientalisms as a pattern of representation which reproduces the dichotomy of Europe and another but introduces a gradation between two poles).

5   Discursive practices of the Mediterranean from Greece, Malta and Morocco

1   Bullock, Stallybrass and Trombley, 1977, 1988, 195.
2   Following its British colonisation in 1814.
3   The third being the Green Party *Alternattiva Demokratika* (Alternative Democratic Party).
4   For more specific details on this issue see Abela, J.S., 1997. *Malta: A Panoramic History*. San Gwann, Malta: Publishers Enterprises Group.
5   An observation which was proven true after Malta signed the accession Treaty in 2003.
6   For an interesting analysis of Maltese ambivalence to Europe see Mitchell, 2002.
7   Sant seemed to play down media discourses/fears of Malta being 'left behind' by the European train.
8   It is worth noting that this is quite a big majority in Maltese terms given the usual closeness of results. The PN was elected with 51.8 per cent of the vote (137,037 votes) while the MLP captured 47 per cent of the vote (124,220 votes).
9   This action was taken with the objective of commencing accession negotiations as had been promised at the Corfu, Cannes, Madrid and Florence EU summits during 1994, 1995 and 1996.
10   Pace, Roderick, 2004. 'Malta's EU Membership: Chapter 1 Concluded, Chapter 2 Just Started', *Mediterranean Politics*, 9(1), Spring, 114–21. London: Frank Cass.
11   This change in policy was also true with the UK Labour Party.
12   In the course of Mediterranean Forum meetings held in Malta, an in-depth discussion on the EuroMed Charter for Peace and Stability was carried out.
13   For more on these issues see Boissevain, J., 1965. *Saints and Fireworks: Religion and Politics in Rural Malta*. London: London School of Economics Monographs on Social Anthropology, 30; and Sultana, Ronald G. and Baldacchino, Godfrey (eds), 1994. *Maltese Society: A Sociological Inquiry*. Msida: Mireva Publications; Mitchell, 2002.
14   For a fascinating debate on identity within a framework of social analysis see Brubaker and Cooper, 2000.
15   Yet language is an area in which Malta will have an advantage over the CEEC. Although half of Malta may be concerned about losing its own language, there is another side of the coin to it: that familiarity with English must be an asset within the EU and will give Malta an advantage over CEEC, in terms of learning how to work the EU system to national advantage, as Greece has learnt so well. Interview in Brussels, January 2004.
16   Labour's vision may have seemed rather backward looking in this respect. However, this attitude was premised on a view of culture and identity (and economy/politics) that assumed that these could flourish in considerable isolation.
17   It might be argued that the 'Greeks' and 'Greece' are a product of the modern era despite their claims to a classical, Hellenistic, Byzantine and early modern continuity. See Herzfeld, Michael, 1989. *Anthropology Through the Looking Glass: Critical Ethnography in the Margins of Europe*. Cambridge: Cambridge University Press. Also Fatouros, Arghyrios A., 1993. 'Political and Institutional Facets of Greece's Integration in the European Community', in Harry J. Psomiades and Stavros B. Thomadakis (eds) *Greece, The New Europe, And The Changing International Order*. New York: Pella Publishing, 23–56. See also Clogg, Richard, 1986. *A Short History of Modern Greece*. Cambridge: Cambridge University Press for more on this.

18 For an interesting discussion on national identity and the politics of alterity see Guillaume, Xavier, 2002. 'Foreign Policy and the Politics of Alterity: A Dialogical Understanding of International Relations', *Millennium: Journal of International Studies*, 31(1), 1–26.

19 On the Greek Orthodox Church, its relation with state authority, in general, and the modern Greek state, in particular, see, Sherrard, Philip, 1959. *The Greek East and Latin West: A Study in the Christian Tradition*. Oxford: Oxford University Press. See also Frazee, Charles A., 1969. *The Orthodox Church and Independent Greece 1821–1852*. Cambridge: Cambridge University Press; Ware, Kallistos, 1983. 'The Church: A Time of Transition', in Richard Clogg (ed.) *Greece in the 1980s*, London: Macmillan in association with the Centre of Contemporary Greek Studies, Kings College, University of London, 208–30.

20 See Clogg, 1986.

21 For more on this issue see Lipowatz, Thanos, 1994. 'Split Greek Identity and the Issue of Nationalism', in Nicolas Demertzis (ed.) *Greek Political Culture Today*. Athens: Odysseas, 115–32.

22 For an excellent analysis of these two schools see Fatouros, 1993 and Couloumbis, Theodore A., 1983. 'The Structures of Greek Foreign Policy', in Richard Clogg, 95–122. Couloumbis refers to these two important slogans as symbolising a crisis in Greek identity in the 1980s. Following the 1981 elections, PASOK's foreign policy approach was one of subjective reluctance but objective active participation in the EEC.

23 Communications with an official. See also Psomiades and Thomadakis, 1993 and Lipowatz, 1994.

24 See Blinkhorn, Martin and Veremis, Thanos (eds), 1990. *Modern Greece: Nationalism and Nationality*. Athens: ELIAMEP.

25 See http://www.monde-diplomatique.fr/en/2000/07/01ramonet. Ramonet, Ignacio, 2000. 'New Hope, Old Frustrations. Morocco: The Point of Change', *Le Monde Diplomatique* (English version), July edition.

26 Greeks were in Egypt since Ottoman times. This 'original' community of Greek settlements in Egypt was prosperous and therefore attracted more Greeks to go there. Greek was even the local *lingua franca* in Egypt for some time. (Communications with an official and presentation by the Director of the Bibliotheca at the permanent exhibition, the Alexandria and the Mediterranean Research Centre, Bibliotheca Alexandrina, October 2003.)

27 See Close, D.H., 1990. *The Character of the Metaxas Dictatorship: An International Perspective*. London: Centre of Contemporary Greek Studies, Occasional Paper 3; Mouzelis, Nicos P., 1986. *Politics in the Semi-Periphery: Early Parliamentarism and Late Industrialisation in the Balkans and Latin America*. Basingstoke: Macmillan, 61.

28 See *The World Factbook 1996* at: http://www.odci.gov/cia/publications/factbook.

29 See Woodhouse, C.M., 1985. *The Rise and Fall of the Greek Colonels*. London: Granada.

30 For an interesting analyses on Greece see, among others, Pridham, Geoffrey (ed.), 1984. *The New Mediterranean Democracies: Regime Transition in Spain, Greece and Portugal*. London: Cass; Verney, Susannah and Couloumbis, Theodore, 1991. 'State-international Systems Interaction and the Greek Transition to Democracy in the mid-1970s', in Geoffrey Pridham (ed.) *Encouraging Democracy: The International Context of Regime Transition in Southern Europe*. Leicester: Leicester University Press, 103–24; Diamandouros, P.N., 1986. 'Regime Change and the Prospects for Democracy in Greece: 1974–1983', in Guillermo O'Donnell, Philippe C. Schmitter and Laurence Whitehead (eds) *Transitions from Authoritarian Rule: Prospects for Democracy*. Baltimore, MD: Johns Hopkins University Press, 138–65; Allison, Graham T. and Nikolaidis, Kalypso (eds), 1997. *The Greek Paradox: Promise vs. Performance*. CSIA Studies on International Security. Cambridge, MA and London: MIT Press.

31 See Lyrintzis, Christos, 1983. 'Between Socialism and Populism: The Rise of the Panhellenic Socialist Movement'. Unpublished PhD dissertation, London: London School of Economics and Political Science; and his 1987. 'The Power of Populism: The Greek Case', *European Journal of Political Research*, 15, 667–86; Clogg, Richard, 1993. *Greece, 1981–89: The Populist Decade*. Basingstoke: Macmillan.

32 For a detailed overview of aspects of the Cyprus issue see Joseph, J.S., 1997. *Cyprus: Ethnic Conflict and International Politics: From Independence to the Threshold of the EU*. London/New York: Macmillan/St Martin's Press. See also his 1996 'Cyprus at the Threshold of the EU', *Mediterranean Quarterly*, 7(2), Spring, 112–22 and Demetriou, Olga, 2004. 'The European Union and the Cyprus Conflict: A Review of the Literature'.

EUBorderConf Working Paper series number 5. Available at: http://www.euborderconf.
bham.ac.uk/publications/files/WP5Cyprus.pdf.

33 The expulsion of the ethnic Greek population from Turkey (in 1922) during the
'purification' of Turkey should be noted here.

34 Under the so-called Zurich and London Agreements, the Constitution divided the people
of Cyprus into two communities on the basis of ethnic origin. The President had to be a
Greek Cypriot elected by the Greek Cypriots, and the Vice-President a Turkish Cypriot
elected by the Turkish Cypriots. The Vice-President was granted the right of final veto on
fundamental laws passed by the House of Representatives and on decisions of the Council
of Ministers which was composed of TEN ministers, three of whom had to be Turkish
Cypriots (representing 18 per cent of the population) and be nominated for appointment
by the Vice-President. Following the Zurich and London Agreements the proper
functioning of the state became virtually impossible. The constitution was conceived at a
time of tension and suspicion and was based on notions aiming at divisions rather than
cooperation and unity.

35 Greek MEPs are notorious for such tactics within the EU framework. Interview at the
European Commission, January 2004, Brussels. For more on this, see Pace, 2004a.

36 Interviews held in Brussels, January 2004.

37 Fatouros, 1993.

38 See Tsoucalas, Constantine, 1993. 'Greek National Identity in an Integrated Europe and
a Changing World Order', in Psomiades and Thomadakis, 57–78.

39 One may query further whether this represents identification with a 'sea within the Sea'
or whether it is just a question of geographic proximity.

40 The movement of the struggle of 1974 for a transition to democratic government.

41 Similar to Spain here – Partido Socialista Obrero Español (PSOE).

42 The Greeks are very proud that the 'euro' includes an inscription in Greek (personal
communications).

43 For more on modern Greece see Fouskas, Vassilis, 1996. 'Interview. Nicos Mouzelis:
Greece and Modernisation in the 1990s', *Synthesis: Review of Modern Greek Studies*,
1(1), 35–8.

44 Spain did not look to Africa until losing most of its colonies in the Americas in the 1820s.
The loss of Cuba in 1898 gave fresh impetus. See Gillespie, Richard, 2000. *Spain and the
Mediterranean: Developing a European Policy towards the South*. Basingstoke: Macmillan,
8 and 9.

45 This is the technical term – hence protectorate.

46 Spain was to take control of a strip of territory along the northern coast, with its capital
in Tetouan and another thinner strip of land in the south, running eastwards from Tarfaya.
With the exception of a small Spanish enclave in Sidi Ifni, what was in-between was to be
French Morocco. Spain was also given rights to the Sahara, stretching south from Tarfaya
to the borders of French Mauritania.

47 In practice it was a military colony but the discourse was of protection of the protectorate.
The French built quite a lot of roads and railways and set up Morocco's administration,
schools and new political institutions. The Spanish protectorate was even more of a
military colony, with less 'development' undertaken. Spain on the other hand showed no
interest in developing the Sahara until the 1960s. In the north, the Spanish saw themselves
more as conquerors than colonists (there were no civilian settlements). The French
resident-general recognised the existence of a functioning Moroccan bureaucracy based
on the Sultan's court with which the French could co-operate – a hierarchy of officials,
with diplomatic representation abroad, and with its own social institutions.

48 Spain suffered some major setbacks (Annual in 1921) and was almost defeated, but Abd
El-Krim made the mistake of taking his rebellion to the French protectorate and thus
France joined the Spanish struggle against him, decisively. See Gillespie, 2000, 12.

49 In practice, even today, the monarch is the main authority in the land. See Leveau, Rémy,
1997. 'Morocco at the Crossroads', *Mediterranean Politics*, 2(2), Autumn, 95–113.

50 See Denoeux, Guilain, 1998. 'Understanding Morocco's "Sanitation Campaign"
(December 1995 to May 1996)', *The Journal of North African Studies*, 3(1), Spring,
101–31. See especially 110–12 on 'Reasserting the Control of the Makhzan', and 118–
21 on 'Regime Strength and Mode of Operation'. See also Leveau 1997, 108 for more on
the *Makhzan*.

51 For an interesting discussion on this see the issue on Tribe and Society in Rural Morocco in the *Journal of North African Studies*, 1999, 4(2), Summer, especially the article by Hart, David M., 'Scratch a Moroccan, Find a Berber', 23–6.

52 Hence, it may be argued that there is hardly a constitutional monarchy in Morocco as in Spain or Britain, for example. See Chapter 3.

53 According to *The World Factbook, 1996*, the main languages in Morocco are Arabic (official), Berber dialects, and French – the latter often the language of business, government and diplomacy. There are also some Spanish speakers but the exact figures are not recorded (Spain claims 2 million).

54 However, bilateral European aid has been more substantial. Yet, lack of donor co-ordination undermines Morocco's priorities (as the recipient). It has put a costly burden on Morocco where public services are already overstretched. Interviews in Morocco, 2002 as part of the MEDA democracy project funded by the European Commission. See report available from: http//www.liv.ac.uk/ewc/pastevents.html under 'The European Union and Democracy Promotion: The Case of North Africa'. Aid allocation is often based on policy selectivity that does not help countries like Morocco with poor policies and weak institutions. This situation is, however, improving on the ground. The said report concluded that the EU as a main donor needs to follow through on its commitments, for example on relieving debts.

55 From Morocco's perspective this still entailed substantial constraints upon Moroccan exports. For Moroccan growers, the minimum entry prices for agricultural imports into the EU were quite high and these prices did not apply to Spanish growers – Morocco's main competitors. Hence, these high entry prices did not allow effective Moroccan agricultural competition in the EU market. Moreover, EU quotas for Moroccan agriculture were restrictive. The quotas had been miscalculated on the basis of three previous years. (This technical detail is important to understand the nature of Morocco–EU relations.) Morocco wanted the calculation to include future (expanded) production. Furthermore, the delivery period was restricted from November until March since the months from April to October were filled by European production. During the restricted period, Moroccan imports had to respect monthly quotas. All in all, these various constraints upon Morocco's agricultural exports to the EU market were a threat to price its products out of this large market. It was clear to Morocco that Spain was the main beneficiary of these new high minimum prices that allowed Spain to sell its agriculture within the EU at any time of the year and at any price: in theory. In practice, there are still short periods when fresh produce of certain items is not available in sufficient volume (even in these days of plastic sheeting).

56 The issue of agricultural products is critical for Morocco because its agricultural economy employs 40 per cent of the country's workforce (that is, it is a welfare issue). On its side, the EU's protectionist CAP works to limit agricultural imports and this leaves little room for flexible negotiations on this issue.

57 Morocco is the leading producer and exporter of fish in Africa and the Arab world. The importance of its fishing sector was evidenced by the creation of the Ministry of Fisheries in 1981. By the mid-1990s, fishing accounted for 11 per cent of the country's GDP and 15 per cent of total exports.

58 The various issues involved were addressed when a very complex and detailed association agreement was initialled in November 1995 and signed on 26 February 1996 together with a new fisheries agreement. It is important to note the timing of this EU offer to Morocco of an association agreement and a new fisheries agreement. The Barcelona Process was also launched during November 1995. The association agreement offered the EU concessions for easier imports of its own agricultural products into Morocco while Moroccan export products were still limited in terms of quotas and delivery periods, and although the set minimum prices were reduced they were still too high for Moroccan growers. Article 18 of the agreement called for a review of import restrictions during the year 2000. One may argue that this is the effect that any common market will have on outside producers.

59 According to *The World Factbook*, 35 per cent of the Moroccan population are between the ages of 0–14 years, 60 per cent between the ages of 15–64 years and 5 per cent aged 65 years and over. See http://www.odci.gov/cia/publications/factbook/geos/mo.html.

60 Statistics in Focus, European Communities, 2003; the *World Fact Book 2003*, the Economist Intelligence Unit, 2003, updated country-by-country information sources.

61 He died in July 1999. On King Hassan's reign see, amongst others, Leveau, Rémy, 1996. 'The Future of the Maghreb', in Josef Janning and Dirk Rumberg (eds) *Peace and Stability in the Middle East and North Africa*. Gütersloh: Bertelsmann Foundation Publishers, 98–101 on 'The Uncertainties of the Monarchic Succession in Morocco'; Köhler, Michael, 1996. 'Stability in Algeria, Morocco and Tunisia', in Janning and Rumberg, 111–20; Gupte, Pranay, 1999. 'The Blood of the Prophet', *Newsweek*, 2 August, 39; Mortimer, Robert A., 1989. 'Maghreb Matters', *Foreign Policy*, 76, Fall, 160–75; Tahi, Mohand Salah, 1988. 'The Maghreb States: Regional and Foreign Policies 1973–1987', PhD thesis, University of Warwick, Coventry; Willis, Michael J., 1999. 'After Hassan: A New Monarch in Morocco', *Mediterranean Politics*, 4(3), Autumn, 115–28; Eickelman, Dale F., 1994. 'Re-Imagining Religion and Politics: Moroccan Elections in the 1990s', in John Ruedy (ed.) *Islamism and Secularism in North Africa*. New York: St Martin's Press, 253–73; Waterbury, John, 1970. *The Commander of the Faithful: The Moroccan Political Elite – A Study in Segmented Politics*. New York: Columbia University Press, 155; Gallagher, Nancy, 1998. 'Interview – The Life and Times of Abdallah Laroui, A Moroccan Intellectual', *Journal of North African Studies*, 3(1), Spring, 132–51.

62 For more on this issue see Hogstad, David, 1995–6. *L'Université et l'Etudiant au Maroc: les fards d'une modernisation naufragée? Essais anthropologiques sur la Cacophonie du Changement*. Mémoire pour l'obtention du Diplôme d'Etudes Approfondies de Science Politique, Institut d'Etudes Politiques, Université de Droit, d'Economie et des Sciences d'Aix-Marseille III (through the author's consent). Although (a degree of) nationalism may be found throughout the Moroccan party system, the USFP is the most 'modern' party and thereby the closest to European parties.

63 Communications with an interviewee.

64 For an interesting account of the king's challenges see *Time Magazine*, 155(25), 26 June 2000 where *Time*'s Cairo bureau chief, Scott MacLeod, interviewed King Mohammed VI. It is important to note how this article personalises the situation in Morocco but Morocco is not the king only. The political and economic elite surely consider their choices and challenges. However, the king does express the reforming tendencies within the elite.

65 According to Ramonet, 2000, the Arab Maghreb Union cannot move forward due to the Western Sahara issue between Morocco and Algeria.

66 The burden of external debt for Morocco is reflected in Moroccan elite discourses. The estimated 2002 figure for Morocco's external debt stood at US$17.7 billion. Source: European Communities, 2003.

67 Mohammed VI wrote his PhD in 'Science Politique' on the issue of EU and Morocco (communication with a colleague).

68 To date there seems to be no development on this issue and no sign of negotiations at present. Morocco continues to wrangle with Spain over fishing rights and immigration and Spain steadfastly insisted on a UN-sponsored referendum on Western Sahara. (The current king is working on modernising Morocco. See interview from *Time Magazine*.)

69 One can argue that, behind the scenes, the only talks will be bilateral in this respect. Only the EU can conclude a fisheries agreement. Portugal is a minor beneficiary of these talks. Currently, the odds are against renewal.

70 And have been in fact for hundreds of years. Spain has ignored Moroccan proposals to establish a working group to discuss the issue.

71 The strength of the mobilisation of the Islamist movement has grown a lot in the last few years. This shows that the Western Sahara issue is now less effective as a nationalist diversion. Divisions exist between Islamists prepared to use the reform agenda of Mohammed and those who refuse to countenance institutional participation (communications with an interviewee). See http://www.lemonde.fr/.

72 The changes to the 'mudawana' family code make polygamy acceptable only in rare circumstances, and only with the permission of a judge and a man's first wife. Tremlett, Giles, 2004. 'Morocco boosts women's rights', *The Guardian*, 21 January, 11.

73 See Clogg, 1986, 39–41.

74 This is to use the criteria of the modern Western state.

75 This of course depends on how this 'modern' era is defined.

76 It may be argued that the modern era in Morocco started in 1912 or, alternatively, in 1956.

77 The monarch serves as head of state on the basis of power defined by a constitution. (Morocco is clearly not a case of a constitutional monarchy in which parliamentary institutions are sovereign.) Although Morocco has a parliament the fact that the parties are usually divided internally leaves the king with a lot of political clout – the current king has been trying to change this. The king, however, is powerful not only due to party divisions but also due to his power base in the military, security apparatus and Makhzen in general. The present king is bringing the military establishment back into public life. (After coup attempts, Hassan distrusted it.)

78 The argument here may extend to whether there is a 'Middle Eastern' identity and whether this could include Israel.

79 See Hart, 1999.

80 This practice is defined as nesting orientalism. See Bakic-Hayden, 1995.

81 PASOK's attitude towards the Mediterranean is pro-Arab but displays some flexibility. See Pace, M., 2004a in Carlnaes *et al.*

82 As Tsoucalas, Constantine, 1969 states 'It is difficult to pin down the historical and cultural character of the Greek nation – Balkan but not Slav, Near Eastern [and once again one may here question whether this Near Eastern category includes Israel] but not Muslim, European but not Western. It may or may not be possible to trace a racial, cultural and national continuity from the classical period through the Byzantine Empire to modern Greece; the undoubted fact is that the origins of the modern social and economic structure are deeply rooted in the long period of Ottoman rule' in *The Greek Tragedy*. Harmondsworth: Penguin, 15. One may question whether it is tenable to claim to be non-Western yet to opt for the EU (even EMU) and NATO.

83 For an interesting insight and an historical approach to the study of Greek political culture, see Diamandouros, P. Nikiforos, 1983. 'Greek Political Culture in Transition: Historical Origins, Evolution, Current Trends', in Richard Clogg (ed.) *Greece in the 1980s*. London and Basingstoke: Macmillan, 43–69.

84 I am indebted to the article of Guillaume, 2002 for being a source of enlightenment here. Thanks also to Iver B. Neumann and an anonymous reviewer for their useful comments.

85 It has become generally recognised in recent years that Berber constitutes Morocco's real linguistic base and that most Moroccans, even the majority of the Arabic speakers, are of Berber descent. For an interesting background on this linguistic issue see Hart, David M., 1997. 'Berber Names and Substrata in Mauritania and the Western Sahara: Linguistic and Ethno-Historical Guidelines for Future Research on a Paradoxical Problem', *The Journal of North African Studies*, 2(1), Summer, 58–71.

86 Erroneously, most Maltese equate Christianity with Catholicism.

87 That is by the creators of European culture, the European intelligentsia.

88 One wonders whether there are any 'Mediterranean' countries that do not present themselves as bridges or intermediaries of some kind. Israel, perhaps.

89 See Clogg, 1993; Mouzelis, 1986. Fatouros, 1993, argues that 'Greece was seen as an intermediary, a bridge, between East and West, as the means by which Western European learning, values, and techniques – literacy, commerce, organization, what we now call economic development – would be brought to the Ottoman empire', 26. Hence Greece gave the West its 'civilisation', in other words, Greece developed the West.

90 See Braudel's works on the Mediterranean for more on this. See also Loti, Pierre, 1892. *Into Morocco*. Translated by E.P. Robins. Chicago, IL and New York: Rand, McNally. All case studies have experienced a different development process of their respective sea transport systems.

91 I owe this insight to Professor Richard Gillespie.

92 See Clogg, 1993.

93 See Loewendahl, Ebru, 1998. *'Promises to Keep': The Reality of Turkey–EU Relations*. Chorley: Action Centre for Europe, where it is stated that 'a more enlightened view of Turkey and its role in Europe and beyond would put Turkey on an equal footing with Eastern European countries'.

94 Also as a pro-Western, stable regime in an 'unstable' region where some political forces are anti-European. Resource-wise, Algeria and even Libya have more to offer. In fact, Morocco's fish resources are heavily outweighed by Algerian gas. The countries most keen to cooperate with the EU, however, are Tunisia (although economically it is not 'important') and Morocco.

95 Which often favours the member over the associate.

96   See http://www.monde-diplomatique.fr/1999/12/DOLHEM/12803.html.
97   See Pace, M., 2004a in Carlnaes *et al*. Relations between Greece and Turkey have improved. Following earthquakes during the year 2000 in both Turkey and Greece, the two countries extended their assistance in humanitarian ways to each other. This relation has been termed *Earthquake Diplomacy* (communications with participants during the Halki International Seminar, 2000).
98   Guillaume, X., 2002.
99   See Horden, Peregrine and Purcell, Nicholas, 2000. *The Corrupting Sea: A Study of Mediterranean History*. Oxford and Malden, MA: Blackwell.
100 Ibid.
101 Both historical (past) and contemporary discourses (present).
102 The case of this only female Greek interviewee points to possible disagreements among respondents from the same country. Elite opinion in each of the countries considered here is therefore not necessarily uniform. In fact, even if this specific case seems to be an exception, it proves the validity of the rule: for example, when there is someone who dissents, there is evidence that there is a near consensus shaped by contingency, history, etc.
103 This dichotomous way of thinking is interesting to note since the 'we' and the 'our' here is clearly relating to Greeks and Greek interests (in a manner totally differentiated from the EU framework yet within it!) and the 'them' and 'theirs' refers to the Mediterranean partners.
104 Nationally, the cultural 'other' are the Turks – this is ingrained in the socialisation processes in Greece including schools, especially in how history is taught. An interesting comment from a Turkish foreign minister which was made to an academic whilst they were viewing a French painting of the Greek revolution: 'Your moment of glory was our moment of descent'. See Müftüler-Bac 1997.
105 One observes that on this matter, Greek academics may be atypical Greek interviewees. This point has been reiterated by Romano Prodi during his latest visit to Ankara, when he repeatedly emphasised that the EU was not taking a different approach with Turkey's membership case: 'In October this year, my Commission will present its recommendation on whether Turkey fulfils the Copenhagen political criteria … Let me assure you that our recommendation will be based on an objective assessment. We will use the same criteria and methodology that so successfully has been used for all the other candidate countries … These criteria were not invented for Turkey, but apply equally to all candidates'. Prodi, Romano, 2004. *Speech of Romano Prodi, The President of the European Commission,* at the Turkish Grand National Assembly, Ankara, 14 January. See also Pace, 2004c. Here is a case of how discourses connect other discourses (specific conjunctions of discourses).
106 These views might be based on Greek Orthodox beliefs. Protestant belief is based on purity while Catholic and Orthodox on the text. Also worth noting here is this positive Greek discourse about Turkey and in favour of Turkey's inclusion in the EU – to the benefit of and in the interest of Greece.
107 This is an example of a discourse that is not uttered.
108 This seems to go against the general thinking in Greece that Greece gave Europe its heritage. Having said this, however, in this light Greece is not probably thought of as Mediterranean but relates back to its Hellenic heritage.
109 My emphasis, reflecting on the dichotomous thinking of Europe on the one hand and the Middle East on the other for Greek interviewees.
110 Others may argue that due to its limited small size, Malta may not be such an important country for Greece to consider. Having said this, not all the Greek interviewees reflected this lack of awareness on Maltese politics. Some did mention that Malta is known through football which reflects the importance of the cultural pillar to bridge understanding between countries. Upon deeper analysis this discourse might also reflect upon the fact that for the Maltese and the Greeks their two countries seem quite apart geographically (with Malta seeing Greece to the East).
111 One questions here whether these are discursive practices or rather reflect a lack of geographical knowledge.
112 This reflects quite a dichotomous mode of thinking.
113 Even though Greek interviewees claimed that the term 'Balkan for Greeks came about after American intervention in the area and this term was coined for South Europe'.
114 This argument may be compared to the categories Europe and Scandinavia. Sweden for example is often categorised under both labels.

115 It is interesting to note here that for the USA the Mediterranean does not exist except as a route to the Middle East/Gulf state area.
116 This term is of course much used in EC and EU documents and is in fact part of the ordained Eurospeak of the EU.
117 This discourse relates to Islamic thinking.
118 Unlike their Greek counterparts!
119 It certainly seems that Europe is perceived as more modern.
120 Note the local framework of this Moroccan discourse and the comparison with France (Morocco's former protectorate).
121 Here, the interviewee might have implied that Berbers are not real Moroccans.
122 This discourse may be interpreted as Morocco's construction of its Mediterranean identity for political reasons since it has been rejected as being European for these purposes amongst others (for instance, its human rights record).
123 Moroccan interviewees stated that Europe itself needs an identity and we all need to tolerate differences. Islam has a lot of taboos and it is just a specific cultural affair of this area (Maghreb).
124 It can be thus observed that each case country has its own set of countries who are in and those who are out of its specific discourse of the Mediterranean when challenged with a pre-given classification of the countries in this area.
125 My own emphasis.
126 These are similar reflections to those of the Moroccan interviewees on the need for tolerance and importance of values that might reflect a religious belief as a basis for these views.
127 Yet, racist sentiments are common amongst some Maltese, for example, *vis-à-vis* Libyans and Arabs in general.
128 It is interesting to note that the female interviewee in Greece stated that she felt 'Mediterranean-European-Arab ... [although] Mediterranean does not mean anything ... it is neutral' whilst most Greek male interviewees claimed to be Greek first. Whether this suggests that male Greek interviewees are more nationalistic remains open for further research.
129 See Horden and Purcell, 2000. The authors distinguish between two prominent models of the Mediterranean: an 'interactionist' one in which the sea links geographically dispersed social groups, and an 'ecologising' one that emphasises the broad geographical and environmental similarities of the circum-Mediterranean lands. The authors' project in this book is to explore the unity of the Mediterranean as an object of historical inquiry prior to Braudel's sixteenth century, broadly speaking from antiquity to the Middle Ages. What the authors have in common with Braudel is the idea of the Mediterranean as a valid object of study, a well-conceived unity.
130 Greeks seem less self-assured yet very nationalistic. This could be an instance of an inferior identification breeding stronger feelings. Interview at the European Commission, January 2004, Brussels.
131 Turkey was omitted from the classification of the Mediterranean presented in the interview guidelines. This Greek inclusion of Turkey reflects the underlying threat from Turkey felt by Greece. The reason why Greek interviewees highlighted Turkey's inclusion in the Mediterranean could relate to Greek discourses of the Mediterranean as a security community for Europe and for the EU to control and manage. It could also have served Greek interviewees to exclude Turkey from an identification with Europe. This has changed recently. Discussions with an official, March 2004.
132 For example, one interviewee stated that Israel is sometimes included as European in international athletic competitions. Israel has not applied for EU membership so far although discussions are underway for a possible application in the near future. (An Israeli, Dana International, won the Eurovision song contest in 1998. In fact, Israel has more than once excelled in 'European' cultural and athletic competitions, including 'European' basketball events.) Israel has an advantageous economic agreement with the EU. Discussions with an official, February 2004.
133 This omission was intentional, to provoke a debate on Turkey's European credentials and observe interviewees' reactions to this.
134 Some see the Mediterranean as a river with two banks rather than a sea – an idea once used by Falangists in Spain to justify Spanish expansionism in Morocco (Gillespie, 2000, 5 and 10).

135 During the initial phase of the interview period, the scandal affecting the Commission was announced in the international media. A report was issued on fraud by some Commission officials, with Commissioners thus held responsible and seen as incompetent/ negligent. The European Commission decided to resign en masse. See http:// www.guardianunlimited.co.uk/Archive/ (*The Guardian*, 16 March 1999).

136 This ambivalence has changed recently. See Pace, 2004a.

137 The Greeks are not alone here. This also happens in the UK and in Denmark, for example.

138 Some may argue that Greeks do not take EU procedures seriously enough to be versed in their content.

139 This is because of discourses of an East against South battle over the allocation of EU funding (even when Mediterranean member states are not beneficiaries).

140 This Greek discourse might be interpreted as an interesting one in that it might also further reflect the need for the EU to construct its own identity through the construction of other areas.

141 This discourse ties up with the analysis in Chapter 2 that discussed foreign policy, specifically the EU's Mediterranean policy as a discursive practice that constructs a 'Mediterranean' area. However, it is interesting to note that the EU's New Neighbourhood Policy acknowledges that 'it is clear that a new EU approach cannot be a one-size-fits-all policy'. Commission of the European Communities, 2003b. *Wider Europe – Neighbourhood*.

142 Ministry of Foreign Affairs, Greece.

143 My emphasis, to highlight the constructed nature of the concept of region.

144 This might reflect the fact that the key interests for Greece lie in the East of the Mediterranean. It would be interesting to examine the different discourses on a holistic approach to the Mediterranean or otherwise from different ministries. From the fieldwork for this book it did emerge that the MFA in Athens has a directorate for the North African states and the Middle East and this might be one of the reasons why Greek interviewees stated that Egypt should be included in the category of North African states. Following the emigration flux of Greeks to Egypt (the attraction of which has been explained earlier in the text), Greek authorities were obviously interested in furthering relations with this country. These issues would be interesting subjects for further research.

145 Once again further research could examine each EU member state's discursive practices of the EU's holistic approach towards the Mediterranean.

146 This attitude might be interpreted as reflecting the myth about Arab states and their 'problem' with trust. One Moroccan interviewee claimed that when a European says 'yes' he or she means 'yes' but when an Arab says 'yes' he/she is usually saying so only to be polite but he/she does not mean yes – in effect reiterating this myth. In this respect, with Morocco's historical links to France this sense of trust has been built over many years. Some may argue that Moroccan references to special European relationships may be a way of embarrassing the Southern Europeans, like Spain, to make concessions! Others may question how it is possible to square this with Spanish and Italian protectionism.

147 Informal discussion with an official, Alexandria, October 2003.

148 In a Commission document on revitalising the EMP, there have been proposals on reforming the CAP (but Spain opposes these, arguing that the areas of Spain that would be hit by agricultural concessions are in Objective 1 regions). The idea would be to reduce subsidies for uncompetitive sectors of European agriculture. EU actors who prioritise competition came up against welfare-based counter-arguments from France and Spain. Of course the whole issue of CAP reform has moved on since – with reform today advocated also on health and ecology grounds. More recent trade talks, however, are less encouraging for Mediterranean countries. A leaked letter from the EU's trade commissioner highlighted the determination of Brussels to continue its US$45 billion-a-year support for farmers. See Elliott, Larry, 2004. 'EU insists on right to subsidise farming', *The Guardian*, 27 March, 25.

149 There is obviously some exaggeration when this interviewee refers to the EU having the same package for the Mediterranean as it does for Latin America. For example, there is no substantial security dimension in EU–Latin American relations.

150 Maltese interviewees also stated that Mediterranean countries need to think more in terms of long-term rather than short-term interests.

151 See Chris Patten's speech, 'A European Foreign Policy: Ambition and Reality', Brussels, 15 June 2000.
152 Interviews in Brussels, January 2004.
153 Libya's recent acceptance back to the international community has been interpreted along the same lines. 'European Union. Selling the deal'. Leader in *The Guardian*, 29 March 2004, 19.
154 The Greeks hope for EU help in controlling Albanian immigration. See Black, Ian, 2001. 'EU Unites to Get Tough on Immigrants', *The Guardian*, 9 February, 14.
155 Tourism is also an important sector in this regard. Tunisia has a population of around nine million and now receives around five million tourists a year. Morocco is also the biggest exporter of hashish to Europe.
156 But there are, increasingly, alternatives. For example, the EU's agreement with Russia on gas. In fact, EU sources of supplies have become more diverse.
157 There was no decision to exclude all Middle East countries (which arguably include North Africa) – just to keep the Middle East Peace Process (MEPP) off the EMP agenda. In any case, the MEPP has so far been US-driven.
158 Indeed, one Moroccan interviewee stated that the EU needs to stimulate and aim for reciprocal, liberated and open markets around the whole Euro-Mediterranean area. Europe cannot just promote projects which will not have any economic repercussions on European markets – that is, it cannot be selectively and purely self-interested in its projects such as the planting of more trees and projects for fishing villages. Europe also needs to promote projects for the poor and for enterprises (reflecting Moroccan interests in attracting foreign direct investment for its economic development).
159 These views may suggest a lack of understanding of the EU's dual structure. See Monar 1998 for an excellent analysis of the EU's policy in the Mediterranean that according to the author 'suffers from a gap between its apparent potential to act and its actual performance'.
160 The economic pillar of the EMP, especially trade, is the most important for Morocco. During my interviews, some Moroccan interviewees referred to the first Gulf War that they claim brought about enhanced economic co-operation in oil between European and Mediterranean partners through the EMP.
161 Interviewees referred to over-complicated EU grant forms and problems encountered by NGOs in Morocco as a result of this. However, one may argue that as long as the EU is funding the EMP, the EU's very imperfect machinery will administer it.
162 Moroccans may be perceived by some readers to be particularly narrowly focused in their views.
163 Perhaps it can be argued that this has been confined to the accession negotiating sessions.
164 Communication with an interviewee. The latter also stated that the Mediterranean used to be 'en vogue' in Greece while solidarity with southern Slavs is not a permanent state of affairs even though it is currently 'there'. The Slav neighbours are felt to be closer to the Greeks not just geographically but also religiously through their Christian Orthodox affiliations and the similar discourses they share on spirituality. In the 1990s especially, Bulgarians and Serbs were perceived by Greeks as Slav brethren and seen as opposing the Turks too. Having said this, however, the said interviewee claimed that since 1999 there has been a European orientation too amongst Greeks (a Europeanisation process that impacted on Greece). Overall, the interviewee claimed that attitudes do change very fast indeed in Greece! He made reference to some patriotic army songs that reveal how discourses of animosity disappear – to a certain extent.
165 Greek preoccupation with immigration concerns might expose why Greek interviewees did not seem to be as well versed in overall EMP matters as their Moroccan and Maltese counterparts. However, it can be noted that Greece has participated less than Malta and Morocco in EMP activities (as seen in conferences, etc.).
166 Although many interviewees were very critical of this and stated that Greece as a state lacks a foreign policy and that it is all based on personalities (which confirms the theoretical work in this regard).
167 Pace, 2004d. 'EU–Turkey Relations', Hydra.
168 Greece has had its specific concerns about Albanians, communication with an interviewee. See also King and Black, 1997.
169 Informal discussion with a colleague, Paris, December 2002.

170 This concern may have receded since. FYROM refers to the former Yugoslav republic of Macedonia. Greece has opposed the name Macedonia ever since its neighbour won independence from Yugoslavia in 1991. Until now it had the support of all NATO allies, except Turkey, for refusing recognition.

171 According to *The World Factbook*, the net migration rate in Greece was 1.97 migrant(s)/ 1,000 population (2000 estimates). In terms of ethnic groups, 98 per cent are Greeks and 2 per cent are classified as other. The estimate for the population in Greece stood at 10,601,527 during the year 2000.

172 Europe does of course import Mediterranean products but only takes a limited volume of agricultural products.

173 Pace, M., 2004a in Carlnaes *et al.*

174 See Paparizos, Antonis, 1995. 'Diafotismos, Thriskeia Kai Paradosi Sti Syghroni Elliniki Koinonia' (translated: 'Enlightenment, Religion and Tradition in Modern Greek Society'), in Nicos Demertzis (ed.) *Elliniki Politiki Koultoura Simera*. Athens: Odysseas, 74–113.

175 See Tabone, Carmel, 1994a and 1994b. 'The Maltese Family in the Context of Social Change and Secularization', in Sultana and Baldacchino, 229–51 and 285–300 respectively.

176 Howard, Michael, 2001. 'Greek Priests Revolt as Church Backs Pope's Visit', *The Guardian*, 20 March, 15.

177 As quoted in Ramonet, 2000, in Morocco these clientelistic politics are also class issues. Morocco is dominated by a system of networks, nepotism, clans and interconnected families 'who would rather give a job to an unsuitable, incompetent relation rather than a highly qualified young person from a poor background'.

178 In Morocco this is mostly drug-trafficking related. See Ramonet, 2000. These common aspects might be perceived as common Mediterranean traits. See Peristiany, J.G. (ed.), 1976. *Kinship and Modernization in Mediterranean Society*. Rome: The Center for Mediterranean Studies. It is important to recall that, as mentioned earlier, Morocco is *the* main supplier of cannabis to Europe (communications with an interviewee).

6 Which 'Mediterranean'?

1   This ties up with the relevance of Giddens' theory of structuration in which the most concrete level of analysis for a thorough investigation of the process of region-formation is concerned with 'elements' of regionalisation. This has been analysed earlier in Chapter 2.

2   That is, multiple (possibilities for) interpretations. Foucault, 1972.

3   The term 'myth' often carries negative connotations in its English usage.

4   At the time of writing, the EU is considering a Greater Middle East Initiative. Discussions with an official. See European Commission, 2004. 'Interim Report on an EU Strategic Partnership With the Mediterranean and the Middle East', *EuroMed Report*, Issue No. 73, 23 March.

5   Brubaker and Cooper, 2000.

6   Interviews in Brussels and informal discussions in Montreal, January and March 2004 respectively.

7   Buzan and Wæver, 2003, 464.

8   During the Council meeting in Tampere, 1999, a Common EU Asylum and Migration Policy was discussed.

9   For an interesting perspective on 'the political' and the literature on identity see Neumann, Iver B., 1997. 'Identity and the Outbreak of War, or Why the Copenhagen School of Security Studies Should Include the Idea of "Violisation" in its Framework of Analysis'. Working Paper No. 578, July, Oslo: Norwegian Institute of International Affairs.

10 *EuroMed Report*, 2001.

11 In the case of the MEPP, for example, there has been a flurry of EU activity around the process since it broke down and before that the EU did try to play a role in fostering horizontal co-operation via various Middle East working groups. However, even if the peace process is delivered it does not make the climate very easy after so many years of conflict. The most recent initiative of the Quartet, the Road Map, is a case in point. Interviews at the European Commission, Brussels, January 2004.

12 Interview, 2 April 1999.

13 Campbell, 1992; Doty, 1993; Larsen, 1997, 1999; Wæver 2002, 2004a, 2004b; Weldes, J., 1999. 'Intervention and Identity: Reconstructing the West in Korea', in Jutta Weldes *et al.* (eds) *Cultures of Insecurity: States, Communities, and the Production of Danger*, 1999. Minneapolis, MN: University of Minnesota Press. Borderlines Series, 14, 91–117.
14 Communication with an official.
15 Wilson, Kevin and van der Dussen, Jan (eds), 1995. *The History of the Idea of Europe.* Milton Keynes: Open University; London: Routledge and Kegan Paul (Series: What is Europe? Book 1) and Delante, Gerard, 1995. *Inventing Europe: Idea, Identity, Reality.* London: Macmillan.
16 See Berger and Luckmann, 1966 on 'reality' and phenomenologies/discourses/perceptions and how these are constructed.
17 Bakhtin, Mikhail (1963) 1991. *Dostojevskijs Poetic.* Gothenburg: Anthropos.
18 Der Derian and Shapiro, 1989.
19 Foucault, 1972, 114.
20 *EuroMed Report*, 2001.
21 European Commission, 2004.
22 Of course, France does not wish to weaken the German–French axis, but Germany is now bigger and stronger and becoming more assertive in the EU. This trilateral relationship involving Germany, France and Britain tends to fluctuate according to issue and context, as witnessed during the recent war in Iraq.
23 Although some may argue that Mauritania is a very weak state, offering little to most EU states. Britain has recently engaged in a similar diplomatic move when it fully endorsed Libya's re-entry into the international community, March 2004.
24 Lacan's mirror image.
25 According to Aliboni, the Mediterranean has been important for Germany for some time and not just recently – see his article of 1990.
26 Interviews at the European Commission, 18 May 1999 and January 2004.
27 Such debates have already started in the context of Turkey's potential membership of the EU: the debates usually enfold in light of the Eastern Mediterranean, the limits of Europe and the inside and outer areas surrounding the EU. See Pace, 2004d. 'EU–Turkey Relations'.
28 In effect, being a member of a collective changes a member state's policy on an area.
29 Keith, Michael and Pile, Steve, 1993. 'Introduction Part 1: The Politics of Place', in Michael Keith and Steve Pile (eds) *Place and the Politics of Identity.* London and New York: Routledge, 1–21.
30 These events have created an uncertain and unstable international climate where fear of what could happen or what might be prevails.
31 Neumann, 2001.
32 I thank Peter Larkin and William Pine-Coffin, librarians at the University of Warwick, for their help in sourcing material on the origin of this concept of the Mediterranean. For more information see the *Cambridge Ancient History* (Astin, A.E. (ed.), 1989. 'Rome and the Mediterranean 218 to 133 BC', *Cambridge Ancient History.* Second edition, volume 8. Cambridge: Cambridge University Press) and Freeman, Charles, 1999. *Egypt, Greece and Rome: Civilizations of the Ancient Mediterranean.* Oxford: Oxford University Press, the *Oxford Classical Dictionary* (Hornblower, Simon and Antony Spawforth (eds), 1996. *Oxford Classical Dictionary.* 3rd edn. Oxford: Oxford University Press) and *The New Encyclopedia Britannica* for a very general overview.
33 Lefebvre, Henri, 1991. *The Production of Space.* Oxford: Blackwell, 27 quoted in Neumann, 2001.
34 This observation does not tally with the process of region building that the EU has set out to implement through the EMP. These regular markers across EU discourses highlight how although the EU fixes a specific meaning to the Mediterranean, this construction is open to change and is therefore made flexible over time. (European Parliamentarians have suggested the case of Mauritania's possible inclusion in the EMP.)
35 Lefebvre, 1991 cited in Neumann, 2001.
36 Foucault, 1972, 112.
37 Schlumberger, Oliver, 2000. 'Arab Political Economy and the EU's Mediterranean Policy: What Prospects for Development?', *New Political Economy*, 5(2), 254. Some analysts may find this discussion of first pillar issues rather strange since security therein often overshadows the political agenda of democracy and human rights.

38 There is also the modest MEDA-Democracy programme as a discursive practice covering democracy-related issues.

39 *EuroMed Special Feature*, 19, 21 February 2001. 'President Prodi's Visit to Jordan, Lebanon and Syria'. Produced by the MEDA Team – Information.

40 See the Tampere conclusions.

41 Hill, 1993.

42 Schlumberger, 2000, 255.

43 But interviewees recognise that this is changing. Interview at the European Commission, January 2004.

44 Pace, Michelle, 2004c (ISA Paper, March).

45 This term refers to the function or purpose of a discourse. See Wæver's work for more on this.

46 The recent EU interest in a Greater Middle East Initiative is mainly driven by economic interests. Interview in Brussels, March 2004.

47 See *Le Monde*, 16 November 2000 on the Euro-Mediterranean summit in Nice and on issues concerning Palestine/Lebanon and how these hampered affectivity at this summit. Available from: http://www.lemonde.fr/. The EU keeps the two separate within the EMP framework.

48 For more on this see Neumann, 2001 who adapts a radical constructivist approach to his work. This is the community of literature which has mostly influenced the approach followed here.

49 Schlumberger, 2000, 267. See Monar, 1998 for more on the intra-European difficulties in implementing the EMP.

50 In hindsight, this seems like a foresight on the New Neighbourhood Policy!

51 This seems to be the hope of many EU-Med players with the transition from the EMP to the ENP (European Neighbourhood Policy).

52 In retrospect, this sounds out the idea behind the Action Plans of the European Neighbourhood Policy.

53 Guillaume, Xavier, 2002.

54 Young, Iris Marion, 1990. *Justice and the Politics of Difference*. Princeton, NJ: Princeton University Press.

55 Young, Hugo, 2001. 'If You Stay Out, Don't Pretend to be In', *The Guardian*, 16 February, 20.

56 Presidency Conclusions of the Euro-Mediterranean Conference of Ministers of Foreign Affairs, Naples, 2–3 December, 2003.

57 The Common Strategy on the Mediterranean confirmed the EU's will to continue to develop the EMP as an EU concern. As suggested, there is, however, some hope that things will be different with the New Neighbourhood Policy, although this is at its early stages (at time of writing).

58 A phrase from Niklas Luhmann. See Luhmann, Niklas, 1979. *Trust and Power*. Chichester: Wiley; Luhmann, Niklas, 1982. *The Differentiation of Society*. New York: Columbia University Press (Series: European Perspectives).

59 Thus, language taken as communication.

60 Benhabib, Seyla, 1996. *Democracy and Difference: Contesting the Boundaries of the Political*. Princeton, NJ: Princeton University Press, 6.

61 As per interview at the European Commission, January 2004.

62 This has been confirmed during interviews. Brussels interviewees agreed that the EMP offered the possibility for Europeans to get to know their Mediterranean partners better while Arab interviewees in Alexandria, October 2003 shared the need for all Arabs to be self-critical. See Pace and Schumacher, 2004.

63 Adler, Emmanuel and Barnett, Michael, 1996. 'Governing Anarchy: A Research Agenda for the Study of Security Communities', *Ethics and International Affairs*, 10, 63–98.

64 Prozorov, 2004.

7 Conclusion

1 Braudel, 1972; Fenech, 1991, 1993; Sant Cassia, 1991; Attinà, 1996.

2 The theory for applying discourse analysis to foreign policy has been worked out by Ole Wæver, amongst others in International Relations (IR). This book has adapted this

approach to EU Mediterranean policy. See Hansen and Wæver, 2002; Wæver, 2004a 'European Integration and Security'; Wæver, 2004b in Wiener and Diez; Larsen, 1997.

3 Agadir refers to the Agadir free trade agreement signed between Jordan, Egypt, Tunisia and Morocco in Agadir, Morocco on 25 February 2004.

4 Marks, Jon, 1996. 'High Hopes and Low Motives: The New Euro-Mediterranean Partnership Initiative', in *Mediterranean Politics*, 1(1), 1–24.

5 Ebeid, Hanaa, 2004. 'The Partnership in Southern Eyes: Reflections on the Discourse in the Egyptian Press'. Lisbon: EuroMesCo Secretariat at the IEEI. *EuroMesCo* paper, No. 37.

6 Maguid, Wahid Abdel (ed.), 2001. *The Public Debate on the Egyptian Euro-Mediterranean Partnership*. Arab Strategic Report 2000. Cairo: Al Ahram Centre for Political and Strategic Studies, 331.

7 Patten, Chris, 2004. 'Agadir and the Road to Prosperity', *Al Ahram*, 25 February (Egyptian newspaper).

8 Ortega, Martin, 2003. 'Some comments on the European Union's Mediterranean Policy', *Perceptions: Journal of International Affairs*, 8(2), June–August. An expanded version of the same article can be found at: http://www.iss-eu.org (in Chaillot Paper no. 64, October 2003, EU Institute for Security Studies, Paris).

9 Pace, 2004e.

10 Ibid.

11 Fabian, 1983.

12 Hansen and Wæver, 2002.

13 Wæver in Hansen and Wæver, 2002.

14 General Affairs and External Relations Council, Conclusions, Luxembourg, 14 June 2004.

References

Abela, J.S., 1997. *Malta: A Panoramic History*. San Gwann, Malta: Publishers Enterprises Group
Adler, Emmanuel and Barnett, Michael, 1996. 'Governing Anarchy: A Research Agenda for the Study of Security Communities'. *Ethics and International Affairs*, 10, 63–98.
—— 1997. 'Seizing the Middle Ground: Constructivism in World Politics'. *European Journal of International Relations*, 3(3), 319–65.
Adler, Emmanuel and Crawford, Beverly 2002. 'Constructing a Mediterranean Region: A Cultural Approach'. Paper presented at the conference on 'The Convergence of Civilizations? Constructing a Mediterranean Region.' Arrábida Monastery, Fundação Oriente, Lisbon, Portugal, 6–9 June.
Agnew, John and Corbridge, Stuart, 1995. *Mastering Space: Hegemony, Territory and International Political Economy*. London: Routledge.
Aliboni, Roberto, 1990. 'The Mediterranean Scenario: Economy and Security in the Regions South of the EC', *The International Spectator*, 25(2), April–June, 138–54.
—— (ed.), 1992. *Southern European Security in the 1990s*. London: Pinter Publishers.
—— 1999. 'Italy and the Mediterranean in the 1990s', in S. Stavridis, T. Couloumbis, T. Veremis and N. Waites (eds) *The Foreign Policies of the EU's Mediterranean States and Applicant Countries in the 1990s*. Basingstoke: Macmillan, 73–97.
Allison, Graham T. and Nikolaidis, Kalypso (eds), 1997. *The Greek Paradox: Promise vs. Performance* (CSIA Studies on International Security). Cambridge, MA and London: MIT Press.
Al-Manì, Saleh A., 1983. *The Euro–Arab Dialogue. A Study in Associative Diplomacy*. London: Frances Pinter.
Almond, Mundt R.A. and Verba, S., 1963. *The Civic Culture*. Boston, MA: Little Brown.
Appadurai, Arjun, 1996. *Modernity at Large: Cultural Dimensions of Globalization*. Minneapolis, MN: University of Minnesota Press.
Arab Human Development Report, 2003. UNDP. Available at: http://www.undp.org/rbas/ahdr/english2003.html.
Aron, Raymond, 1967. *Main Currents in Sociological Thought 2: Durkheim, Pareto, Weber*. Harmondsworth: Penguin Books. Translated by Richard Howard and Helen Weaver.
Ashley, Richard K., 1984. 'The Poverty of Neorealism', *International Organization*, 38(2), Spring, 225–86.
Astin, A.E. (ed.), 1989. 'Rome and the Mediterranean 218 to 133 B.C.', *Cambridge Ancient History*. 2nd edn, vol. 8. Cambridge: Cambridge University Press.
Attinà, Fulvio, 1996. 'Regional Cooperation in Global Perspective. The Case of the "Mediterranean" Regions', Jean Monnet Working Papers in Comparative and International Politics, April, 6.
—— 2003. 'The Euro-Mediterranean Partnership Assessed: The Realist and Liberal Views', *European Foreign Affairs Review* 8, 181–99.
Augelli, Enrico and Murphy, Craig, 1988. *America's Quest For Supremacy and the Third World: A Gramscian Analysis*. London: Pinter.
Bagge Laustsen, Carsten and Wæver, Ole, 2000. 'In Defence of Religion: Sacred Referent Objects for Securitization', *Millennium: Journal of International Studies*, 29(3), 705–39.
Bakhtin, Mikhail, [1963] 1991. *Dostojevskijs Poetic*. Gothenburg: Anthropos.

Bakic-Hayden, M., 1995. 'Nesting Orientalisms: The Case of Former Yugoslavia', *Slavic Review* 54(4), 917–31.

Barber, James and Smith, Michael (eds), 1974. *The Nature of Foreign Policy: A Reader*. Milton Keynes: Open University Press.

Barth, Fredrik (ed.), 1969. *Ethnic Groups and Boundaries – The Social Organization of Culture Difference*. Oslo: Universitetsforlaget.

Benhabib, Seyla, 1996. *Democracy and Difference: Contesting the Boundaries of the Political*. Princeton, NJ: Princeton University Press.

Berger, Peter L. and Luckmann, Thomas, 1966. *The Social Construction of Reality: A Treatise in the Sociology of Knowledge*. New York: Penguin Books.

Bicchi, Federica, 2003. 'European Foreign Policy Making Towards the Mediterranean Non Member Countries'. Unpublished PhD thesis, European University Institute, Florence.

Black, Ian, 2000. 'Aspirants vow to obey EU code' (European Parliament Special Report), *The Guardian*, 16 February, 13.

—— 2001. 'EU Unites to get Tough on Immigrants', *The Guardian*, 9 February, 14.

Blinkhorn, Martin and Veremis, Thanos (eds), 1990. *Modern Greece: Nationalism and Nationality*. Athens: ELIAMEP.

Boissevain, J., 1965. *Saints and Fireworks: Religion and Politics in Rural Malta*. London: London School of Economics, Monographs on Social Anthropology.

Borneman, John, 1995. 'American Anthropology as Foreign Policy', *American Anthropologist*, 97(4), December, 663–72.

Braudel, F., 1972. *The Mediterranean and the Mediterranean World in the Age of Philip II* (vols I and II). London: Collins.

Bretherton, Charlotte and Vogler, John, 1999. *The EU as a Global Actor*. London: Routledge.

Browning, Christopher Stephen, 2001. 'Constructing Finnish National Identity and Foreign Policy, 1809–2000'. Unpublished PhD dissertation, University of Wales, Aberystwyth.

Brubaker, Rogers and Cooper, Frederick, 2000. 'Beyond "identity"', *Theory and Society*, 29, 1–47.

Bulletin of the EU, Bulletin 2/95. 'Strengthening the Mediterranean policy of the EU: Establishing a EMP'.

Bullock, Alan, Stallybrass, Oliver and Trombley, Stephen, 1977. *The Fontana Dictionary of Modern Thought*. London: Fontana Press.

Burchill, Scott and Linklater, Andrew, 1996. *Theories of IR*. London and New York: Macmillan.

Buzan, Barry, 1991. *People, States and Fear: An Agenda for International Security Studies in the Post-Cold War Era*, 2nd edn. Hemel Hempstead: Harvester.

Buzan, Barry, Waever, Ole and de Wilde, Jaap, 1998. *Security: A New Framework for Analysis*. London: Lynne Rienner Publishers.

Buzan, Barry and Wæver, Ole, 2003. *Regions and Powers: The Structure of International Security*. Cambridge: Cambridge University Press.

Calleya, Stephen C., 1997. *Navigating Regional Dynamics in the Post-Cold War World: Patterns of Relations in the Mediterranean Area*. Brookfield, VT: Dartmouth Publishing Company.

Campbell, David, 1992. *Writing Security: United States Foreign Policy and the Politics of Identity*. Minneapolis, MN: University of Minnesota Press.

—— 1998. 'MetaBosnia: A Review of Narratives of the Bosnian War', *Review of International Studies*, 24(2), 261–81.

Cantori, Louis J. and Spiegel, Steven L., 1970. *The International Politics of Regions: A Comparative Approach*. Englewood Cliffs, NJ: Prentice-Hall.

Carlnaes, W., Sjursen, H. and White, B. (eds), 2004. *Contemporary European Foreign Policy*. London: Sage Publications.

Carr, Fergus (ed.), 1998. *Europe: The Cold Divide*. Basingstoke: Macmillan.

Caracciolo, Luciano and Korinman, Michel (eds), 1998. *Italy and the Balkans*. Washington, DC: Center for Strategic and International Studies.

Cassell, Philip (ed.), 1993. *The Giddens Reader*. Basingstoke: Macmillan.

Centre for European Policy Studies (CEPS) Bulletin, *Turkey in Europe*, Monitor Issue 1, January 2004.

Chase-Dunn, Christopher, 1981. 'Interstate System and Capitalist World-Economy: One Logic or Two?', in W. Ladd Hollist and James N. Rosenau (eds) *World System Structure: Continuity and Change*. Beverly Hills, CA: Sage Publications.

Chérigui, Hayète, 1997. *La Politique Méditerranéenne de la France: entre diplomatie collective et leadership*. Paris: L'Harmattan.

Chourou, Béchir, 1999. 'A Challenge For EU Mediterranean Policy: Upgrading Democracy From Threat to Risk'. Paper presented at the international workshop on The Human Dimension of Security and the EMP. Malta, 14–15 May.

Clogg, Richard, 1986. *A Short History of Modern Greece*. Cambridge: Cambridge University Press.

—— 1993. *Greece, 1981–89: The Populist Decade*. Basingstoke: Macmillan.

Close, D.H., 1990. *The Character of the Metaxas Dictatorship: An International Perspective*. London: Centre of Contemporary Greek Studies, Occasional Paper 3.

Cohler, Anne M., Miller, Basia Carolyn and Stone, Harold Samuel (eds), 1989. *Montesquieu: The Spirit of the Laws*. Cambridge: Cambridge University Press.

Commission of the European Communities, 1991. Communication from the Commission to the Council on *The Implementation of Trade Arrangements Under the New Mediterranean Policy*. COM(91)179 final, 22 May.

—— 1993. *EEC Mediterranean Agreements*. Bureau D'Informations Europeennes, Brussels, Belgium. TM 392, 8 October.

—— 1994a. Report from the Commission to the Council and the European Parliament on *The Implementation of Financial and Technical Cooperation with Mediterranean non-Member Countries and on Financial Cooperation with Those Countries as a Group*. COM(94)384 final, 18 November.

—— 1994b. *A Strategy for Euro-Mediterranean Partnership*. Essen: IP/94/1156, 6 December.

—— 1994c. *The European Union Relations With the Mediterranean*. MEMO/94/74, 6 December.

—— 1995a. *Strengthening the Mediterranean Policy of the European Union: Proposals for Implementing A EMP*. COM(95)72 final, 8 March.

—— 1995b. *Proposal for a Council Regulation (EC) on Financial and Technical Measures to Support the Reform of Economic and Social Structures in Mediterranean Non-member Countries and Territories*. COM(95)204 final, 7 June.

—— 1995c. *Barcelona Euro-Mediterranean Conference (27–28 November 1995) – Declaration and Work Programme*. DOC/95/7, 4 December.

—— 1996. *Amended Proposal for a Council Regulation (EC) on Financial and Technical Measures to Support the Reform of Economic and Social Structures in Mediterranean Non-member Countries and Territories*. COM(96)113 final, 25 March.

—— 1999. *Survey on Free Trade and Economic Transition in the Mediterranean*. DG1B/A/4, April.

—— 2001. 'Mid-term Evaluation of the Euromed-Youth Programme' ref. no. MEI/B7–4100/1B/0418, 24 August.

—— 2002a. Action Plan, Valencia Conference at: http://europa.eu.int/comm/external_relations/euromed/conf/val/action.pdf.

—— 2002b. Valencia Conclusions at: http://europa.eu.int/comm/external_relations/euromed/conf/val/concl.pdf.

—— 2003a. Strategy Paper and Report of the European Commission on the Progress Towards Accession by Bulgaria, Romania and Turkey, November 2003. *Turkey in the Enlargement Process – Progress and Challenges*.

—— 2003b. *Wider Europe – Neighbourhood: A New Framework for Relations with our Eastern and Southern Neighbours*. Brussels, 11.3.2003. COM(2003) 104 final.

—— 2003c. *European Union and the Mediterranean: Towards Integration*. Final conference of the 'UNIMED Business Network' project. CONFINDUSTRIA, Rome, 11 March. Accessed through the EuroMed Calendar.

—— 2003d. Naples Conclusions: http://europa.eu.int/comm/external_relations/euromed/publications.htm and

Annex to the final Conclusions of the 6th Euro-Mediterranean meeting of Foreign Ministers, Naples, December 2003. 'Recommendation from the Euro-Mediterranean Parliamentary Forum to the Sixth Euro-Mediterranean Ministerial Conference on setting up a Euro-Mediterranean Parliamentary Assembly' (2 December 2003).

—— 2004. Commission's Regular Report on Turkey, 6 October.

Connolly, William, E., 1991. *Identity/Difference: Democratic Negotiations of Political Paradox*. New York: Cornell University Press.

—— 1995. *The Ethos of Pluralization*. Minneapolis: University of Minnesota Press.

Couloumbis, Theodore, A., 1983. 'The Structures of Greek Foreign Policy', in R. Clogg (ed.) *Greece in the 1980's*. London: Macmillan, in association with the Centre of Contemporary Greek Studies, 95–122.

Cowen, Michael P. and Shenton, Robert W., 1995. *Doctrines of Development*. London: Routledge.

Cox, Robert, 1981. 'Social Forces, States and World Orders: Beyond IR Theory', *Journal of International Studies*, 10(2), 126–55.

——— 1987. *Production, Power and World Order: Social Forces in the Making of History*. New York: Columbia University Press.

Cox, Robert and Sinclair, Timothy J., 1996. *Approaches to World Order*. Cambridge: Cambridge University Press.

Craib, Ian, 1992. *Modern Social Theory: From Parsons to Habermas*. New York and London: Harvester Wheatsheaf.

Croft, Stuart, Redmond, John, Wyn Rees, G. and Webber, Mark, 1999. *The Enlargement of Europe*. Manchester: Manchester University Press.

Delante, Gerard, 1995. *Inventing Europe: Idea, Identity, Reality*. London: Macmillan.

Demetriou, Olga, 2004. 'The European Union and the Cyprus Conflict: A Review of the Literature'. EUBorderConf working paper series number 5. Available at: http://www.euborderconf.bham.ac.uk/publications/files/WP5Cyprus.pdf.

Denoeux, Guilain, 1998. 'Understanding Morocco's "Sanitation Campaign" (December 1995 to May 1996)', *The Journal of North African Studies*, 3(1), Spring, 101–43.

Der Derian, James and Shapiro, Michael J., 1989. *International/Intertextual Relations: Postmodern Readings of World Politics*. Lexington, MA: Lexington Books.

Derrida, Jacques, 1976. *Of Grammatology*. Baltimore, MD: Johns Hopkins University Press.

——— 1992. *The Other Heading: Reflections on Today's Europe*. Bloomington, IN: Indiana University Press.

Deutsch, *et al.*, 1957. *Political Community and the North Atlantic Area: International Organisation in the Light of Historical Experience*. Princeton, NJ: Princeton University Press.

Diamandouros, P.N., 1983. 'Greek Political Culture in Transition: Historical Origins, Evolution, Current Trends', in R. Clogg (ed.) *Greece in the 1980s*. London and Basingstoke: Macmillan, 1983, 43–69.

——— 1986. 'Regime Change and the Prospects for Democracy in Greece: 1974–1983', in Guillermo O'Donnell, Philippe C. Schmitter and Laurence Whitehead (eds) *Transitions from Authoritarian Rule: Prospects for Democracy*. Baltimore, MD: Johns Hopkins University Press, 138–65.

Diez, Thomas, 2001. 'Europe as a Discursive Battleground. Discourse Analysis and European Integration Studies', *Cooperation and Conflict*, 36(1), 5–38.

Dokos, Thanos, 2003. *NATO's Mediterranean Dialogue: Prospects and Policy Recommendations*. ELIAMEP Policy Paper No. 3. Athens: Hellenic Foundation for European and Foreign Policy (ELIAMEP).

Doty, Roxanne Lynn, 1993. 'Foreign Policy as Social Construction: A Post-Positivist Analysis of US Counterinsurgency Policy in the Philippines', *International Studies Quarterly*, 37(3), 297–320.

——— 1997. 'Aporia: A Critical Exploration of the Agent-Structure Problematique in IR Theory', *European Journal of International Relations*, 3(3), 365–92.

Ebeid, Hanaa, 2004. 'The Partnership in Southern Eyes: Reflections on the Discourse in the Egyptian Press', EuroMesCo paper, No. 37. Lisbon: EuroMesCo Secretariat at the IEEI.

Echeverría, J.C., 1999. 'Spain and the Mediterranean', in S. Stavridis, T. Couloumbis, T. Veremis, N. Waites (eds) *The Foreign Policies of the EU's Mediterranean States and Applicant Countries in the 1990s*. New York: St Martin's Press, 98–112.

Economist Intelligence Unit country reviews available at: http://www.economist.com/countries.

Egyptian Businessmen Association, 2000. 'The World Trade Organisation and the Arab countries'. Communication to the 4th forum of Arab Businessmen Society, Kuwait, May.

Eickelman, Dale F., 1994. 'Re-Imagining Religion and Politics: Moroccan Elections in the 1990s', in John Ruedy (ed.) *Islamism and Secularism in North Africa*. New York: St Martin's Press, 253–73.

Eliassen, K.A. (ed.), 1998. *Foreign and Security Policy in the EU*. London: Sage.

Elliott, Larry, 2004. 'EU insists on right to subsidise farming', *The Guardian*, 27 March, 25.

El-Sayed, Selim Mohammed, 1995. *Mediterraneanism: A New Dimension in Egypt's Foreign Policy*. Kurasat Istratijiya, Strategic Papers, 27.

Emirbayer, Mustafa, 1997. 'Manifesto for a Relational Sociology', *American Journal of Sociology*, 103(2), September, 281–317.

Escobar, Arturo, 1995. *Encountering Development: The Making and Unmaking of the Third World*. Princeton, NJ: Princeton University Press.

Escribano, Gonzalo and Jordán, Josep María, 1998. 'Subregional Integration in the Southern Shore of the Mediterranean and the Euro-Mediterranean Free Trade Area'. Paper presented at the Valencia Forum on the Euro-Mediterranean Free Trade Area, organised by the Centro Español de Relaciones Internacionales, 20–21 November.

Europe Documents, 1995. *Council Report on Relations Between the EU and the Mediterranean Countries*, in preparation for the conference on 27–28 November in Barcelona: No. 1930/31, 27 April.

European Commission 1999. 'Conclusions: Third Euro-Mediterranean Conference of Foreign Ministers', Stuttgart, 15–16 April 1999. Available at: http://europa.eu.int/comm/external_relations/euromed/conf/stutg/conc_en.htm. Accessed January 2001.

—— 2000. *The Barcelona Process: Five Years On, 1995–2000*, Luxembourg: Office for Official Publications of the European Communities.

—— *Euromed Information Notes*. 'Euro-Mediterranean Partnership and MEDA Regional Activities', June. Also available at: http://europa.eu.int/comm/europeaid/projects/med/regional_en.htm.

—— 2001. *EuroMed Report*, Issue 25, 9 February. 'Final Declaration of the Second Session of the Euro-Mediterranean Parliamentary Forum'. Brussels, 8–9 February, 3.

—— 2002. *EuroMed Report*, Issue 52, 28 November. Romano Prodi, President of the European Commission, Europe and the Mediterranean, Time for Action. Louvain-la-Neuve: Université Catholique de Louvain-la-Neuve, 26 November.

—— 2003. *EuroMed Report*, Issue 57, 22 May. 'Building a Euro-Mediterranean Area'. Speech by Romano Prodi, President of the European Commission at the opening of the 22nd 'Giorntae Dell'Osservanza', Bologna, 17 May.

—— 2004. *EuroMed Report*, Issue 73, 23 March. 'Interim Report on an EU Strategic Partnership with the Mediterranean and the Middle East'.

European Communities, 2003. 'The Israeli Economy and the European Union'. *Statistics in Focus* (Stéphane Quefelec). Also available at: http://www.europa.eu.int/comm/eurostat/.

Euro-Mediterranean Conference on Regional Cooperation. Valencia, 28–29 January 1999. *Concluding Statement by the Chairman State Secretary Dr Hans-Friederich Von Ploetz*.

Euro-Mediterranean Market at: http://www.euromedmarket.org/.

EuroMed Special Feature, Issue 19, 21 February, 2001. *President Prodi's Visit to Jordan, Lebanon and Syria*. Produced by the MEDA Team – Information.

Euromed Special Feature, Issue 30, 27 May 2002. Available at: http://www.deljor.cec.eu.int/en/images/special_features/special_features_30.htm.

EuroMed Synopsis, EuroMed Special Features, EuroMed Reports, EuroMed Calendars and EuroMed Information Notes. Various: available at: http://europa.eu.int/comm/europeaid/projects/med/index_en.htm; http://europa.eu.int/comm/external_relations/euromed/publication.htm; http://europa.eu.int/comm/europeaid/index_en.htm.

EuroMed Synopsis, Issue 254, 8 January 2004.

EuroMed Synopsis, Issue 255, 15 January 2004.

EuroMed Synopsis, Issue 257, 29 January 2004.

Euro-Mediterranean summit in Nice, 2000. *Le Monde*, 16 November. Available from: http://www.lemonde.fr/.

EuroMeSCo, 2003. *European Security and Defence Policy – Latest News*. Available at: http://www.euromesco.net/euromesco/artigo.asp?cod_artigo=88651. Accessed on 22 September 2003. Section on 'EU-Morocco: Positive Appraisal of the Partnership'.

European Union reports and sources available at: http//europa.eu.int/.

EU–Libya: http://europa.eu.int/news/index_en.htm.

EU–Syria talks at: http://europa.eu.int/comm/external_relations/syria/intro/index.htm.

Fabian, Johannes, 1983. *Time and the Other: How Anthropology Makes Its Object*. New York: Columbia University Press.

Falk, Richard, 1986. *Reviving the World Court*. Charlottesville, VA: University Press of Virginia.

—— 1987. *The Promise of World Order*. Philadelphia, PA: Temple University Press.

Faria, Fernanda, 1996. 'The Mediterranean: A New Priority in Portuguese Foreign Policy', *Mediterranean Politics*, special issue on Western approaches to the Mediterranean, 1(2), Autumn, 212–30.

—— 1999. 'The Making of Portugal's Mediterranean Policy', in S. Stavridis, T. Couloumbis, T. Veremis, N. Waites (eds) *The Foreign Policies of the EU's Mediterranean States and Applicant*

Countries in the 1990s. New York: St Martin's Press, 113–39.

Fatouros, Arghyrios, A., 1993. 'Political and Institutional Facets Of Greece's Integration in the European Community', in Harry J. Psomiades and Stavros B. Thomadakis (eds) *Greece, The New Europe, and the Changing International Order*. New York: Pella Publishing, 23–56.

Fenech, Dominic, 1991. 'Mediterranean Regionality', in S. Fiorini and V. Mallia-Milanes (eds) *Malta: A Case Study in International Cross-Currents*. Malta: Malta University Publications, 267–77.

—— 1993. 'East–West to North–South in the Mediterranean', *GeoJournal*, 31(2), 129–40.

Ferguson, James, 1990. *The Anti-Politics Machine: 'Development', Depoliticization and Bureaucratic Power in Lesotho*. Cambridge: Cambridge University Press.

Foucault, Michel, 1972. *The Archaeology of Knowledge*. London: Tavistock.

—— 1973. *The Order of Things*. New York: Pantheon.

—— 1977. *Discipline and Punish*. Translated by Alan Sheridan. London: Allen Lane.

—— 1979–86. *The History of Sexuality* (3 volumes). London: Allen Lane.

—— 1980. *Power/Knowledge: Selected Interviews and Other Writings, 1972–1977*. Colin Gordon (ed.). New York: Pantheon Books.

—— 1989. *Archaeology of Knowledge*. London: Routledge.

—— 1991. 'Governmentality', in G. Burchell, C. Gordon and P. Miller (eds) *The Foucault Effect: Studies in Governmentality*. Chicago, IL: University of Chicago Press, 87–104.

Fouskas, Vassilis, 1996. 'Interview. Nicos Mouzelis: Greece and Modernisation in the 1990s', *Synthesis: Review of Modern Greek Studies*, 1(1), 35–8.

Frazee, Charles A., 1969. *The Orthodox Church and Independent Greece, 1821–1852*. Cambridge: Cambridge University Press.

Freeman, Charles, 1999. *Egypt, Greece and Rome: Civilizations of the Ancient Mediterranean*. Oxford: Oxford University Press.

Galtung, Johan, 1971. 'A Structural Theory of Imperialism', *Journal of Peace Research*, 2, 81–98.

Gallagher, Nancy, 1998. 'Interview: The Life and Times of Abdallah Laroui, A Moroccan Intellectual', *Journal of North African Studies*, 3(1), Spring, 132–51.

Gamble, Andrew and Payne, Anthony, 1996. *Regionalism and World Order*. Basingstoke: Macmillan.

General Affairs and External Relations Council, 2004. Conclusions, Luxembourg, 14 June.

George, Jim, 1994. *Discourses of Global Politics: A Critical (Re)Introduction to IR*. Boulder, CO: Lynne Rienner.

Geradin, Damien and Petit, Nicolas, 2003. 'Competition Policy and the Euro-Med Partnership', *European Foreign Affairs Review*, 8, 153–80.

Germain, Randall and Kenny, Michael, 1998. 'International Relations Theory and the New Gramscians', *Review of International Studies*, 24(1), January, 3–21.

Giammusso, Maurizio, 1999. 'Civil Society Initiatives and Prospects of Economic Development: The Euro-Mediterranean Decentralized Co-operation Networks', *Mediterranean Politics*, 4(1), Spring, 25–52.

Giddens, Anthony, 1976. *New Rules of Sociological Method: A Positive Critique of Interpretative Sociologies*. London: Hutchinson.

—— 1984. *The Constitution of Society: Outline of the Theory of Structuration*. Cambridge: Polity Press.

—— *Sociology*. Cambbridge: Polity Press, 32.

Gill, Stephen (ed.), 1993. *Gramsci, Historical Materialism and International Relations*. Cambridge: Cambridge University Press (Cambridge Studies in International Relations Series, 26).

Gillespie, Richard, 1996. 'Spain and the Mediterranean: Southern Sensitivity, European Aspirations'. *Mediterranean Politics*, special issue on Western approaches to the Mediterranean, 1(2), Autumn, 93–211.

—— 2000. *Spain and the Mediterranean: Developing a European Policy towards the South*. Basingstoke: Macmillan.

Gilpin, Robert, 1975. *U.S. Power and the Multinational Corporation*. New York: Basic Books.

Grieco, Joseph, 1990. *Cooperation Among Nations: Europe, America and Non-Tariff Barriers to Trade*. Ithaca, NY: Cornell University Press.

Grugel, Jean and Hout, Wil (eds), 1999. *Regionalism Across the North–South Divide: State Strategies and Globalization*. Routledge: London.

Guardian, The, 2003. 'Blair hails Libya deal on arms', Saturday, 20 December.

Guardian, The, 2004. Leader: 'European Union. Selling the deal', 29 March, 19.

Guillaume, Xavier, 2002. 'Foreign Policy and the Politics of Alterity: A Dialogical Understanding of International Relations', *Millennium: Journal of International Studies*, 31(1), 1–26.

Gupte, Pranay, 1999. 'The Blood of the Prophet', *Newsweek*, 2 August, 39.

Haas, Ernst B. 1980. 'Why Collaborate? Issue-linkage and International Regimes', *World Politics*, 32, 357–405.

Hall, Stuart, Held, David and McGrew, Tony, 1992. *Modernity and its Futures*. Oxford: Polity Press, in association with the Open University.

Hansen, Lene and Wæver, Ole, 2002. *European Integration and National Identity: The Challenge of the Nordic States*. London: Routledge.

Hart, David M., 1997. 'Berber Names and Substrata in Mauritania and the Western Sahara: Linguistic and Ethno-Historical Guidelines for Future Research on a Paradoxical Problem', *The Journal of North African Studies*, 2(1), Summer, 58–71.

—— 1999. 'Scratch a Moroccan, Find a Berber', *Journal of North African Studies* (issue on tribe and society in rural Morocco), 4(2), Summer, 23–6.

Hasenclever, A., Mayer, P. and Rittberger, V., 2000. 'Integrating Theories of International Regimes', *Review of International Studies*, 26(1), 3–33.

Henley, Jon, 2004. 'Libya Agrees Payout for French Jet Bombing', *The Guardian*, 10 January, 14.

Herzfeld, Michael, 1989. *Anthropology Through the Looking Glass: Critical Ethnography in the Margins of Europe*. Cambridge: Cambridge University Press.

Higgott, Richard A., 1983. *Political Development Theory: The Contemporary Debate*. London and Canberra: Croom Helm International.

—— 1994. 'Ideas, Identity and Policy Coordination in the Asia-Pacific', *The Pacific Review*, 7(4), 367–79.

Hill, Christopher, 1993. 'The Capability-Expectations Gap, or Conceptualising Europe's International Role', *Journal of Common Market Studies*, 31(3), 305–28.

Hirst, Francis W., 1998. *Liberalism and the Empire: Three Essays*. London: Routledge.

Hodge, Carl Cavanagh, 1999. 'Turkey and the Pale Light of European Democracy', *Mediterranean Politics*, 4(3), Autumn, 56–68.

Hogstad, David, 1995–1996. *L'Université et l'Etudiant au Maroc: les fards d'une modernisation naufragée? Essais anthropologiques sur la Cacophonie du Changement*. Mémoire pour l'obtention du Diplôme d'Etudes Approfondies de Science Politique, Institut d'Etudes Politiques, Université de Droit, d'Economie et des Sciences d'Aix-Marseille III.

Holland, Martin (ed.), 1997. *Common Foreign and Security Policy: The Record and Reforms*. London: Pinter.

Holmes, John W. (ed.), 1995. *Maelstrom, the United States, Southern Europe, and the Challenges of the Mediterranean*. Cambridge, MA: World Peace Foundation.

—— 1996. 'Italy: In the Mediterranean, but *of* it?', *Mediterranean Politics*, special issue on Western approaches to the Mediterranean, 1(2), Autumn, 176–92.

Horden, Peregrine and Purcell, Nicholas, 2000. *The Corrupting Sea: A Study of Mediterranean History*. Oxford and Malden, MA: Blackwell.

Hornblower, Simon and Spawforth, Antony (eds), 1996. *Oxford Classical Dictionary*, 3rd edn. Oxford: Oxford University Press.

Howard, Michael, 2001. 'Greek priests revolt as church backs Pope's visit', *The Guardian*, 20 March, 15.

Howorth, Jolyon, 1996. 'France and the Mediterranean in 1995: From Tactical Ambiguity to Inchoate Strategy', *Mediterranean Politics*, special issue on Western approaches to the Mediterranean, 1(2), Autumn, 157–75.

Huband, Mark, 2000. World News: Trade: 'Mediterranean region facing marginalisation', *Financial Times*, 9 March, 16.

Human Development Report, 2003. UNDP. Available at: http://www.undp.org/hdr2003/pdf/hdr03_HDI.pdf.

Huysmans, Jef, 1998. 'Security! What Do You Mean? From Concept to Thick Signifier', *European Journal of International Relations*, 4(2), 226–55.

Ioakimidis, P.C., 1993. 'Greece in the EC: Policies, Experiences and Prospects', in Harry J. Psomiadis and Stavros B. Thomadakis (eds) *Greece, The New Europe and The Changing International Order*. New York: Pella Publishing, 405–20.

—— 1999. 'The Model of Foreign Policy-Making in Greece: Personalities Versus Institutions', in S. Stavridis, T. Couloumbis, T. Veremis, N. Waites (eds), 1999. *The Foreign Policies of the EU's Mediterranean States and Applicant Countries in the 1990s*. New York: St Martin's Press, 140–70.

Jackson, Patrick Thaddeus and Nexon, Daniel H., 1999. 'Relations Before States: Substance, Process and the Study of World Politics', *European Journal of International Relations*, 5(3), 291–332.

Jameson, Frederic, 1981. *The Political Unconscious: Narrative as a Socially Symbolic Act*. London: Metheun.

Joenniemi, Pertti and Wæver, Ole, 1992. 'Regionalization Around The Baltic Rim: Notions on Baltic Sea Politics'. Prepared for the Presidium of the Nordic Council for the 2nd Parliamentary Conference on Co-operation in the Baltic Sea Area, Oslo, 22–24 April.

Joffé, George, 2000. 'Europe and the Mediterranean: The Barcelona Process Five Years on', RIIA Briefing Paper Number 16.

—— 2001. 'European Union and the Mediterranean', in Mario Tele (ed.) *The European Union and the New Regionalism*. Burlington, VT: Ashgate, 207–25.

Jørgensen, Knud Erik (ed.), 1997. *European Approaches to Crisis Management*. London: Kluwer.

Joseph, S.J., 1996. 'Cyprus at the Threshold of the EU', *Mediterranean Quarterly*, 7(2), Spring, 112–22.

—— 1997. *Cyprus: Ethnic Conflict and International Politics: From Independence to the Threshold of the EU*. London/New York: Macmillan/St Martin's Press.

Keith, Michael and Pile, Steve, 1993. 'Introduction Part 1: The Politics of Place', in Michael Keith and Steve Pile, eds. *Place and the Politics of Identity*. London and New York: Routledge, 1993, 1–21.

Keohane, R. O., 1989. *International Institutions and State Power: Essays in International Relations Theory*. Boulder, CO: Westview.

Kinacioglu, Muge, 2000. 'From East–West Rivalry to North–South Division: Redefining the Mediterranean Security Agenda', *International Relations*, 15(2), August, 27–39.

King, Russell and Black, Richard, 1997. *Southern Europe and the New Immigrations*. Brighton: Sussex Academic Press.

Kofman, Eleonore and Youngs, Gillian, 1996. *Globalisation: Theory and Practice*. London: Pinter.

Köhler, Michael, 1996. 'Stability in Algeria, Morocco and Tunisia', in Josef Janning and Dirk Rumberg (eds) *Peace and Stability in the Middle East and North Africa*. Gütersloh: Bertelsmann Foundation Publishers, 1996, 111–20.

Knudsen, Olav F. and Neumann, Iver B., 1995. *Subregional Security Cooperation in the Baltic Sea Area: An Exploratory Study*. Olso: Norsk Utenrikspolitisk Institutt.

Kuus, Merje, 2004. 'Europe's Eastern Expansion and the Re-inscription of Otherness in East-Central Europe', *Progress in Human Geography*, 4(1), August, 472–89.

Lacan, Jacques, 1977. *Écrits: A Selection*. Translated by Alan Sheridan. New York: W.W. Norton.

Laclau, Ernesto and Mouffe, Chantal, 1985. *Hegemony and Socialist Strategy: Towards a Radical Democratic Politics*. London and New York: Verso.

Laffey, Mark and Weldes, Jutta, 1997. 'Beyond Belief: Ideas and Symbolic Technologies in the Study of IR', *European Journal of International Relations*, 3(2), 193–237.

Lake, David A. and Morgan, Patrick M. (eds), 1997. *Regional Orders: Building Security in a New World*. University Park, PA: Pennsylvania State University Press.

Larsen, Henrik, 1997. *Foreign Policy and Discourse Analysis: France, Britain and Europe*. London: Routledge.

—— 1999. 'British and Danish European Policies in the 1990s: A Discourse Approach', *European Journal of International Relations*, 5(4), 451–83.

—— 2002. 'The EU: A Global Military Actor?', *Cooperation and Conflict: Journal of the Nordic International Studies Association*, 37(3), 283–302.

Latter, Richard, 1992. *Mediterranean Security*. London: HMSO, Wilton Park papers, 48.

Laursen, F. (ed.), 2003. *Comparative Regional Integration: Theoretical Perspectives*. Aldershot: Ashgate.

Lefebvre, Henri, [1974] 1991. *The Production of Space*. Oxford: Blackwell.

Leveau, Rémy, 1996. 'The Future of the Maghreb', in Josef Janning and Dirk Rumberg (eds) *Peace and Stability in the Middle East and North Africa*. Gütersloh: Bertelsmann Foundation Publishers, 93–110.

—— 1997. 'Morocco at the Crossroads', *Mediterranean Politics*, 2(2), Autumn, 95–113.

Lewis, Martin W. and Wigen, Kären E., 1997. *The Myth of Continents: A Critique of Meta-geography*. Berkeley, CA and London: University of California Press.

Lipowatz, Thanos, 1994. 'Split Greek Identity and the Issue of Nationalism', in N. Demertzis (ed.) *Greek Political Culture Today*. Athens: Odysseas, 115–32.

Lister, Marjorie, 1997. *The EU and the South: Relations with Developing Countries*. London: Routledge/UACES.

Loewendahl, Ebru, 1998. *'Promises to Keep': the Reality of Turkey–EU Relations*. Chorley: Action Centre for Europe.

Loti, Pierre, 1892. *Into Morocco*. Translated by E.P. Robins. Chicago, IL and New York: Rand, McNally.

Luhmann, Niklas, 1979. *Trust and Power*. Chichester: Wiley.

—— 1982. *The Differentiation of Society*. New York: Columbia University Press. (Series: European Perspectives).

Lyotard, Jean-François, 1984. *The Postmodern Condition: A Report on Knowledge*. Manchester: Manchester University Press.

Lyrintzis, Christos, 1983. 'Between Socialism and Populism: The Rise of the Panhellenic Socialist Movement'. Unpublished PhD dissertation. London School of Economics and Political Science, London.

—— 1987. 'The Power of Populism: The Greek Case', *European Journal of Political Research*, 15, 667–86.

MacLeod, Scott, 2000. (Cairo bureau chief) 'Interview with King Mohammed VI'. *Time Magazine*, 155(25) or Internet Edition (Online), 26 June. Available at: http://www.time.com/europe/magazine/2000/0626/kingqa.html.

Maguid, Wahid Abdel (ed.), 2001. *The Public Debate on the Egyptian Euro–Mediterranean Partnership*. Arab Strategic Report 2000. Cairo: Al Ahram Centre for Political and Strategic Studies, 331.

Marks, Jon, 1996. 'High Hopes and Low Motives: The New Euro–Mediterranean Partnership Initiative', *Mediterranean Politics*, 1(1), 1–24.

Martín, Iván, 2004. 'Social consultation and the impact of the Euro-Mediterranean free trade areas and the MEDA programme on economic and social rights: A case for surpassing the division between the three baskets of the EMP'. Paper presented at an international workshop on the impact of European Union involvement in civil society structures in the Southern Mediterranean. Friedrich Ebert Stiftung, Rabat, Morocco, 4–5 December.

Martinson, Jane, 2001. 'Quebec Rioters cry Foul, but Free Trade Deal is Done', *The Guardian*, 23 April, 12.

McSweeney, Bill, 1996. 'Identity and Security: Buzan and the Copenhagen School', *Review of International Studies*, 22(1), November, 81–93.

MEDA democracy project funded by the European Commission. Report available at: http//www.liv.ac.uk/ewc/pastevents.html under 'The European Union and Democracy Promotion: The Case of North Africa'.

Mediterranean Politics, 1996. Special issue on Western approaches to the Mediterranean, 1(2), Autumn.

Merritt, Richard L., 1975. *Foreign Policy Analysis*. Toronto and London: Lexington Books.

Meyer-Resende, Madalena, 2004. Paper presented at the panel on Europe and the Mediterranean, ECPR, Bologna, June.

Meyrede, Laurent, 1999. 'France's Foreign Policy in the Mediterranean', in S. Stavridis, T. Couloumbis, T. Veremis and N. Waites (eds) *The Foreign Policies of the EU's Mediterranean States and Applicant Countries in the 1990s*. New York: St Martin's Press, 40–72.

Milliken, Jennifer, 1999a. 'The Study of Discourse in IR: A Critique of Research and Methods', *European Journal of International Relations*, 5(2), 225–54.

—— 1999b. 'Intervention and Identity: Reconstructing the West in Korea', in Jutta Weldes, Mark Laffey, Hugh Gusterson and Raymond Duvall (eds) *Cultures of Insecurity: States, Communities, and Danger*. Minneapolis, MN: University of Minnesota Press. Borderlines Series, 14, 91–117.

Mingolo, Walter D., 1998. *The Darker Side of the Renaissance: Literacy, Territoriality, and Colonization*. Ann Arbor, MI: University of Michigan Press.

Mingst, Karen, 1999. *Essentials of IR*. New York and London: W.W. Norton.

Mitchell, Jon P., 2002. *Ambivalent Europeans: Ritual, Memory and the Public Sphere in Malta*. London: Routledge.

Monar, Jörg, 1997. 'Political Dialogue with Third Countries and Regional Political Groupings: The Fifteen as an Attractive Interlocutor', in E. Regelsberger *et al.* (eds) *Foreign Policy of the EU: From EPC to CFSP and Beyond.* London: Lynne Rienner Publishers, 263–74.

—— 1998. 'Institutional Constraints of the EU's Mediterranean Policy', *Mediterranean Politics*, 3(2), Autumn, 39–60. Available at: http://www.monde-diplomatique. fr/1999/12/DOLHEM/ 12803.html.

Montesquieu, Charles de Secondat, 1989. *The Spirit of the Laws.* Translated and edited by Anne M. Cohler, Basia Carolyn Miller and Harold Samuel Stone. Cambridge: Cambridge University Press.

Moravcsik, Andrew, 1998. *Centralization or Fragmentation? Europe Facing the Challenges of Deepening, Diversity and Democracy.* New York: Council on Foreign Relations.

Moré, Iñigo, 2004. 'The Economic Step Between Neighbours: The Case of Spain–Morocco', *Mediterranean Politics*, 9(2), 185–200.

Mortimer, Robert A., 1989. 'Maghreb Matters', *Foreign Policy*, 76, Fall, 160–75.

Mouzelis, Nicos P., 1986. *Politics in the Semi-Periphery: Early Parliamentarism and Late Industrialisation in the Balkans and Latin America.* Basingstoke: Macmillan.

Müftüler-Bac, Meltem, 1997. *Turkey's Relations With a Changing Europe.* Manchester and New York: Manchester University Press.

Murphy, Emma (ed.), 2001. *Mediterranean Politics*, special issue on the state and the private sector in North Africa, 6(2), Summer.

—— 2002 'Navigating the Economic Reform in the Arab World: Social Responses, Political Structures and Dilemmas for the European Union', in C.P. Hanelt, F. Neugart and M. Peitz (eds) *Europe's Emerging Foreign Policy and the Middle East Challenge.* Munich: Bertelsmann Foundation, 33–57.

Neugart, F. and Schumacher, Tobias, 2004. 'Thinking about the EU's Future Neighbourhood Policy in the Middle East: From the Euro-Mediterranean Partnership to "Barcelona Plus"', in Christian-Peter Hanelt, Giacomo Luciani and Felix Neugart (eds) *Regime Change in Iraq,* Florence: EUI-RSCAS, 169–99.

Neumann, Iver B., 1994. 'A Region-building Approach to Northern Europe', *Review of International Studies*, 20(1), 53–74.

—— 1996a. 'European Identity, EU Expansion and the Integration/Exclusion Nexus'. Paper presented at the conference: Defining and Projecting Europe's Identity: Issues and Trade-Offs. Institut Universaire de Hautes Etudes Internationales, Geneva, 21–22 March.

—— 1996b. 'Collective Identity Formation: Self and Other in International Relations', *European Journal of International Relations*, 2(2), 139–74.

—— 1996c. *Russia and the Idea of Europe: A Study in Identity and International Relations.* London: Routledge.

—— 1997. 'Identity and the Outbreak of War, or Why the Copenhagen School of Security Studies Should Include the Idea of "Violisation" in its Framework of Analysis'. Working Paper No. 578, July, Oslo: Norwegian Institute of International Affairs.

—— 1998. *Uses of the Other: The 'East' in European Identity Formation.* Minneapolis, MN: University of Minnesota Press.

—— 2001. 'From Meta to Method: The Materiality of Discourse'. Paper presented at ISA 2001.

Neumann, Iver B. and Welsh, Jennifer M. 1997. '"The Turk" as Europe's Other', in Peter, J. Burgess (ed.) *Cultural Politics and Political Culture in Postmodern Europe.* Amsterdam and Atlanta, GA: Rodopi.

New Encyclopaedia Britannica, The, 1995. 15th edn. Chicago, IL: Encyclopedia Britannica.

Norton-Taylor, Richard, 2000. 'Comment and Analysis. Analysis: Intelligence Test'. Features. *The Guardian*, 20 December, 17.

Núñez Villaverde, Jesús A., 2000. 'The Mediterranean: A Firm Priority of Spanish Foreign Policy?', *Mediterranean Politics*, 5(2), Summer, 129–47.

Nuttall, Simon, 1992. *European Political Cooperation.* Oxford: Clarendon Press.

Official Journal of the European Communities, 2000. 'Common Strategy of the European Council of 19 June 2000 on the Mediterranean Region'. Santa Maria da Feira.

Ohmae, Kenichi, 1990. *The Borderless World: Power and Strategy in the Interlinked Economy.* London: Collins.

—— 1995a. *The Evolving Global Economy: Making Sense of the New World Order.* Boston, MA: Harvard Business School.

—— 1995b. *End of the Nation State: The Rise of Regional Economies.* London: Harper Collins.

Ortega, Martin, 2003. 'Some Comments on the European Union's Mediterranean Policy', in *Perceptions: Journal of International Affairs*, 8(2), June–August. An expanded version of the same article can be found at: http://www.iss-eu.org (in Chaillot Paper No. 64, October, EU Institute for Security Studies, Paris).

Ó Tuathail, Gearóid, 1996. *Critical Geopolitics: The Politics of Writing Global Space.* Minneapolis, MN: University of Minnesota Press. Borderlines Series, 6.

Paasi, Anssi, 1996. *Territories, Boundaries and Consciousness: The Changing Geographies of the Finnish-Russian Border.* Chichester: Wiley.

Pace, Michelle, 2000. 'Regionalism in International Relations: The Mediterranean as a Social Construct', *Agora Without Frontiers*, 5(3), 207–19 (translated into Greek). Athens: Institute of International Economic Relations.

—— 2002. 'The Ugly Duckling of Europe: The Mediterranean in the Foreign Policy of the European Union', *Journal of European Area Studies*, 10(2), 189–209.

—— 2004a. 'Collective Identity: The Greek Case', in W. Carlnaes, H. Sjursen and B. White (eds) *Contemporary European Foreign Policy.* London: Sage Publications, 227–38.

—— 2004b. 'The Euro-Mediterranean *Partnership* and the *Common* Mediterranean Strategy? European Union Policy from a Discursive Perspective', *Geopolitics*, 9(2), 292–309.

—— 2004c. 'Governing Border Conflicts: When Can the EU Be an effective mediator'. Paper presented at the International Studies Association convention, Montreal, 17–20 March.

—— 2004d. 'EU–Turkey Relations', presented at Britain and Greece: 5th Annual Bilateral conference. Hydra, Greece, 8–10 October. Available at: http://www. euborderconf.bham. ac.uk/publications/files/EU-TurkishrelationsHydra.pdf.

—— 2004e. 'The Role of "Political Dialogue": A Dialogic Understanding of EU-Mediterranean Relations'. Paper presented at the ECPR Standing group on the European Union. 2nd Pan-European conference on EU Politics. 'Implications of a Wider Europe: Politics, Institutions and Diversity', Bologna, June 25.

Pace, Michelle and Schumacher, Tobias, 2004. 'Report: Culture and Community in the Euro-Mediterranean Partnership: A Roundtable on the Third Basket, Alexandria 5–7 October 2003', *Mediterranean Politics*, 9(1), 122–6.

Pace, Roderick, 2004. 'Malta's EU Membership: Chapter 1 Concluded, Chapter 2 Just Started', *Mediterranean Politics*, 9(1), Spring, 114–21.

Paparizos, Antonis, 1995. 'Diafotismos, Thriskeia Kai Paradosi Sti Syghroni Elliniki Koinonia' (translated: Enlightenment, Religion and Tradition in Modern Greek Society), in Nicos Demertzis (ed.) *Elliniki Politiki Koultoura Simera.* Athens: Odysseas, 74–113.

Patten, Chris, 2000. *A European Foreign Policy: Ambition and Reality.* Brussels. Internet Edition (Online), 15 June. Available at: http://europa.eu.int/comm/external_relations/news/06_00/ ip_00_624_en.htm; http://europa.eu.int/comm/external_relations/cfsp/intro/index.htm.

—— 2004. 'Agadir and the Road to Prosperity', *Al Ahram,* 25 February (Egyptian newspaper).

Peristiany, J.G. (ed.), 1976. *Kinship and Modernization in Mediterranean Society.* Rome: Center for Mediterranean Studies.

Peterson, John and Sjursen, Helene (eds), 1998. *A Common Foreign Policy for Europe? Competing Visions of the CFSP.* London: Routledge.

Philippart, Eric, 2003. 'The Euro-Mediterranean Partnership. A Critical Evaluation of an Ambitious Scheme', *European Foreign Affairs Review*, 8(2), Summer, 201–20.

Piening, Christopher, 1997. *Global Europe: The EU in World Affairs.* Boulder, CO: Lynne Rienner.

Price, Richard and Reus-Smit, Christian, 1998. 'Dangerous Liaisons? Critical International Theory and Constructivism', *European Journal of International Relations*, 4(3), 259–94.

Pridham, Geoffrey (ed.), 1984. *The New Mediterranean Democracies: Regime Transition in Spain, Greece and Portugal.* London: Frank Cass.

Prodi, Romano, 2004. Speech of Romano Prodi, The President of the European Commission, at the Turkish Grand National Assembly, Ankara, 14 January.

Prozorov, Sergei, 2004. 'Three Theses on Governance and the Political', *Journal of International Relations and Development*, 7(3), 267–93.

Psomiades, Harry J. and Thomadakis, Stavros B. (eds), 1993. *Greece, The New Europe, and the Changing International Order.* New York: Pella Publishing.

Pye, L., 1962. *Politics, Personality and Nation Building: Burma's Search for Identity.* New Haven, CT: Yale University Press.

Quefelec, Stéphane, 2003. '2002 in the Mediterranean Countries: Selected Indicators'. *Statistics in focus.* European Communities.

Ramonet, Ignacio, 2000. 'New Hope, Old Frustrations. Morocco: The Point of Change', *Le Monde Diplomatique* (English version), July. Also available at: http://www.monde-diplomatique.fr/en/2000/07/01ramonet.

Regelsberger, Elfriede, de Schoutheete, Philippe and Wessels, Wolfgang (eds), 1997. *Foreign Policy of the EU: From EPC to CFSP and Beyond*. Boulder, CO: Lynne Rienner.

Rein, R. (ed.), 1999. *Spain and the Mediterranean Since 1898*. London and Portland, OR: Frank Cass.

Richardson, John T.E. (ed.), 1996. *Handbook of Qualitative Research Methods for Psychology and the Social Sciences*. Leicester: British Psychological Society.

Rozakis, Christos, 1986. 'Greek Foreign Policy 1974–85: Modernization and the International Role of a Small State', in A. Manessis *et al.* (eds) *Greece in Motion*. Athens: Exandas (in Greek).

Rumelili, Bahar, 2004a. 'The European Union's Impact on the Greek–Turkish Conflict. A Review of the Literature'. EUBorderConf project working papers series, No. 6. Available at: http://www.euborderconf.bham.ac.uk/publications/files/WP6GreeceTurkey.pdf.

—— 2004b. 'The Talkers and the Silent Ones: The European Union and Change in Greek–Turkish Relations'. EUBorderConf project working papers series, No. 10, October. Available at: http://www.euborderconf.bham.ac.uk/publications/files/GreeceTurkey2.pdf.

Said, Edward W., 1978. *Orientalism: Western Conceptions of the Orient*. London: Penguin Books (reprinted in 1979, New York: Vintage Books).

—— 1981. *Covering Islam: How The Media And The Experts Determine How We See The Rest Of The World*. Pantheon Books: New York (reprinted in 1997, New York: Vintage Books).

—— 1993. *Culture and Imperialism*. London: Vintage.

Sánchez Mateos, Elvira, 2003. 'European Perceptions of Southern Countries Security and Defence Issues: A Reflection on the European Press'. EuroMeSCo Paper 23. Lisbon: EuroMeSCo Secretariat at the IEEI.

Sant Cassia, Paul, 1991. 'Authors in Search of a Character: Personhood, Agency and Identity in the Mediterranean', *Journal of Mediterranean Studies*, 1(1), 1–17.

Schlumberger, Oliver, 2000. 'Arab Political Economy and the EU's Mediterranean Policy: What Prospects for Development?', *New Political Economy*, 5(2), 247–268.

Searle, John R., 1995. *The Construction of Social Reality*. London: Penguin Books.

Shapiro, Michael J., 1981. *Language and Political Understanding: The Politics of Discursive Practices*. New Haven, CT: Yale University Press.

—— 1992. *Reading the Postmodern Polity*. Minneapolis, MN: University of Minnesota Press.

—— 1994. 'Moral Geographies and the Ethics of Post-Sovereignty', *Public Culture*, 6, 479–502.

—— 1997. *Violent Cartographies: Mapping Cultures of War*. Minneapolis, MN: University of Minnesota Press.

Shapiro, Michael J. and Alker, Hayward R. (eds), 1996. *Challenging Boundaries: Global Flows, Territorial Identities*. Minneapolis, MN and London: University of Minnesota Press. Borderlines Series, 2.

Sherrard, Philip, 1959. *The Greek East and Latin West: A Study in the Christian Tradition*. Oxford: Oxford University Press.

Shields, Rob, 1990. *Places on the Margin: Alternative Geographies of Modernity*. London: Routledge.

Smith, Karen E., 1999. *The Making of EU Foreign Policy*. Basingstoke: Macmillan.

Smith, Michael E., 2004a. 'Institutionalization, Policy Adaptation and European Foreign Policy Cooperation', *European Journal of International Relations*, 10(1), 95–136.

—— 2004b. *Europe's Foreign and Security Policy: The Institutionalization of Cooperation*. Cambridge: Cambridge University Press.

Smith, Steve, 1999. 'Social Constructivisms and European Studies: A Reflectivist Critique', *Journal of European Public Policy*, 6(4), special issue, 682–91.

—— 2000. 'Wendt's World'. *Review of International Studies*, 26, 151–63.

Sofos, Spyros, 2001. 'Reluctant Europeans? European Integration and the Transformation of Turkish Politics', in K. Featherstone and G. Kazamias (eds) *Europeanization and the Southern European Periphery*. London: Frank Cass. Originally appeared in 2000, 'Reluctant Europeans? European Integration and the Transformation of Turkish Politics', *Southern European Society and Politics*, 5(2).

Stavridis, Stelios, Couloumbis, T., Veremis, T. and Waites, N. (eds), 1999. *The Foreign Policies of the EU's Mediterranean States and Applicant Countries in the 1990s*. New York: St Martin's Press.

Sultana, Ronald G. and Baldacchino, Godfrey (eds), 1994. *Maltese Society: A Sociological Inquiry.* Msida: Mireva Publications.

Tabone, Carmel, 1994a. 'The Maltese Family in the Context of Social Change', in R.G. Sultana and G. Baldacchino (eds) *Maltese Society: A Sociological Inquiry.* Msida: Mireva Publications, 229–51.

—— 1994b. 'The Maltese Family in the Context of Secularization', in R.G. Sultana and G. Baldacchino (eds) *Maltese Society: A Sociological Inquiry.* Msida: Mireva Publications, 285–300.

Tahi, Mohand Salah, 1988. 'The Maghreb States: Regional and Foreign Policies 1973–1987'. University of Warwick, PhD thesis, February.

Tampere conclusions. Available at: http://europa.eu.int/council/off/conclu/oct99/oct99_en.htm.

Tassinari, Fabrizio, 2004. '*Mare Europaeum.* Baltic Sea Region Security and Cooperation from post-Wall to post-Enlargement Europ'. PhD dissertation. Department of Political Science, University of Copenhagen, Copenhagen.

Taylor, Simon, 1999. 'Turkish Poll Will do Little to Thaw Ice', *The European Voice*, 8–14 April, 12–13.

Thomson, Janice, 1995. 'State Sovereignty in International Relations'. *International Studies Quarterly*, 39, 213–33.

Thompson, John B., 1984. *Studies in the Theory of Ideology.* Cambridge: Polity Press and Oxford: Basil Blackwell.

Todorov, Tzvetan, 1984. *Mikhail Bakhtin: The Dialogical Principle.* Ttranslated by Wlad Godzich. Minneapolis, MN: University of Minnesota Press.

Tonra, Ben, 2000. 'Mapping EU Foreign Policy Studies', *Journal of European Public Policy*, 7(1), March, 163–9.

Tovias, Alfred, 1997. 'The Economic Impact of the Euro-Mediterranean Free Trade Area on Mediterranean Non-Member Countries', *Mediterranean Politics*, 2(1), 113–28.

—— 2001. 'On the External Relations of the EU 21: The Case of the Mediterranean Periphery', *European Foreign Affairs Review*, 6, 375–94.

Tremlett, Giles, 2004. 'Morocco Boosts Women's Rights', *The Guardian*, 21 January, 11.

Tsoucalas, Constantine, 1969. *The Greek Tragedy.* London: Penguin.

—— 1993. 'Greek National Identity in an Integrated Europe and a Changing World Order', in H.J. Psomiades and S.B. Thomadakis (eds) *Greece, The New Europe, And The Changing International Order.* New York: Pella Publishing, 57–78.

Vasconcelos, Álvaro and Joffé, George 2000. 'Towards Euro-Mediterranean Regional Integration. Introduction', *Mediterranean Politics*, special issue on the Barcelona Process. Building a Euro-Mediterranean Regional Community, 5(1), Spring, 3–6.

Verney, Susannah and Couloumbis, Theodore, 1991. 'State-international Systems Interaction and the Greek Transition to Democracy in the Mid-1970s', in Geoffrey Pridham (ed.) *Encouraging Democracy: The International Context of Regime Transition in Southern Europe.* Leicester: Leicester University Press, 103–24.

Wæver, Ole,1995. 'Securitization and Desecuritization', in R.D. Lipschutz (ed.) *On Security.* New York: Columbia University Press, 46–86

—— 2002. 'Identity, Communities and Foreign Policy. Discourse Analysis as Foreign Policy Theory', in Lene Hansen and Ole Wæver (eds) *European Integration and National Identity: The Challenge of the Nordic States.* London: Routledge, 20–49.

—— 2003. 'Securitization: Taking Stock of a Research Programme in Security Studies'. Draft paper discussed at a PIPES (Program on International Politics, Economics and Security) seminar at the University of Chicago, February 24.

—— 2004a. 'European Intergration and Security: Analysing French and German Discourses on State, Nation and Europe'. Paper presented at a conference on Security and Integration, 6–7 February 2004. Article downloaded from the author's website. Available at: http://www.polsci.ku.dk/people/Faculty/Waever_Ole.htm.

—— 2004b. 'Discursive Approaches', in Antje Wiener and Thomas Diez (eds) *European Integration Theory.* Oxford: Oxford University Press, 197–214.

Wæver, Ole, Buzan, Barry, Kelstrup, Morten and Lemaitre, Pierre, 1993. *Identity, Migration and the New Security Agenda in Europe.* London: Pinter.

Walker, R.B.J., 1993. *Inside/Outside: International Relations as Political Theory.* Cambridge: Cambridge University Press.

Wallerstein, Immanuel, 1979. *The Capitalist World-Economy.* Cambridge: Cambridge University Press.

Waltz, Kenneth N., 1979. *Theory of International Politics*. Reading, MA: Addison-Wesley.

Ware, Kallistos, 1983. 'The Church: A Time of Transition', in Richard Clogg, ed. *Greece in the 1980s*, London: Macmillan (in association with the Centre of Contemporary Greek Studies, Kings College, University of London), 208–30.

Waterbury, John, 1970. *The Commander of the Faithful: The Moroccan Political Elite – A Study in Segmented Politics*. New York: Columbia University Press.

Weldes, J. 1999. 'Intervention and Identity: Reconstructing the West in Korea', in Weldes, Jutta, Laffey, Mark, Guterson, Hugh and Duval, Raymond (eds) *Cultures of Insecurity: States, Communities and the Production of Danger*, Minneapolis, MN: University of Minnesota Press. Borderlines Series, 14.

Weldes, Jutta, Laffey, Mark, Gusterson, Hugh and Duvall, Raymond (eds), 1999. *Cultures of Insecurity. States, Communities and the Production of Danger*. Minneapolis, MN: University of Minnesota Press. Borderlines Series, 14.

Wendt, Alexander E., 1987. 'The Agent-Structure Problem in IR Theory', *International Organization*, 41(3), Summer, 335–70.

—— 1992. 'Anarchy is What States Make of it: The Social Construction of Power Politics', *International Organization*, 46(2), 391–426.

—— 1999. *Social Theory of International Politics*. Cambridge: Cambridge University Press.

Wendt, Alexander E. and Duvall, Raymond, 1989. 'Institutions and International Order', in Ernst-Otto Czempiel and James N. Rosenau (eds) *Global Changes and Theoretical Challenges: Approaches to World Politics for the 1990s*. Lexington, MA: Lexington Books, 51–73.

Wessels, Wolfgang, 1982. 'European Political Cooperation: A New Approach to European Foreign Policy', in David Allen, Reinhardt Rummel and Wolfgang Wessels (eds) *European Political Cooperation: Towards a Foreign Policy for Western Europe*. London: Butterworths, 1–20.

White, Brian, 1999. 'The European Challenge to Foreign Policy Analysis', *European Journal of International Relations*, 5(1), 37–66.

Whitaker, Brian, 2003. 'British Firms set Sights on Libya as Hopes Rise of an End to Sanctions', *The Guardian*, 2 September, 12.

—— 2004. 'Egypt Rebuffs US over Regional Reform', *The Guardian*, 8 March, 15.

Willis, Michael J., 1999. 'After Hassan: A New Monarch in Morocco', *Mediterranean Politics*, 4(3), Autumn, 115–28.

Wilson, Kevin and van der Dussen, Jan (eds), 1995. *The History of the Idea of Europe*. What is Europe? series, 1. Milton Keynes: Open University; London: Routledge and Kegan Paul.

Woodhouse, C.M., 1985. *The Rise and Fall of the Greek Colonels*. London: Granada.

Woods, Clyde, 1998. *Development Arrested. The Blues and Plantation Power in the Mississippi Delta*. London: Verso.

World Bank Group. Available at: http://www. worldbank.org/data/.

World Factbook, The. Available at: http://www.odci.gov/cia/publications/factbook.

Young, Hugo, 2001. 'If you Stay out, Don't Pretend to be in', *The Guardian*, 16 February, 20.

Young, Iris Marion, 1990. *Justice and the Politics of Difference*. Princeton, NJ: Princeton University Press,.

Index